Paper Palaces

Venetian palace façade, from Sebastiano Serlio's fourth book (Venice, 1537), fol. xxxivr/156r.

Paper Palaces

THE RISE OF THE RENAISSANCE
ARCHITECTURAL TREATISE

Edited by Vaughan Hart
with Peter Hicks

Yale University Press
New Haven and London

Designed by Laura Church
Printed in Hong Kong

Library of Congress Cataloging-in-Publication Data

Paper palaces: the rise of the Renaissance architectural treatise /
edited by Vaughan Hart, with Peter Hicks.
p.   cm.
Includes bibliographical references and index.
ISBN 0-300-07530-8 (cloth)
1. Architecture – Early works to 1800.
2. Architecture – Textbooks.   3. Architecture, Renaissance – Textbooks.
I. Hart, Vaughan, 1960– .   II. Hicks, Peter, 1964– .
NA2515.P36   1998
720 – dc21   98-15257
CIP

A catalogue record for this book is available from
The British Library

Contents

Part Two
THE TREATISE IN CONTEXT

Contributors

VAUGHAN HART
(co-translator of Serlio), University of Bath

PETER HICKS
(co-translator of Serlio), University of Bath

MARIO CARPO
University of Saint-Etienne

KRISTA DE JONGE
Catholic University, Leuven

FRANCESCO PAOLO FIORE
University of Rome

MARCO FRASCARI
University of Pennsylvania

LUISA GIORDANO
University of Pavia

JEAN GUILLAUME
Centre d'Etudes Supérieures de la Renaissance, Tours

FREDERIQUE LEMERLE
Centre d'Etudes Supérieures de la Renaissance, Tours

NIGEL LLEWELLYN
University of Sussex

INDRA KAGIS McEWEN
(translator of Perrault), McGill University/
National Theatre School of Canada, Montreal

JAMES McQUILLAN
University of Portsmouth

MANUELA MORRESI
University of Venice

ALBERTO PEREZ-GOMEZ
McGill University, Montreal

INGRID D. ROWLAND
(translator of Vitruvius), University of Chicago

JOSEPH RYKWERT
(co-translator of Alberti), University of Pennsylvania

ROBERT TAVERNOR
(co-translator of Alberti and Palladio), University of Bath

RICHARD J. TUTTLE
Tulane University

Acknowledgements

W E ARE GRATEFUL TO Professor Nicholas Adams, Timothy Anstey, Dr Andrew Ballantyne, Dr Deborah Howard, Neil Leach, Professor John Onians, Professor Richard Schofield and Dr David Watkin for their advice in preparing this book. We should also like to thank David Hicks and Elisabetta Da Prati for translating several essays, Dr Jennifer Nutkins for her editorial advice, and Richard Tucker and Joe Robson for providing technical assistance. Gillian Malpass of Yale University Press has been a consistent supporter of our project at first to translate and here to interpret the content of the Renaissance architectural treatises for an English-speaking readership. The librarians of the Rare Books Departments in Cambridge University Library, the Bibliothèque Nationale in Paris, and the British Library were of special assistance. In particular we should thank Nicola Thwaite, who collaborated (with Vaughan Hart) on an exhibition of architectural books from Cambridge University Library (again entitled *Paper Palaces*), which was held in the Fitzwilliam Museum, Cambridge, from January to April 1997 (see Hart and Thwaite 1997). Our research has received generous funding from the British Academy and the Graham Foundation for Advanced Studies in the Fine Arts.

Preface

THE RENAISSANCE ARCHITECTURAL TREATISES discussed in this book played a fundamental, if neglected, role in the development of western architecture. Whilst illustrating the importance of these works, this collection of essays complements the English translations which are now available of the treatises by Vitruvius (1931 and forthcoming 1998), Alberti (1988), Filarete (1965), Serlio (1996 and forthcoming 1999), Palladio (1997) and of the post-Renaissance treatise by Perrault (1993). For the most part the translators of these works have supplied the corresponding chapter in this volume. The first section of this book also deals with the no less important treatises which remain, to date, inaccessible to the English reader, most notably those by di Giorgio, Colonna, Sagredo, Philandrier, De l'Orme, Vignola and Scamozzi. In addition, two chapters in this first section focus on the central role of illustrations in these early architectural books.

The scope of this study allows for a thorough comparison of the treatises, and in particular their often unique adaptation of the antique rules of architecture to suit both traditional building practices and modern needs. The second part of the book goes on to discuss this native content with respect to Renaissance architectural books published in England, the Low Countries, and in Italy itself as the 'birthplace' of the treatise in script and print.

The European architectural literature discussed here documents the ideas behind Renaissance building practices which evolved at first in mid-fifteenth-century Italy and then in sixteenth-century Europe as a whole. Despite the importance of these books, however, a traditional bias towards issues of practice and patronage made manifest in actual built work has led in the past to a certain neglect of these texts by English-language architectural writers. Since Rudolf Wittkower's pioneering study of the architectural principles in the 'age of humanism' was published in 1949, a limited number of English-language works has appeared which take various treatises and their writers as chapter topics (Onians 1988) or as the sole subject (Kruft 1994; see also Choay 1980/97; Wiebenson 1982; Guillaume 1988; Hart and Thwaite 1997). However, the present study is the first collection of essays to offer the English-language reader a spectrum of opinion on the role and significance of the treatise tradition.

Many of the most important Renaissance theorists were also architects, although a number – like Colonna, Sagredo and Philandrier – built little or nothing at all. Where appropriate, reference has been made to an individual author's experience as an architect and their built works, although the principal focus of this book is the theoretical texts rather than their author's buildings, which are well enough covered elsewhere. Nor is the focus here the influence of any particular treatise upon architecture through the ages, since this topic would be enormous.

Publications on the theory (or theories) and practice of architecture are commonplace today, but the idea for a book on architecture can be traced to a particular time and group of authors. This collection of essays traces these origins of architectural bibliography, and as a consequence charts the early development of modern notions of architectural education, of the dichotomy between the theory and practice of architecture, and of the central role of the architect as the 'designer' of buildings.

Vaughan Hart
Department of Architecture
University of Bath, 1997

Introduction

'PAPER PALACES'
FROM ALBERTI TO SCAMOZZI

Vaughan Hart

FROM CRAFT SECRET TO PUBLISHED CODE:
THE RISE OF ARCHITECTURAL LITERATURE

COLLECTIVELY, ARCHITECTURAL TREATISES chronicle the development of the art of building from the early Italian Renaissance onwards. Often written by architects for fellow architects, as well as for patrons and builders, these books illustrate ideal projects for villas, temples and even cities; they record the ideas which directly shaped such architectural masterpieces as Leon Battista Alberti's Tempio Malatestiano in the fifteenth century, Andrea Palladio's Villa Rotonda in the sixteenth, and Claude Perrault's Louvre colonnade in the seventeenth. It follows that to understand these buildings fully we must study their architects' books (Rykwert 1996b; Hart and Thwaite 1997).

With a very few exceptions the authors of the treatises were experienced architects, and their books were not intended as abstract discussions on theory but as practical aids for the purpose of building. Even the philologist Guillaume Philandrier had some practical experience as an architect, building a gable on Rodez cathedral in the 1550s (although this, rather like his commentary to Vitruvius, sits remote from the Gothic architectural context and is to a large extent a self-contained, formal exercise). To emphasise the interrelationship between book and building, authors often illustrated examples of their own work as models. Sebastiano Serlio included a woodcut of one of his Venetian ceiling designs (in Book IV) and drawings of a house in Fontainebleau (called the Grand Ferrara) and the château of Ancy-le-Franc (both in Book VI), whilst Philibert De l'Orme illustrated his own house on the rue de la Cerisaie, Paris, and his design for the front façade of the château at Saint-Maur. But Palladio's and Scamozzi's villas illustrated in their respective treatises were probably the most influential

'paper palaces'. Without them, England would not boast its own
Palladian villas, and perhaps most notably Burlington's interpretation of
Scamozzi's Rocca Pisani in the form of the famous villa at Chiswick.

The appearance of the first manuscripts on architecture in the
middle of the fifteenth century, together with the first printed treatises
after 1486, closely followed the renewed use in Italy of the five 'styles'
of building, as the antique Orders were called. Renaissance architecture was accompanied by its own literature almost from the start. Early
writers on architecture sought to emulate the Roman author Vitruvius
whose *De Architectura Libri Decem* was the only comprehensive treatise
solely on the theory of architecture to survive from antiquity. Vitruvius
recorded the foundation rituals which inaugurated ancient cities, the
arrangement of forums and basilicas, of temples and theatres, and of
more exotic structures such as the Roman tower of the winds. He also
records the origins and characteristics of the Greek columns, that is of
the Doric, Ionic and Corinthian Orders. In codifying the rules for the
'correct' carving of these Orders, early authors surveyed the (often
conflicting) use of the column on ancient Roman remains and also
studied the writings of Pliny on specific monuments such as the
Pantheon, of Polybius on Roman camps and of Julius Frontinus on
aqueducts. But it was Vitruvius's treatise which provided Renaissance
theorists with the principal antique precedent for a treatise on architecture, and as such largely determined the content of Renaissance architectural books. Indeed, without the chance survival of Vitruvius's
manuscript, Renaissance architectural literature would not have been
able to explain with such certainty the relationship, for example,
between architectural and human proportion or between the timber
hut and the origins of ornament. Moreover, without the Vitruvian
models of hut and body, Renaissance architecture would itself surely
have looked very different.

The first treatise on the Vitruvian model was Alberti's *De re
aedificatoria* which was presented in manuscript form to Pope Nicholas
V around 1450. It offered a coherent account of the principles of
antique architecture, addressed to patrons rather than to architects
(Borsi 1986; Alberti 1988; Kruft 1994, 44). Although Alberti clearly
sought to emulate the Roman author in producing a treatise on
architecture in ten books, it was perhaps Alberti's training in canon law
which lay behind his decision to record 'laws' for the art of building.
The nobility of the art of architecture and its basis in the proportions
of the human body, notions fundamental to Vitruvius and elaborated
by Alberti, were subsequently defended in the manuscript on architecture by Antonio Averlino, called 'Filarete', the various versions of
which were written in the early 1460s (Onians 1988; Kruft 1994, 51–
5). The text is composed as a dialogue between Filarete and a lord (or,

on occasions, his son) and outlines the circumstances which lead this lord (a thinly disguised Francesco Sforza, Duke of Milan) to employ Filarete to build a new city, Sforzinda, to reflect the architect's anthropomorphic theory. Filarete's fortified city, with its central square, ducal palace and cathedral, is the first thoroughly planned ideal city of the Renaissance. Moreover, unlike Alberti, with his abstract consideration of Vitruvian concepts, Filarete sought to apply these concepts, and that of decorum in particular, in a series of illustrations of house types designed to be expressive of the social order of fifteenth-century Italy. Following Filarete's example, the next set of manuscripts on architecture (of the 1480s and late 1490s), by Francesco di Giorgio, included an illustration of a plan for a citadel laid out as a human body, thereby interpreting the anthropomorphic basis to *all'antica* architecture more literally still. The early manuscript treatises thus clearly presented Vitruvian architecture as the 'embodiment' of civic harmony, necessarily modelled on the image of bodily harmony.

Without exception, these pioneering architectural writers sought to explain how Vitruvius's threefold requirement of *firmitas* (strength), *utilitas* (utility) and *venustas* (beauty) could be satisfied through his somewhat enigmatic concepts of order (*ordinatio*), arrangement (*dispositio*), proportion (*eurythmia*), symmetry (*symmetria*), decorum (*decor*) and distribution (*distributio*) (Vitr.I.ii.1–9; Kruft 1994, 24–7). Alberti complained that Vitruvius's terminology was difficult to understand (Alberti 1988, Book VI ch. 1). Di Giorgio even went to the trouble of translating Vitruvius himself in order to refine his use of the Roman's terminology. Francesco Maria Grapaldi in his *De Partibus Aedium* (On the Parts of Buildings) published in Parma in 1494 attempted to define these Vitruvian terms for an Italian readership just as Henry Wotton in his *Elements of Architecture* (1624) was to do for an English audience over a century later. Architectural practice thereby developed, for the first time since antiquity, a body of theoretical terms and a literature which described it. These treatises thus established 'norms' against which buildings could be compared and judged.

The principles of Gothic architecture had been transmitted orally, within secretive guilds and craft lodges, and were not intended for publication (Rykwert 1988): and as an *ars mechanica*, architecture occupied a relatively low status in the medieval hierarchy of knowledge (Kruft 1994, 40). As a consequence, in sharp contrast to the enormity of the building enterprise undertaken during the Middle Ages and the production of manuscripts on diverse subjects, surviving literary evidence on Gothic building procedures is scarce. Xylography or woodcut printing had been in existence for some seventy years before production of the first printed books in the 1440s (Febvre and Martin 1993, 47), but no works on Gothic design were printed before 1486.

Surviving works (with a didactic purpose) on Gothic architecture are limited to Villard de Honnecourt's 'lodge-book' (c.1225–50), which was an illustrated sketch-book rather than a publication (Kruft 1994, 36–7), and two books published in the German lands, where printing began. These were Matthias Roriczer's *Das Büchlein von der Fialen Gerechtigkeit* (The little book about the right way for setting out pinnacles), published in Regensburg in 1486, and the so-called *Fialenbüchlein* (Small book on pinnacles), published without title or date in Nuremberg and written not by a mason but a goldsmith, Hans Schmuttermayer – goldsmiths frequently made architectural models in precious materials, and numbered amongst the earliest printers (Febvre and Martin 1993, 49). De Honnecourt's 'lodge-book' mostly dealt with geometric procedures, the two German books more specifically with the application of *ad quadratum*, but it is impossible to say to what extent they reflected the mason's legendary craft 'secret' (Rykwert 1988; Kruft 1994, 38–9).

This limited material on Gothic architecture was, curiously enough, not greatly added to by *incunabula* on Vitruvian architecture. The early Renaissance manuscripts on the subject certainly circulated widely enough and were evidently much studied – di Giorgio's was even admired as far afield as Spain (Rykwert 1988). Book production had itself spread rapidly following the 'invention' of printing with movable type, most probably at Mainz in the 1440s, and its introduction into Italy in 1464/5 (Febvre and Martin 1993, 51–5, 182–6). But architectural books were not a product of this development, despite the evident market for such works and the manifest suitability of the subject for woodcut illustration. One reason for this reticence may have been the poor reception of the printed book, as an artifact, by certain patrons of architecture. According to Bernardino Baldi the works in the library of Federico da Montefeltro, the Duke of Urbino and sometime patron to Alberti, were 'all written by hand, and not one printed, for he would have been ashamed to own such a thing' (Borsi 1986, 135). Alberti seems never to have attempted to prepare his treatise for mechanical reproduction despite the relative novelty of the technique. Indeed, early printing does not appear to have played much of a part in the development of subjects of a scientific or technical nature (Febvre and Martin 1993, 259), with books in this area accounting for only 10 per cent of the works published before 1500 (with 45 per cent theological, just over 30 per cent classical and medieval literature, and just over 10 per cent legal works (Febvre and Martin 1993, 249)).

In 1486 (or shortly thereafter), thirty or so years after printing had been 'invented', the first printing of Vitruvius (edited by Giovanni Sulpicio of Veroli and published anonymously in Rome) finally appeared, as did, coincidentally, Alberti's treatise (printed by Niccolo di Lorenzo Alemani in Florence) and Roriczer's anachronistic book (Kruft 1994, 66–7). Planned treatises by Peruzzi, Bramante and Leonardo are either lost or were never developed from the surviving fragmentary studies (Kruft 1994, 59, 62). Thus, despite the fact that the late fifteenth and early sixteenth centuries were seen as the 'Golden Age' of architectural practice in Italy by later authors such as Serlio and Vasari, the masterpieces of this 'High Renaissance' were destined to match their medieval counterparts in not being accompanied by a corpus of published writings. The early Italian Renaissance was certainly not the child of the printing press.

It is clear that during the early Italian Renaissance architectural practice evolved from being governed by principles of geometry, as recorded by Euclid, to applying those of proportion, as recorded by Vitruvius (Rykwert 1988). Although this shift was encouraged by architectural writers, the novelty to contemporaries of the content of the early architectural manuscripts can be over-emphasised. Vitruvius had been discussed at Charlemagne's court (Ungers 1994, 308), and manuscript copies of the Roman author were common enough in medieval libraries (Krinsky 1967; Rykwert 1988); indeed, his text lies behind the entry for architecture in the most important of the medieval encyclopedias, the *Speculum majus* of Vincent de Beauvais (*c.*1190–1264) (Kruft 1994, 36, 39). Roman buildings, much in evidence, were also not ignored during the Middle Ages, as pilgrim guides such as the thirteenth-century *Mirabilia Urbis Romae* prove. Despite this interest, however, and the obvious compatibility of the Greek Orders as recorded by Vitruvius with the much-studied conceptions of human form outlined by Plato (in the *Timaeus*) and of architectural decorum (or magnificence) outlined by Aristotle (in the *Nicomachean Ethics*), the porticoes and pediments of antique architecture remained things of the past. Moreover, there was no literary call to the Orders amongst builders and patrons before Alberti's treatise of around 1450. Although Gothic architecture is by necessity structurally symmetrical, it is clearly not an ornamental (that is, 'Ordered') interpretation of antique principles. The antique Orders were considered too overtly 'pagan', or at best 'Jewish', by medieval builders and clergy north of the Alps; whilst in contrast Gothic arches and buttresses, the tangible expression of scholasticism, were identified as the architecture of the true Church and became celebrated as such in Giotto's paintings (Panofsky 1957; Onians 1988, 113–19, 126–9).

What, then, led Alberti to break the silence of a millennium and a half and write expressly on the virtues of Roman architecture, and on the Orders in particular, as an aspect of nascent 'Renaissance' culture evident in Italy from the 1420s? The decisive stimulus came less from

single events such as the legendary 'rediscovery' of a Vitruvius manuscript by Poggio Bracciolini in 1416 at the monastery library of St
Gallen in Switzerland (Kruft 1994, 39, 66), than from more fundamental cultural changes in early fifteenth-century Italy. Of greater
importance was the growing quest for national identity amongst Italian
humanists, which led Alberti (and later Filarete) to favour the Orders
as the legitimate expression of Italian nationalism, and of Christian
morality and civic decorum as outlined in his treatise (Onians 1988,
147–57, 181; Kruft 1994, 53). Moreover, philosophical developments
during this period, such as the reinterpretation of the Platonic concept
of bodily harmony by Nicholas of Cusa (Rykwert 1996a), and later by
Marsilio Ficino and Pico della Mirandola, may have given new vitality
to the role in architecture of Pythagorean musical ratios and bodily
proportions as outlined by Vitruvius and re-emphasised by Alberti
(Vitr.III.i; Alberti 1988, Book IX ch. 5). The early Renaissance treatises
certainly promoted these important Platonic themes in the Roman's
treatise through their illustration of the 'Vitruvian man', whilst the
basis of *all'antica* architecture in (God-given) human proportion which
this figure emphasised provided a path for the assimilation of the
Orders into Christian iconography throughout Europe (see Hart,
chapter 17, below). Alberti's treatise and subsequent Vitruvian literature thus effectively put the case for building – and magnificent
building at that – as a Christian enterprise, in the wake of traditional
doubts amongst many clerics as to the virtue of ecclesiastical and
private building works (Onians 1988, 112–29; 147–57).

The craft secrecy which surrounded the procedures of pointed arch
construction almost certainly prohibited their open inclusion in the
early treatises as codified 'rules'. Equally, this suggests that the content
of these books – notably the proportions ordering the column-and-
beam system of Vitruvian architecture which these treatises sought
principally to describe – lay outside Gothic procedures as understood
by the master masons (if not the medieval clerical student of Vitruvius)
(Rykwert 1988). From being a secretive craft discipline and lore,
complemented by a Vitruvian culture studied and discussed by a
narrow band of clergy and nobility, after 1500 the art of building
became openly dependent on published rules for the five Orders which
were argued over by a much wider cross-section of society. Filarete's
and di Giorgio's early drawings of various types of private dwellings,
and Serlio's subsequent manuscript Book VI illustrating house types
suitable to all social grades (*c.*1541–7), perfectly illustrate the increased
relevance of an architecture based on Vitruvian domestic principles
(Vitr.VI.iii-vii) to middle-ranking merchants and even, for the first
time, to the poor. Clearly, even if printing did not start the Italian
Renaissance, it certainly greatly encouraged the fashion for *all'antica*

architecture amongst a diverse body of patrons eager to emulate the grandeur of ancient Rome: and printed images came to provide a unique source for architects who practised in lands remote from the principal Roman remains by providing easy-to-use design patterns. Indeed these 'antique' patterns were used by architects throughout the ducal, papal and republican states of Italy, and in Catholic and Protestant countries alike.

It might thus appear at first glance that the printed book helped to establish throughout sixteenth-century Europe a design 'orthodoxy' whose signature was no longer the pointed arch but the antique column. However, a consistent feature of the Vitruvian treatise (subsequent to the uniquely 'classical' model provided by Alberti) was the integration of this 'foreign', antique ornament with local medieval forms and building techniques – by di Giorgio and Cesariano in Italy, by Serlio, De l'Orme, Martin and du Cerceau in France, by Sagredo in Spain, by Shute, Dee and Wotton in England, by Vredeman de Vries in the Low Countries and by Dürer and Ryff in the German lands (Onians 1988, 158; Kruft 1994, 71). De l'Orme went so far as to invent a sixth Order, for example, which he terms 'French'. Through this regional interpretation of antique models and ornament, treatise writers clearly attempted to make the *all'antica* style acceptable to the religious and historical sensibilities of their intended readership. The Gothic was, after all, the established architecture of salvation, and its integration with *all'antica* forms in Vitruvian literature can only have served to validate this new architecture in Christian terms. The project of making Vitruvius accessible and relevant to modern needs was further facilitated by the fact that all the authors listed above wrote their texts or commentaries in their national language. For example, whereas Alberti had followed Vitruvius in writing in Latin, Filarete, di Giorgio, Serlio, Vignola and Palladio all wrote in their native Italian.

The continuity of building traditions is further illustrated as a theme in the early sixteenth-century treatises by the integration of Vitruvian concepts with the more established ones of Euclid. Most dramatically, the first Italian Vitruvius had included a plan, section and elevation/ section through Gothic Milan cathedral: these projections were ordered using the medieval geometry known as *ad triangulum*, and were employed to illustrate the Roman author on architectural representation (see Hart, chapter 9, below). Subsequently, Dürer applied established Euclidean techniques to the new ornamental forms, notably to demonstrate the problem which Vitruvius had himself promised to illustrate of how to draw the entasis of a column. In Elizabethan England Vitruvius's text was first introduced not as a work in its own right but cited as a 'preface' to Euclid (by John Dee), and the 'hero' of eighteenth-century masons remained Euclid, not Vitruvius (Rykwert 1988). Indeed, in France in particular, the vault constructions in Serlio's second book, the novel illustrations of stereotomy in De l'Orme's *Premier tome* (a topic later expanded upon in Mathurin Jousse's *Le Secret d'architecture*), together with the masons' outcry against Gerard Desargues's new Cartesian stereotomy methods of 1636–44, all testify to the masons' continuing preoccupation with geometry. This was in sharp contrast to the proportional debate more recently established amongst architects.

Gothic practices were thus an important element in the Vitruvian treatises produced in Italy and, less surprisingly, in northern Europe. The integration of medieval with Vitruvian architecture was, after all, perfectly in accord with Alberti's respectful superimposition of antique architectural forms on the Gothic churches of Santa Maria Novella in Florence and San Francesco in Rimini. Indeed, although the early Vitruvian manuscripts advanced the use of *all'antica* architecture largely at the expense of native building traditions, in stressing as di Giorgio did the 'rediscovery' of true architecture (Kruft 1994, 57), the subsequent Vitruvian books had the opposite effect. From 1500, with the appearance of the first translations of Vitruvius and of architectural texts in national tongues accompanied by illustrations of Gothic practices, architectural books promoted vernacular culture and in so doing ironically enough effectively undermined the universal status of ancient (Latin) texts such as that of Vitruvius (Febvre and Martin 1993, 319–32; Grafton 1992).

Moreover the 'licentious' integration of antique models and traditional forms by treatise writers, and the growing fashion for Mannerist superfluity and similar Vitruvian 'errors' popularised in particular through the fame of Michelangelo's work, helped prompt an equally 'licentious' type of Vitruvian pattern-book, which appeared in northern Europe after 1550 (for example, the treatises by Serlio (1551), de Vries (1577–81), Sambin (1572) and Dietterlin (1598)). These works, with their illustrations of grotesque decoration and broken pediments, were complemented by the Mannerist aesthetics of Giovanni Lomazzo (of 1583) and Federico Zuccaro (of 1607). It was in the context of such early 'errors' and Mannerist tendencies that the 'Accademia Vitruviana' (Accademia della Virtù) was established in Rome in 1540–41 to carry out philological work on the Roman author's text and thereby encourage a strict adherence to Vitruvian authority (Tolomei 1547; Kruft 1994, 69–70). The most notable outcome of this study was Guillaume Philandrier's *Annotationes* to

Vitruvius published in Latin in 1544 (see Lemerle, chapter 10, below). Philandrier's commentary was the most accurate to date, and he even commended the work to his dedicatee François I, with the assertion that 'I have a firm interpretation except for a few places which not even Apollo could have deciphered' (Wiebenson 1982, 1–14).

FROM PALLADIO TO PERRAULT

Despite the spread of Mannerist architecture in northern Europe after 1550, the *all'antica* style was destined to enjoy a continued vitality through the enormous popularity of Palladio's design models as illustrated in his *Quattro libri*. Palladio also produced illustrations for Daniele Barbaro's 1556 Italian translation of Vitruvius, which itself breathed new life into Vitruvian debate by correcting the misinterpretations of the earlier editions of Fra Giocondo and Cesariano (Kruft 1994, 72). Whilst Serlio had illustrated the application of the Orders to such modern elements as house façades, fireplaces and even church domes (Bramante's dome for St Peter's is illustrated in Book III), this spirit of Vitruvian invention reached its full expression in Palladio's treatise. Most notably, in the absence of any surviving antique houses other than in ruined form, Palladio illustrated a series of *all'antica* villas and palazzos which, unlike Serlio's and De l'Orme's northern European prototypes, were now independent of Gothic forms and fully adapted to suit modern needs of comfort and convenience. Indeed Palladio, more than any other treatise writer, shifted the content of architectural books from the lengthy theoretical interpretations of Vitruvius initiated by Alberti towards the architect-orientated practical designs found in the later pattern-books. Although the treatises of Serlio, Vignola and Palladio could not replace Vitruvius's text from which they had evolved, in the second half of the sixteenth century they held equal rank alongside it (Kruft 1994, 72). Moreover, Palladio's many woodcuts of his own domestic architecture underline the growing bond between 'paper palaces' and actual ones. They illustrate the fact that the content of architectural treatises was increasingly determined not by philological concerns but by active areas of contemporary patronage, chief amongst which was domestic architecture.

The 'Palladian' spirit was most notably continued early in the following century by the next major Vitruvian-style treatise, produced in 1615 by Palladio's pupil, Vincenzo Scamozzi (see Frascari, chapter 14, below). Scamozzi's treatise was, however, destined to be the last in the Renaissance tradition of such works. His *L'Idea della architettura universale* lies at the crossroads between the old body-centred Neoplatonic cosmology and the new age of mathematical order which would be exemplified by the French theorist Claude Perrault. The growing popularity of the Baroque in seventeenth-century Italy limited the relevance of Vitruvian literature, and meant that practising architects were less concerned with the 'correct' interpretation of Vitruvian rules than they were with the breaking of them. However, neither Bernini nor Borromini published any 'rules' or models, whilst the principal work of one of the main Baroque theorists, Guarino Guarini's treatise on civil architecture, was not published until 1737 (Kruft 1994, 101–8). With no systematic theoretical defence of Italian early- and high-Baroque, printed literature on architectural theory remained dominated during the first half of the seventeenth century by the increasingly anachronistic treatises of the previous century. This inertia is illustrated by the many new editions and translations of Serlio (1618–19, 1663), Vignola (1603 etc.), and Palladio (1601, 1616, 1642) (Wiebenson 1982; Bury 1988). These new editions of the old masters were especially popular in northern European countries where the Renaissance ideals had only been embraced relatively recently.

The gradual loss of vitality in Vitruvian debate is perfectly illustrated by the development of the theory of the Orders. The early theorists had quickly discovered that Vitruvius and Roman building practice as evidenced by the actual remains could not be reconciled with regard to determining the 'correct' proportions of the Orders. Matters were further confused by the apparent need to adjust the proportion of elements according to optical effect, as alluded to by Vitruvius (Vitr.VI.ii) and facilitated by the Renaissance rules of perspective. Such variations and calculations rendered the absolute relative. Consequently Vitruvius's key discussion of the human form as the absolute basis of the proportions of the Greek columns was to be supplanted in the sixteenth-century Order books by ever more practical instructions directed towards establishing a consistent mathematical method for the proportioning of elements. In Serlio's pioneering codification of 1537 the columns had progressed in clear modular ratios which, in the case of the Greek Orders, followed Vitruvius in reflecting the human 'types' of each column, although the pedestals were based, independently and confusingly, on the harmonic proportions. First Hans Blum (in 1550) and later, most successfully of all, Vignola (in 1562) sought to embrace the proportions of every element in much-reprinted, easy-to-use systems now defined without any reference to the human body (see Tuttle, chapter 11, below).

The rise of such abstract mathematical systems meant that by 1600 a riot of conflicting advice concerning architectural proportion was available in print. This conflict undermined faith in the possibility of establishing any 'absolute' set of ratios for the five columns based on human form. Observing this conflict, the French architect Roland

Fréart, Sieur de Chambray, was the first writer to compare and criticise the various rules given by modern authors when conservatively advancing the Greek Orders as absolute models in 1650. But in contrast the 'arch-Modern' Claude Perrault, after once again comparing the published ratios but now recommending their 'mean', famously redefined architectural proportion as a form of 'arbitrary', changeable beauty in his French Vitruvius of 1673 and *Ordonnance* of 1683. 'Positive' (or absolute) beauty was henceforth to be limited to the apparently rational criteria of bilateral symmetry, solid construction and fitness for use (see McEwen, chapter 18, below). Thus the immutable basis of architecture in universal harmony as recorded by Vitruvius, a concept which was reinterpreted in early fifteenth-century Italy and which was so effectively wed to medieval traditions yet modern needs throughout sixteenth-century Europe, in seventeenth-century France came to be seen as founded on nothing more than human judgement and taste.

ILLUSTRATING VITRUVIUS

The printed treatises were conceived for use by architects at the point of design, that is with compasses and dividers in hand. Hence these books utilised woodcuts, and later copperplate engravings, to illustrate and thereby shorten and clarify any accompanying text. The illustrations in the sixteenth-century treatises should be seen as 'technical' rather than 'artistic' in nature, their principal purpose being to convey practical information concerning proportion, dimension and, with regard to the column and specific building types, character or decorum. Vitruvius's text made reference to illustrations, promising figures of the volute of the Ionic column and the curve of entasis, for example, although none of these has survived. The first scale woodcuts to be published in a Vitruvian book were those of Milan cathedral in Cesariano's *Vitruvius* (see Hart, chapter 9, below). Editions of Vitruvius's treatise, and of architectural treatises based on the Vitruvian model, were amongst the earliest fully illustrated printed books. However, the development of the illustrated architecture book in the first half of the sixteenth century formed part of the growth of illustrated printing which was in fact well-established before 1500 in works of a non-technical nature (comprising theological, legal, classical and medieval literature; Febvre and Martin 1993, 90–104). In its use of the woodcut, the architectural treatise was again surprisingly slow to exploit the available printing technology.

Alberti's manuscript was, it is thought, intended to be read aloud, and as such included no illustrations in its early editions (Alberti 1988, xxi; Serlio 1996, xvii–xx). Indeed, it was not until 1550 that the first illustrated edition was to appear (in Florence). Filarete's and di Giorgio's manuscripts, although well illustrated in their various versions, remained unpublished (Onians 1988; Kruft 1994, 54, 58). Grapaldi's *De Partibus Aedium* published in Parma in 1494 was unillustrated. With its descriptive maze of antique monuments, the first illustrated book to touch on architecture was the *Hypnerotomachia Poliphili* supposedly by Fra Francesco Colonna, printed in 1499 by the great Venetian printer Aldus Manutius. Ten years later Fra Luca Pacioli's *De divina proportione* was published in Venice with illustrated sections on architecture. A number of manuscript copies of Vitruvius had been illustrated, notably the so-called Ferrara manuscript of the late fifteenth (or early sixteenth) century and an Italian translation of Vitruvius produced by Fabio Calvo under Raphael's direction around 1514 (Sgarbi 1993, 48; Kruft 1994, 67). Both manuscripts were to remain unpublished, however. The first printed edition of Vitruvius's treatise, that of around 1486, was unillustrated, whilst the first illustrated version to be published, and as such the first illustrated book with the rules of antique architecture as its central concern, was that edited by Fra Giocondo, published in Venice by the learned Giovanni de Tridino in 1511. Cesariano matched illustrations with text in the first Italian edition of Vitruvius, published by Gottardo da Ponte of Como in 1521, and pre-empted Serlio by introducing the popular comparative illustration of the Orders in a line. A number of illustrations of the Orders also appeared in the short architectural treatise entitled *Medidas del Romano* (Roman measurements) published not by an Italian, but by a Spaniard, Diego de Sagredo, at Toledo in 1526 (see Llewellyn, chapter 6, below). In subsequent decades Fra Giocondo's and Cesariano's plates were destined to form the basis for the illustrations (and text) of numerous Vitruvius editions (Wiebenson 1982; Kruft 1994, 70–72). As but one example, Cesariano's illustration of Halicarnassus was adapted by Walther Ryff in his German Vitruvius of 1548 to include late-Gothic architecture of Nuremberg, indeed echoing Cesariano's own representation of Gothic architecture (Milan cathedral) to illustrate Vitruvius (Kruft 1994, 71).

The honour of being the first to develop the idea of a fully illustrated treatise, however, goes to the Bolognese theorist Sebastiano Serlio (Serlio 1996; see Hart and Hicks, chapter 7, below). In publishing the first-ever treatise to deal with the five Orders in a systematic way (in the form of the *Regole generali di architettura* of 1537), Serlio introduced the hugely influential type of craft-orientated, illustrated rule-book for the carving of the antique columns which Blum and, ultimately, Vignola were to rationalise still further. Serlio's prescriptions for the Orders reflected the teachings of his master Peruzzi, and more particularly an anonymous illustrated manuscript on the Orders apparently produced under Peruzzi's guidance in Siena after 1520 (Juřen 1981; Kruft 1994, 64). Serlio also illustrated the Orders applied to the design of a range of modern elements – from fireplaces to house façades – which were without any surviving antique models. In the case of the survey drawings in the third book of his treatise, on ancient monuments, each of the illustrations was intended as an accurate record of the measurements (and proportions) of the original architecture, to be scaled-off with compasses as the text itself suggests. Serlio's text remains more or less strictly 'bounded' by the outline of these figures, in both its content and its physical shape.

A mere glance at one of Serlio's pages shows the astonishing detail which the early printers achieved in their woodcuts (plate 1). Indeed, from the inception of the printed architectural image onwards it has become impossible to construct a building without reference to such mass-produced images, whether to woodcuts, engravings or, more recently, to photographs (see Carpo, chapter 8, below).

TOWARDS AN EDUCATION IN THE 'THEORY' AND 'PRACTICE' OF ARCHITECTURE

The Renaissance treatises were largely responsible for defining the now familiar role of the architect as the 'designer' of buildings, a role increasingly independent of that of the site-based builder or master mason. Following Vitruvius, these books outlined to their architect-readership design procedures that required the application both of antique models to provide form to buildings and, of greater novelty, of an individual column (or columns) to govern the ordered arrangement and the character (decorum) of façades. Serlio, for example, explains this process to the would-be architect through matter-of-fact descriptions of façade compositions (Serlio 1996). Moreover, the Italian term *disegno* means both a 'design' and a 'drawing', and the latter became the preferred representational medium for architects in the early Renaissance. For in line with Alberti's *De pictura*, early Vitruvian manuscripts had included a justification for drawing as the means by which optical and geometric aspects of a design could best be expressed (Onians 1988, 159, 172–3; Kruft 1994, 58). Consequently, the early treatises recommended that designs should be represented not only in the well-established three-dimensional form of scale models and perspectives, but also in the more abstract projections (types of 'arrangement') recommended to architects by Vitruvius of plan (Vitruvius's 'ichnography'), section and elevation (both termed 'orthography' by Vitruvius) (Vitr.I.ii; see Hart, chapter 9, below). Hence di Giorgio and

Serlio, for example, both make full use of these projections in order to illustrate their utility.

The architect's emerging independence from, and mastery over the mason and craftsman in matters of design was further defined in the early Italian Renaissance by the sharp distinction between the published 'theory' of *all'antica* architecture, with which the architect was naturally conversant, and the many traditional craft 'practices' carried out on-site. Vitruvius had himself made a clear distinction between the *fabrica* (craft) and *ratiocinatio* (theory) of architecture (Vitr.I.i; Kruft 1994, 24). The very existence of such relatively novel artifacts as books on architecture necessarily constituted a 'theoretical' discourse remote from actual 'practice'. Such remoteness was underlined by the principal concern of these publications with the enigmatic terms of Vitruvius, as opposed, say, to the actual building practices and craft achievements of the previous three centuries. This emerging dichotomy was openly characterised by the illustration of twin figures – 'Theory' and 'Practice' – in the frontispieces of the treatises by Vignola, Palladio and Scamozzi, three of the most active practitioner-authors of the sixteenth century. Giorgio Vasari lamented that theory, when separated from practice, was of little use: if only Alberti had had more practical experience he would, according to Vasari, have been a better architect. Certainly Alberti had stressed in the prologue of his treatise that the architect 'must have an understanding and knowledge of all the highest and most noble disciplines' (Alberti 1988, 3). True to the ideal of the Renaissance man, the Vitruvian architect was expected to have encyclopedic knowledge of the theory of many arts. Vitruvius had himself defined the architect as 'a man of letters, a skillful draughtsman, a mathematician, familiar with historical studies, a diligent student of philosophy, acquainted with music; not ignorant of medicine, learned in the responses of jurisconsults, familiar with astronomy and astronomical calculations' (Vitr.I.i; Kruft 1994, 24).

Whilst Alberti and Filarete had principally written for princes and noble patrons, Serlio was the first treatise writer with the express aim of educating the architect, and hence whilst Alberti wrote in Latin, Serlio followed Filarete and Cesariano's example in writing in Italian, of use to architects and scholars alike. Serlio notes at the outset of Book IV that his rules were formulated not only for 'exalted intellects', but for 'every average person' (Serlio 1537, fol. IIIr/126r); and in Book III he states that 'my whole intention is to teach those who do not know and who think it worthwhile listening to what I say' (Serlio 1540, fol. CVI/99v). Moreover, Vitruvius's text was not clearly organised from a didactic point of view, and Alberti had ordered his text around philosophical concepts (particularly the Vitruvian triad of *firmitas* (II–III), *utilitas* (IV–V) and *venustas* (VI–IX)) rather than, say, the Orders or distinct building types (Kruft 1994, 43–4, 51; Serlio 1996, xix). In short, none of the earlier writers, with their various philological, utopian and anthropomorphic priorities, answered the practical needs of a practising architect. This need was addressed by Serlio through his unprecedented design patterns or *invenzioni*. His pioneering conception of a clear 'programme' of instruction for the would-be architect, which he outlined in his first book of 1537 (but entitled Book IV), was to be realised through a series of separately published books designed to form a complete work (Kruft 1994, 73–9; Serlio 1996).

Serlio's didactic scheme commences with a fully illustrated instruction in the traditional craft and painterly rules of geometry and perspective (Books I and II respectively), moves on to a study of Roman building types (Book III) and of the rules for the carving and use of the five Orders, arranged sequentially from Tuscan to Composite (Book IV), then descends through sacred and secular architectural projects (Books V and VI respectively) to conclude with practical problems which an architect might encounter, such as building on irregular or sloping sites (Book VII). This conception of a didactic programme in seven books reflected contemporary rhetorical-mnemonic theory (as well as di Giorgio's revised manuscript, reduced from ten to seven books), rather than Vitruvius's 'classical' ten-book organisation as revived by Alberti (Serlio 1996, xxvi). Serlio's books largely defined the categories of subsequent Vitruvian literature, not least the ever-popular idea of a separate book on the Orders (as published by Blum in 1550, Vignola in 1562 and Shute in 1563).

Thus, in parallel with the theory and lore of *all'antica* architecture which the early treatises made public for the first time, techniques of architectural practice also became the subject of publications during the early sixteenth century. Indeed, although Vitruvius's treatise was enigmatic with regard to the details of such matters as Roman hydraulics, perspective and carving, Vitruvian theorists expanded on these allusions with publications on the use of hydraulics in engineering and garden design (by di Giorgio and De Caus), of perspective in stage design (by Serlio) and of geometry in stonecarving (by Dürer and Serlio). Hence it was also in this 'technical' content that Vitruvian literature assisted the rise of the architect, as distinct from the master mason, by challenging the absolute monopoly of the crafts in techniques of construction (see Morresi, chapter 15, below). In France, for example, sections in treatises, and indeed entire works, dealt for the first time with the non-Vitruvian, traditional craft subjects of stereotomy (books by De l'Orme and Jousse) and carpentry (again by De l'Orme). Indeed, the practical bias of these books, and of Serlio's in particular, was a central reason for their success in introducing *all'antica* architecture into the building practices of northern Europe.

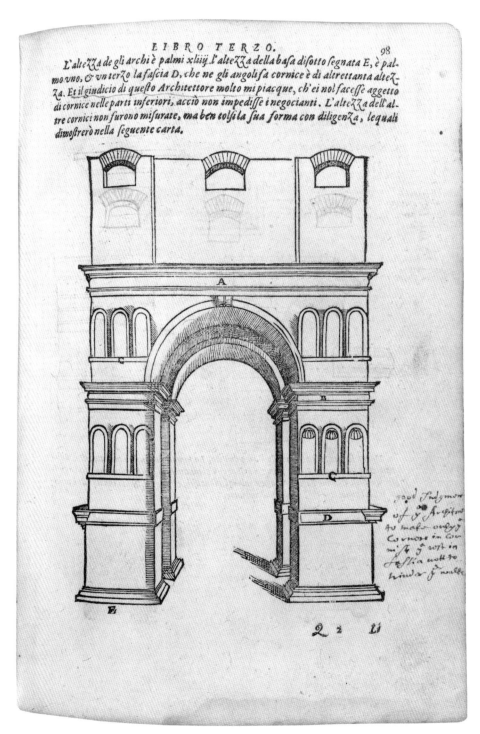

L'altezza de gli archi è palmi xliiij. l'altezza della basa disotto segnata E, è palmo vno, & vn terzo la fascia D, che ne gli angoli sa cornice è di altrettanta altezza. Et il giudicio di questo Architettore molto mi piacque, ch'ei nol facesse aggetto di cornice nelle parti inferiori, acciò non impedisse i negocianti. L'altezza dell'altre cornici non furono misurate, ma ben tolsi la sua forma con diligenza, lequali dimostrerò nella seguente carta.

1 (above and facing page) Inigo Jones's annotations to his copy of Serlio's Book III (1600 edition, published by Francesco de' Franceschi: fols. 98r and 100r). Collection Centre Canadien d'Architecture/Canadian Centre for Architecture, Montréal.

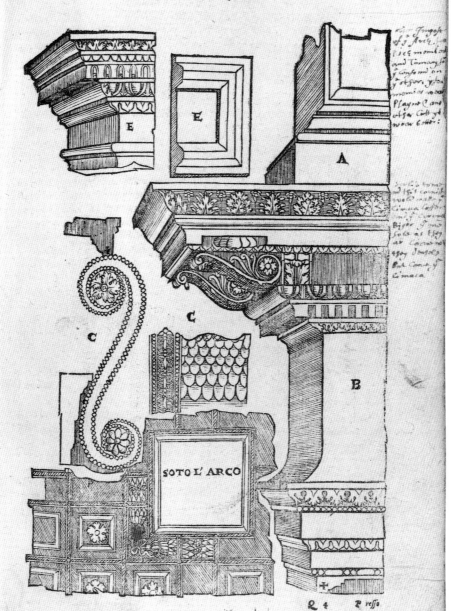

SOTO L'ARCO

E · E · A · C · C · B

Through such works it was now perfectly possible for architects to become masters of masons, independent of traditional craft initiation (although Palladio's training as a mason and Inigo Jones's as a joiner both point to the endurance of the craft apprenticeship). Up to the early sixteenth century, the education of would-be architects in the Vitruvian subjects was, in the majority of cases, through a period in a painter's studio: Serlio and Vignola were taught the Renaissance art of perspective in this way. But by the mid-sixteenth century the art of building had been largely transformed from an oral, secretive craft to a public art almost fully defined in print, a fact which reduced the architect's traditional dependence on the painter. I say 'almost' defined in print, because in the absence of large-scale ecclesiastical building programmes up to this time, books on church design had not been produced by market-orientated printers (excepting, that is, Serlio's Book v). This transformation was unique in that other medieval craft activities – such as tailors and the town guilds – retained a monopoly on their techniques, whilst the professional disciplines of law and medicine were by tradition less secretive, university-based subjects.

The printed book had made self-education relatively easy and established reliable and clear versions of texts which would otherwise have been subject to scribal error and restricted circulation (Onians 1988, 172). The novice architect was not to copy slavishly the patterns and models which accompanied these texts, but was rather to study them as illustrations of the application of Vitruvian principles and as starting points for further invention within the general rules (Serlio's *regole generali*). A library of Renaissance treatises on the scale of Inigo Jones's richly annotated collection, which included Vitruvius, Alberti, Serlio, De l'Orme, Vignola, Palladio and Scamozzi (plate 1), in effect prefigured the institutionalised courses to be taught in the newly founded architecture schools of the late seventeenth century. Indeed, the first courses in schools such as the Académie Royale d'Architecture, founded by Louis XIV in Paris in 1671, were themselves naturally enough centred on these canonical texts; these courses led in turn to new treatises, as, for example, with François Blondel's *Cours d'architecture* of 1675–83, which was based on his twice-weekly lectures at the Académie.

THE 'VITRUVIAN MAN': THE EVOLVING MODEL OF DECORUM, SYMMETRY AND PROPORTION

Vitruvius had described two 'models' which the Orders imitated, namely the hut supposedly built by primitive man (Vitr.II.i.2–8) (plate 2) and the proportions and features of the human body (Vitr.IV.i.6–8).

EX PRIMA MVNDI HOMINVM AETATE AEDIFICATIO· MVLTI ENIM AB
ANIMALIBVS EXEMPLA VITAE CONSERVAMÕ͗ IMITATI SVNT & Cᴬ

2   Building the primitive hut, from Cesare Cesariano, *Di Lucio Vitruvio Pollione De Architectura Libri Dece*
(Como, 1521), Book II, fol. xxxIIr. Cambridge University Library.

In particular, he recorded that the body had dictated the proportions
and gender of the Greek columns which ranged from the 'masculine'
Doric and 'matronly' Ionic to 'maidenly' Corinthian. In describing the
principle of decorum, these types had been linked by Vitruvius to
temples dedicated to particular gods: Doric for Minerva, Mars and
Hercules; Ionic for Juno, Diana and Bacchus; and Corinthian for
Venus and Flora (Vitr.I.ii.5). Vitruvius's characterisation of the columns
was developed by early theorists to form a 'language of use', in which
particular Orders were matched to particular modern building types
with regard to dedication, function or character and status of the
patron. Hence, according to Filarete, the Doric column was suited to
the residence of a gentleman, the Corinthian to that of a merchant and
the Ionic to that of a craftsman: according to Serlio, the Tuscan was
suited to fortresses, the Doric to buildings for men of arms, Ionic to
those for men of letters, and Corinthian to convents. Indeed, Serlio's
was the most complete development to date of this principle of
decorum based on human types.

The simile of the architectural 'body' frequently recurred in Vitruvian literature and represented an important departure from Gothic practices in which the body was not, as far as the evidence suggests, a principal model – although geometrical studies of the face feature in De Honnecourt's 'lodge-book' (Wittkower 1988, 102; Kruft 1994, 37). Hence Alberti famously defined architectural beauty with reference to the 'reasoned harmony of all the parts within a body, so that nothing may be added, taken away, or altered, but for the worse' (Alberti 1988, Book VI ch. 2, 156); and, as was noted earlier, Filarete's text is a 'celebration' of the anthropomorphic principle in architecture. Di Giorgio interpreted Vitruvius more literally still by drawing the body inside columns, and the face inside entablatures (to represent the idea of dentils as a row of teeth-like blocks) and also inside capitals to show their proportion. Sagredo in 1526 again illustrated the relationship between the entablature and the features of the face. Vitruvius's body–column simile was to be interpreted most inventively by the English theorist John Shute; the personifications of the five columns in his treatise of 1563 reflected moral archetypes illustrated in Renaissance emblem and heraldry books (see Hart, chapter 17, below). In contrast, the ideal of the column as a perfect body was disfigured by Sambin and Dietterlin through their grotesque and bestial herms.

Moreover, in describing the planning of temple architecture, Vitruvius famously observed that the extremities of a man with outstretched limbs conformed to the geometry of a circle (centred on the navel) and a square (with an unspecified centre) (Vitr.III.i.3). Vitruvius goes on to describe the human body as the ultimate source of Platonic 'perfect' numbers – particularly six and ten – and of units of measurement (the 'finger' or inch, 'palm', 'foot', and 'cubit' or forearm from elbow to fingertips). Following the celebrated drawings of this so-called Vitruvian man by di Giorgio (1482–6) and Leonardo (c.1490), the Roman's description was to become one of those most frequently illustrated in Renaissance editions of his treatise. Di Giorgio and Leonardo had both united the square and circle in one drawing, but Fra Giocondo in his 1511 Vitruvius showed two versions – the square, centred on the phallus, and the circular, following Vitruvius's description, centred on the navel (plate 3). Cesariano, in his Italian translation of 1521, illustrates one figure inside an overlapping square and circle and another, quite different figure with his feet extending below a square (Sgarbi 1993, 44) (plate 4). Dürer in 1528 illustrated the back of the male torso, once again centred on a circle but now only partly indicated, thereby 'fragmenting' the absolute geometry of human form for the first time.

Vitruvius's description of the perfection of the male form was given force by the Platonic conception of the human body as an elemental

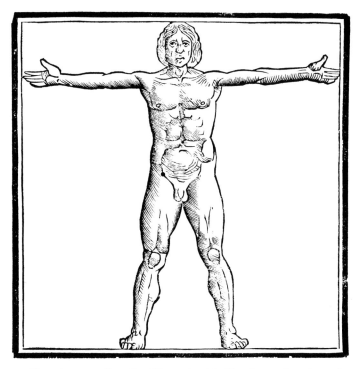

3   Vitruvian man, from Fra Giocondo, *M. Vitruvius per Iocundum solito castigatior factus* (Venice, 1511), Book III, fol. 22v. Cambridge University Library.

model, or microcosm, which embodied the harmony of the planetary bodies, or macrocosm. 'Cosmological man' had been represented in medieval manuscripts, notably the twelfth-century codex by Hildegard of Bingen (Sgarbi 1993, 44; Kruft 1994, 35; Rykwert 1996a, 80) and, not surprisingly, this figure became fused with Vitruvian man in Renaissance books on cosmic harmony. Francesco Giorgi illustrated Vitruvian man in his *De harmonia mundi* (Venice, 1525), in a chapter entitled 'Why man in the figure of the circle is an image of the world' (Wittkower 1988), and Heinrich Cornelius Agrippa illustrated men in various postures surrounded by the astrological signs in his *De occulta philosophia libri tres* (Cologne, 1533) (plate 5). In Elizabethan England the first reference to Vitruvian man was made by John Dee in his famous mathematical Preface to *Euclid* of 1570 (Hart 1994), but Robert Fludd was the first Englishman to illustrate the Vitruvian figure in his all-embracing work on cosmic harmony, the *Utriusque Cosmi . . . Historia* (Oppenheim, 1617–19), with its sections on fortification and mnemonic architecture.

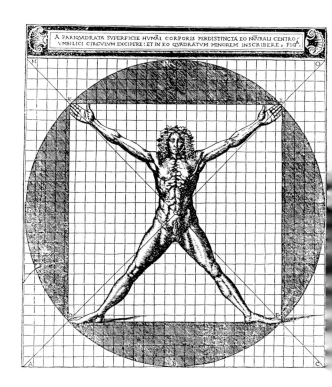

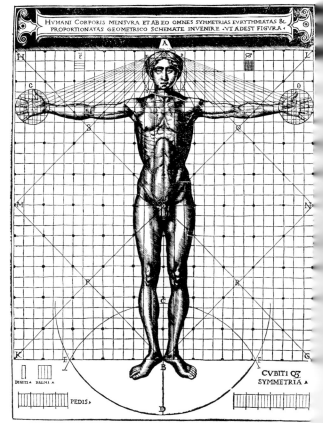

4 Cesariano illustrated one
figure inside an overlapping
square and circle and another,
quite different, figure with feet
extending below a square. The
latter version presents the
Vitruvian man as a Christ-like
figure. From Cesare Cesariano,
*Di Lucio Vitruvio Pollione De
Architectura Libri Dece* (Como,
1521), Book III, fols. XLIXr, Lr.
Cambridge University Library.

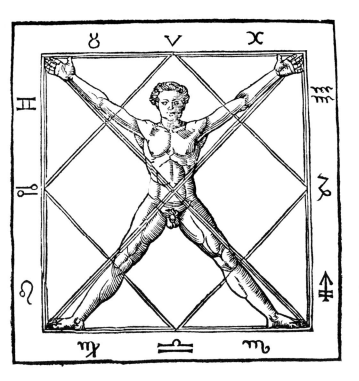

5 'Cosmological man', from Heinrich Cornelius Agrippa, *De occulta philosophia libri tres* (Cologne, 1533), Book II, p. CLXIIII. Cambridge University Library.

The conception of human proportion as the divinely inspired 'pattern' of all human works, outlined in Vitruvius and thus developed by Neoplatonists, underlies the Renaissance treatises' central concept of a 'new' architectural order in harmony with nature and the cosmos. Hence, in his second book of 1545 Serlio described the lineaments of a given plan as the *linee occulte* (or 'hidden lines' of nature), whilst Scamozzi went on to relate these lines to palace plans in 1615 (Hersey 1976; Serlio 1996, 458). Dee advanced his conception of Vitruvian man as 'the Lesse world . . . called *Microcosmus*' as proof of the need to 'reharmonise' traditional English arts through the application of geometric principles (Dee 1570, sig. ciiij). Wotton echoed this aspiration in 1624 by again contemplating 'the Fabrique of our owne Bodies, wherein the *High Architect* of the world, had displaied such skill, as did stupifie, all humane reason' (Wotton 1624, 7).

This attempt by treatise writers to harmonise architecture, from part to whole, with the proportions of the human body led naturally to the concept of a licentious or neglected architecture which was 'out of harmony', as it were, with nature. Filarete, in outlining his organic concept of *all'antica* architecture, maintained that since 'a building is really a living being', 'it can be cured of illness by a good doctor' (Filarete 1972, 29). In his *De divina proportione* (Venice, 1509), Luca Pacioli linked the capitals of the various Orders to a range of human emotions, the Corinthian to joy and the Ionic to melancholy, for example. If bodies which lacked harmony and eurythmia became ill, then so, in theory, could buildings: the author of the *Hypnerotomachia Poliphili* (Venice, 1499) used the simile of bodily health to explain the harmonious arrangement of antique architecture, where, quoting Robert Dallington's 1592 translation, 'as in a mans body one qualitie being contrarie to another, sicknesse dooth follow . . . so in building if the adjuncts be unaptly disposed, and undecently distributed there will fall out a fowle deformitie' (Colonna 1592, 22). In this vein Teofilo Gallacini, a student of medicine, used the methods of a physician in his *Trattato . . . sopra gli errori degli architetti* (written in 1621) to diagnose deformities in Mannerist ornament, pointing to licentious elements which jarred with the Vitruvian system of anthropomorphic proportion and character.

Vitruvius's treatise was presented by Dee as recording a Christian Golden Age, written as it had been around the time of Christ's nativity during the age of Augustus (see Hart, chapter 17, below). Moreover, Vitruvius's description of human proportion was apparently reinforced by the biblical conception of man created in the image of God (Genesis 1:26). Early Vitruvian literature underlined the moral virtue of 'perfect' human proportions. In the *Hypnerotomachia Poliphili* Poliphilo's object of desire, Polia, is presented as the ultimate embodiment of the divine proportions of which the antique temples, arches and tombs encountered by Poliphilo were but pale reflections. Ten years later Pacioli made this relationship between the Orders and the divine origin of their proportions explicit in the *De divina proportione* (identified, following Euclid, as the Golden Section).

The biblical ideal of man made in the image of God, and the traditional cultivation of Christ's body as the ultimate human embodiment of divine proportion, naturally enough led early Vitruvian commentators to 'christianise' the Vitruvian form. The so-called Ferrara manuscript of Vitruvius dating from the late fifteenth, or the early sixteenth, century shows a figure whose attributes are those of a crucifixion (Sgarbi 1993, 44–6), and Cesariano adapted Leonardo's drawing by representing the man within the square more explicitly as a crucified figure, with palms exposed (unlike in Leonardo's version but exposed by Cesariano no doubt in part to indicate the palm as a unit of measure). Cesariano's Christ-like man is, significantly enough, a different character from that in the circle: the animation of this 'circular' figure, with flowing hair and erect phallus, is in sharp contrast to the static nature of the Christ-like form (Sgarbi 1993, 44). Whilst there were no illustrations of Vitruvian man in the literature of Elizabethan England, in the English *Lomazzo* a plate added to Lomazzo's section on human proportion was loosely based on Dürer's famous engraving of Adam and Eve (of 1504), and again it is implied that the

Orders which follow should be formed in imitation of divine prototypes. This intention was underlined in Lomazzo's text which urged
his reader 'to represent any columne after the similitude of mans body,
which is the perfectest of all Gods creatures' (Haydocke 1598, Book 1,
85) (see Hart, chapter 17, below).

Filarete's famous drawing of a naked Adam in need of shelter from
the rain sought to emphasise the original purpose behind architecture
in the Christian story, that of providing 'clothing' to the perfect body
which Adam represented as the First Man (Onians 1988, 159; Rykwert
1996a; Sgarbi 1993, 44). Moreover, St Augustine had related the
proportions of the human body to the dimensions of Noah's Ark, as
Alberti was to point out, whilst medieval writers linked the traditional
Latin-cross church plan to the human form, and especially to that of
Adam and the Saviour (Augustine, *De civitate*, xv.26; Alberti 1988,
Book IX, ch. 7; Rykwert 1996a, 39, 77). These medieval associations,
together with the fact that Vitruvius's description of the perfection of
human form was made in the context of the design of a temple or
sacred building (*sacra aedes*), prompted Vitruvian commentators to
apply the divine 'pattern' of the body to church design in particular. Di
Giorgio drew a male figure ordering the plan of a Latin-cross church
and a church façade (Wittkower 1988, 21; Kruft 1994, 56; Rykwert
1996a, 63). Indeed, he even used the figure of a man as the outline of
a walled town, with a church situated in the breast. Pietro Cataneo in
his *I quattro primi libri di architettura* (Venice, 1554) again illustrated the
anthropomorphic qualities of the Latin-cross church with a Christ-like
form (plate 6), and in discussing Solomon's temple, Juan Bautista
Villalpanda in his *In Ezechielem explanationes et apparatus urbis* (Rome,
1604/5) was to illustrate the plan of the porticoes of the archetypal
temple organised around a loin-clothed figure with arms now folded
towards the breast.

In the Renaissance treatises the Vitruvian body-temple analogy was,
however, also extended to the planning of secular building types. The
model of the human body obviously informed the inventive application of Vitruvian principles to various house types, at first by Alberti,
Filarete and di Giorgio, and later by Serlio, De l'Orme and Palladio;
indeed, at the outset of his section on domestic architecture in the
Quattro libri, Palladio directly compared the proportions of the human
body with the planning of private dwellings (and not with the layout
of churches, which are not discussed in the treatise). Palladio's explicit
application of a divine prototype to a secular purpose, and one with
questionable moral authority at that (Onians 1988, 176), was echoed by
his unprecedented use of the pediment and dome, traditional features
of church architecture, to form his famous Villa Rotonda. Palladio's
woodcut views inside the 'body' of his buildings have been compared

6   The Vitruvian man and a church plan, from Pietro Cataneo, *I quattro primi libri di architettura* (Venice, 1554), Book III, fol. 37r. Cambridge University Library.

to Andreas Vesalius's early dissection drawings, published in 1543 (see Tavernor, chapter 13, below); Vesalius pictured the parts of the human body as the object of anatomical investigation, cut open, rather than as being based on a divine pattern established by external qualities of proportion and profile. Indeed, Palladio's drawing of the Vitruvian figure, published in the 1567 'Barbaro' edition, takes a step in this practical direction in illustrating the human figure as a study of measured relationships between parts, that is no longer encompassed by the Vitruvian geometric outline so resonant of divine ideals to earlier commentators.

Whereas the Vitruvian figure had embodied a perfect unity between geometry and proportion, the tendency throughout the sixteenth century was towards an evermore abstract understanding of the two. This divorce was encouraged by the development of geometry as a technical discipline and the rise of an independent body of literature devoted to defining geometric procedures for architects based, initially at least, on the theorems of Euclid (as outlined, for example, in the Euclidean treatises by Serlio of 1545, Bartoli of 1564 and Pomodoro of 1603). The potent mix of Euclidean practicality with mystical and numero-logical ideals associated with the body, found most notably in the works of Dürer and Dee, was gradually replaced in the seventeenth century by the strictly mathematical view of architectural practices outlined in France by Jean Dubreuil and Gérard Desargues. The divorce of geometry from a human and, therefore, divine archetype would ultimately lead to the ever-increasing preoccupation of late eighteenth-century architects with abstract geometrical purity, manifest in the grid architecture of Jean-Nicolas-Louis Durand (Pérez-Gómez 1988). This development had been heralded clearly enough during the sixteenth century by the advent of the modern geometric science of fortification, rendering redundant the Roman camp layout alluded to by Vitruvius and described by Polybius. This building science was again informed by a separate class of literature in which the application of geometry was, for the first time, independent of any human-based system of proportion or ornament.

The anatomical conception of the human body advanced through the rise of medical science in the second half of the seventeenth century, and the consequent decline of Neoplatonism with its anacronistic microcosm–macrocosm simile, inevitably undermined the status of the human body as a divine harmonic model. It was noted earlier that the Cartesian Claude Perrault did the most during this period to demote the human form as the absolute basis of architectural proportion, in stressing the relative influences of human judgement and taste. Perrault was, significantly enough, a doctor and anatomist (who was to die from an illness contracted during dissection). By the time of Marc-Antoine Laugier's famous reassessment of architectural principles published as the *Essai sur l'architecture* in 1753, the Orders were to be solely derived from the scale-less, man-made structure of the primitive hut, rendering redundant the divine pattern of the human body whose potency had been so central to the Vitruvian canon over the previous three centuries.

FROM VITRUVIAN TREATISE TO ARCHITECTURAL PATTERN-BOOK

The decline in the status of the human body as the absolute guarantor of architectural beauty serves to underline the decline of the Vitruvian book itself as the sole authority on design principles and practices. This decline also took place in the wake of the growing availability of new

forms of architectural literature and the discovery of ancient monuments in the New World and the Near and Far East which did not
accord with the 'classical' view of antiquity as recorded by Vitruvius
(Grafton 1992; see McQuillan, chapter 19, below).

In Victor Hugo's *Notre-Dame de Paris*, the scholar, gazing at the first
printed book which has come to disturb his collection of manuscripts,
turns to the vast cathedral and exclaims that the printed word will
destroy the sacred building. The inevitable, if gradual, popularisation of
the theory and practice of architecture, encouraged at first by printing
and then by the use of illustrations and the vernacular in early
sixteenth-century books, reached its fulfilment in the eighteenth century with the appearance of practically orientated pattern-books, many
of which were now exclusively aimed at a more humble readership of
builders and craftsmen. Although the art of building lost a sense of its
esoteric meaning through this process, as Hugo's scholar predicted,
architecture gained through its literature a public accessibility and a
power to express more secular themes. Furthermore, just as the
woodcut once played a part in a fundamental change in the popular
style of European architecture, through the replacement of esoteric
Gothic principles by a pictorially defined order, so contemporary
digital imagery may again lead to a shift in architectural style. For the
first time in five centuries, the printed book may be destined to play
only a supporting role in this development. From the tradition of the
didactic treatise we may be in the process of returning to an exclusive
form of architectural communication, this time developed through the
less accessible world of computer-aided design software (see Carpo,
chapter 8, below).

The effectiveness of the Vitruvian system lay in its ability to embody
the Renaissance view of an animistic, interconnected natural world in
which man was at the centre and the ultimate 'pattern'. Indeed, in
seeking to explain this architecture, the early treatises naturally aspired
towards a poetic or metaphorical imitation of nature, rather than one
of scientific exactitude. Absolute values of proportion and measure
were always to be modified with respect to human optical perceptions:
the early aim was to offer inspirational patterns rather than complete
prescriptions. The works of Palladio and Scamozzi mark the fulfilment
of this project to make manifest *all'antica* architecture, adapting it to
suit modern needs so that, following Scamozzi's title, it might become
a truly 'universal' design language. Indeed, their treatises were largely
responsible for the exportation of what we now call Palladianism to the
New World.

It follows, however, that the gradual replacement of the Renaissance
view of nature by instrumental, mathematical concepts during the
seventeenth century would be paralleled by, and would help stimulate,

the substitution of an architecture regulated by antiquity with one of Mannerist forms no longer dependent on models offered by either the human body or the past. In fact, the published treatises had themselves participated in this process, since the particular desire from the early sixteenth century onwards to codify the Vitruvian column 'types' assisted the rise of rational modes of thought that, ironically enough, rendered obsolete the body-centred analogies which had underpinned the very meaning of the antique Orders. With the advent of 'modernity' the architectural treatise became replaced by the manual or pattern-book, a transformation which Serlio's variant woodcut designs had initiated in introducing the concept of the 'architect-as-selector' as opposed to an inspired designer of unique buildings in the tradition of Alberti (Choay 1997, 190–91).

Each one of the Renaissance treatises represents a unique response to topics which were once of great controversy, the most notable being the correct carving of the five columns. Yet the works share one central theme, for they record each generation's attempt to formulate new architectural ideals through a reinterpretation of antiquity. Behind the façades of the 'paper palaces' illustrated in these treatises lies the enduring need to forge links with the origins of European civilisation through the medium of architecture.

Detail of plate 2, introduction.

Part One

EMULATING VITRUVIUS

1 Bronze portrait-plaquette of Alberti, usually called his 'self-portrait'.
36 × 27 mm. Paris, Bibliothèque Nationale.

Chapter One

THEORY AS RHETORIC:
LEON BATTISTA ALBERTI
IN THEORY AND IN PRACTICE

Joseph Rykwert

L EON BATTISTA ALBERTI is well known, too well known to be 'introduced', yet he is known badly, which makes any such introduction difficult. The eulogies of the standard handbooks speak of him as the father 'of the architectural profession of the Renaissance', or even 'of modern architecture', and refer to his treatises on sculpture, painting and architecture which are alleged to have laid down the law on how these arts are to be practised (Alberti 1966; 1972; 1988a). These references are often illustrated with black and white, usually rather shabby photographs of his buildings in Rimini, Florence and Mantua, giving generations of students the impression that his designing and building had only the vaguest relation to the principles he expected others to follow (Gadol 1969; Borsi 1986).

The difficulty is compounded by a somewhat misleading view of Alberti and of his architecture which has been prevalent for over a century. The architecture of the Italian Renaissance was created, the conventional view has it, by two very different figures: there was first Filippo Brunelleschi, the practical man, the mason and contractor, his clothes often dingy with stone dust; and secondly Alberti, the theorist and man of letters, the strikingly handsome and elegant courtier and showy athlete, who would never sully his hands or clothes with building-site mire. This image and the poor illustration of his buildings both tend to obscure the fact that for Alberti the often messy business of practice was necessarily related to matters of theory.

The courtly image of Alberti also owes a good deal to the bronze portrait-plaquette, usually called his 'self-portrait': a proud, graceful face, shown in profile, is labelled with an abbreviated form of his name and his personal device, the winged eye (Rykwert and Engel 1994,

474) (plate 1). Students of Renaissance bronzes maintain that it was modelled in Ferrara and by an inexpert hand, which has suggested that it might indeed be a self-portrait. However clumsy the modelling and casting, this image is perhaps the first of its kind, and seems to have stimulated Pisanello to initiate – with his splendid medal of the Byzantine emperor, John VIII Paleologus, come to Ferrara for the Ecumenical Council – the series of portrait medals which are one of the high points of Italian fifteenth-century sculpture.

The court of Ferrara was perhaps the most brilliant literary and artistic centre in Italy during the 1430s. At that time Alberti, in the Pope's following, was in Ferrara for the same council (which would within a matter of weeks be moved to Florence, and is therefore known as the Council of Florence). Pisanello was working there and the great Greek scholar Theodore of Gaza was teaching at the university. The Flemish composer Guillaume Dufay was master of the Pope's chapel, and another Fleming, the painter Rogier van der Weyden, also worked in the small town.

Alberti was not yet involved in architecture, although he was known as a theorist of the arts, since he had already written his brief book on painting which he produced in two versions – the first one in Latin and, shortly after, another one in Italian which he dedicated to Brunelleschi, with whom he had struck up a friendship (Baxandall 1974).

Tuscan though he was, Alberti had first come to Florence as a mature man, since he was born in the exile to which his family had been condemned during the Florentine disorders at the end of the fourteenth century. Born in 1404 in Genoa – and illegitimate, like his only brother Carlo – he was educated in Padua (his father had moved to Venice meanwhile) and at the University of Bologna, the best in Italy at the time. He took his – normal – double doctorate in canon and civil law, and was almost certainly ordained deacon and perhaps also priest. His first employment was in the suite of the austere Cardinal Albergati, papal legate (effectively governor) in Bologna, with whom he may have travelled to northern Europe – Germany and the Low Countries – although the only evidence about this journey is an occasional reference Alberti makes to ice-skating or half-timbered building in his architectural treatise.

From Albergati's entourage he moved into the papal court, as a pontifical abbreviator. A college of these officials was in effect a chancery, which wrote the Pope's pronouncements and ran his diplomatic correspondence. Alberti also received a number of Church preferments which made him financially independent. Although the first Pope he served directly was the Venetian Eugenius IV, Martin V (his predecessor) had intervened with the government of Florence to have the ban on the Alberti clan removed, and it is probable that Battista took the opportunity to visit Florence soon after this, in 1428. He was certainly there for some time after Pope Eugenius was forced out of Rome by a rebellion in 1434.

Alberti's Florentine stay was important for his literary reputation; he had written a number of minor works on various subjects, satirical, moral, mathematical – some to commissions from illustrious patrons – and he had begun his major socio-economic work *On the Family* (Alberti 1969), which was to become his best-known book, apart from those on architecture and painting. Since Alberti had had the greatest difficulties with some of his relations, who tried to exploit his illegitimacy to dispossess him, it was a paradoxical work for him to write, dealing as it does with the double importance of the family for the individual and for the city. The book on painting was written early in the 1430s in a Latin version (Alberti 1972). Among other things, it showed exactly how to construct the *perspectiva artificialis* which had been formulated by Brunelleschi and first consummately practised by Masaccio; it was to fascinate painters for several centuries to come. Alberti's long stay in Florence also allowed him to apply himself to the Tuscan 'language', for which he produced what was in effect its first grammar. He organised a number of competitions for the best Tuscan poems, and was appointed canon of the cathedral, a post which certainly increased his income – although his being a salaried official adds to the difficulties of establishing his authorship of those monuments with which he is linked by tradition (and even documents), since his name would probably not appear in building accounts if his services were 'borrowed' from Church or princely authorities.

During the 1430s Alberti had befriended Lionello d'Este, the young, learned and humane Marquess of Ferrara, and dedicated to him yet another of his Latin manuals – on the training and care of horses. At Lionello's suggestion he also acted as 'juror' in a competition for a statue of the marquess's father, Niccolo. In the preface to the horse-book, Alberti records his Solomonic judgement, awarding the first prize for the figure of the horse to one sculptor, and that of the marquess to another. It seems that it was again Lionello, during one of Alberti's Ferrarese visits, who asked him to provide a commentary and a 'reading' of Vitruvius's *Ten Books* on Architecture, the one acknowledged and reliable text dealing with the architecture of the ancient world.

This invitation and the first explicit involvement of Alberti in architecture may have been connected to the marquess's proposal to build a bell-tower for his cathedral, which he wanted to do in the newly revived antique manner, though it was not really begun until about 1450, and its building continued into the eighteenth century. Its

general outline and detail seem to flout much of the advice (about the
relation of columns to arches and the succession of storeys) which
Alberti was later to incorporate in his treatise on architecture and it is
difficult to connect him with this building in any explicit way. In fact,
Alberti's career until that time would seem to correspond to the
conventional view of him as a theorist with no real interest in the
practicalities of building. However, from the late 1440s the scholar and
the brilliant man of letters becomes increasingly involved with construction, engineering and even site organisation.

This change seems to have been influenced by the election to the
papacy, after the death of Eugenius IV in 1447, of Thomas Parentucelli
of Sarzana, a Tuscan scholar, diplomat and theologian (whom Alberti
had known since his student days in Bologna) who styled himself
Nicholas V. Pious and ascetic as he was in private, the new Pope was
enormously ambitious for the spiritual as well as the secular power of
his office. Building was to be his main investment. He moved the
principal papal residence from the Lateran to the Vatican – from the
palace adjoining the Pope's own cathedral, the basilica of the Saviour
founded by the Emperor Constantine and better known as St John
Lateran, to the (incidentally, more defensible) martyrium of St Peter,
prince of the Apostles and the first Pope.

The papal residence at the Vatican was in fact a country retreat, a
fortified villa known as the Belvedere, and Nicholas's scheme involved
the first attempt to link the villa with St Peter's, the other venerable
but rather decrepit and weather-beaten Constantinian basilica (Westfall
1974). In the first two of his 'Ten Books on Architecture' Alberti
shows himself to be very well informed about the mechanical and
constructional problems of the old church. Some drawings of uncertain
authorship show proposals to enlarge the apse of the church and to
fortify the whole east end, which bordered on the city wall. Houses to
the north of the church were unified, decorated and turned into a
papal residence. Plans were made for the ramshackle approach through
the Borgo, the suburban area that lies between the river and the
church, to be ordered and made more solemn, while the piece of open
ground before the church was planned as a colonnaded and paved
square. The low cloister through which the church was entered was
given an imposing, four-tiered façade in the form of a loggia from
which the Pope could bless the crowds, but it was left incomplete, and
was destroyed in the course of the late sixteenth-century rebuilding.

The Holy Year of 1450 attracted great crowds. At some point a
group of pilgrims seems to have broken through the balustrades of the
main bridge which connected the Vatican with the city; many were
trampled in the panic, others drowned in the river. The bridge was
vital and had to be quickly rebuilt. Alberti himself – for once – records

that he was consulted and had it reconstructed with a covered colonnade replacing the old balustrade. In the sixth chapter of his eighth book he is almost certainly describing the bridge which he designed on that occasion (Alberti 1988a).

Of all this prominent and large-scale work nothing but small fragments remain. Echoes of Alberti's ideas may be seen in the detail of the Palazzo Venezia, which Cardinal Pietro Barbo, later Pope Paul II, extended vastly during the later 1450s when he added a barrel-vaulted entry from the square, a colonnaded courtyard and – to the ninth-century basilica of San Marco round which the palace is built – a 'benediction loggia' based on the column-and-arch arrangement of the Colosseum and the Theatre of Marcellus, both of which also provided a basis for the much bigger loggia fronting St Peter's.

By 1450 therefore Alberti, the intellectual and courtier, was treated by the papal government, if not by the Pope himself, as a reliable and highly original architect-builder. No other builder or mason in Rome is known to have formulated such new and clear ideas about architecture, and many of these ideas are reflected by the buildings of the period, even where his participation in the project is at best conjectural. He is also known to have devised surveying instruments and pumping gear which were used to recover parts of the imperial Roman barges that had sunk in Lake Nemi, and the rebuilding of the Trevi fountain is attributed to him.

The treatise on architecture in ten books had probably reached the end of the fifth book by about 1450, when a version of it may have been presented to the Pope (Grayson 1960). There is evidence to suggest that the treatise was known in Rome soon after that, while the opening of the sixth book implies that the author was returning to it after a long break. Alberti was to leave this treatise almost complete at his death in 1472, although there are several blank spaces left in the latter part of the manuscript where references had to be verified (Alberti 1966; 1988a).

Alberti's title, *De re aedificatoria*, seems, in its fastidious Latinity, to invoke comparison with Vitruvius's treatise, written a millennium and a half earlier, also set out in ten books and known by the Greekifying title, *De Architectura* (Grayson 1960; Choay 1979). Vitruvius's and Alberti's works were, respectively, the first ancient and the first 'modern' treatises on architecture, and the difference in titles reflects the difference between the two enterprises. While Vitruvius was codifying the practice of Hellenistic architects in the preceding three or four centuries, Alberti was projecting an architecture of the future, and his appeal to the past was largely literary, since such famous ancient buildings as he quoted were either ruined or buried or both – and in any case accessible only to the most adventurous travellers. The few mentioned that were actually known to him and to his readers, such as the Roman Pantheon or the tomb of Theodoric in Ravenna, were the products of a building industry which bore no relation to practice current in Alberti's time.

The two treatises were also written for entirely different readers: Vitruvius wrote as the representative of an antiquarian tradition, and hoped his manuscript would obtain imperial patronage for that tradition as well as for himself. Alberti was attempting the constitution or the re-establishment of architecture as a liberal profession (Westfall 1969). He wrote in Latin to be read by great merchants, princes and pontiffs: by the men who were his patrons, rather than by artists and craftsmen. His treatise is a rhetorical exercise, to be read as a literary text and it was much admired by his contemporaries as a stylistic masterpiece of modern Latin, to be set beside Cicero rather than Vitruvius – about whose style Alberti himself made some unflattering reflections.

As it happened, pilgrims of that Holy Year of 1450 seem to have brought the plague with them and later in the year the Pope exiled himself to a castle at Fabriano in the Romagna, where he was visited by the commander of the papal army, Sigismondo Malatesta, Tyrant of Rimini. Sigismondo had that year undertaken to reconstruct the old and poor brick church of the Franciscan brothers (Rimini had an important place in the legend of the order's foundation), transforming it into a stone 'temple' rededicated to his patron, the saintly Burgundian king Sigismond (Ricci 1974). He wanted it to be a dynastic 'pantheon' for his family and a personal declaration of the triumph of himself and his mistress (later his wife) Isotta degli Atti.

It may well be that the Pope suggested Alberti as the right architect for Sigismondo's enterprise; by the time he was consulted, work on the interior had been going on for some years already. Sigismondo's building campaigns were erratic and the building was never completed, yet Alberti's involvement with the Riminese project seems to have been his first employment as an independant consultant and architect, whose authority was dependent (at least in part) on the masterly way in which he had stated ideas that he would now be able to apply in practice. Unfortunately, all that now remains is the lower part of the proud stone shell that Alberti designed to encase the poor brick church, but neither the upper part nor the vault and the dome that were certainly planned, were even begun. The project is otherwise documented miserably: there is an enigmatic elevation of the domed church on a small medal by the sculptor Matteo de'Pasti (Rykwert and Engel 1994, 484–5) (plate 2), who became the site architect, and a squiggle on a reproachful letter Alberti addressed to him about the work (Alberti 1957). Of course, there must have been drawings and

2   The Tempio Malatestiano, Rimini. Medal cast by Matteo de'Pasti. Inscription
dated 1450, cast c.1454? 40 mm dia. London, British Museum.

models also (even more than one), since there is evidence that one was
taken to pieces so that the masons might ascertain its detailed construction; many years after Sigismondo's (and Alberti's) death, a showy cake
for a Malatesta wedding reproduced such a model of the finished
church 'in fine sugar'.

For all that, a good deal can be inferred about the design and the
intentions of both patron and builder, primarily because the lower part
of the façade reproduces, with some variations, the details and the
dimensions of the nearby triumphal arch of the Emperor Augustus
(Borsi 1986, 106). As it is only a five-minute walk away, the reference
would have been unmistakable to any visitor; moreover the width of
the triple arches of the façade of the church is exactly double that of
the ancient arch. Alberti was very conscious of the status of such
triumphal arches as a building type; he knew several such arches in
Rome and had written rather lyrically about them in the sixth chapter

of his eighth book (Alberti 1988a). The numerical adjustments in the façade which have puzzled some historians were almost certainly due to a desire to achieve a numerical harmony between the rather long Rimini foot and the ancient Roman one.

The front of the building is in fact a brilliant and wholly original interpretation of the medieval church with a high nave and lower aisles as a composition which would make sense in 'antique' terms, that is, one which can be 'read' as a mosaic of themes assembled to make a coherent statement. The sides of the building recede in a series of arches, each one containing a sarcophagus in which one of the famous members of Sigismondo's court was to be buried. Of the three arches on the front, the middle one frames the main door, but there is no certain evidence about how the side arches were to be filled: almost certainly they would not have been left blank, as they are now. The most probable hypothesis seems – to me at any rate – that they were to contain the tombs of Sigismondo and Isotta, so that the whole construction could be read as a triumph (the notion of a triumph as a work of art rather than a procession and festival had become a literary commonplace after Petrarch) and perhaps also as a dynastic monument. This would really be the only way to explain the enormous expense and effort which the execution of the project would seem to have required.

As in all his other buildings, so in the Rimini church, the usual difficulties of overambitious builders (sporadic financial problems, site restrictions, shortage of materials) were compounded by the sheer originality of Alberti's proposals. There was no precedent for the sort of building he had proposed in Rimini and the documents are full of his reproofs as well as the masons' obvious puzzlement and even incredulity about his proposals – such as the one for the wooden barrel-vault over the nave at Rimini. Alberti had clearly expressed his preference for barrel-vaults in the fourteenth chapter of his third book. His examination of the structure convinced him that it was not strong enough to carry such a vault in stone or brick; in any case, as he points out in the ninth chapter of his fifth book, a wooden roof makes for better acoustics.

In Florence as in Rome Alberti's authorship is not always linked explicitly to buildings which tradition has firmly awarded him: namely the four constructions patronised by Bernardo Rucellai – the palace (plate 3) and loggia in the Via della Vigna Nuova, the façade of the Dominican church of Santa Maria Novella (plate 4) and the chapel containing the model of the Holy Sepulchre in the Rucellai family church of San Pancrazio (long since deconsecrated and much altered). Giorgio Vasari, who was a little censorious about Alberti, thought San Pancrazio Alberti's most successful ensemble, though he is rather

3 (left) Palazzo
Rucellai, Florence.
Computer study of
the façade.

4 (below) Santa
Maria Novella,
Florence.

scathing about the loggia. This little building has been something of a puzzle to Alberti's commentators, since it breaks one of the rules he formulated clearly in the fifteenth chapter of his seventh book: that arches should not be allowed to rest directly on cylindrical columns. Indeed on a quasi-imaginary portrait of Rucellai, which his descendants still conserve and in which his buildings are lined up in the background, the porch is represented with pilasters carrying the cornice, and the arches rest on imposts as they do in the two Roman benediction loggias.

The Rucellai palace and the church of Santa Maria Novella have this in common: they are both façades which Alberti added to existing buildings (plates 3 and 4). In the case of Santa Maria Novella, he was given a roomy, majestic vaulted late-Gothic basilica and his design develops the formal devices of Rimini. The motif of the triumphal arch is stretched and articulated to incorporate a series of older tombs in variegated dark green and white Tuscan marbles built into the wall of the church at ground level. Alberti extended this colour treatment to the whole façade of the Florentine church. As in Rimini, he was appealing to a nearby antique example: in Florence it is the cathedral Baptistery, which in the fifteenth century was considered the ancient temple of Mars adapted to church use, though its finish was to be seen on a number of other Florentine buildings, notably in the small twelfth-century basilica of San Miniato al Monte, which Alberti preferred to all the other Florentine churches. The triumphal arch at Santa Maria Novella becomes the base for a flattened image of a temple front which is the centre-piece of the upper façade, linked to the lower storey by great scrolls on either side. While neither church façade corresponds exactly to the rules for a portico belonging to a sacred building as Alberti set them out in the fifth chapter of his seventh book, the combination of the triumphal arch and the temple front to make a frontispiece for a basilican building accords very much with his ideas about composition. The façades in Rimini and Florence are effectively the first essays in devising a church front which could be read as being composed in the antique architectural language that was to dominate western architecture until the twentieth century. Alberti also used this marble intarsia technique to construct the model (at a scale of 1:2) in San Pancrazio of the Holy Sepulchre in Jerusalem. Rucellai was concerned to have the dimensions faithfully reproduced and sent a team of masons to Jerusalem to check them.

As the Riminese church was cut in the hard and pale limestone much used in the region (supplemented by Istrian stone imported from across the Adriatic), so the Tuscan buildings also make use of local techniques and local materials inventively and creatively, as Alberti himself recommended in the fourth chapter of his second book. Moving into the more usual Florentine stone, *pietra serena*, for the Rucellai Palace, he reinvented the three-storey Florentine house. The palace was the product of a refacing of an older untidy building, as was Santa Maria Novella, and was almost certainly built in two stages as Rucellai bought adjoining property. This building, too, was never finished.

The traditional three-storey structure of the Florentine patrician house had already been refined, through the use of antique proportions and mouldings, by Brunelleschi. Alberti devised a form of façade in which each storey corresponded to an Order of columns – or at least pilasters. Commenting on the ornament of private buildings in the fourth chapter of his ninth book, Alberti insists that there is nothing more agreeable than the representation of a stone colonnade. However, since Vitruvius and Pliny provided no real account of the façade of a palace, and no ruined palaces with intact façades remained, the model which Alberti used in Florence was based on the account that Vitruvius gave of the permanent set of the Roman stage – which, for tragedies, almost always had to represent a royal palace with its façade of superimposed columns (Vitr.v.vi.8; Alberti 1988a, Book VIII ch. 7, 273). Although, again, no theatres survived in full columnar splendour, there were enough ruins in Rome itself and in Orange, in Provence, to show that Vitruvius's account was credible. The Palazzo Rucellai was not designed as a whole building, however, but only as a façade to a family home which was being constantly extended, a fact which makes it difficult to reconstruct. Moreover, the two upper storeys are taller than the lower ones – against Alberti's recommendation that each storey should be shorter than the one below (Alberti 1988a, Book IX ch. 4, 301). Rather than considering this an inconsistency on Alberti's part, some scholars have suggested that he was deliberately taking account of the very narrow street on which the palace stood, and was adjusting the height to allow for the forced vision of the façade (Tavernor 1998).

This three-storey articulation was almost immediately taken up by Bernardo Rossellino, the sculptor-mason-architect who seems to have worked several times with Alberti in Rome and to have been on very good terms with the older man. The opportunity for this experiment was offered by another Pope, Pius II, who succeeded Nicholas V (after the disastrous but brief pontificate of Calixtus III Borgia) in 1458. Like Nicholas, Pius was a scholar and a builder; christened Aeneas Silvius, he revived the papal name Pius (used only once, in the second century) since Virgil persistently referred to his hero as 'pius Aeneas'. Born in a small country town, Corsignano, Pius transformed it into a palatial residence and renamed it Pienza after himself. Rossellino was commissioned to build a cathedral, palaces for the local bishop and the Pope, and a town hall. Some cardinals followed suit and built themselves residences there. However, it was the papal palace and the episcopal palace which presented themselves in proper Albertian guise (unlike the constrained Palazzo Rucellai), in following Alberti's prescription about the height of each storey diminishing as the palace rises.

At the end of the 1450s Alberti, who had liked to pass the summer in the palace and at the court of another mercenary commander and bibliophile, Federico da Montefeltro, Duke of Urbino, began to spend more time with the Gonzagas in the Mantovano (Baldi 1824; Dennistoun 1851). Lodovico Gonzaga would consult him on many matters – from draining schemes to points of learning as well as building projects: the restoration of Lodovico's castle at Cavriano was one such project about which some documents have survived.

Lodovico had intervened in Alberti's life, during his Florentine period, by involving him in a construction which had been started some time earlier, the circular choir added to the church of Ssma Annunziata in the Piazza degli Innocenti, which neighbours Brunelleschi's Ospedale of the same invocation. Alberti proposed to cover it with a hemispherical dome and so it was built – against the advice of some of the clergy and other Florentine 'experts'. The roof on the exterior had a much shallower curve than the interior one and this allowed for an intervening ring-wall to buttress the dome. It was one of the first of such domes to be built in modern times, constructed in emulation of the Pantheon, a building Alberti admired and mentioned as a model several times in his treatise. In the extended correspondence which the building provoked, it becomes clear that Alberti was the one architect whose word the Lord of Mantua would take against others.

Sometime in 1459/60, Lodovico Gonzaga had a dream (or nightmare) which instructed him to build a church dedicated to St Sebastian at one of the southward gates of Mantua. Alberti's design was for a Greek-cross church in plan, with a hemispherical dome on pendentives over the central space, one arm of the cross opening on to a porch (Calzona and Volpi Ghirardini 1994). It was without any recent precedent and there were difficulties from the beginning. Ecclesiastical authorities – including Lodovico's cardinal-son Francesco – found it strange, looking 'neither like a mosque nor a synagogue nor yet like a church'. Nevertheless, together with Brunelleschi's Santa Maria degli Angeli (though that, also, was never completed) it stands as an early example of the centralised church which became increasingly important in the late fifteenth and sixteenth centuries.

The marquess wanted this church built quickly, but its construction was full of problems. Alberti – or perhaps Lodovico – seems to have underestimated the instability of the soil as well as the humidity. There was therefore rising damp in the walls, and as soon as the vaults over the arms of the cross were built it became clear that the sideways thrust was not fully taken up and the walls went out of true, while the vaults settled rather ominously. (This last defect must have been clearly visible at the time, but has been disguised by later building and was not brought to the notice of students until recent photogrammetric surveys allowed precise measurements.) Emergency decisions to remedy these defects had to be taken. A crypt was introduced under the body of the church to ventilate both the foundations and the lower part of the walls, which were doubled in thickness, particularly at the corners. Another Florentine sculptor-mason, Luca Fancelli, was acting as the site architect – and doing so in concert with Alberti, as Rossellino had done in Rome and Matteo de'Pasti in Rimini. The correspondence in the Gonzaga archives shows clearly that Fancelli and the marquess were aware of these structural problems but also that Lodovico never wavered in his loyalty to Alberti. Construction of San Sebastiano was slow. At the marquess's death in 1478 (Alberti had died earlier, in 1472) the level of the aisle roofs had barely been reached and the central space was still covered with timber boards.

The subsequent history of the building is melancholy. Stone mouldings intended to frame some of the openings were instead used on the façade; pilasters and cornices were added and an entrance to the upper church was made to one side. A groined vault was built over the central space instead of a dome. In the nineteenth century the church was deconsecrated and reopened, with new grandiose stairways, as a monument to the war dead of 1915–18.

Lodovico had other more ambitious building projects as well. The old market-place and the big abbey church of Sant'Andrea (which housed the phials of Christ's blood, the most venerated relic in Mantua) were both neglected. Pius II, long intent on another crusade – the Turks had captured Constantinople in 1453, and were moving into the Balkans – summoned a conference of Christian rulers to Mantua in 1459/60. The old market square was paved for the occasion and new colonnaded loggias as well as a clock-tower were planned. In all of this Alberti is known to have had a part, although the exact nature of his contribution is difficult to establish. The abbey was taken away from the monks, placed more directly under Gonzaga authority, and a plan to rebuild and enlarge it was made by another architect. Alberti was consulted and, politely enough, had the project set aside in favour of his own. Again, his intentions cannot be read from the existing building, since transepts and a deep chancel were added to the three-bay church in the sixteenth century, while a dome was set over the crossing in the eighteenth (Carpeggiani and Tellini Perina 1987; Soggia 1991) (plate 5). However, the 'original' three-bay church has very striking parallels in proportion and arrangement both to the holy of holies of the Jerusalem temple of Solomon and to the basilica of Maxentius in Rome, which in the fifteenth century was believed to be the Temple of Peace; moreover, the passage on the Etruscan temple in the fourth chapter of book seven could be interpreted as being related to such a plan (Rykwert and Tavernor 1986).

The subsequent building history of the church is very confused. The original window openings were bricked in, new ones cut in the walls, and then bricked up again. A huge circular window – a feature Alberti particularly disliked, as he told Matteo de'Pasti, his site architect in Rimini, in the much-quoted letter (Alberti 1957) – was cut over the porch, and the whole interior was decorated in Neoclassical grisaille early in the nineteenth century. The Mantuan churches are therefore like a grimy and overpainted Old Master canvas which needs cleaning to show its real colours.

In the case of Sant'Andrea, this is almost literally true, since the bright colouring of the façade has only recently reappeared (Rykwert and Tavernor 1986; Soggia and Zuccoli 1994). The brick-red of the stone mouldings and capitals, and the painted chequer marbling of the walls all came as something of a surprise when the stucco facing was restored and analysed. Since building work only began after Alberti had died, there is no knowing his intentions about the colour: certainly the whole conception of the church depends on it being a brick structure. A recently discovered eighteenth-century painting of the square and the façade shows not only the colouring of the architectural members, but circular panels by or after Andrea Mantegna in the pediment and over the main door. Mantegna had a funerary chapel and monument in Sant'Andrea, and had built himself a house opposite San Sebastiano; one of two altarpieces of St Sebastian that Mantegna painted may have been intended for that church.

Mantegna was a master of geometric perspective as well as an antiquarian; he painted (as did Botticelli) an interpretation of the Allegory of Calumny, which the satirist Lucian describes as being one of the most famous paintings of the ancient world, the work of Apelles, Alexander the Great's favourite artist. Lucian was one of Alberti's favourite writers, and in the treatise on painting Alberti describes this very picture as the type of subject a modern artist should undertake. In a small country town such as Mantua, centred on a princely court, it is inconceivable that the marquess's favourite painter and his favourite architect did not meet, but no documents tell of such a meeting, which suggests that their relationship was unremarkable.

Alberti's painting treatise did not enjoy the immediate acceptance and enthusiasm that the one on architecture provoked. *De re aedificatoria* was not printed until some years after his death, finally appearing in 1486 at the behest of Lorenzo the Magnificent, who as a

5   Sant'Andrea, Mantua.

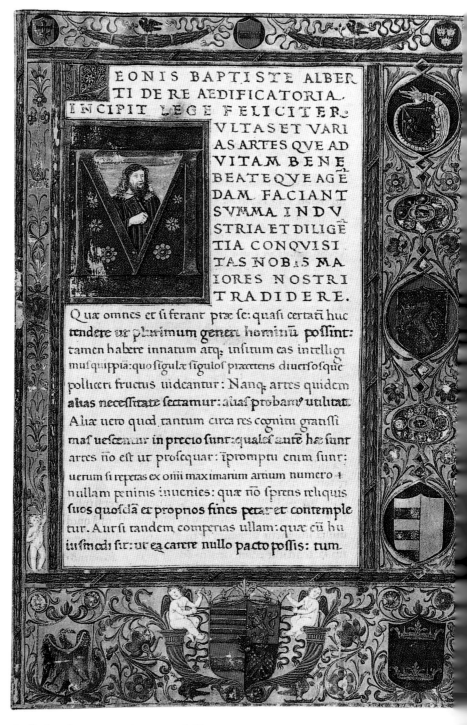

6 Preface from manuscript copy of Alberti, *De re aedificatoria*, fifteenth century, belonging to Matthew Corvinus, King of Hungary. MS α.O.3.8 = Lat.419, Modena, Biblioteca Estense.

PROHOEMIVM

LEONIS BAPTISTE ALBERTI DE RE AEDIFI
CATORIA INCIPIT LEGE FELICITER

young man had been shown the sights of Rome by the ageing Alberti and was known to admire the treatise as a masterpiece of modern Latin prose. However, before it was printed, two other great bibliophiles, Alberti's friend Federico da Montefeltro of Urbino and Matthew Corvinus, King of Hungary, each had two splendid illuminated manuscript copies of it made (Rykwert and Engel 1994, 414–17) (plate 6). Another fine if less showy manuscript belonged to Bernardo Bembo, the Venetian ambassador to Florence, and through Henry Wotton (in his turn British ambassador to Venice) this passed to Eton College (plate 7). Yet another, that owned by Lorenzo, is lost, but must have been the source of the printed text which went through two Latin and one Italian versions before 1550, when the best-known Italian translation was printed, the first to be illustrated. By then it had reached the status of a classic. A French version was made by Jean Martin – who also translated Vitruvius, Serlio and the *Hypnerotomachia Poliphili* – and it appeared in 1547. The English version had to wait for the eighteenth century and the German for the early twentieth.

All subsequent theorists had to come to terms with both Alberti and Vitruvius. Vitruvius had described various actual buildings he was familiar with as well as the basilica at Fano which he had designed, but since they were either not recorded or destroyed, later theorists felt free to reconstruct these buildings in conformity with their own ideas. Alberti's buildings on the other hand were familiar and much published; even when later theorists took exception to details (as Roland Fréart de Chambray to Alberti's Doric Order which he found 'coarse and Gothic'), there was little doubt that what he said and wrote was borne out by what he designed and built.

One sentence of Alberti's, which was taken up a century later by Palladio, sums up much that is important (but still not fully appreciated) in his teaching: that 'the city is like some large house, and the house is in turn like some small city' (Alberti 1988a, Book 1 ch. 9, 23). Since it is always with the city that his teaching and his designing were concerned, the whole of his treatise should be read – perhaps more than any other – as an instruction for piecing together a new urban fabric. The same is true of his buildings. Even the Florentine façades only make sense as functions of the public spaces which they address, rather than of the buildings they clothe. If we are to read Alberti as the father of any one notion, it is perhaps as the true ancestor of urbanism.

Chapter Two

ON FILARETE'S
LIBRO ARCHITETTONICO

Luisa Giordano

THE TREATISE OF THE Florentine Antonio Averlino, otherwise known as 'Filarete' (from the Greek *philaretos* meaning 'lover of virtue'), was the second work of architectural theory in the Renaissance following that by Alberti. Like Alberti, the author was an architect who dedicated himself to theoretical studies. Filarete began as a sculptor and became an architect only in a much later stage of his career. As far as we know, he received all of his most important commissions outside his homeland, Tuscany. He executed the central portal, signed and dated 1445, of St Peter's Basilica in Rome, for Pope Eugenius IV (plate 1). The bronze plates which cover the door remained in place even after the reconstruction of the Vatican basilica and are the principal testimony to Filarete's sculptural activity. His stay in Rome was suddenly interrupted in 1447, when he was accused of stealing some relics, considered at that time a most serious offence. Filarete went first to Venice and then Milan, where he worked for Francesco Sforza, who had become duke in 1450. In Lombardy up until the mid-1460s, Filarete worked mainly as an architect, becoming (along with Benedetto Ferrini, the other Tuscan master in the service of the court) the major representative of Renaissance culture in the state. All Filarete's Milanese work is connected to his patron, Francesco Sforza. At the duke's behest, Filarete worked on the reconstruction of the castle of Milan and on the design for the Ospedale Maggiore, founded in 1456. In 1457 he was granted a brief period of leave in order to go to Bergamo, where he received the commission for the new cathedral. The cultural and formative differences between Filarete and Lombard architects, however, eventually led to the Florentine master distancing himself from them and the project of Milan cathedral, to which he had been assigned by the duke. In 1465 Filarete also gave up the Ospedale Maggiore project, although he had already

1 Detail of Filarete's central portal to St Peter's Basilica, Rome, for Pope Eugenius IV, signed and dated 1445. Scene from the martyrdom of St Peter.

contributed a design for it, and had, indeed, overseen the first stages of its construction. Sometime in the 1460s he returned to Florence. The year of his death is unknown; the last thing we know is that, in 1465, he was planning a trip to Constantinople.

THE DATE AND CONTENT OF FILARETE'S TREATISE

Filarete wrote the treatise (called by him the *Libro architettonico*) in the latter stages of his period in Milan, and he dedicated it to Francesco Sforza. As his activities in Lombardy drew to a close, and with the aim of strengthening his ties to Florence, the author added a chapter (Filarete's term is *libro*, or 'book') dedicated to the patronage of the Medici family, and wrote a second dedication, this time to Piero de' Medici. According to Vasari (1906, 457), this last addition and second dedication were written in 1464, and modern scholars have confirmed this date. For the preceding twenty-four books, Spencer (1956, 93–103) proposes 1461–2 for Books I–XXI, and 1464 for the books on drawing (XXII–XXIV) and the book dealing with the contemporary architectural commissions of the Medici (XXV). Grassi, on the other hand, dates most of the work to the years 1460 and 1461, although he allows a final date of 1464, taking into account the various revisions of the author (Filarete 1972, xi–xiii).

The manuscripts reflect the stages of composition of the work, and can be divided into two groups. The first group, which comprises the original version in Italian vernacular, can in turn be broken down into two branches, the first of which derives from the version written for Francesco Sforza, while the second contains a revised text prepared to go with the new dedication to Piero de' Medici. Of this second branch, the Codex Magliabechiano,[1] the best witness to the text and the most complete as regards the illustrations, contains the author's final revision of the text as well as the dedication to Piero.

The second group of manuscripts consists of the Latin version of the text. This was written for Mattia Corvino by the humanist Antonio Bonfini; Bonfini did not translate literally but instead made cuts and revisions which were guided by the text of Vitruvius (Hajnóczi 1992).

Filarete's treatise was not printed until modern times. Its characteristics, such as the continuous narrative dense with parentheses and anecdote, and the patchy treatment of architectural theory, made the treatise of little interest to later generations. Vasari (1906, 457–8) mentions the work and the codex owned by the Medici, but criticises harshly both the treatise and its author: 'And even though there may be some good things in it, it is nevertheless for the most part ridiculous and stupid such that it is probably useless'.[2] The first studies of Filarete's treatise date from the nineteenth century: in 1890 von Oettingen published a first, partial edition and a summary of the treatise, while an ample summary with excerpts was included in a volume by Lazzaroni and Muñoz in 1908 (242–77). More recently Filarete's theory has been considered in the context of the architectural practice of his time by Saalman (1959), whilst the theory was systematically analysed in a study by Tigler of 1963. Filarete's treatise thus acquired a well-defined position in the field of architectural theory (Kruft 1994, 51–5). Furthermore, an English translation and a critical edition in Italian have both been published, in 1965 and 1972 respectively.

Of all the architectural treatises of the Renaissance, Filarete's is the only one which has a narrative structure (if we discount the *Hypnerotomachia Poliphili*). In the text, the author imagines that his patron, Francesco Sforza, has given him the task of designing a city with the flattering name of Sforzinda. He goes on to describe the plan, the necessary materials and the organisation of the project. While working on the port, a 'Golden Book' is found which tells of an ancient king, Zogalia, and a city of Plusiapolis. The buildings of this mythical city, described in the 'Golden Book', become the model for those in the new city.

---

[1]   Florence, Biblioteca Nazionale, II, I, 140.

[2]   'E comecchè alcuna cosa buona in essa si ritruovi, è nondimeno per lo più ridicola, e tanto sciocca, che per avventura è nulla più.'

Filarete chooses to tell this story in the form of a dialogue between the architect-narrator and the members of the Milanese ducal family: Francesco Sforza, Duchess Bianca Maria Visconti, and their first-born son Galeazzo Maria. It seems that Filarete took as his model the works of Plato (Onians 1971), who addresses arguments relevant to the city and to creative activity in particular in the three dialogues *Timaeus*, *Critias* and *Laws*. Filarete was probably introduced to Plato by the humanist Francesco Filelfo, who might also have brought to Filarete's attention medieval works which cited the activity of the builder as one of the qualities of a prince, a theme which is clearly fundamental to Filarete's treatise (Lang 1972).

The continuous narrative structure and the fact that each building is proposed as a unique project makes the text ideally suited to being accompanied by illustrations. In fact, Filarete often refers to illustrations in order to explain his intentions more clearly. The illustrations were therefore not devised simply as an optional ornament to the manu-script, but are instead integral to the text. Filarete's treatise can only be considered complete when it is seen as a synthesis of word and image.

The continuity of the narration is interrupted after Book XXI with three subsequent books dedicated to drawing. The dialogue structure is retained, but the interlocutor is now solely Galeazzo Maria Sforza. The books on drawing are based on the work of Alberti, that is, the *De pictura* and the *Elementi di pittura*. Filarete repeats the principles of Alberti, although in a less organic fashion and with additional points derived from his own experience and personal taste. Furthermore, he excuses this digression on drawing by citing the subject's traditional importance in the education of a young prince. However, in order fully to understand this digression, one must remember that Alberti had asserted in *De re aedificatoria* (Book IX, ch. 10) that the principles included in his *De pictura* were essential to the education of an archi-tect. The twenty-fifth and final book of Filarete's treatise deals with Medici buildings in general, and is particularly important for the information it contains about the palace which was the Milanese seat of the Medici bank.

CONTEMPORARY WORKS REFLECTED IN THE TREATISE

As can be seen from the above summary, Filarete's treatise is a text which can be read on different levels. The author uses the narrative system principally to interject ample references to his own professional experience, therein describing his projects for the Ospedale Maggiore (Book XI) and for the cathedral of Bergamo (Book XVI). The fact that the work's dedicatee, Francesco Sforza, also becomes a protagonist in the treatise echoes a common characteristic of the literature written for the courts of the fifteenth century. The encomium of the ducal family of Milan thus becomes one of the principal components of the text. This is expressed not only with outright praise, but also in a more elaborate and symbolic way. The name of the mythical king, Zogalia, is for example an anagram of Galiazo (Galeazzo), the Sforza heir. Moreover, while building Sforzinda the duke baptises the ports of the city in terms which allude to his wife and children (Book v, 145–6). He leaves the naming of the last port to the architect, who designates his own name, exalting his role as creator and emphasising his pride as member of the court. As to the court itself and his work there, Filarete introduces into the text some references which record certain contemporary circumstances and events. He cites the humanist Tommaso Morroni da Rieti and the poet Francesco Filelfo as the authors of the dedicatory inscriptions set up on the Ospedale Maggiore (Book xi, 320–21); Filelfo is also remembered as the interpreter of the 'Golden Book', and this hints at both his possible position at the Sforza court and his role as Filarete's guide to ancient texts. As to the organisation of the workers in the treatise, the figure of the *commissario* – who is often referred to as the site administrator, second only to the duke and in close contact with the architect – reflects the historical role in the Sforza court of the commissary general, Bartolomeo Gadio.

Considering the treatise in this light, one becomes conscious of the numerous references to situations and initiatives which, although clear to the author and the reader of the time, are quite difficult to interpret today. This kind of difficulty is exemplified in a passage from Book vii, in which Filarete describes with great detail the structure of the dome of the cathedral in Sforzinda and which Spencer (1959) has in turn linked hypothetically with Filarete's work on the cathedral of Milan. A passage in Book xvi is even more specific. Here Filarete responds to the duchess's request for a new church and monastery for the Gerolamites by providing an actual design: this episode has been related to the ducal project for San Sigismondo in Cremona, for which Filarete is reputed to have drawn up a design in *c.*1460 (Spencer 1956, 99–100; Filarete 1972, 458–9; Giordano 1988, 117–20) – although when the church was begun in 1463 it was based on a design which cannot be attributed to Filarete. It is therefore evident that Filarete's treatise, in contrast to the other theoretical works of the fifteenth and sixteenth centuries, can be seen as an explicit historical document, albeit of arduous interpretation.

The role that Filarete claims for himself and, consequently, for the profession of the architect, is of great significance. A comparison with Alberti's treatment of the same subject proves informative. In the prologue to *De re aedificatoria* Alberti had described the exemplar architect, identifying this figure as one who designs in a rational manner and realises works which fulfil the most important human needs. In chapters 10–11 of the ninth book, Alberti had specified the ideal education and professional qualities of the architect, insisting upon the need for a knowledge of painting and mathematics. Filarete does not advance such clear and precise propositions as these. Nonetheless, he exalts the role of the architect as being of primary importance, emphasising his activity as a builder as fundamental to human existence, and pointing out how difficult it is to master the profession. Furthermore, by demonstrating that every project is conceived and completed first in the mind of the architect, becoming a technical application only thereafter, Filarete plays a significant part in the process which culminates in the recognition of architecture as a liberal art.

A characteristic feature of Filarete's outlook is the relationship which develops in the treatise between the architect and the patron. Alberti had already addressed this issue, arguing that the person who, in the fullest intellectual sense, practises architecture had the right to retain control over their professional activity: this independence would include the architect's right to choose his own projects, with the option of simply acting as a consultant, or of offering no more than a design to the many potential patrons who sought the services of a successful architect (*De re aedificatoria*, Book IX ch. 11). For Filarete, the design process always goes hand-in-hand with the process of building. The intellectual theory cannot be divorced from the workshop practice. Furthermore, the architect, who has the task of creating and defining in his mind the project requested by the patron, assumes the role of 'mother' of the project, while the patron plays that of 'father'. This is a metaphor which grants the architect a much more dignified role than that afforded him in the Middle Ages. On the other hand, it defines his position not as an autonomous artist, but rather as a privileged figure within the confines of the court. Also related to the emerging status of the artistic profession is Filarete's mention of contemporary craftsmen such as architects, sculptors, painters and glassmakers: these act in the treatise as a *complement* to the group of ancient craftsmen whose effigies are depicted in the house of the architect, Onitoan (an anagram of Filarete's first name), and which in the treatise appear as a sort of gallery of famous men.

★   ★   ★

ON ARCHITECTURAL THEORY

The theory of architecture is not presented by Filarete following a defined organic structure but is instead proposed within his narrative, through both affirmations of a general nature as well as examples and descriptions of particular buildings. There is, therefore, a radical difference in method compared to Alberti. Alberti constructs a very coherent treatise, in which he first delineates the conceptual structure of the arguments, then the general characteristics of the pertinent themes, and finally the definition of the particular details. In this way, his propositions have a normative function. Filarete, on the other hand, when presenting anything other than a mere general definition, chooses to describe one or more particular examples from which his readers must deduce the theoretical criteria for themselves.

In the opening of the treatise, Filarete declares the principles on which his theory is founded. All architecture is modulated on the form and the proportions of Man. Man, too, is the inventor of the very act of building, because the first building was the hut. Regarding this particular theme, the author integrates Vitruvian theory into Christian history, affirming that the first builder was Adam. From the very beginning, then, it becomes evident how Filarete uses the ancient theoretician: Vitruvius is a supreme authority (*auctoritas*), and his principal concepts are repeated; but Filarete does not go on to explain Vitruvius, an omission that often results in a text which distorts the Roman author's meaning. At this point it should be noted that, in order to compose a text which is a combination of information on materials, construction rules and mythical and historical anecdotes, Filarete uses not only the theoreticians cited with deference in his opening – Vitruvius and Alberti – but also a series of sources that range from the ancients – for example Pliny and the Latin poets – to medieval literature – from Isidore of Seville to Dante.

As to the morphology of individual architectural elements, a point of significance is Filarete's stand against the use of the ogival arch (Book VIII, 230–32), comprising one section of many in his diatribe against the 'modern' style, that is, the Gothic. This passage dedicated to the pointed arch reflects the differences that had distinguished the Tuscan architect Filarete from the Lombard masters. Architectural morphology now takes on a meaning which Alberti had not even remotely intended: the problem is so important for Filarete that he not only notes, as had Alberti, that the ogival arch was not used in antiquity, but he also goes on to create an aesthetics of form. He observes that although the ogival arch and the round arch are both very strong supports, the round is better because the eye can follow its outline in a single, unbroken movement.

THE PLANNING OF SFORZINDA

The central argument of Filarete's treatise is the planning of a city. Sforzinda is the first ideal city of the Renaissance, and as such it is of great importance for the history of the idea of the city, even though Filarete's actual designs were not of any great influence (Kruft 1989, 13). Sforzinda has the form of an eight-point star, circumscribed in a circle (plate 2). The interconnecting piazzas and the seats of public offices, together with the royal palace, are all arranged in the centre. No detailed description is offered for either the quarters inside the walls or the relationship between the parts, but Filarete does describe both the general sub-division of the city and particular projects. The physiognomy of certain parts of the city thus remains nebulous, and the architectural theory must be deduced from what Filarete writes on single buildings.

As to the *spezie* (species) of the buildings, whilst Alberti had classified all of the possible categories, distinguishing whether buildings were public or private, religious or secular, and whether they were built out of necessity or for beauty or indeed pleasure, Filarete proposes even more complex distinctions (Book II, 48ff), which are based on the function of the building and on criteria of an aesthetic and social nature. He first categorises the buildings in order of priority as public, private or sacred. He then distinguishes the sacred buildings as either communal, public or private, next analysing those of public function on the same terms, lastly subdividing the buildings of private citizens into categories for gentlemen, craftsmen or the poor.

After having affirmed along general lines these last criteria, which link the quality of the buildings to the social hierarchy, Filarete reconfirms this principle when he elaborates on private, domestic architecture, by proposing specific designs in Sforzinda for the ducal palace (Books VII, VIII and IX), the house of a gentleman (Books XI and XII), the house of a merchant and the house of a craftsman (Book XII). In this way he defines the categories of urban buildings, wherein their grandiosity and size correspond to the different divisions which make up the society. Concerning churches, Filarete goes on to indicate the general and the symbolic reasons for the cross plan, affirming that 'the reason why churches are made in the shape of a cross is because with the coming of Christ, the shape became used out of reverence for Him, in that He was put on a cross'[3] (Book VII, 186). Filarete does not propose any one form as better than another. The different types of cross plans can be deduced from the individual examples which he

---

[3]   'Il perché le chiese si fanno in croce si è perché poi che venne Cristo s'è usato per riverenza sua, perché fu posto in croce.'

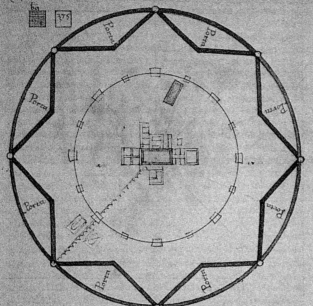

La discripuone della
Cura...

I nella testa doriente Io fo lachiesa maggiore & inquella doccidente fo
ilpalazzo reale lequali grandezze alpresente non tocho pche quando la
faremo allora intenderete tutto dalla porte della piazza inuer setten
trione Io fo lapiazza demercatanti laqual fo largha uno quarto dista
dio aoe nouanta tre braccia & tre quarti & lungha mezzo stadio & dalla
porte merediana della piazza fo unaltra piazza oue sara come due uno
mercato & iui suendera cose damangiare & come e labeccheria & frutte &
herbe & altre simile cose plobisogno della uita delhuomo & questa sara lar
gha unterzo distadio & lungha due terzi aoe braccia dugento cinquanta a
ppresso diquesta intesta gliso ilpalazzo delcapitano dacanto appresso lacor
te, che solo lastrada lasporte & inquella demercatanti dauna testa fo ilpa
lazzo delpodesta & dallaltra parte opposita quello doue siriene laragione de
comune. Dalla parte settentrionale fo laprigione comune laquale uiene aesse
dirieto alpalazzo della ragione. Dalla parte orientale dacanto della pia
zza fo lerario aoe doue sifa & conserua lamoneta & appresso ladoghana
nella piazza delmercato sara come o detto ilpalazzo delcapitano & dauna

proposes and which include both the longitudinal and the centralised plan. The latter is statistically the most frequent and, from the compositional point of view, the most original (Spencer 1958). Disregarding the particular characteristics of the examples described, it can be said that Filarete generally proposes a Greek cross with a centralised plan and barrel-vaults covering the arms of the cross, while an octagonal dome rises over the central intersection. Tall bell-towers are placed at the corners of the building, a compositional feature derived from the antique monument of San Lorenzo in Milan. The recurring proposition of the centralised plan probably had an effect within the court of Francesco Sforza. The church of Santa Maria di Guadalupe in Bressanoro, begun in 1465 on a plan furnished by the court, is a centralised building with five, domed sectors. The differences between the church and Filarete's proposals are clear enough, but the church cannot be explained without the intermediary role of the treatise (Giordano 1988, 124–6).

In presenting buildings that are based on reminiscences or studies of ancient monuments, the author showed himself to be interested in the architectural heritage of antiquity, as well as being capable of understanding, in approximate terms, the historical function of the buildings: significant is his differentiation in the text between 'long' theatres and 'round' ones, which make allusion to the typologies of the amphitheatre and of the circus (Tomasi Velli 1990, 119–21). Projects of monumental scale, inspired by antique forms, are presented as exemplar architecture, and can be invested with symbolic meaning. The most famous example is that of the House of Virtue and of Vice (Book XVIII), where each of its parts has a symbolic function and meaning drawn from the didactic theme of Hercules at the Crossroads (Hidaka 1988). In other examples, Filarete did not reach such levels of complexity, choosing instead to concentrate on very elaborate projects such as the plan of the temple in the city of Plusiapolis.

ON DECORATION

Concerning the decoration which complements the architecture, once again Filarete does not openly specify a hierarchy of styles, but this can be deduced from the text. On mosaic he pays homage to the examples in St Mark's, Venice, and he proposes this type of decoration for the most prestigious buildings, such as the cathedral of Sforzinda (Book IX, 248ff.) and the church of the Ospedale (Book XI, 317–18). One can therefore conclude that Filarete thought highly of this technique which emphasises the preciousness of the materials and their luminosity. Indeed, the excellence of mosaic is re-emphasised throughout the books on drawing: in Book XXIV Filarete even explains in detail the mosaic technique, but admits realistically that it is a 'lost art which has been little used since Giotto'[4] (Book XXIV, 671–2). This preference for mosaic goes hand-in-hand with the indications as to iconographic themes, which are of medieval derivation. Hell and purgatory, for example, are suggested as subject matter for the pavement of the cathedral of Sforzinda, complementing the theme of paradise in the upper section of the building (Book IX, 250). *Dipinti*, or frescoes, are recommended for the decoration of public buildings, for the gentleman's residence (Book XII, 327) and for the cloisters of the Gerolamite monastery (Book XVI, 467). For the public buildings, didactic allegories and exemplar figures from Roman history are specifically proposed as subject matter (Book X, 283ff). As noted earlier, the effigies of ancient craftsmen are also painted in the residence of the architect Onitoan (Book XIX, 563).

ON THE ORDERS OF ARCHITECTURE

Filarete's position regarding the architectural Orders – a term he does not use – is completely original. The process of codification of the Orders with reference to Vitruvius and to ancient monuments began in the fifteenth century; but it is a commonplace that Alberti is the only one of the fifteenth-century theorists to have correctly interpreted the Greek Orders as described by Vitruvius. Alberti equally drew conclusions from his own study of ancient monuments, from which he described a fourth Order (the 'Composite' or Italic) besides those previously classified by Vitruvius. Alberti's definition, however, was evidently only advanced at a theoretical level, because in practice he, like all architects of the mid-fifteenth century, widely employed licentious capital types which he discouraged in theory (Thoenes 1980). Filarete's position on the Orders is unique, even with respect to a panorama as diverse as that of fifteenth-century opinion on the subject. Furthermore, his classification has nothing in common with those of other theoreticians. In Book VII Filarete paraphrases a passage in which Vitruvius links the Orders to the dedication of temples (Book VII, 187), but in his following definition of the Orders (Book VIII), Filarete freely departs from the ancient source. Moreover, unlike Alberti, who had correctly identified all of the components of the column-and-beam system as constituant parts of the Order, Filarete defines a particular Order by making reference solely to the column, that is, solely to the vertical element of the system. There are three *maniere* (styles) of

---

[4] 'Arte perduta, ché da Giotto in qua poco s'è usata.'

columns with distinct proportions: the Doric, formulated on the ratio of 1:9, which is the most slender and ornate; the Corinthian, on the ratio 1:8, which is the median Order; and the Ionic, on the ratio 1:7, the squattest and therefore the poorest. As to the morphology of the individual parts, the only fluted and cabled column is the Doric, a fact illustrated in the drawing which compares the three Orders (plate 3). Concerning the capitals, the Ionic is illustrated with its typical volutes, but in the text the proportions of the capital are specified using a unitary method which dictates, for all the Orders, the addition of a band of leaves that decorate the lower two-thirds of the capital (Book VIII, 216–17). Consequently, in the illustration both the Doric and the Corinthian Orders have capitals with S-shaped volutes which join above a band of acanthus leaves; and these capitals can thus only be differentiated by what becomes secondary decoration; the Ionic capital beneath its volutes is also uncharacteristically ringed with leaves.

Although the author's formulation of the *maniere* of the columns may seem bizarre even in the context of the series of fifteenth-century attempts to follow Vitruvius, Filarete elaborates a very organic and functional theory regarding the Orders. The proportions of the Orders respect those of the various human morphologies, and are made to correspond to social classes (Onians 1973; 1988a, 172–3). Thus the Doric, the most slender and ornate Order – and that also intended to dictate the proportions for doorways – is recommended for the house of a gentleman, the Corinthian Order for that of a merchant and the Ionic for that of a craftsman. The unique position of Filarete with respect to Vitruvius and Alberti is further accentuated by the fact that, once again regarding the Orders, the author declares explicitly that he would rather not consider the merits of Vitruvius's interpretation because the ancient text uses terms which 'are ugly and not in use'[5] (Book VIII, 216). It has been pointed out that Filarete basically recommends a column of a Corinthian-like style as the privileged Order, and that he reserves for the Ionic column a humble role, thereby continuing the Florentine tradition of the first part of the fifteenth century initiated by Brunelleschi (Bruschi 1992, 23–5).

ON THE DESIGN PROCESS

The steps indicated by Filarete as essential to the passage from the idea to the definition of the project consist of a series of graphic designs and a final realisation of a wooden model. The first 'idea' of the building, after its development in the architect's mind, is expressed in a rough

---

[5] 'Sono scabrosi e non si usano.'

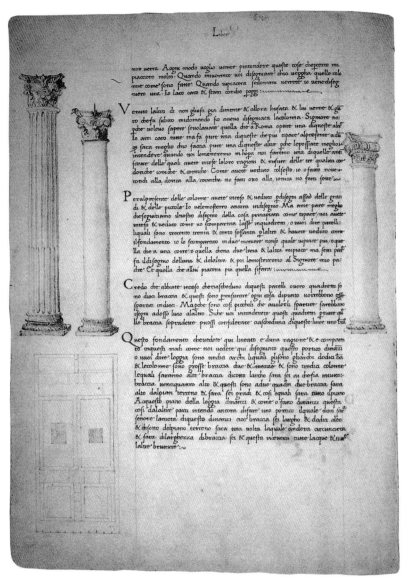

3   Filarete's comparative drawing of the three Orders, Doric, Corinthian and
Ionic, from the Codex Magliabechiano, fol. 57*v*. Florence, Biblioteca Nazionale.

sketch, otherwise known as *congetto* or *disegno di grosso*; this is followed
by a scale drawing and a wooden model, that is, a *modello* or *disegno
rilevato*, which serves to illustrate fully the architect's project to the
patron and builders. The method used to define the building's plan
consists of first transferring on to an axis the measurements – to scale

– of the sides of the area to be built upon. Next, the surface is divided into squares: every square has sides equal to a certain number of *braccia*, which varies from project to project. It is upon this grid – which serves as a base, and which is designed to reflect the scale of the concept that the architect wishes to realise and its relationship to the available space – that Filarete distributes the various parts of the building. Drawing, then, is the method which allows the project to be given form. From the technical point of view this method of elaboration is similar to modern systems which involve the division of square units and the combination of whole-number values based on a unit of measurement – which in Filarete's case is the *braccio*.

ON SFORZINDA AND THE IDEAL CITY OF MILAN

It was noted earlier that the outstanding feature of Filarete's treatise is its concentration on the planning of Sforzinda, the first modern, utopian city. Filarete's project for the distribution of the central piazzas has certain characteristics which significantly distinguish it from the Vitruvian forum and from Albertian theory. Alberti had clearly differentiated between the characteristics of an ancient city and the needs of a modern one. To describe the former, he had paraphrased Vitruvius, and to characterise the form of the latter, he had proposed a rectangular piazza with sides of a ratio 1:2, surrounded by buildings with porticoes which were in proportion to the grandeur of the piazza. Filarete does not show any interest in a reconstruction of the ancient forum, basilica or other public place such as the curia. For the centre of the city he proposes an arrangement of three interconnecting piazzas, each proportioned to the ratio of 1:2 (Book VI, 165–6). The main piazza is sited in the centre of the composition: the cathedral is located on its east side, the ducal palace on its west side. The northern side of the main piazza opens up on to a smaller one, that of the merchants. In this piazza, the seats of the civil administration can be found: the palace of the *podestà*, the town hall, the prisons and the treasury. The southern side of the main piazza opens on to a further small piazza (although bigger than that of the merchants), which is a market place and is enclosed by the palazzo of the *capitano*, the taverns, the brothel and the public baths.

At the beginning of Book X, Filarete contradicts in part his previous statements, since he gives slightly different measurements for the main piazza and, more importantly, he states his intention to locate the town hall (that is, the *Palazzo della Ragione del Comune*) in the centre of the merchants' piazza rather than on its edge. This public building is to be built upon a series of pillars linked by arches, these running along both the perimeter and the longitudinal centre-line of the ground floor, so as to create an open space comparable to a great hall.

Filarete emphasises the fact that the three-piazza arrangement is linked by streets directly to the city gates. Along these streets are still more piazzas, all proportioned using the ratio 1:2, and each designed to host markets of various types and surrounded by shops. The streets which lead from the main piazza to the towers on the walls of the city are, on the other hand, lined by monasteries, whilst parochial churches face the piazzas of these streets. It is evident from the particular functions of each building, and from the systematic naming of these buildings, that the centre of Filarete's Sforzinda fulfils the needs of the society of the time, in which the city is dominated by the duke and is governed by public administrators of medieval tradition (which Filarete signifies by the names still in use). Filarete's city is, then, in its distribution of the seats of religious and civil power and of the market-places, a rationalisation of the late-medieval city; and especially a rationalisation of the form that the urban centre had acquired in the region of the Po, where the arrangement of three interconnecting piazzas linked to the cathedral and the public buildings was the norm (as, for example, in Pavia and Lodi).

Hence, although utopian, Filarete's city reflected the arrangement of certain actual cities. Indeed, Filarete's project bears many significant similarities to, and was perhaps influenced by, the real city of Milan and its idealisation in medieval cartography. To confirm this hypothesis it is necessary to recall some historical facts particular to this Lombard city. In 1228 the *comune* had founded, next to the piazza of the cathedral, a new piazza, in the centre of which was located the *broletto*, or *Palazzo della Ragione*, whose ground floor was entirely composed of pillars and so open to the surrounding piazza. This urban project, of great political significance because it affirmed the full sovereignty of the *comune*, had not been limited to the piazza alone but had also addressed the streets which linked the new public space to each of the city gates. The radial structure of Milan, which in the early Middle Ages had prevailed over the Roman grid system, following this excep-tional intervention also took on a symbolic meaning. Indeed a fourteenth-century map of Milan accompanying a text of Galvano Fiamma, the most important historian of the period, illustrates the city as completely circular and self-contained within the urban walls. Fur-thermore, it shows the civic piazza in the centre, adjacent to the cathedral and the ducal palace. Filarete must have meditated upon the history and on the *forma urbis* of Milan, furnishing an idealised re-elaboration of this idea contained within his homage paid to the duke. In this way the treatise reconfirms its dual nature as theoretical work and courtly tribute.

Chapter Three

THE *TRATTATI* ON ARCHITECTURE BY FRANCESCO DI GIORGIO

Francesco Paolo Fiore

Francesco di Giorgio di Martino (Martini) was born in Siena on 23 September 1439, the son of Giorgio, an official of the *comune* (as documentary evidence records). Francesco, whose humble origins have been exaggerated, took advantage of the connections and influences deriving from his father's position to take up his first artistic apprenticeship in the city. Probably as early as 1460 he was practising under Lorenzo di Pietro (called 'il Vecchietta'), one of the leading painters and sculptors in Siena. At that time, di Pietro was working on a commission for Pope Pius II Piccolomini, the panel of the *Assumption of the Virgin* which is still today over an altar in the duomo in Pienza. It is possible that di Pietro also worked as an architect in Pienza, despite the fact that the pontiff had rejected his design for the Piccolomini loggia in Siena and had employed Bernardo Rossellino in Pienza. A decade later, di Giorgio was active in the Ospedale di Santa Maria della Scala, painting works near to the principal frescoes executed by di Pietro and decorating the church (1470–71); he was also perhaps influential in deciding the church's architectural programme (Gallavotti Cavallero 1985). Nevertheless, di Giorgio's paintings of the 1470s, when he worked with the painter Neroccio di Bartolomeo (de'Landi), are distinct from those of his putative master in that di Giorgio's have a more dynamic and a freer interpretation of the images and *all'antica* architectural backgrounds. Thus, for di Giorgio in Siena it is possible to discern a fruitful relationship with Liberale da Verona (in Siena from 1467 to 1476), and the profound influence of Donatello (in Siena from 1457 to 1459) (Christiansen et al. 1988).

Nor was di Giorgio's education limited to painting and sculpture. In 1469 he shared with Paolo d'Andrea the post of overseer of the *bottini*, that is, the underground conduits which brought water into Siena. Di Giorgio must therefore have been qualified to direct the complex work of excavating and arranging waterways, tasks which required a good knowledge of geometry applied to the problems of plotting and gradation, and the principles of hydraulics, and he must have become known for his ability to organise a building site. Interest in this sort of work, which today is called engineering, drove him to consult amongst other things the codices on machines by Mariano di Jacopo (called 'il Taccola') (Prager and Scaglia 1972), a Sienese notary who had a passion for mechanics and who had been in contact with Filippo Brunelleschi on these matters. From this study there resulted in around 1465 what could be considered as di Giorgio's first codex, known as the *Codicetto* or small codex owing to its pocket-sized parchment pages.[1] The physical appearance of the *Codicetto*, with its small pages literally covered with rapid autograph notes and sketches, underlines the raw interest which di Giorgio had for this part of architecture, called *machinatio* by Vitruvius. Di Giorgio's interest in this field was to last the whole of his life and it was present throughout the rest of his treatises. He took Taccola's work as a starting point and already here in the *Codicetto* are his own improvements to many of the mechanisms, and to these he added remarks from ancient authors such as Vegetius, Frontinus, Vitruvius, Marco Greco and Ptolemy, and (probably after his arrival in Urbino) some fortress plans (Michelini Tocci 1989) (plate 1). His work is so significant that the *Codicetto* has been seen as the originator of a Sienese tradition of *ingegni* (inventions) for military and civil use (Galluzzi 1991).

Di Giorgio came to Urbino around 1476, having ended his Sienese partnership with Neroccio the year before. Probably immediately on arrival (or very shortly thereafter), in order to highlight his knowledge of mechanical *ingegni*, he presented to Duke Federico da Montefeltro a new codex of machines which was a reflection and elaboration of the rapid jottings of the *Codicetto*. The elegant parchment presentation codex was entitled *Opusculum de architectura*[2] and it was kept until the seventeenth century in the library of the palace in Urbino. The Latin dedication to Federico (which compared the duke to Alexander the Great and Augustus in that, like them, Federico was a lord who needed an architect such as Dinocrates or Vitruvius) is almost too explicit in its attempts to attract the condottiero-duke's attention; although it should be remembered that Leonardo too was later to present himself to Lodovico il Moro, the lord of Milan, as an architect of *ingegni*. Here it is significant that di Giorgio opted for a codex with no text beyond the Latin dedication, and that, like Taccola, he developed the theme of *machinatio* through designs alone. His designs included ancient and

---

[1]   Biblioteca Apostolica Vaticana, Cod. Urb. 1757.
[2]   British Museum, Cod. 197.b.21 (previously Harley 3281).

modern war machines (amongst which were self-propelled carts for transporting siege towers into attack and for carrying other similar heavy objects), civil machinery indispensible for the construction of the new *all'antica* architecture (screws and cranes for hauling and raising, respectively, large pieces of stonework), hydraulic machinery (pumps, mills and norias), and finally plans for fortresses capable of resisting modern arms such as cannons and light firearms, and also capable of using such weapons in their own defence.

As previously in the *Codicetto*, the machines show improvements and new elements with respect to those by Taccola, and the fortresses (even though in some cases they are somewhat simplistic and impractical) reveal innovative solutions in which geometry is utilised, either to establish the novelty of the proposal (especially in reference to circular fortresses) or in response to the geometry of the firing lines. Di Giorgio was later to write that, regardless of the difficulty of defending against bombard shots, it was not the thickness of the walls but the geometry of the fortresses which facilitated resistance, and that in this the military architect was pursuing a new path, independent of the ancients. In the *Opusculum* there are fortresses with concentric walls on circular plans with four towers on the axes (one tower, being larger than others, is set across the two perimeter walls to control both, as for example in plate 1) (fols. 20*v*, 69*v*, 73*v*, 82*r*), there are polygonal fortresses with circular corner towers and a semi-circular or triangular core (fols. 21*v*, 73*r*), and there are fortresses in the shape of rhombuses (fols. 21*r*, 69*r*), one of these showing cannon emplacements in the flanks of the circular corner towers so as to be able to cover the whole perimeter with flanking fire.

In fact it was the rhombic form which di Giorgio was to declare that he in the end preferred, whilst he was to consider circular forms as unsuitable for fortresses, particularly if they were of a large diameter, because of the impossibility of defending such forms with flanking fire. Doubtless this conclusion was reached as a result of his service as architect to Federico da Montefeltro, one of the greatest condottieri of the period. Despite this, however, one of the fortresses built by di Giorgio, Sassocorvaro, has a circular perimeter, and for this reason and also because of the height of its walls it has been judged by some to be 'backward' (Hale 1965; Pepper and Huges 1978). Sassocorvaro was built for Ottaviano Ubaldini, Federico's cousin, who collaborated with Federico in the government and defence of the state of Urbino (not least in the renovations performed in the town itself and the construction of the new ducal palace). The very functions of Sassocorvaro, not merely a fortress but also a palace, justify its circular shape, and this so-called 'backward' form was employed at the same time as di Giorgio was building for Federico the forward-looking acute-angled ravelin

War machines and fortresses, from the *Codicetto*, fols. 58*v*–59*r*. Rome, Biblioteca Apostolica Vaticana, Cod. Urb. Lat. 1757.

with separated flanks fronting the village of Costacciaro (1477) (Fiore 1987).

Di Giorgio remained in Urbino for more than ten years until 1489, fully occupied in the execution of 136 works, as he himself recorded in the *Trattati* (or 130 if we are to believe Giovanni Santi). These probably included adaptations and renovations of existing architecture and perhaps work on civil and military machines. He was at any rate exceedingly active. He completed the ducal palace, the duomo, the convents of Santa Chiara and San Bernardino in Urbino, and reconfigured the palace and the fortress of Gubbio (Fiore and Tafuri 1993); he also built the fortresses of San Leo, Cagli, Sassofeltrio, Tavoleto and Serra Sant'Abbondio, scattered throughout the state, to which should be added Giovanni della Rovere's fortresses at Mondolfo and Mondavio (Adams 1993) (plate 2). In Urbino di Giorgio had to hold his own in one of the liveliest Italian courts of the period and also live up to the legacy of Piero della Francesca and Leon Battista Alberti, as well as to what had been built by the architects who had been his predecessors, namely, Maso di Bartolommeo and Luciano Laurana. Indeed Pedro Berruguete, Ambrogio Barocci, Baccio Pontelli and the humanist Sulpicio da Veroli were all present in Federico's court at the same time as di Giorgio. Di Giorgio records that it was the duke himself who encouraged him to study Vitruvius and the architecture of antiquity, subjects which together with discussions of machines and fortresses constituted the nucleus of his *Trattati*.

DI GIORGIO'S *TRATTATI*: THE FIRST VERSION

Of the *Trattati* by Francesco di Giorgio, two principal versions remain. The first version is represented by the parchment codices L[3] and T[4] and the second version is preserved in the paper codices S[5] and M.[6] After the hasty edition of M by Promis (1841), it is Salmi (1947) who should be credited with the first serious study of the two different versions. He was followed by Maltese (1967), who printed the texts with the variant readings of both versions integrated. The chronological watershed between the two editions according to Maltese is the *editio princeps* of the *De Architectura* by Vitruvius, dated by Maltese to 1486. There have been many (often dissenting) contributions since then, ranging from the counter-arguments of Betts (1977), and the facsimile edition of the codex L (Marani 1979) to the most complete studies to date by Mussini (1991; 1993) (who, amongst other things, discovered the *Fogli Reggiani* – the missing pages from L) and by Scaglia (1992). Despite the differences of opinion, I believe that on the basis of the considerations expressed briefly here in the Appendix we may conclude that the first version of the *Trattati* is to be placed after the long preparation period begun in Siena and continued in Urbino, in other words, between the very end of the 1480s and the beginning of the 1490s. The second version is therefore to be set between 1496 and di Giorgio's death in 1501. One important question, however, remains unanswered. Was the completion of L and T influenced by di Giorgio's journey to Milan in 1490? If so, how can we find the necessary time for the passage of L to T, both being very similar but nevertheless T being a copy made after a certain interval? Despite leaving these questions open, it still seems clear that the intense work undertaken to establish a sequence and chronology for the *Trattati* of Francesco di Giorgio has already produced appreciable results; and it also seems clear that, in trying to fit this sequence into the frame of his life and work, it is not possible to omit discussion of the actual contents and architectural propositions, often very mature for the 1490s.

[3] Florence, Biblioteca Mediceo-Laurenziana, Ashburnham 361.
[4] Turin, Biblioteca Reale, Saluzziano 148.
[5] Siena, Biblioteca Comunale, S.IV.4.
[6] Florence, Biblioteca Nazionale, Magliabechiano II.I.141.

The fortress of Mondavio, Urbino.

The *Trattati* were the concluding synthesis, not the prelude to di Giorgio's activities as an architect. The differences between the *Trattati* and the *De re aedificatoria* by Alberti are thus striking, not only because, unlike Alberti's writings on architecture, the *Trattati* were written in Italian and illustrated with an enormous number of designs (plates 3–8), but also because of the form and expository structure of the *Trattati* as well as the different personality, education and activities of their author. In the first version of the *Trattati* as represented by L and T (but following the classification of Maltese and citing the fuller version in T) the subjects treated on are as follows: fortresses; fortress draw-bridges and other types of defences; cities; hydraulic works; temples; theatres; columns; ancient and modern architecture and building prac-tices; geometry and methods for measuring distances, heights and depths; levers for wheels and mills; springs and how to raise and channel water; metals; water-pipes, reservoirs, winches and cranes; the military art and war machines; convents (not in L); machines and various pieces of practical advice; campanili and gardens (both not in L); extracts from the 'Book of Fires' by Marco Greco; surveys of ancient monuments (not in L).

Di Giorgio began each subject with the *ragioni* (the theories), for the most part represented by translated extracts from Vitruvius, and progresses to propositions which he wishes to be seen as his own invention distinct from the Vitruvian or antique models which are also reconstructed by him. For example, in the treatise on sacred buildings, highly dubious reconstructions of ancient temples are found alongside new, original designs for churches. In this case the illustrations of the reconstructions differ considerably from the accompanying text of Vitruvius, which di Giorgio had translated but not really understood. From this, it is very clear that the function of the illustrations is to amplify the invention whilst attempting to remain faithful to the translated text of Vitruvius.

The *ragioni* also take precedence in the first treatise, dedicated to fortifications (plate 3). The treatise opens with a statement concerning the principal aim of the fortress, namely defence, and his citation of Vitruvius refers to the general anthropomorphism of architecture which di Giorgio had deduced from the Latin text. Di Giorgio's text proclaims that 'it seemed good to me to form the city, fortress and castle in imitation of the human body'[7] (T, fol. 3*r*) and is accompanied by an illustration of a pentangular citadel superimposed upon a human body, with the fortress on the head, the towers on the limbs, the church on the breast, the piazza on the stomach and the gates between the legs. Clearly this is a distortion of Vitruvius's discussion of architec-

---

[7] 'Parmi di formare la città, rocca e castello a guisa di corpo umano.'

ffiuore derfoure fichon
lnaggo Lentrorto dall torre
pale upto alspanto di frante
te Lentrorto fichurer fio Es
i porete di drento itrutti op
neffore hoffoff hordenarife
ypo miporte bertefiche cho
nopelle pororj dore bonbore
iffano p che fono molto orte
ffe deffe fortege

mio baffo giuditio dar hore
dore che quando fuffero piu
itj di torerj Cadore due ho
ore oureffe eche effe torij f
unoi olouter reinnno im
me chelle i teorte i torlmo
riposte flero che p ono flo
fichonde porch fiurencha
ctitiorj evoreiortj ponrj al
expefto p che noneffendo e
chomune chonchordio al fi
no poffo Efimil mente fofi
reagiorj chonposfe fereano
tore voote fitte loironcho
fovore debo

into chonfiderore opotuto
effe delle bonbarede affai difi
xe dareffe poterfi difenbore
ij modi che neder ripofffi fie
pere mirco chonortteredepe

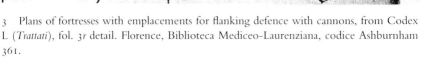

3   Plans of fortresses with emplacements for flanking defence with cannons, from Codex
L (*Trattati*), fol. 3r detail. Florence, Biblioteca Mediceo-Laurenziana, codice Ashburnham
361.

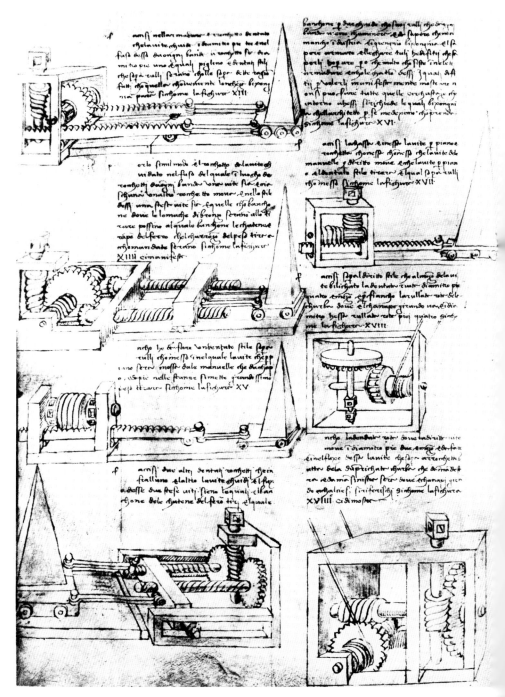

4 Machines for dragging or raising large blocks of stone, from Codex L (*Trattati*), fol. 45*v*. Florence, Biblioteca Mediceo-Laurenziana, codice Ashburnham 361.

5 The sculptor Callimachus and the birth of the Corinthian Order, from Codex T (*Trattati*), fol. 14*v* detail. Turin, Biblioteca Reale, codice Saluzziano 148.

tural proportions being derived from the human body, echoed by Alberti in his sophisticated comparison between architecture and the *animans* (the animated organism), but di Giorgio's design is nevertheless very powerful, both in the way in which it stimulates the reader's comprehension and imagination and in the way it evokes the symbolic values of architecture. The extensive use of the anthropomorphic metaphor in the first version of the *Trattati* (judged by some to be almost a verbal tick) (plate 5), was reduced in the second version, and, more in keeping with Vitruvius, was discussed in the sections on temples and the Orders (plate 8).

The novelty of di Giorgio's treatise on fortresses puts in high relief the force and realism of his propositions. His final remarks on how to deal with the most recent developments in warfare, namely the use of firearms, are particularly à propos. The arrangement of a fortress, he says, should be closely related to the site, the walls should be low so as to be protected from the raking fire of the besiegers and should also have a surrounding moat in order to make scaling them difficult on all sides. Furthermore, the walls should be angled 'with the defences low down in the flanks'[8] (T, fol. 3v) so these 'defences' too will be protected in turn from the grazing fire of cannons in protected positions. All this is clearly shown in the illustrations, and these reveal some very secret but important solutions for achieving the total defence of fortress perimeters which cannot be entirely provided with flanks: solutions such as *capannati* (forward towers) and other defence emplacements which guard the fortress from the side forward of the moat. That di Giorgio had planned defences which were external to the fortress (whether fortified moats or detached towers in advanced positions) is almost a greater sign of the novelty of his defensive thought than is his adoption of polygonal and flankable forms for fortresses. As a conclusion to this first treatise, di Giorgio mentions the acutely-angled bastion 'in the shape of a rhombus, with many facets to the front and detached from the wall . . . and the wall cut back in so that, with the projection of the corners, the bombard emplacement in the flanks of those corners are protected and hidden by that projection'[9] (T, fol. 5v) (here resembling the plan in plate 3).

The value of di Giorgio's work as a precursor to sixteenth-century defensive developments is clear, explaining nineteenth-century interest in the *Trattati* and the emphasis placed on this aspect of his activity. This definition of his fortifications as 'transitional' is unsatisfactory, however – I have argued elsewhere against the existence of a classical period of fortification (Fiore 1988); rather, it is much more worthwhile to consider the close relationship between di Giorgio's propositions and the contemporary military works commissioned from him by Federico da Montefeltro. This relationship is particularly evident in the previously mentioned interconnection between the fortresses, their dimensions and the site, taking into account the mountainous areas and the small settlements of the state of Urbino (Adams 1993). When di Giorgio gave advice and prepared some fortress plans for Alfonso di

[8]   'Colle difese per fianco e da basso.'

[9]   'A guisa di rombo, in nella fronte sua di più facce, e partisi dal muro . . . e lì el muro venga a risegare acciò che lo sporgiare degli angoli le bombardiere ne' fianchi d'essi coverte e occulte per lo sporto d'essi sieno.'

Calabria in the 1490s, the geographical imperatives were of a completely different nature (Dechert 1990), and the ideas which were
produced on that occasion were to be echoed in the second version of
the *Trattati* and in the *Raccolta* (the 'collection').

Like di Giorgio's fortresses, his cities are also surrounded by walls on
a polygonal plan, and the treatise on these cities similarly begins with
the anthropomorphic metaphor, the *ad circulum* and *ad quadratum* man
as discussed by Vitruvius. But di Giorgio goes beyond this comparison
and proposes a model of a centralised octagonal city with a central
piazza whose form matches that of the perimeter, whilst the city gates
are either in the centre of the sides or in the corners. However, next
to this he places particularly interesting alternative figures for cities on
hills and in plains, on the sea or by rivers, with orthogonal grid street-
plans which represent the precursor of sixteenth-century developments
but at the same time are probably linked to the newly founded cities
of the medieval tradition. After the treatise on cities comes one on
embankments, bridges and dykes, all works of infrastructure which are
connected with, and at the same time qualify the nature of, the city
walls; these walls in turn follow the new defensive theories, determining the shape of the city with a greater rigidity than before. This is
perhaps the part of the *Trattati* that is closest to presenting the idea of
an urban utopia, a long way from di Giorgio's work for Montefeltro,
although di Giorgio is here once again clearly referring to the reality of
the restricted city-states of his time.

With his treatise on temples, just as in Book III of Vitruvius, di
Giorgio concentrates entirely on architectural themes, and after a long
and innacurate translation of Vitruvius he illustrates his own propositions for churches with centralised plans of different shapes. These
shapes include the pentagon, the Greek cross with a single nave and
semi-circular chapels within the thickness of the wall (as in the
churches built by di Giorgio and in many of those built in Rome at
the end of the fifteenth century), and the Greek cross with three naves
and a cupola, resting on pointed supports, which is even wider than
the central nave. Tafuri (1993) has emphasised that in fact two of these
plans (T, fol. 12*v*), and particularly that with the doubled cupolas on
the transepts and the triple-domed choir, could be related to the
Certosa di Pavia, which di Giorgio visited in 1490. Nevertheless, the
same plan appears in the Zichy codex (fol. 138*r*), a manuscript which
was copied from a version of the *Trattati* perhaps already completed in
Urbino prior to this visit, and a similar arrangement is repeated on two
survey drawings of ancient monuments in T (fols. 74*r*, 85*v*), which are
based upon an earlier sketch by di Giorgio.[10] And so it is uncertain as

---

[10]   Uffizi 320, sig. A*r*.

to whether di Giorgio took the motif adapted in his designs from the antique or directly from the Certosa di Pavia. However, the more significant feature remains the cupola wider than the nave, a feature to be developed by Bramante for St Peter's in Rome and which occurs in a study design by him where the cupola rests both on columns distanced from the corner columns and on intermediary columns.[11] But it is unclear as to how exactly di Giorgio would have developed the vertical elements, particularly considering the frequently proposed dactylic rhythm (that is, large column, small column, small column, large column, etc.). All this would lead us to think that his propositions took as their model the duomo in Siena (with its broadened cupola) and, more generally, certain Romanesque models (with naves with altered rhythms).

In the treatise on the architectural Orders, di Giorgio tried once again to follow Vitruvius, fixing specific proportional relationships for the Doric, Ionic and Corinthian, and to these he added a more elegant and ornate Order which he called 'Tuscan', the Order which was later to be called Composite and which had previously been presented by Alberti as 'Italic'. Right from the very start di Giorgio, following Vitruvius, puts the emphasis on the proportions of the Orders rather than on the forms of the individual parts. These parts, too, are principally defined according to the proportions, and for these proportions anthropomorphism is once more called into play. Only in the second version of the *Trattati* was di Giorgio to arrive at an unequivocal proportional progression (based on the ratio of the diameter at the base of the column to the column height including base and capital) of $1:7$ for the Doric, $1:8$ for the Ionic and $1:9$ for the Corinthian.

The treatise on houses follows, and here di Giorgio proposes appropriate models for different ranks of inhabitant, from king to citizen, as Alberti and Filarete had done before him. Di Giorgio discusses only houses for cities, with the exception of two houses for the countryside (one in the form of a monumental *belvedere* and the other a rustic house with strictly agricultural functions). Whilst the considerations of use and distribution are fundamental, nonetheless the many divers inventive and even heterodox propositions are far removed from initial considerations as to function and distribution. Let us take the plan for the palace of a king first. Here there are two different, successive courtyards on a single axis of symmetry, and a *viridarium* (pleasure garden) completed by a loggia between wings matching the body of the facing building. This geometrical combination plays a decisive role in generating almost infinite variations in the other plans, and these plans are characterised by the presence of U-shaped schemes with

---

[11] Uffizi 7945, sig. Ar.

loggias and internal courtyards and circular schemes for *sale* (halls) and courtyards. This latter arrangement was a complete innovation (especially with respect to Vitruvius), only comparable to Mantegna's (contemporary) house in Mantua, but it was to be so popular in the following century that it was even used for Charles V's palace in Granada. There is also an example of a D-shaped courtyard, as mentioned by Pliny and reworked and transformed once again into a circular form in the Villa Madama for Pope Leo X in Rome. Finally, there are the centralised palaces with hexagonal, octagonal or circular perimeters, propositions which should be considered separately because they were destined never to be built and only found future influence in the imagination and in projects of such architects as Giulio Romano and Sebastiano Serlio. Related to the subject of palaces is the description, a few pages on in the first version of the *Trattati*, of some bathhouse complexes. Here, after the usual reference to Vitruvius, there is a discussion of the sequence of rooms in Federico's bath complex in the ducal palace in Urbino. Even though di Giorgio mentions no names, this reference to his work built for Federico was to anticipate the explicit comments on his fortresses for Montefeltro and on the Data stables included in the second version of the *Trattati*. It goes without saying that, with the passing of the years, di Giorgio felt able more openly to publicise his works for the duke.

There then follows the treatment of moles, dykes and conduits, a prelude to the section on geometry and machines. Even though this part may not be physically separable from the preceding part on houses (it begins on the *verso* side of a parchment sheet in both L and T), nevertheless this first version of the *Trattati* was almost immediately subdivided into two books, one on architecture and the other on machines, as in a copy made in Naples in 1492. But the possibility cannot be ruled out that di Giorgio had himself by that time already reworked the part of the first version dealing with civil architecture, as appears likely from his subsequent *Opera di architettura* on civil architecture (above all with respect to his shifting comprehension of Vitruvius), and given also the likely development of the material on machines and fortifications in the direction of what can be seen in the *Raccolta* (Fiore 1978).

At the end of T there follows the section on the surveys of ancient monuments (plate 6), and whilst these are in part directly based on di Giorgio's survey sketches preserved in the Uffizi, they should be seen rather as fair copies of these sketches either with additions or variations. This section owes its great importance to the fact that it is one of the first collections of studies, though brief and over interpretative, representing ancient monuments in central Italy and Rome. The plans and elevations of the invented palaces which are also here, combined with

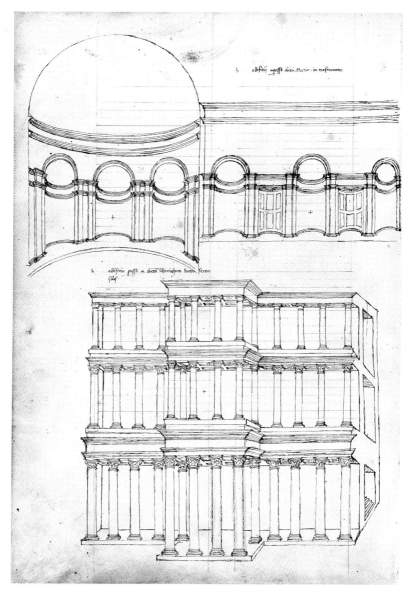

6 Ancient buildings in Rome, near Santa Maria in Trastevere, and the
Septizonium, from Codex T (the antiquarian additions to the *Trattati*), fol. 84*v*.
Turin, Biblioteca Reale, codice Saluzziano 148.

reconstructions of complexes such as the baths or the imperial palace
on the Palatine, show clearly di Giorgio's eclectic method and his
procedure with respect to his reading of the antique.

THE SECOND VERSION OF THE *TRATTATI*

The second version of the *Trattati* as preserved in S and M is characterised by many new features, notably the previously absent Aristotelian structure with the development now going from general to
particular, the more formal language, the removal of a majority of the
translations from Vitruvius (here these parts are abridged or interpreted), the reordering of the treatises, and the addition of new illustrations next to a selection of the initial ones. It is clearly not a simple
rewriting entrusted to humanist friends, but a complete rethinking and
critical reordering of the whole, for which a certain period of time
must have been required. Di Giorgio probably only had such a length
of time after 1496, in other words after his continuous travels which
followed his return to Siena in 1489. It remains, however, difficult to
say when di Giorgio reached the point of considering the first version
of the *Trattati* as out of date, not least because the chronological
watershed between the two versions rests on the appearance of the
undated *editio princeps* of Vitruvius (which should probably be dated
slightly later than its commonly accepted date of 1486; Bentivoglio
1992).

Codices S and M differ in the order of the treatises, even though
they are very similar as regards the text – so similar that Maltese was
able to integrate the two versions of the text into one. Whilst S placed
the treatise on fortresses fourth in order, M has the following order
(the order in which Maltese listed the titles): preamble; necessary and
common principles and norms; parts of houses, methods for finding
water; castles and cities; temples; forms of fortresses; parts and forms of
ports; machines for moving weights and drawing water, presses and
mills; conclusion.

After the general, introductory treatise, M starts immediately on the
subject of houses, this time going from houses in the countryside to
houses in the city, and from those destined for craftsmen to those for
princes (plate 7). That there is no house for a king would lead to the
conclusion that this section was written in Siena, where royal patrons
such as the House of Aragon were no longer in evidence. Irrespective
of the absence of a design for a royal house, the propositions are of
notable complication and articulation, and with characteristic features
such as U-shaped forms, circular bodies within quadrilateral plans
(generated through a clear process of geometrical variation), whilst the
only propositions to be omitted are the centralised plans related to the
ancient amphitheatre. References to the ancient house, on the other
hand, were more developed; this was both because di Giorgio understood intuitively the relationship between the atrium and the courtyard
or Vitruvian *cavedium* (even though he did not know that they were in

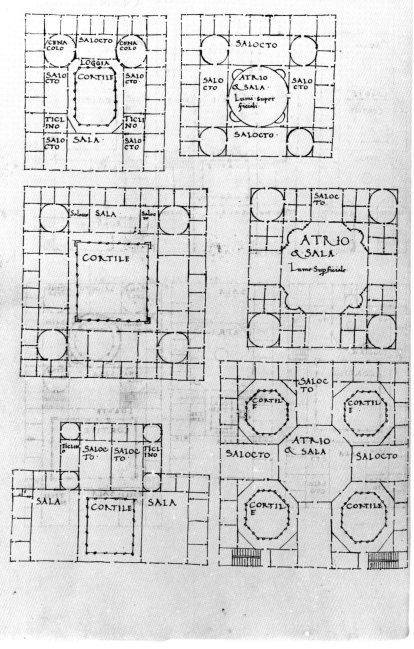

7   Plans of houses for *signori* (the nobility), from Codex M (*Trattati*), fol. *20v*. Florence, Biblioteca Nazionale, codice Magliabechiano II.I.141.

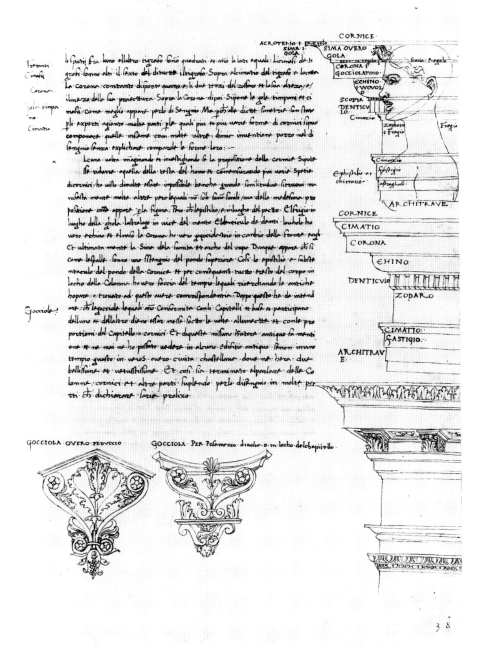

8 Anthropomorphic interpretation of an entablature, with details of entablatures and corbels, from Codex M (*Trattati*), fol. 37r. Florence, Biblioteca Nazionale, codice Magliabechiano II.I.141.

fact synonyms; Pellecchia 1992), and because he included *sale* (halls) and *salotti* (smaller halls) amongst other ground-floor rooms in designs for houses and palaces with only one floor, propositions which even he admitted were extraordinary, but which for him were 'pleasing and useful' (M, fol. 24*v*). In this section di Giorgio also spends some time discussing the stables for three hundred horses which he built for the Urbino palace.

The treatise on temples likewise presents noteworthy innovations with respect to the previous version, and all the subjects it treats are derived from Book III of Vitruvius on temples; to this treatise is added that on the architectural Orders (plate 8). Di Giorgio, with more coherence than before, here collects the only references to anthropo-morphic metaphors in the second version of the *Trattati* and signifi-cantly develops the subject of the proportions of sacred buildings and their parts, as well as the proportions of the Orders. On the other hand, numerous examples of ancient and modern temples presented in L and T are omitted. Only two interesting schemes remain: one with a centralised plan, and the other with a longitudinal plan with transepts and a cupola again wider than the central nave and set on columns (M, fols. 42*r* and *v*).

As mentioned above, in M the treatise on fortresses comes fifth, and with it opens the second part of this version, the part dedicated to military architecture and *machinatio*. After discussing ancient machines, di Giorgio moves straight on to the subject of bombards, and after a panegyric on Federico d'Urbino passes on to assess the utility of the different parts of fortresses; he gives many examples of fortresses, amongst which are those built by the author himself for Montefeltro, as previously mentioned. After the opening dedication to princes, where di Giorgio selected from amongst the themes and illustrations of the first version of the *Trattati*, here he seems to let himself go, using examples which have no precedent. With the machines in the follow-ing, concluding treatise of the manuscript M, di Giorgio returns to editing the first version, rationalising the material by arranging it according to the main principles of mechanics (Galluzzi 1991), perhaps influenced by his meeting and conversations with Leonardo in Milan and Pavia in 1490.

THE INFLUENCE OF DI GIORGIO'S *TRATTATI*

The influence of di Giorgio's *Trattati* was very widespread. Leonardo depended on di Giorgio's propositions when revising his ideas on the best forms for fortresses, opting for broken forms rather than circular ones (Marani 1984). His influence on treatises on architecture and mechanics was even wider, as is shown by the Sienese codex now held in the British Library,[12] by the designs of Giuliano da Sangallo and Antonio da Sangallo the Younger, Baldassare Peruzzi (who owned some designs by di Giorgio and annotated them), Pietro Cataneo and Oreste Biringucci and as is shown by the *Pirotechnia* of Vannoccio Biringucci. However, apart from the Accademia codex, we should not forget the huge amount of material which di Giorgio made in preparation for the *Trattati*, and from which derive the many designs in the Ashburnham 1828 codex of the Laurentian Library in Florence (Burns 1974). Amongst these, there is a plan for the rectangular palace with circular *sale* in the corners (present in the antiquarian additions to T) which, disseminated through the designs by Pietro Cataneo and Oreste Biringucci, influenced the design of the Palazzo Thiene in Vicenza by Andrea Palladio (Morresi 1989). Sebastiano Serlio certainly knew di Giorgio's work, although he took di Giorgio's ideas more directly from Peruzzi. Furthermore, di Giorgio's designs were greatly admired by Ignazio Danti, the mathematician and geographer from Perugia, brother of the sculptor Vincenzo and biographer of Vignola.

Di Giorgio's death in November 1501 coincided with fundamental political changes in Italy which marked the passing from the fifteenth to the sixteenth century – notably the invasion of Urbino by Cesare Borgia and the preventative destruction of many of the fortresses built by di Giorgio for Federico da Montefeltro, on the orders of Federico's son Guidubaldo who was concerned that he would never be able to re-enter his state if the fortresses had been occupied by enemies. The innovations introduced in Rome by Bramante were soon to render obsolete di Giorgio's architectural experiments and their representation in the *Trattati*. However, the wealth and inventive freedom of di Giorgio's propositions, together with the breadth of interests which they revealed, were to continue to be the starting point for many different lines of research in the sixteenth century.

---

[12]   British Museum, Cod. Add. 34113.

Chapter Four

THE *HYPNEROTOMACHIA POLIPHILI* BY FRANCESCO COLONNA: THE EROTIC NATURE OF ARCHITECTURAL MEANING

꙰

Alberto Pérez-Gómez

Do not be bewildered by the surfaces; in the depths all becomes law. And those who live the secret wrong and badly, lose it only for themselves and still hand it on, like a sealed letter, without knowing it.

Rainer Maria Rilke, *On Love*

POLIPHILO'S 'STRIFE OF LOVE IN A DREAM', published in Venice by Aldus Manutius in 1499, is one of the most beautiful books ever produced. Although today it is often excluded from standard histories of architecture with a more scientific bias, and its reading is not considered to be as essential as the works of Alberti or Palladio, this book was immensely influential in its own time. Turning its pages, the experience of ancient architecture becomes accessible to the reader, deployed in the space of human desire, through a precise description of all its sensuous components and geometrical 'lineaments', always meticulously coherent with the beautiful woodcuts that accompany the text. The images, a source of architectural ideas in Europe for at least three hundred years, represented monuments, gateways, sculptural details, hieroglyphs, fountains, festivals and processions, plans of buildings and gardens, geometric shrubbery and ritual objects, and were absolutely crucial for the meaning of the text. *Hypnerotomachia* was translated into French in 1546 and republished in 1551, 1554 and 1561. Transformed French versions with different titles appeared in 1600,

1657 and 1772. More recent free translations, some of which have been reprinted in the twentieth century, appeared in 1803, 1811 and 1883. A critical edition of the 1499 text with notes (in Italian) by Giovanni Pozzi and Lucia Ciapponi was published in 1968 and reprinted in 1980. In English, however, only a large section of the first part was translated under the title *The Strife of Love in a Dream*, published in 1592 and 1890.

We probably will never know with certainty who the author was. From the beginning his identity was clouded with mystery, his name known only through an anagram. Given the enigmatic character of the book and its alchemical and hermetic symbolism, revealing a syncretic mentality – both mythical and rational – sometimes at odds with dogmatic Christianity, the authorship question has produced abundant speculation. The author could certainly have been the friar Francesco Colonna (1433–1527), a Dominican from Venice. This is the most widely held hypothesis, one argued admirably by Claudius Popelin, the translator and writer of a vast and learned introduction to a terse French edition of the work (Colonna 1971, I, vii–ccxxxvii), and more recently by Maria Teresa Casella and Giovanni Pozzi (1959). The name Francesco Colonna is common, and it is therefore not difficult to raise questions about this hypothesis, particularly in relation to the pagan themes and the intense erotic content of the book. Maurizio Calvesi, in *Il Sogno di Polifilo Prenestino* (1983, 15–62), argued that the author was a Roman, lord of Palestrina after 1484 and member not of a religious order but of a pagan confraternity, the Roman academy of Pomponio Leto. Calvesi offers much evidence that points to a relationship between the Roman site and the iconography of *Hypnerotomachia*. Starting from this assumption, and from a statement in the dedication about the text having been written twice (which may in fact be an allusion to the double dream of the plot, or any number of other double meanings common in alchemical treatises), Emanuela Kretzulesco-Quaranta (1986, 26) has constructed a detective story in which she claims that the author of a 'first' text (now lost) in Latin was none other than Leon Battista Alberti, engaged in this project while he was in Rome (before 1464), under papal patronage. Kretzulesco-Quaranta argues that once the papacy became more conservative, Alberti left Rome and that Prince Francesco Colonna rewrote the text in an 'invented' vernacular, to make it more difficult to read and avoid censorship from the 'dark' forces of the Church. While this is an entertaining story, the evidence is circumstantial and the 'plot' heavily dependant on a miss-reading of early Renaissance humanism and its interest in a primordial theology as a proto eighteenth-century Enlightenment. The vernacular of *Hypnerotomachia*, despite its idiosyncrasies, would have been more accessible than the learned Latin of the humanists, and its Venetian flavour is impossible to disregard. Further-more, while the authorship of the outstanding woodcuts is also contro-versial, it is generally agreed that they are most probably the work of an artist from the Veneto. More recently Liane Lefaivre (1997) has also speculated that Alberti was the author of the work.

The architectural treatises of the European tradition, starting with Vitruvius, are easily understood in relation to the aspirations of phi-losophy and science. These books often appear dry and technical to the uninitiated or impatient reader. The philosophy and science in ques-tion, however, at least well into the eighteenth century, was hardly positivistic. It always incorporated answers to the most pressing ques-tions concerning human action and the ordering of the world, mostly in the form of an implicit mythical dimension. In other words, archi-tectural treatises until the end of the eighteenth century served as articulations of the metaphysical dimension of architecture in a tradi-tional world; referring the generation of forms to a coherent cosmos and its transcendent values, they elucidated the meaning of an architec-ture that was itself beyond question (Pérez-Gómez 1983). Thus it could be argued that European architectural theory has for the greatest part of its history clarified in the language of reason (words and proportions) the meaning of built work and, perhaps more impor-tantly, has helped to articulate the possibilities of an ethical practice, addressing the issue of the common good through architecture, that is, the appropriateness of forms to certain cultural situations and ritual actions.

The Renaissance was a seminal time for our own architectural practice. Architecture was 'promoted' to acquire the status of a liberal art. Its theory, in the tradition of the Greek *techné* and articulated through *mathemata* (meaning that which could be taught because it was invariable, deriving both from the tradition of the crafts and humanity's rational capacity) became a potentially prescriptive set of rules, the origin of later scientific and technological methodologies. Yet in *Hypnerotomachia Poliphili* the Renaissance also developed potential alter-natives to this sort of theory, proposing instead a lengthy story, a love story of sorts, bent on disclosing the presence of meaning in the space of Eros, while de-emphasising the canonic aspect of technical rules.

The theocentric universe had already been exhausted by the late fifteenth century. Cleverly, the hero of *Hypnerotomachia* reveals that architectural creation could no longer be directly inspired by the gods through its contemplation as a mere liberal art, in the sense of Alberti, nor could it come about as the *ars* or craft of the medieval mason acting as the hand of God characterised as the Augustinian 'architect'. The answer lay somewhere in between yet in a different place, where a radically different role for the personal imagination might emerge.

The original edition of *Hypnerotomachia* (1499) contains, as part of the preface, a synopsis of the story (here freely paraphrased):

You should know that Poliphilo dreamed about being in a threatening dark forest and narrates the myriad things he saw, a veritable strife for love, which is the meaning of the Greek words in the title. With elegant style and great care, he tells of many ancient marvels deserving of a place in the theatre of memory, architectural monuments encountered in his search for Polia, his beloved: a pyramid and obelisks; the great ruins of classical buildings; the precise measurement and characteristics of columns, their capitals, bases, entablatures with their diverse architraves, friezes and cornices, and their respective mouldings and ornaments; a great horse; a magnificent elephant; a hollow, half-buried colossus; and a triumphal gateway with its harmonic measurements and ornamentation. After suffering a major scare at the threshold, passing the test of a frightening tunnel, and being brought back to life by a wonderful encounter with the five senses in the form of five nymphs, he describes how he deciphers mysterious hieroglyphs and is shown several fountains and quenches his thirst by drinking the tepid water springing from a stone nymph's breasts. He is then taken to a magnificent bath where he is teased by the five senses before eventually arriving at the palace of the queen, who is the embodiment of free will. And being invited by her to partake of a splendid meal, he expresses his admiration for the variety of precious stones and materials worn by all present, and describes a game in dance and other measurements of sound. After the festivities, he is taken to visit three gardens, the first made of glass, the second of silk and the third a labyrinth, which is human life. In its midst was trinity itself, expressed through hieroglyphs, as in sacred Egyptian sculpture. He describes three important doors where one must make a choice and how, behind one, Polia awaits him. Without either character realising the meaning of their physical proximity, she takes him to admire the four triumphs of Jove: four processions whose chariots and artifacts celebrate the stories of the Classical poets explaining the effect of various kinds of love. Then follow the triumph of Vertumnus and Pomona, the ancient sacrifice of Priapus and the description of a magnificent temple of great beauty where the sacrifices of miraculous rites and ancient religion once took place. It is here that the couple fully acknowledge their loving encounter. Poliphilo then proceeds to narrate how he and Polia arrive at the coast to wait for Cupid at the site of a ruined temple, where she persuades him to explore in search of admirable ancient things. There he finds, among many enlightening epitaphs, a mosaic mural depicting hell. Scared again, he returns to Polia, just in time to meet Cupid, who has arrived in his ship propelled by beautiful rowing nymphs. Both climb aboard, and Love uses his wings as sails. Sea gods, goddesses and nymphs pay tribute to Cupid and the vessel arrives triumphantly at the island of Cytherea. Poliphilo then tells about the forests, gardens, fountains and rivers on the island, as well as the procession of triumphal chariots and nymphs in honour of Cupid who, blindfolded, guides them. In the centre of the island, the final place of arrival, he describes the venerean fountain with its precious columns and the actions that take place after the appearance of Mars, followed by a visit to the innermost enclosure containing the tomb of Adonis, where the nymphs tell the story of the hero's death and of the sad celebration of his anniversary commemorated every year by Venus, the lover.

The nymphs finally ask Polia to tell the story of her own love, its origins and difficulties. Polia acquiesces and her words fill the second book, giving a genealogy of her family, explaining her initial inclination to ignore Poliphilo, and providing a detailed account of the final success of their love. Following Polia's account, Poliphilo concludes by describing their embrace in the happy place of dwelling, until he is awakened, sad and alone, by the song of the nightingale.

This story is a sensuous and obsessive search for love that is not fulfilled. Polia is absent at the end of the story. Yet, the space of architecture appears through the text in the fulness of its meaning, including details about sites, materials, proportions, procedures and specifications, obviously a lesson most helpful for any aspiring architect. The ideal is not of this world (as modernist utopias might assume), the perfect garden/city/architecture remains otherworldly, yet the narrative legitimises a utopic vector for the imagination – the construing of the good life in the 'here and now' of our human world, the legitimate task of modern architecture.

Indeed, *Hypnerotomachia* is the first narrative articulation of architectural intentions at the very inception of the modern age. It expounds a poetic vision that sets a temporal boundary to the experience of architecture, emphasising that architecture is not only about form and space but about time, about the presence of man on earth. Architecture had always fulfilled its inveterate cultural task of disclosing a symbolic order at the intersection between a 'situation', a ritual or liturgy, and its material, constructed frame. Both aspects were perceived as indispensable and intimately related, yet traditionally they were never, even remotely, assumed to be related in an absolute and permanent fashion as two terms in an unambiguous equation. Ritual actions were obviously narrative (temporal) forms that articulated, together and within

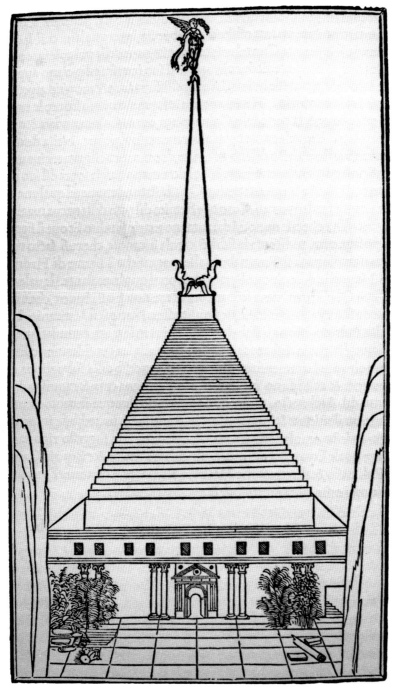

1   The first, immense monument encountered by Poliphilo, dedicated to propitious destiny, from Colonna, *Hypnerotomachia Poliphili* (Venice, 1499), sig. b*v*.

their architectural (spatial) sites, the order of human purpose in the gap between a mortal humanity and an overwhelming external reality. During the Renaissance sacred and profane rituals remained a fundamental part of the culture, and this is clearly reflected in *Hypnerotomachia*. The effective public function of ritual would be questioned eventually as a result of both the scientific revolution and its political consequence, the emergence of democracy at the end of the *ancien régime*. Therefore, the issue of 'situation' was not to become an explicit problem for architecture until the early eighteenth century, when it appears in the form of questions about 'character' and 'type' related to architectural meaning in the theoretical writings of Jacques-François Blondel, Germain Boffrand, Sébastien Le Camus de Mézières and others. It became a crucial theoretical problem during the late eighteenth century in the works of Etienne-Louis Boullée and Claude-Nicolas Ledoux, and has remained so until our own time.

However, given the dominant instrumental turn taken by architectural theories in the last two hundred years, it is easy to understand that our historical tradition has maintained in high regard Alberti's *De re aedificatoria* and Palladio's *Quattro libri* and has had less time for *Hypnerotomachia*. Indeed, it could be argued that European architecture followed the models of Alberti, Palladio and Vignola, projecting architecture as a liberal art guided by mathematical and geometric principles, precisely because these treatises were the precursors of a 'scientific' theory of architecture that allowed for the objectification of form. In a retrospective reading, these works have been interpreted as anticipations of a theory that eventually became obsessed with prescription and instrumentality, culminating in the work of Jean-Nicolas-Louis Durand, and nineteenth- and twentieth-century rationalism.

Today, in the wake of modernism, after witnessing the failures of instrumental theories and functionalism to generate meaningful architecture, we are perhaps better prepared to appreciate the great relevance of *Hypnerotomachia*. This 'didactic' dream, told in the form of a narrative that articulates the appropriateness and ethical values implicit in the making of 'Classical' architecture, reveals much that remains hidden in the other canonic treatises of the Renaissance. The book's narrative form itself prevents us from reducing the 'content' to an instrumental reading, as the making of the architecture it describes implies a self-transformation of the maker. It thus opens up ways to articulate ethical questions pertinent to our own architectural practice.

Hypnerotomachia fulfils its objective by demonstrating how architectural meaning is not something intellectual, a 'formal' question of proportional relationships or abstract aesthetic values, but rather originates in the erotic impulse itself, in the need to quench our physical

thirst: the existential condition to which humanity can only be reconciled within the realm of *poiesis* (the making of culture, that is, art and
architecture) and its metaphoric imagination. Poliphilo first experiences
the overwhelming harmony of Classical architecture and then, as soon
as he measures the wonderful monuments he encounters, discloses the
presence of precise proportional relationships (plates 1–3). In his sensuous narrative this discovery of *mathemata* is constantly synthesised
with a recollection of love; the effect of architecture is always beyond
the purely visual or theoretical, evoking the memory and expectation
of erotic fulfilment in a dense and vivid present. The harmony of
architecture is always mater-ial (related to the Latin *mater*, the Mother
of All) and tactile, the formal exactness of number coinciding with the
sensuous qualities of the materials, akin to the harmony that stems from
our wholeness as human beings in love, and analogous to the experience of wholeness that is prompted by the beautiful melodies often
accompanying Poliphilo's encounters. Poli-philo is, indeed, the lover
of Polia, the absent woman, whose name stands for the city (*polis*) and
perhaps also for multiple knowledge or wisdom (in the biblical sense of
carnal knowledge) and thus alludes to the primordial existential orientation conveyed by architecture to one's embodied consciousness. She
is represented as the missing 'sixth sense' in the episode in which
Poliphilo, after experiencing the mortal threat of the labyrinth,
encounters five nymphs whose names are those of the senses (Colonna
1971, I, 123ff.). The wholeness of love and architecture is sensuous yet
beyond the senses, it is a wholeness underscored by alchemical themes
and operations of fragmentation and union that structure the narrative
(Fierz-David 1987).

The emphasis on desire as the 'origin' of meaning cannot be dis-
counted, even in our sceptical times. The architectural meanings
to which we have access, those that touch us and leave us in awe, do
not occur as 'associations' in the mind alone, despite our Cartesian
'common sense'. This restricted understanding of meaning is, indeed, a
seventeenth-century prejudice first articulated for architecture in the
theoretical works of Claude Perrault (Pérez-Gómez 1993, 1–44).
Architectural meaning, like erotic knowledge, is primarily of the body
and happens in the world, in that pre-reflective ground of existence
where reality is first 'given', and as such it can never be reduced to
pure objectivity or subjectivity.

Although less explicit for architects than the Vitruvian tradition,
Hypnerotomachia also belongs to a Classical lineage. The understanding
of art (poetry and handicrafts, including architecture) revealing its
meaning *as* and *in* erotic space, has its roots at the inception of Graeco-
Roman culture (Carson 1986; Gadamer 1986). Artistic meaning is

2   The gateway in the first monument, from Colonna, *Hypnerotomachia Poliphili*
(Venice, 1499), sig. c.viiir.

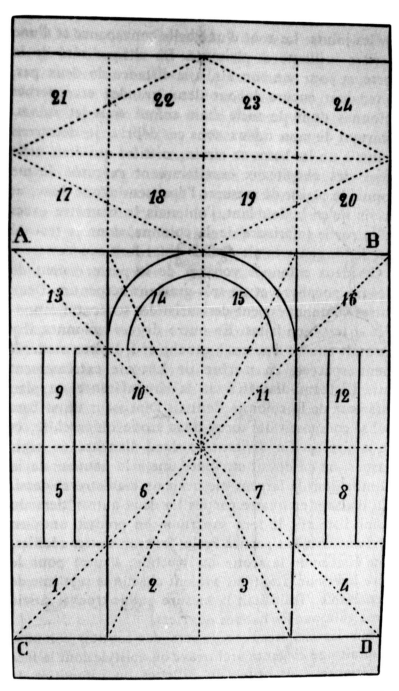

3 The proportions of the gateway in the first monument, (plate 2, after the French edition of 1546).

disclosed as the place and moment of 'recognition' when a work conveys its truth and may thus change our life, where the work appears utterly new, yet uncannily familiar.

In order to understand this tradition we should briefly recall that in Hesiod's *Theogonia* (seventh century BCE) Eros was one of three primordial divinities, responsible for the permanent copulation of the other two, Gaia (the earth) and Ouranos (the sky), united in the perpetual darkness that preceeded the age of man. Primordial Eros was itself complete, androgynous. Only when Time (Kronos) irrupted into the scene and castrated Ouranos was human reality set in motion – the cycles of day and night, the yearly seasons. At this point Eros was reborn, together with Aphrodite, from the blood and semen of Ouranos as it fell into the Mediterranean. In his new incarnation, Eros (Cupid) became the god of desire (Vernant 1990, 465–78). Eros, in the work of Sappho, who gave us some of the earliest and most moving poems in our tradition, is always 'bitter-sweet'. Eros is about a lack, a desire for what is missing, yet a space must be maintained or the desire ends. In Classical mythology only a god's desire can reach without lack, and only Eros is never-endingly filled with lack itself (Carson 1986, 11, 26, 30). Thus Eros defines the space/time of human culture as inherently bounded, pierced by an arrow of infinite desire yet always limited, suggesting that in the recognition and embracing of this tension, humanity may also recognise its purpose.

Later in the Greek tradition Plato and Aristotle translated this narrative into the language of philosophy. Indeed, the discovery of self-consciousness associated with the birth of philosophy, science, and architectural theory is inconceivable without the awareness of a 'distance' between the mind and world that is revealed through desire (Snell 1960; Carson 1986, 38). Aristotle established an analogy between Eros and knowing, claiming that men, by their nature, reach out to know, both deriving delight from reaching and pain from always falling short. Starting from the known, men try to give names to nameless things by transference (*metaphora*) from things similar in appearance. For Plato (in the *Symposium*), Eros is capable of revealing beauty in itself, the supreme good, 'in the one moment of man's life that is worth living' (Vernant 1990, 472), the same power of revelation that makes valuable the products of human handicraft (*techno-poiesis*). Homosexual or heterosexual love is for Plato either engendering (the best form of love), or a revelation of beauty in the eyes of the beloved, always transcending the mortal sphere. Through love the soul becomes winged and ascends to the stars. Echoes of Eros also resound in Plato's *symbolon* theory, according to which men were once whole (spheres), but now must live their lives looking for their other half. A *symbolon* was the name given to a clay token that was broken and given to a friend so that they might be recognised as such by the giver's family or institutional group (Gadamer 1986, 31–2). The issue (for 'symbolic' art and architecture) is one of recognition and participation, the possibility of understanding our potential wholeness through the experience of the work.

This is the central issue for Greek tragedy, whose cathartic effect is well described by Aristotle. The event was framed by the theatre, one of the most cosmologically resonant building 'types' of antiquity (see Vitruvius, v.vi.1), while the space 'in between', of the chorus, was the focus of the spectators' attention. Indeed, while before the Classical era 'spectators' and 'actors' remained undifferentiated, united in the action of Dionysian rituals, Greek tragedy introduced a 'distance' analogous to the space of Eros. The cathartic effect of the plot, a profound form of knowledge that disclosed a potential reconciliation between personal destiny and the designs of the immortal gods, would become a model for European art and architecture. The theatre itself stood for over two thousand years as a metaphor for architecture and the world, with architecture conceived as a form of knowledge capable of answering to man's most pressing existential questions.

The revelation of erotic space 'as such' was an important concern in the early Greek and Roman literary tradition. Some of the earliest prose narratives (proto-novels) that have survived are love stories, yet differing substantially from our common conception of such plots. The issue in these texts is never the fulfilment of a romantic relationship, but rather the erotic tension itself, either never resolved or resolved only in the last pages, evidencing the presence of a human space where wholeness is possible through a mode of participation that we now term 'aesthetic'. The best known of these narratives is perhaps Longus's *Daphnis and Chloe* from the second century AD, the story of two peasants living in nature who become progressively educated in love, while their environment changes from wilderness to a delectable garden (Zeitlin 1990, 417–60).

Imbued with the passion and temporality of Christianity, erotic narratives were also important allegories of knowledge during the Middle Ages, the most notable being the *Roman de la Rose*, and culminating with the epiphanies of Dante. *Hypnerotomachia Poliphili*, self-consciously connecting itself to the Classical tradition, addresses the meaning of architecture in particular, in its relations to nature (the garden) and self-knowledge. By incorporating other 'modern' interests that emerge in the culture of the Italian Renaissance, it opens up relevant possibilities for architecture.

In Poliphilo's Renaissance world of magic and alchemy the primacy of the pre-reflective ground as the origin of meaning is explicit. The elements of nature are never stable and *physis* is alive, constantly transforming. In alchemy the process is more important than its product, because the world of nature is in perpetual motion and change, never fully objectified and stable. The alchemist/architect must strive to find the primordial unity yet understands that the end is never fully attainable. Architecture is a verb rather than a noun; this is its true nature as a mimetic art.

In *Hypnerotomachia* the work of architecture was perceived to have a propitiatory role, its purpose to bring about good fortune and a happy life. *Hypnerotomachia* helps to legitimise the possibility and desirablity of actually changing the world of human affairs through constructions of the human imagination, never an obvious option before this time. Fortune is identified with Fortuna Primigenia and also with Venus Physizoa, the primordial mother, Earth. Architecture is a propitiation of Fortuna, which indeed could be understood as the Heideggerian 'earth', an element ever-present in the work of art that reminds mankind of its mortal nature and discloses 'being' as being-towards-death. This theme, in line with the necessity of cultivating prudence to develop a sound architectural practice, is constant throughout *Hypnerotomachia*. When Poliphilo arrives at the Palace of Free Will, the question of the role of individual freedom versus predestination becomes explicit (Colonna 1971, I, 151ff.). The power of architecture as a form of white astral magic is evidenced in the astrological ordering of the queen's abode. As a result, a number of relevant questions, eminently modern in their implications, can then be articulated. What are the limitations and responsibilities of the new man, whose newly acquired dignity was being celebrated by the Renaissance? What is the role of the individual imagination in a world that recognises the need for man to transform the order of creation and celebrates its artifacts while demanding that such acts of human *poiesis* be reconciled with the 'given' order of experience? In this context, where is architecture? Where is the beloved Polia?

These fundamental questions are eventually confronted at the three doors, where Poliphilo must make his most important choice (Colonna 1971, I, 221–30) (plate 4). The two nymphs that accompany him, Logistica (Reason) and Thelemia (Desire/Will/Fulfilment), fail to convince him to take either the right or the left door. For Poliphilo, at the crossroads, chooses neither *vita contemplativa* – a life of contemplation associated with classical metaphysics and theology but also with architecture as a liberal art and science – nor *vita activa* – the world of human action and 'being as production' in the old medieval sense, notions associated with architecture as a mechanical art (but which, undergoing secularisation, would lead to technology being seen as the physical fulfilment of material desires through a will-to-power and male-oriented, punctual cycle of toil, pleasurable reward and endless

ΘΕΟΔΟΞΙΑ
GLORI DE I

ΕΡΩΤΟΤΡΟΦΟΣ
MATERAMORIS

ΚΟΞΜΟΔΟΞΙΑ
GLORIAMVNDI

4 The three doors at
the crossroads. Poliphilo
is accompanied by the
nymphs Logistica and
Thelemia, from
Colonna,
Hypnerotomachia Poliphili
(Venice, 1499), sig.
h.viiir.

disillusion). Rather, Poliphilo's choice leads him through the middle
door to *vita voluptuaria*, a life of desire where fulfilment is never fully
present nor fully absent. A life of desire as both recollection and
projection and of ethical responsibility and respect for the otherness of
his beloved, leading to an architecture mindful of its necessary appropriateness and wholeness: this, we thus learn, is the life that the good
architect must pursue.

Indeed, Poliphilo meets Polia beyond that central door. She carries
a lighted torch, and they walk together. After witnessing the divine
effects of love through many works of human creation and ritual
processions, they eventually recognise each other in the circular temple
of Venus, the place where the architecture is most perfect (Colonna

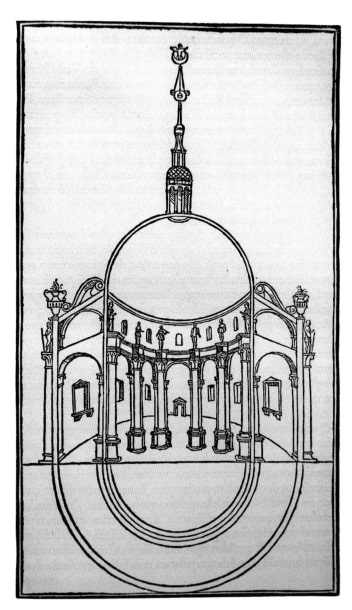

5 The circular temple
of love, epitome of
architectural
perfection, from
Colonna,
*Hypnerotomachia
Poliphili* (Venice, 1499),
sig. n.iii*r*.

1971, 1, 330ff.) (plate 5). Under the dome an eternally glowing lamp
and a well mark the *axis mundi* where a priestess of Venus performs
rites that lead to a miraculous germination of life, while Poliphilo
extinguishes Polia's fiery torch in the water.

   Although the only extant English edition ends 'happily' with the
alchemical fusion of water and fire, in the original version we soon
learn that in order to fulfil their desire the couple must still cross the

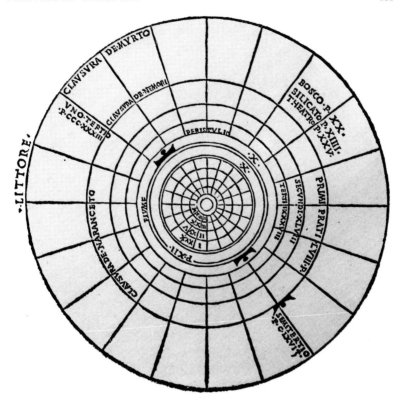

6 Plan of the circular island of love, from Colonna, *Hypnerotomachia Poliphili*
(Venice, 1499), sig. t.viiir.

sea of death. In fact, immediately after acknowledging the wholeness
brought about by love, Poliphilo must visit, alone, a cemetery under a
ruined temple where he finds many funerary monuments, also identified as poignant architectural works, the epitaphs of which describe the
tragedy of lovers separated by death. Scared by a vision of hell and
overtaken by anguish, Poliphilo returns to the coast to find Polia, just
in time to board Cupid's ship (Colonna 1971, II, 110ff.). It is no
coincidence that Cupid plays the role of navigator and that Love
becomes Tecton, the mythical carpenter, ship-builder and pilot, the
Homeric ancestor of the architect. Cupid's wings become the sails of
the ship, another archaic theme associated with the role of the architect
in the myth of Daedalus and Icarus, as father and son attempt to escape
from Crete and the architect is credited with the invention of wings/
sails (Pérez-Gómez 1985).

   On the other side of the water, on the island of love (plate 6), Polia
and Poliphilo are finally together, but not before having been meta-
phorically blindfolded by Cupid. The possibility of meaningful architecture depends upon a realisation that visible form and language refer

to something other, recognised only when the dominant sense of sight (and Renaissance perspective) is mediated by the body's primary synaesthetic (tactile) understanding. At the privileged place described as a Classical theatre, the centre of centres as *theatrum mundi*, the two lovers witness an ultimate ritual of love, now performed by the immortal gods themselves (the tragic story of Venus and Adonis). There they endure the last painful delay in their quest for love (Colonna 1971, II, 263ff.). Polia's version of the story is then heard. At the end of her narration, however, Poliphilo finally wakes up from his dream, alone yet complete in the presence of an architecture that evokes the memory of fulfilment, the final recognition of the mystery of depth, the wholeness that, however 'weak', grounds us as purposeful beings in the universe.

Hypnerotomachia Poliphili was never intended as a work of high literature. Its themes, as suggested here, were common in the Middle Ages and in the works of the early Renaissance Italian poets. Clearly, the main concerns of Colonna were architectural and alchemical, a concern for the disclosure of a symbolic order in the world of human action. Yet the language is highly imaginative, an idiosyncratic vernacular Italian with much Latin syntax and vocabulary. The erotic content is blunt and effective, though often full of clichés, interspersed with abundant specialised architectural and botanical technical terms. It is a strange dialect, constructed yet 'popular'. Predating the inception of the modern novel (before Rabelais and Cervantes) and the normalisation of prose in European languages, the language of *Hypnerotomachia* displays a texture prophetic of the present quest to reconcile personal creation and a political common ground in art and literature, suggesting a potential collapse of the difference between poetic forms and the language of popular culture.

The woodcut images of *Hypnerotomachia Poliphili* represent the loci of classical architecture visited by the hero. The text provides minute descriptions of the monuments, including the colours and textures of materials and iconography of these buildings, usually referring to the Roman goddesses Fortuna and Venus and furthering the propitiation of human destiny through love, harmony and fertility. In this way the Classical loci were intended to function as models for a superior fifteenth-century architecture. In addition, Poliphilo is often fascinated by the enigmatic presence of hieroglyphs inscribed in buildings and fragments, the meaning of which is analogous to that of the architecture (Colonna 1971, I, 106–7). In the case of these discoveries, Poliphilo deciphers and renders the images in language, yet, unlike other Renaissance authors such as Filarete, he seems to acknowledge that the ultimate meaning of such evocative figures must remain hidden. Thus, he is prepared to accept the ambiguity of architectural meaning, one recognised as inhabiting the surface of the image yet resistant to clarification in language.

We learn much from *Hypnerotomachia Poliphili* as soon as we are willing to see, in the wake of the recent demystification of positive science, that there is truth in myths. This strange text is difficult, yet eloquent, a brave attempt to speak about that obscure subject first named by Plato: the space of meaning in the western tradition, the place of our dwelling. *Chora*, Plato acknowledged, can only be grasped with great difficulty, it is like the substance of our dreams, and we may only conceptualise it indirectly, through spurious reasoning. Yet, without it we simply cannot account for reality. Elsewhere (Pérez-Gómez 1994, 1–34) I have associated the space of Eros and meaning with this term *Chora* used by Plato in his *Timaeus* to name the 'third' element of reality, distinct from Ideas (being) and Things (becoming) whilst grounding their relationship, a realm identified with both cultural space (the matrix of becoming) *and* the primordial material of the craftsman (the *prima materia* of the demiurg) yet distinct from natural place (*topos*). *Hypnerotomachia* tried to describe such space for the sake of 'improving' architecture, a space/matter that is definitely controlled by the architect (since the Renaissance was responsible for the preoccupation with generating architectural 'ideas' or images), while it still coincides with cosmic place, a site whose meaning grounds the architect's work and is not prejudiced by the products of his making.

Once the original covenant between man and god was broken, whether it be with the Cthonic gods of the Myceneans, or the God of Israel in the ancient Near East, European man had to make up for a lack. How to build and yet not to dominate nature, how to avoid imposing an order on the creation while making up for our fallen condition became pressing issues. The architect learned from Eros how to seduce, as Eros is present everywhere in nature. Thus Poliphilo's virtual work is an act of seduction. The power of Eros is the power of magic, the power of *techno-poiesis*. The architect's works must incite love, they are spellbinding, like the image of the beloved. Yet in order for the work to be good the architect must first fall in love, put himself under the sway of that which is given. Much closer to us, Friedrich Nietzsche wrote late in his life that only a vigorous lover can be a good artist; the work of art, a model of man's will-to-power, must nevertheless engage the love of fate in order to bring about the appropriate configurations of time and space.

The essential intention of *Hypnerotomachia*, to articulate a possible ethical position through a narrative that acknowledges important models for the practice of architecture, is still valid today. This is so particularly in view of the current philosophic understanding of truth – shared by Heidegger (1977), Hans-Georg Gadamer (1986), and

Gianni Vattimo (1988) – as embodied in human works through 'art', and of a diagnosis of the postmodern condition in which the only alternative to the strong Being of traditional religion and science seems to be the weak truth that shines forth through recollection of historical works. Also important is the basic phenomenological lesson of *Hypnerotomachia* connecting architectural meaning to embodied experience through discourse, rather than simply accepting meaning (the transhistorical meaning of the works that constitute our cultural traditions) as an effect of exclusively mental or intellectual processes liable to be dismissed as logical impossibilities, or at best delusory constructs, in the age of immanent reason.

The tactical know-how that we may derive for architecture from hermeneutic ontology and phenomenology thus seem to have been partially prefigured by *Hypnerotomachia Poliphili*. Indeed, an understanding of the architect's potential as a creative artist whose imagination is not reduced to the function of either romantic production *ex nihilo*, or classical reproduction of a transcendent order, seems crucial today. This strategy is the most appropriate on which to found an ethical practice of architecture that is capable of avoiding both solipsism and nostalgia in a world where images, simulations that are merely reflections of reflections, have acquired the status of reality. *Hypnerotomachia* suggests the importance of resisting the temptations of technology (cyberspace) with its implicit collapse of erotic distance: the overcoming of desire has of course been a prime objective of much late modern utopian thinking. In this context, such a strategy of resistance becomes an instrument to deconstruct technological 'common places' seen merely in terms of their utilitarian value, revealing their mysterious origin and thus enhancing the possibility of creating a truly eloquent architecture.

Chapter Five

VITRUVIUS IN PRINT AND IN VERNACULAR TRANSLATION: FRA GIOCONDO, BRAMANTE, RAPHAEL AND CESARE CESARIANO

Ingrid D. Rowland

IN THE 20S BC, Vitruvius dedicated his *De Architectura Libri Decem* (Ten Books on Architecture) to the Emperor Augustus. He did so in the belief that his own profession had entered a new age, affording unprecedented prospects for the invention of new forms and the new synthesis of disparate styles. Rome's extensive political dominion in turn inspired Vitruvius to attempt something still more significant: to include architecture as part of a universal language, not only of form, but of cultural expression as a whole. Fifteen centuries later, that grand project still exerted its forceful pull. In the first printed editions of Vitruvius, from the Latin edition of Giovanni Sulpicio da Veroli (*c.*1486) to the vernacular translation of Cesare Cesariano (1521), a similar conjunction of creative energy and penetrating synthesis once again aimed at formulating a universal expressive language.

Renaissance Italy, as a peninsula filled with diverse small states subjected to constant threat of foreign invasion and internecine war, may, politically, have borne little resemblance to the nascent Augustan Empire. When Vitruvius wrote his treatise, however, that empire, still less than ten years old, must have looked a good deal less secure than it would turn out to be. Vitruvius had spent most of his life in conditions of civil war; his synthetic vision of the builder's art, like that of his Italian disciples, must have been largely the creature of hope.

Rather than prescribing strict canons for Classical style, the *Ten Books* sought instead to include architecture within a systematic theory of design, one based on the workings of nature, herself described as an architect (Vitr.IX.i.2–6). In Vitruvius's account, nature's designs,

manifested on a large scale in the structure of the cosmos (Vitr.IX) and
more immediately in the measure of the human body (Vitr.III.i.2–4),
formed the reliable core for every kind of human creation: hence, he
insisted that the layout of cities should follow the quirks of their
individual sites, buildings should accommodate the size of their human
users, ornaments should conform to the shapes and laws of nature,
the twisted ropes that propel a catapult should be tuned to perfect
pitch.

Vitruvius also claimed repeatedly that this large conception of his
subject and the rigorous order in which he treated it were features
entirely new to architectural writing. The ordered exposition of the
Ten Books must be counted, then, as his own original contribution to
the field (see esp. Vitr.I.i.18; IV.praef.; V.praef.; VI.praef.7; VII.praef.11–
18). For the next fifteen centuries, his readers took him at his word,
preserving his text alone among all the treatises of ancient architectural
writers. Whether they mined his work for moral precepts, information about the properties of stone and timber, guidelines for well-
proportioned ornament, educational curricula or designs for artillery,
they regarded him as an *auctor*, a word that in Latin bore connotations
of divinity and fertility as well as authority (as evident in words like
'augur', 'Augustus' and 'augment'). In the words of Vitruvius himself,
'authors' in this exalted sense:

> not only produce ever fresh and flourishing fruit for their own
> fellow citizens, but also for all the nations who have come after
> them. And those who from an early age enjoy an abundance of
> learning develop the best judgment, and in their cities they have
> established civilized customs, equal justice, and those laws without
> which no community can exist safely (Vitr.IX.praef.2).

The changing economy of the late Middle Ages and early Renaissance gave Vitruvius a fresh relevance when, just as in ancient Rome,
the flowering of trade exposed receptive Italians to a wide variety of
cultural influences. In antiquity, Vitruvius had faced the challenge of
eclecticism by insisting that the mind take in a broad range of ideas but
maintain them in a strict order, what he called *disciplina*. He described
the process of architectural design as an orderly, reasoned progression
from initial idea to final ornament, and attempted to impose the same
order on the composition of his treatise. For designers and patrons
alike, he advocated a broad liberal education that tempered its welter
of intellectual stimuli by strict observance of disciplinary rigour. The
humanists of the fifteenth century found these precepts enduringly
sound.

Unlike Vitruvius himself, however, who was an educated man with
a command of both Greek and Latin in addition to his professional

skills, many Italian architects of the fifteenth and sixteenth centuries could speak and write only in their own vernacular, despite their ever-growing mastery of Classical form as a kind of visual language. Nor were their patrons necessarily much better equipped; a figure as influential as Pope Julius II famously protested 'I'm no scholar'. Powerful merchants and mercenaries, important patrons of art, often knew far less than he. For these interested but linguistically limited parties, the guidance of a vernacular Vitruvius may have been a desirable goal long before it became practicable.

The problem lay with the Vitruvian text itself, which had survived from antiquity in considerable disarray. As medieval scribes had struggled with words whose immediacy had been lost over the generations – like the Greek and Latin technical terms with which Vitruvius worked and which peppered his treatise, or the names of long-dead architects and remote cities – these words became garbled approximations of what they once had been. Particular torments were reserved for three Greek poems whose text Vitruvius had cited complete; their Greek letters began to look more and more like Cyrillic script and eventually much of the verse simply dropped away. The Roman numerals by which Vitruvius expressed dimensions proved especially susceptible to corruption; a moment of careless copying could transform 'xxviii' to 'xxvii' or garble the special symbols by which the ancient Romans denoted weights and measures. Not until the humanist movement of the fifteenth century did Vitruvius's detailed measurements of pagan temples seem to hold any interest for Christian readers; earlier marginal notes in manuscripts indicate a greater preoccupation with Book I and its curriculum of liberal education, Book II's discussion of building materials, Book VIII's treatment of hydraulics and the final technological flourishes of Books IX (cosmology and sundials) and X (machines).

For humanists, however, details mattered; in them lay the secrets to the graceful proportions and structural durability of ancient architecture, and as the humanist scholars began to demand a more accurate text of Vitruvius, so their contemporaries with interests in art and architecture demanded every possible key to unlocking and recreating the beauties of the ancient world. By the 1480s the learned Sienese architect Francesco di Giorgio Martini had begun to try his hand at drafting a vernacular Vitruvius (Scaglia 1985, 17). Significantly, this was the same decade in which the first definitive Latin edition of Vitruvius went to press in Rome (in 1486 or shortly thereafter) at the hands of Giovanni Sulpicio da Veroli, professor of grammar and rhetoric at the city university, the *studium urbis* (Scaglia 1985, 52–3; Daly Davis 1989). Both Sulpicio's printed Latin text and Francesco di Giorgio's fragmentary translation show the extent to which establishing a definitive version of Vitruvius's treatise was still work-in-progress by that time; in fact, Sulpicio's preface to his readers actively invited them to send him their comments so that he might eventually improve upon his published text. The same acute awareness that he was dealing with unfinished business led Sulpicio to leave wide margins in his printed book where readers could supply their own illustrations – the nine to eleven geometric diagrams to which Vitruvius referred in his text have not been preserved in the manuscript tradition – and their own readings of the Greek poems, which generations of Greek-less scribes had rendered nearly unintelligible in all the extant manuscripts.

A generation later, in 1511, the Veronese architect and scholar Fra Giovanni Giocondo took a boldly different approach to publishing Vitruvius (Ciapponi 1984). His edition, printed in Venice by Giovanni Tacuino and dedicated to Pope Julius II, was a big folio book, copiously illustrated in a spare graphic style, probably by Giocondo himself. All Vitruvius's Greek terms and Greek poems were now carefully printed in Greek, restored as the result of Giocondo's brilliant detective work among the manuscripts of the Medici library in Florence. Furthermore, unlike his cautious predecessor Sulpicio, Giocondo made a sweeping attempt to correct troubled passages in the preserved Latin text of the *Ten Books*, often replacing traditional manuscript readings with his own informed conjectures as to what Vitruvius might once actually have written. While many of these 'corrections' (the technical term is 'emendations') are no longer accepted by modern Classical scholars, many have withstood every subsequent test.

Giocondo's edition, for its lavish physical presence, its intellectual daring and its impressive scholarship, was intended to make an impact on contemporaries, and it succeeded. It must have sold well, too, for the last decade of the fifteenth century and the early years of the sixteenth favoured the publication of big illustrated books, both in Latin and in vernacular, many obviously issued by their publishers as moneymakers. As a result, Giocondo's *Vitruvius* would be instrumental in shaping more than the content of the first complete vernacular versions of the *Ten Books*; like his Latin edition, the first vernacular translations of the text were designed as large-format printed books with abundant illustrations. (The importance of Giocondo's edition may also be gauged by the fact that two subsequent revised editions from the Florentine firm of Giunta, printed in 1513 and 1522, opted for the more economical octavo format with rudimentary woodcuts to reach less well-heeled readers.)

If Fra Giocondo provided the scholarly stimulus for translating Vitruvius, the achievements of a contemporary architect afforded an equally strong push from the artistic quarter when, by bedazzled consensus, his designs began to equal the lofty elegance of the ancient

Romans. That architect was Donato Bramante, a native of Urbino who had worked extensively in Milan before transferring to Rome around 1500. In the Eternal City, at his own expense, he began to study the remnants of its ancient architecture, painting and sculpture, refusing other work to eliminate distractions. Eventually, however, he began to accept commissions again, first from powerful cardinals and then, in the last days of 1503 or early in 1504, from the newly elected Pope Julius II (Bruschi 1967, xxix).

Bramante was more than an architect for Julius; he was a close friend to that driven and difficult Pope. Like Leonardo da Vinci, a companion of his Milanese days, Bramante had never been educated in Latin; they were both classified by contemporary humanist scholars as *illitterati*. 'Illiterate' or not, their intellectual lives, like that of Pope Julius himself, spanned an impressive range of interests. Bramante's skill at reciting Dante and at improvising the popular songs known as *strambotti* often prompted the Pope to require his services as a performer as well as a designer. (The architect from Urbino was also surely the author of a tongue-in-cheek poem about Rome's antiquities published as a cheap pamphlet under the pseudonym 'Prospectivo melanese depintore' – 'Mr Perspective, the painter from Milan'. Dedicated to Leonardo and composed in a clumsy version of Dante's poetic metre, *terza rima*, this pamphlet, the *Antiquarie prospettiche Romane*, and its country-bumpkin verse are entirely too clever to be what they seem.)

Julius II, in turn, despite his denials of scholarly prowess, showed himself an extraordinarily shrewd patron of the arts; in his pell-mell ten-year reign (1503–13) he forced the Florentine sculptor Michelangelo Buonarroti to turn fresco painter for the Sistine Chapel ceiling against the artist's outraged protests. At the same time, he declared the sprawling early Christian basilica of St Peter's structurally unsound, and ordered Bramante to design a replacement while proceeding to demolish the venerable old building, temporarily disabling the city's chief attraction for the flocks of pilgrims who descended every year in search of spiritual benefits. In the midst of these ambitious plans, Pope Julius also began to refurbish a suite of rooms in the Vatican palace to serve as his private apartments, for which Bramante recommended a young nephew, Raffaello Sanzio of Urbino (Raphael) to join the team of fresco painters assigned to the project. Julius's satisfaction with the young painter's work soon won Raphael exclusive rights to complete the entire suite. In the meantime, Julius and Bramante conspired to reshape the very urban fabric of Rome to their own grandiose designs, carving parallel boulevards through cramped medieval neighbourhoods and sparsely settled garden plots to create a verdant garden city where the Tiber flowed past the Vatican (Frommel

1988, 50–53). As focal points for their scheme, they laid the foundations of churches and a massive courthouse, all designed on a scale to
rival the imposing ruins that Bramante proved to have studied to such
brilliant effect.

It was no wonder, therefore, that Fra Giocondo chose to dedicate
his epic edition of Vitruvius to Pope Julius late in the latter's reign; the
book's preface states openly that like Augustus before him, the pontiff
was proving to be a masterful patron of the builder's art. Indeed, Julius
himself, as his pontifical name suggested, made a point of comparing
his renewal of Christian Rome to the great undertakings of the city's
imperial past. It may not be surprising, in this context of grand
experiment and self-conscious renewal, that the first two completed
projects to translate Vitruvius into the Italian vernacular each acknowledged Donato Bramante as mentor and inspiration, singling him out as
the first contemporary architect truly to rival the ancients for purity of
design and magnificence of scale. One of these vernacular Vitruvius
translations originated in the creative heart of papal Rome, the other as
a personal odyssey in the regional isolation of Milan. Both, however,
were modelled on the imposing size, copious illustration and financial
success of Fra Giocondo's Latin edition.

The Roman project took its impetus from Raphael, whose artistic
development in the fervid atmosphere of Julian Rome was as meteoric
as that of Bramante and Michelangelo. Raphael became the most
sought-after painter in Rome. At the same time, he extended his
interests to every aspect of design: architecture, sculpture, metalwork
and engraving, supplying designs for work in all these media for
execution by his large, thriving workshop. When Pope Julius died in
1513, the succeeding pontiff, Leo X, continued to entrust greater and
greater responsibility (and an ever-widening set of commissions) to the
personable young artist. When Bramante himself died in 1514, Raphael
and the elderly Fra Giocondo succeeded jointly as chief architects to St
Peter's, still little more than a ruinous hulk. It must have been the
challenge of formulating a suitable aesthetic for St Peter's that
prompted Raphael to solicit the guidance of a vernacular Vitruvius –
like Bramante, he was 'illiterate'. To carry out the translation, Raphael
engaged the services of an eccentric, impoverished, but rigorous
scholar named Marco Fabio Calvo, who lodged in one of Raphael's
own houses for the duration of the project. A third participant, the
wealthy curial official Angelo Colocci, must have served as consultant
and scribe out of his own passionate interest in the ancient writer
(Rowland 1994). The head of a scholarly confederation called the
Roman Academy, Colocci was also Italy's supreme expert on ancient
weights and measures, the owner of an extensive collection of antiquities in which stone weights and images of architects' tools featured
prominently. He shared his collections and his marvellous personal

library (which included some manuscripts of Vitruvius as well as important illustrated texts of ancient technical writers) with his wide circle of friends, facilitating the development of what they all acknowledged as an intellectual renaissance in Rome. Furthermore, Colocci became a close friend of Fra Giocondo during the friar's last sojourn in Rome, eventually inheriting much of the latter's library upon his death in 1515. It seems likely, therefore, that Giocondo must also have been a significant presence in the shaping of Calvo's translation.

Colocci, an important early editor of printed vernacular texts and a vocal champion of vernacular literature, would certainly have foreseen the Calvo translation's potential for publication, as would a marketer as shrewd as Raphael, whose personal experience with engraving would have made it easy for him to improve drastically on Giocondo's illustrations. Work was already well under way on revising the text of the Calvo translation and selecting and drafting its illustrations when Raphael died of a sudden fever in 1520 (Nesselrath 1993). Neither the artist's extensive workshop nor Calvo, nor Colocci himself ever mustered the heart to return to the project.

In Milan, meanwhile, a dedicated architect named Cesare Cesariano had been at work on translating Vitruvius for nearly twenty years. When Bramante departed from that city in 1500, he left behind a Milan in political turmoil but also a city of intense creative ferment, to which he and Leonardo da Vinci had been signal contributors. Both had been lured in the 1490s to the court of Ludovico Sforza 'il Moro', a warlord whose combination of political ruthlessness and penetrating taste made for a most effective patron (just as with Julius II). Together with his cultured wife Beatrice d'Este and his formidably gifted brother Cardinal Ascanio, il Moro in a few years had succeeded in making Milan a city whose cosmopolitan flair combined with pride in a distinct regional individuality. Even the French invasion of 1499 could not suppress the continuing development of the arts in Lombardy.

As one of the Milanese artists caught up in this inventive tide, Cesariano, a university-educated painter and military engineer, envisioned producing a vernacular Vitruvius; with its help, he would eventually declare, Lombard architects might achieve still greater success at rivalling the magnificence of the ancients. Cesariano took for granted that this accessible Vitruvius should appear in print, in vernacular translation and with explanatory illustrations, but even these expedients, to his mind, would not suffice to make the ancient author's meaning plain. Word by word, therefore, he set about writing a commentary to the text, explaining obscure terms, comparing information supplied by other authors ancient and modern, and inserting a good deal of contemporary material, whether descriptions of buildings, tales about other architects, or ancedotes from his own life. As in many medieval manuscripts of ancient authors and in contemporary printed

1   Page layout, from Cesare
Cesariano, *Di Lucio Vitruvio
Pollione De Architectura Libri Dece*
(Como, 1521), Book V, fol.
LXXIIIr. Reyerson and Burnham
Libraries, Art Institute of Chicago.

books, these comments would eventually appear in fine print, filling
the ample margins of Cesariano's published text (plate 1).

By 1513, he had completed much of the translation. To underwrite
the expensive process of publication, Cesariano formed a company
with an aristocratic dilettante, Luigi Pirovano, and a well-placed official
in Como, Agostino Gallo, who may have been instrumental in choosing a local Comasco printer, Gottardo da Ponte, to carry out the work.
The new company engaged two humanist scholars, Luigi Benedetto
Giovio and Bono Mauro, to act as copy-editors. The book's design
presented no mean logistical challenge, sporting its two varieties of
type intermingled with woodcut prints on full folio pages. From the
outset the company deferred publication over an extraordinary six
years. Six years stretched into nine as Cesariano, dividing the work on
his magnum opus with a variety of commissions as a military engineer,

procrastinated with commentary and plates (Gatti 1971; 1991). In 1521 Cesariano's exasperated associates wrested what they could of the remaining text and plates from the author's hands; the erstwhile copy-editors Giovio and Mauro brought the commentary to a hasty conclusion while Pirovano and Gallo engaged another artist to supply a missing woodcut. Later that year the book was out, a work of epic idiosyncrasy, and with its two final books, IX and X, executed in a palpably different manner from the rest. Cesariano, outraged, preserved his own autograph draft for these same books, work which has recently been published after its rediscovery in a Madrid library (Vitruvius 1996), and he sued his former partners, winning a favourable judgement in 1523 (Gatti 1991; Vitruvius 1996, 2).

Manfredo Tafuri has noted, perceptively, that Cesariano's subsequent legal wrangles with these erstwhile associates revolved around a fundamental point of pride: by undertaking the tasks of translation, illustration and commentary himself, Cesariano sought personally to embody Vitruvian liberal education (Tafuri 1978, 410–11). Indeed, as a military engineer with university training, he conformed as closely to Vitruvius's own biography as any of his contemporaries. In Milan and Rome alike, 'illiterate' Bramante had exerted a degree of influence that promised increased cultural authority for architects, an authority for which Vitruvius's text pleaded its own poignant case.

For Pirovano and Gallo, Cesariano's partners, as for their philological consultants Giovio and Mauro, the point of the Vitruvius project was its teamwork, an indication of Lombardy's continued cultural vibrancy. The lone hero and the erudite team were contradictory visions, and because the team eventually seized control of the book's publication, as teamwork it would emerge from the press. Yet if the team won the battle of the book's acknowledgements, Cesariano handily won the war of authorial attribution, even in his own day. Everyone knew that the work was his, and a highly individual work it was.

Though clearly inspired in its format and the layout of some of its illustrations by Giocondo's Latin edition of 1511, Cesariano claims, plausibly, to have established his own working text of Vitruvius by comparing ('collating') the readings of eleven manuscripts available to him in Milan (Krinsky 1971; Fiore 1989). However, whereas Fabio Calvo carried out his translation within a close-knit community of scholars and artists, Cesariano's labour was, despite his associates' claims to the contrary, heroically, sometimes perversely, single-handed, his visual world bounded by the local architecture of northern Italy just as his vernacular hewed close to the local dialect.

As a matter of professional principle, Calvo and Colocci both held high standards for vernacular; by observing these standards they hoped to elevate contemporary speech to a common language rather than a

regional idiom; whatever their personal differences of opinion about
how to carry out this enterprise in detail, they consistently emphasised
clarity of expression and elegance of style. Furthermore, the pooled
expertise of their intellectual community in Rome, not to mention the
presence of the ancient ruins, enabled them to discern the meaning of
obscure Latin words and then to translate those words intelligibly.
Cesariano was largely forced to puzzle it all out on his own; characteristically, when a Latin word eluded him, he simply Italianised it, which
usually meant no more than putting it into the ablative case. Valiantly
he might try to explain its meaning in his commentary, but the
translation itself remained, on occasion, a peculiar hybrid between
Classical Latin and Milanese *volgare*. More confusing still are the places
where he attempted (like Alberti before him) to insist upon a seamless
continuity between the ancient and modern worlds, as when he speaks
of ancient temples as if they are one and the same with Christian
churches, designating them both by the Italianised Latin word *ede*,
which really means nothing more specific than 'building'.

Cesariano seems to have spent at most only a brief time in Rome.
His illustrations suggest why he may have felt no need to do more than
this; northern Italy had impressive monumental architecture of its own,
both ancient and medieval. To his own eye, Milan's Gothic cathedral
embodied most of the aesthetic principles enunciated by Vitruvius:
qualities like durable structure, harmony (under which rubric he classified both Vitruvian 'symmetria' and 'eurythmia'), and economy of
means. Hence, he used the Duomo rather than a Classical building to
illustrate Vitruvius's introductory discussion of those very principles at
the beginning of Book I (plate 2), rendering the cathedral in Vitruvius's
three recommended ways: plan, elevation and perspectival *scaenographia*
(Vitruvius 1521, fols. xiiiir, xvr, xvv). Only detailed scrutiny could
have shown him the extent to which such a building partook of a
formal idiom quite different from that of Rome itself. He seems to
have assumed that Vitruvius's discussion of temples referred to the
placement of engaged columns and pilasters on a façade. In a sense, he
was quite right to do so; Vitruvius himself seems to assume that his
readers will extrapolate from his discussion of freestanding temple
colonnades to designing with engaged columns (as in his basilica at
Fano), but as a result Cesariano also misinterpreted the double rows of
exterior columns that characterised Vitruvius's dipteral temples as an
interior loggia, effectively turning the Classical scheme inside out.
Romanesque buildings imprinted their own variety of Roman style on
his vision as surely as Classical structures like the arenas of Verona and
Padua. Local tradition had it that Lombard houses preserved intact the
forms of ancient domestic architecture, and he approached Vitruvius's
discussion of houses in Book VI with this conviction firmly in place
(Pellecchia 1992).

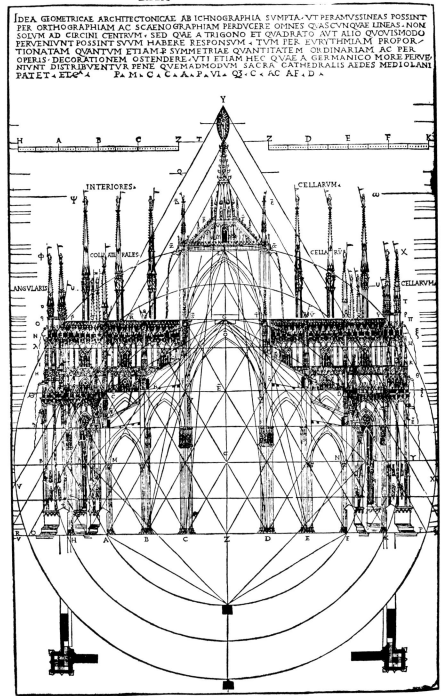

2   Milan cathedral as example of Classical proportion, from Cesariano, *Di Lucio Vitruvio Pollione De Architectura Libri Dece* (Como, 1521), Book I, fol. xvv. Reyerson and Burnham Libraries, Art Institute of Chicago.

For its Lombard visual sense alone, therefore, Cesariano's edition is a decided anomaly among sixteenth-century architectural treatises, but the anomalies hardly stop there. Its language, its approach to Vitruvian theory and its copious commentary are equally peculiar. In many respects, Cesariano seems to have drawn his inspiration from another lengthy, equally anomalous printed book, the provocatively titled *Hypnerotomachia Poliphili* issued authorless by the Venetian press of Aldus Manutius in 1499. Published in a quixotic effort to raise money among affluent antiquarian readers, the *Hypnerotomachia* combined woodcuts of crumbling ancient buildings, Egyptian hieroglyphs, pagan statues and Greek and Roman inscriptions with a tale about a scholar's romance with one of the nymphs who cavorted among the ruins. The hero's desire to know antiquity verges upon, and occasionally merges with, sexual longing: a woodcut 'triumph of Priapus' flaunted that phallic god's chief attribute as plainly as the satyr who, in another woodcut, unveils a voluptuous sleeping water-nymph. The erotic transports of the protagonists thus met the reader's own presumed longing for bygone antiquity in a seductive visual mix that can still work its beguiling charms.

As for the narrative itself, it strove mightily to infuse Italian vernacular with something of Latin's stately gravitas, with decidedly mixed results. Sometimes it rises to the enigmatic pitch of the woodcuts, but just as frequently the story lumbers along under its burden of Latinate words; somehow, they fail to create a spell as binding as the picture-magic of the illustrations. And yet for some readers the *Hypnerotomachia*, both words and images, has always proved utterly intoxicating. Raphael's friend Angelo Colocci was one such enchanted reader. Another, all too clearly, was Cesare Cesariano. Perhaps the prose into which the Lombard architect chose to put his Vitruvius aimed, like the *Hypnerotomachia*, to create an antiquarian aura simply by mimicking the solemn movement and the word-sounds of Latin.

Cesariano's illustrations, in combination with his Latinate text, may also have sought to recreate the *Hypnerotomachia's* evocative aura of sound and image. As with the *Hypnerotomachia*, his Vitruvius evinces a fascination with the other languages of the Mediterranean: while the Aldine romance includes inscriptions in Hebrew, Greek, Egyptian hieroglyphs and (anachronistically) Arabic, Cesariano boasts one in Etruscan (a pastiche of two still-extant inscriptions from Volterra which he lifted from another large printed book, Raffaele Maffei's *Commentaria Urbana* of 1506 (Massa Pairault 1991)). As in the *Hypnerotomachia* also, Priapus reigns supreme: one of the figures by which Cesariano illustrates the basic geometry of the human body sports a conspicuous erection quite absent from the Vitruvian text.

Both Fabio Calvo and Cesariano wrote their translations just before the architectural Orders had been codified; like their fifteenth-century predecessors, both use Italian equivalents to the Vitruvian term *genus* in referring to the various column types. 'Order', in the Vitruvian text and *ordine* in their vernacular versions of it, denoted the basic sequence of the book, its overarching order of ideas. On a more specific level, it also referred to a row of columns or to a sequence of instructions or designer's decisions. In 1519 or so, Raphael and Angelo Colocci began to use the word 'order' in a different way, to classify the various types of columns and to limit their canonical number. They did so in connection with yet another papal commission from Leo X, a request to draw a series of reconstructions of Imperial Rome – implementing Julius II's garden city in the real Rome was proving incompatible with his successor's extravagant ways. As with the Vitruvius translation, the manuscript project showed signs of adaptation for publication before it was abandoned altogether at Raphael's death: the portfolio's letter of presentation, a vernacular document drafted initially with the help of the gifted Mantuan aristocrat Baldassare Castiglione, was subsequently revised to transform a personal letter to the Pope into a more broadly conceived document of interest to the general reader (Raphael *c.*1519–20; Thoenes 1986). This latest draft of the preface, written in Angelo Colocci's hand in 1519 or early 1520, not only touts drawing to scale with the help of a magnetic compass but also presents the 'five Orders' as the fundamental units of Classical design (Rowland 1994; De Teodoro 1994). These five Orders comprised the four Vitruvian *genera* (Doric, Ionic, Corinthian and Tuscan), and square piers, to which Raphael and Colocci applied the evocatively Hellenic term, 'Attic'. Thanks to Raphael's fame, to Rome's central place in early sixteenth-century architectural culture, and to the general inclinations already established by contemporary practice, both men's formulation, like their drawing method, would quickly become definitive.

Raphael's articulation of the Orders clearly built on Bramante's preoccupation with the subject, a preoccupation evident above all in the latter's built work. By basing his own designs on a highly restricted set of ancient models, Bramante, especially in his Roman period, seemed to be moving towards establishing a canonical form for each column type (Denker Nesselrath 1990). Individual built studies, like his Doric Tempietto, or superimpositions of several Orders, like his famous Belvedere staircase, reflected close study of the ancient monuments, but also an effort to systematise what he had absorbed. Raphael's own architecture built on Bramante's precedent, to observe still greater degrees of restriction in the design and proportioning of canonical forms. The usual term for Raphael's procedure is 'archaeo-logical accuracy', but, as with Bramante, his evocations are no mere copying; they reveal a profound analytical component as well.

In a large illustration at the beginning of Book IV, Cesariano's *Vitruvius* presents the same group of five canonical *genera* as Raphael's letter to Leo X (Doric, Ionic, Corinthian, Tuscan, square 'Attic' piers), adding an additional 'matronal' Doric form to create six types in all; he does not call them Orders, but rather *genera* in the plate and *generatione* in the commentary (Vitruvius 1521, fols. LXv, LXIIIr). The striking synoptic image provides a capsule overview of Classical architectural design. Like Raphael's letter, it does so, moreover, in a spirit quite alien from that of Vitruvius himself, who set no limits on the number of *genera* that human ingenuity might devise, but admitted somewhat apologetically to knowing the names of only four. Cesariano, on the other hand, has created a commanding synthesis of canonical design; remarkably, moreover, given vast differences in basic visual sense, this move toward synthesis is virtually at one with what Raphael and his friends were doing at the same time in Rome. Bramante forms one obvious point of connection between the two projects, and if the Bramante who worked with Cesariano in Milan was a far less sophisticated interpreter of Classical style than the Bramante who worked with Julius II and Raphael in Rome, he had still achieved more than enough to galvanise Cesariano. In effect, therefore, both Calvo's translation and Cesariano's edition of Vitruvius represent the formulation of the Classical Orders at the precise moment before their lexical identification as 'the Orders' had become an indispensable part of that formula.

In another suggestive parallel with the Raphael project, Cesariano's illustrations include a remarkable set of composite diagrams, images designed to present several types of information at once. As a medium, print had already proved a stimulus to the formulation of new graphic styles, but the same impulse shows up in other media as well: Raphael's *School of Athens* of 1505–11 presents Pythagoras with a tablet on which two musical ideas, the diapason and perfect numbers, are presented in ingenious combination. Giocondo's *Vitruvius*, especially in its smaller octavo reprints, also explores the use of graphs but not, for the most part, as composite entities.

Yet the basic impulse to draw parallels among different kinds of information reached to the heart of Vitruvian thought, to the conviction that all phenomena must be ordered by generic classification or by proportion before they had meaning. If Cesariano's systematic presentation of the six architectural *genera* departs from Vitruvius's openended sense of invention, his combination drawing of optical illusions seems Vitruvian to the core (Vitruvius 1521, fol. LXr; plate 3). Again, the graphic ingenuity with which he presents Ionic details alongside instructions for entasis, for the hollowing of flutes and for the articulation of the three fascias of the Ionic architrave is a remarkable achievement.

A more enigmatic connection links Cesariano's drawings for Book v with a series of sketches for the Calvo *Vitruvius* made by Angelo

3. Optical refinements of Ionic architecture, from Cesariano, *Di Lucio Vitruvio Pollione De Architectura Libri Dece* (Como, 1521), Book III, fol. LXr. Reyerson and Burnham Libraries, Art Institute of Chicago.

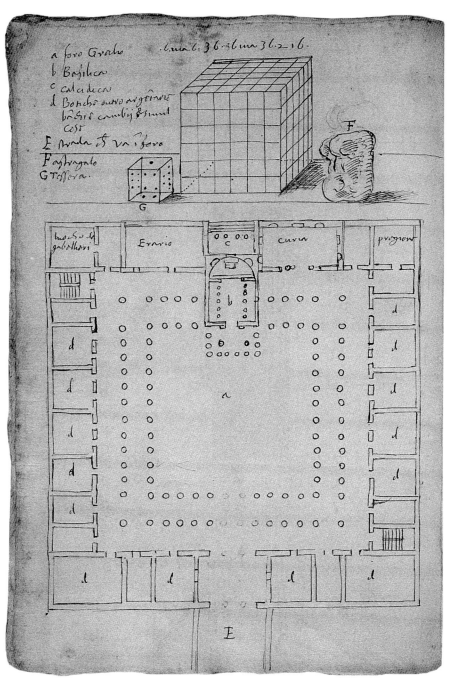

4 Harmonious proportions in cubes and a 'Greek forum', *c.*1519, fol. 58*v*. MS It. 37a, Munich, Bayerische Staatsbibliothek.

Colocci. In one of the more opaque passages of the *Ten Books*, the preface to Book v, Vitruvius links effective writing to Pythagorean numbers. The mind, he states, is best equipped to absorb 216 lines of text, because this number is the cube of sixteen, a perfect number that is itself the sum of two perfect numbers, six and ten, and because the cube is the most stable of the regular polyhedra. Fortified by this premise (to which he never himself adheres, from what we can tell), Vitruvius proceeds to describe the proper layout of an urban forum and civic centre. Colocci's sketch for this section of the text collapses its successive discussions into the single image of a forum surmounted by a scored hexahedron, which is itself flanked by a knuckle-bone and a cubical die (plate 4). In effect, the image seems to suggest that the geometrical and numerical basis for proper prose composition should also be seen to inform the proportions of well-planned cities. And indeed, this is the way in which Colocci himself thought about the world: as a great chain of interlocking numerical harmonies. By acknowledging a similar synthetic bent in Vitruvius, his sketch may say as much about the true meaning of the *Ten Books* to Renaissance thought as Leonardo da Vinci's famous 'Vitruvian man'.

Interestingly, Cesariano also seems to read this section of Vitruvius as a continuing numerological argument rather than a succession of discrete topics (Giocondo's drawings in this part of the text, by contrast, seem to act as distinctly separate entities); Cesariano's image of a cube is juxtaposed with dice; the two following cuts show a comparison of Greek and Latin fora in plan and cutaway elevation (Vitruvius 1521, fol. LXXII*v*) and a still more ambitious rendering of Vitruvius's basilica at Fano in plan, elevation, cutaway and two schematic diagrams (Vitruvius 1521, fol. LXXIIII*r*). These composite images, as powerful as Colocci's, would exert considerable influence on subsequent representations. Both Colocci and Calvo may well have been thinking back to the architectural illustrations of Luca Pacioli's *De divina proportione* (On Divine Proportion) of 1509, where architecture is explicitly related to number theory, but the ingenuity of their graphic solutions, generated independently but almost simultaneously, seems to bespeak a larger spirit of their age. It is ironic that Raphael's unpublished Vitruvian studies, bolstered by the Roman intellectual community (notably Angelo Colocci) and by papal ideology, would set the standard for nearly all subsequent development in the analytical understanding and practice of Classical architecture. Cesariano's *Vitruvius*, on the other hand, despite its publication in print, brought him few architectural commissions outside continuations of the military work in which he had already been engaged for years. His edition, with its pungent local flavour and personal idiosyncrasy, still testifies above all to one man's personal obsession.

Chapter Six

'HUNGRY AND DESPERATE FOR KNOWLEDGE': DIEGO DE SAGREDO'S SPANISH POINT OF VIEW

Nigel Llewellyn

SAGREDO, ITALY AND THE VITRUVIAN TRADITION

'OF ALL MEN, I am the most hungry and desperate for knowledge': the interlocutor 'Picardo' is thus unabashed at setting out his needs, at the opening of Diego de Sagredo's short treatise *Medidas del Romano*, or 'Roman measurements', published in Toledo in 1526.[1] After some rhetorical pleasantries, Sagredo's protagonist 'Tampeso' sets about offering the information necessary to satisfy Picardo's curiosity, proclaiming 'The measurements of the Romans begin . . .' (Sagredo 1526, sig. A.iv*v*).

Yet the apparent innocence of Sagredo's assemblage of words, pictures and numbers, working together in a conversational way and to a format more akin to a handbook or manual than to a polemical treatise, tends to mask the author's true purposes. These were to offer Spanish readers ready access to the rules of Classical architecture, to bring them up-to-date with Italian theory and to construct a particularly Spanish manifestation of a famous Classical locus, the Vitruvian book. The fulfilment of these aims required considerable skill on

---

[1] 'Yo soy el hombre del mundo mas desseoso y perdid por saber' (Sagredo 1526, sig. A.iv*v*). For a full account of the complex publishing history of the several editions and versions of the treatise, see Marañon 1947 and Llewellyn 1975, 80–83. There are few useful secondary sources for Sagredo: however, see Rosenthal 1958; Llewellyn 1977; Marias and Bustamente 1986; Llewellyn 1988; Kruft 1994, 219–20. Dr Valerie Fraser of the University of Essex is preparing an English translation and edition of the *Medidas*.

Sagredo's part, for he had to satisfy his readership with a sufficiency of local reference and subject accessibility as well as carry authority in his treatment of the Classical canon and of the body of learning developed in Renaissance Italy.

Indeed, across Europe sixteenth-century authors, editors and commentators were seeking to establish for their national cultures decent credentials in the Vitruvian tradition; cultural interest groups beyond the Alps felt a powerful urge to revive the antique along the lines already established in Italy. Sagredo had to balance the tension between two demands, for sufficient conformity to the Italian model and for sufficient local originality, and this tension runs as a powerful current through the *Medidas*, applying even on the level of language. The potential verbal problem for Sagredo, of using Spanish terms and prose in an idiom generally regarded as Latinate, recurred on the more elevated level of intellectual achievement. For his efforts were directed at establishing a body of theoretical and practical building concepts that could be regarded as both acceptably and authentically Classical as well as local in the sense of being compatible with Spanish interests, tastes and traditions. Sagredo's Spanish text on the rules for correct building – in fact, the first book of its type published in any European language other than Latin or Italian – belonged to a wider European cultural ambience unified in discourse through a common heritage in Classical antiquity and focusing on an international community of Latinate scholarship. Significant sets of players within this community were the clerics, professionally oriented toward Rome, and the patron class with its interests in establishing a Spanish dialect of the language of Classical architecture. Sagredo was a member of both sets.

The necessary understanding of the local interests of Sagredo's readership should be placed in the particular context of Spanish architecture in the early years of the sixteenth century. In geo-political terms, the recently unified 'most Catholic' nation was, of course, positioned between the rest of Europe and the Pagan and Muslim worlds of the Americas and Africa. In cultural terms, Spain was seeking to establish its legitimate rights over the inheritance of Classical antiquity, and the development of the country's architecture is a potent sign of its high artistic ambitions. The economic framework upon which the new buildings were founded was relatively unstable, since the national population of fewer than ten million people had suffered substantial losses late in the 1400s through emigration and the forced repatriation of skilled workers amongst the ranks of the *conversos*, Jews who had converted to Christianity. In the early years of the sixteenth century, Spain attracted large numbers of itinerant workers in the arts of design, from Italy, France and many regions of northern Europe, all of whom contributed to the development of the characteristic local style.

A significant mass of Spanish Renaissance building survives – little of it widely studied or familiar outside a narrow circle of enthusiasts – and it forms an instructive parallel with Italian examples and other Italianate traditions. In terms of both genre and style, the pattern of Renaissance building across the huge Spanish land-mass was very varied. There were episodes in sixteenth-century Spanish building when the architects observed a comparatively decorous aesthetic and designed on lines that were modelled closely on High Renaissance prototypes (the *estilo desornamentado*); the plans and elevations of the new royal palaces erected at Granada (from the late 1520s) and at El Escorial near Madrid (from the 1560s) typify this trend (Wilkinson Zerner 1993). But much other secular building (especially in Old Castile and in Andalucia), as well as a great deal of ecclesiastical building and furnishing, was strikingly ornamental. Indeed the style has been called 'Plateresque', a term meaning 'silversmith-like' and traditionally connoting both superimposed ornament and fanciful invention; moreover this style is often assumed to represent a challenge to the Classical canon in its Vitruvian form (Bury 1976).

Sagredo's view of antiquity was unremarkable: he used it as a flexible, cultural metaphor capable of synthesis and able to resist the tensions between barren antiquarian demands for authenticity and a potentially heretical and destabilising yearning for originality. His solution was to make reference to the ancient rhetorical principle of decorum or appropriateness, now widely understood as having played a dominant role in the development of architectural theory during the post-Classical period (Onians 1988, esp. 36–99). Decorum demanded that Sagredo tailor sound principles or procedures to fit local conditions and interests and the *Medidas del Romano* manifests this process through a form of practical application. His main concern was to demonstrate how Spanish architecture could legitimately be presented within a Latin or Roman idiom (Rosenthal 1958).

Sagredo differed from many Italian treatise writers in that he seems never to have been employed as an architect *per se*, although he did oversee the completion of complex building works and he was associated with ambitious building patrons. His book is dedicated to his patron Alfonso de Fonseca, Archbishop of Toledo, Primate of Spain and Lord Chancellor of Castile (Sánchez Cantón 1923–41, 1, 6; Pita Andrade 1958; Sendin Calabuig 1977). In the text itself, Sagredo refers to his post as chaplain to Queen Juana 'the Mad', mother of Emperor Charles V, and he also knew well – and in 1517 witnessed the will of – Francisco Jimenes de Cisneros, the key patron of Spanish humanism at the University of Alcalà.[2] As I have argued elsewhere, Sagredo knew

---

[2] The few biographical facts known about Sagredo can be gleaned from the text of *Medidas* and research undertaken by Professor Fernando Marias of Madrid (see Marias and Bustamente 1986).

Italy and was *au fait* with contemporary currents in Italian architectural theory (Llewellyn 1988). He had to be in Burgos in 1523–4 to oversee the construction of a funeral monument erected to the memory of Bishop Juan Rodriguez de Fonseca (Léon 1960), and his Italian journey must have taken place between then and 1517, the most likely date being early in 1522 when many of the prelates in his immediate circle were in Rome at the enthroning of Hadrian of Utrecht as Pope.[3]

So close is the relationship between Sagredo's book and Italian Renaissance architectural theory and so rich is the pattern of cultural, political and economic links between Spain and Italy around 1500, that Sagredo's book needs to be more precisely contextualised by means of some observations on his Italian predecessors. As is well known, Vitruvius's *De Architectura* – the only substantial ancient survival – represented a crucial intellectual justification for the genre. However, Vitruvius was poorly expressed, lacking in a useful tradition of illustration, ambiguous in its terminology, incomplete and (in patches) irrelevant to Renaissance needs. Nevertheless, it played a vital symbolic role and it set the course for its successors; *De Architectura* established the thematic range for later theoreticians and its structure was also influential (Onians 1971). Before the publication of the *Medidas del Romano*, Latin editions of Vitruvius had appeared in Lyons, Florence, Venice and Rome and within another generation translations had been published in Italian, French, German as well as Spanish. Key texts for Sagredo were Fra Giocondo's Latin Vitruvius of 1511, published in Venice, and Cesariano's Italian commentary on the Roman author of 1521, published in Como. Alberti's *De re aedificatoria*, widely but wrongly regarded in the Renaissance as an enlarged, improved and modernised version of Vitruvius, was influential on Sagredo not in its scale but for its imaginative historical analyses of the development of architectural form and for the example set by its nationalistic theme, for Alberti (1404–72) had argued strongly for Tuscany as the legitimate Italian heir to Roman antiquity. Sagredo also seems to have had knowledge of Italian theory in manuscript form, namely the elaborately illustrated treatises of Antonio Averlino, called Filarete (c.1400–69?) and Francesco di Giorgio Martini (1439–1501), both of whom worked in courtly environments and were open to regional and political interests (Onians 1988, chs. 11–12).

Despite the apparent chronological difficulty, Sebastiano Serlio (1475–1554) can be shown to have been a powerful Italian influence on Sagredo, as were the authors of two other books printed in Venice, neither of them strictly within the genre of architectural theory: Francesco Colonna's fantastical *Hypnerotomachia Poliphili* (1499) and the

---

De divina proportione (1509) by Luca Pacioli (*c.*1445–*c.*1514) (Onians 1988; Serlio 1996, xi–xxxv). Amongst these Vitruvian books we find both full-scale *compendia* and briefer handbooks, types which continue into the later sixteenth century (with Palladio and Vignola for example): Sagredo's book fits into this second category. The *Medidas del Romano* also follows its Italian forebears in presenting, as do they, adaptations of standard material and theory for local or special needs. In addition, the text is clearly addressed at a wide artisan readership ready to receive instruction, as well as at prospective patrons and an educated public. Throughout, an imaginative use is made of illustrations, for example the woodcut prints running down the edge of several early pages which display the Euclidean sequence of forms: the point, the line, the circle, the square and the angle (the sequence starting on sig. A.viiir; plate 1).

MORAL QUESTIONS

Treatises are inevitably theoretical and building is unavoidably practical, and in Italian architectural theory the issues raised by this mix resolve into two discernible currents. There are books which seek only to establish a vocabulary of architectural forms and there are those which attempt to describe the theoretical principles by which architecture should be created and experienced. The dominant theoretical problem was, of course, the establishment of rules for the Orders of architecture, that system of parts linked together by proportion, location and motif, whose key signifiers, the columns themselves, were also understood as the secondary signifiers of the new *all'antica* (or, *allo romano*) style that was held in such wide regard: Alberti notes that 'in the whole art of building the column is the principal ornament without any doubt' (Alberti 1966, Book VI ch. 13).[4] In the earlier theory of the fifteenth century even the most basic identification of the Orders had remained uncertain; for example, there was endless confusion over the form and shape of Doric. However, by the 1520s the canon had been established – partly, I would argue, with Sagredo's assistance – and he assumes a relatively confident understanding of the issue in his description of the Orders and their interrelations.[5]

Sagredo chose the dialogue form for his treatise because he intended his book to adopt a strongly didactic tone. The book comprises a series of conversations between a painter called 'Picardo' and his teacher, a

---

[4] 'In tota re aedificatoria primarium certe ornamentum in columnis est.'

[5] See Llewellyn 1988, where I have argued that the *Medidas* fills a gap in development between the publication of Pacioli (1509) and that of Serlio's Book IV (1537). A key work is Bramente's Tempietto, for which see Lotz 1995, 11 and notes.

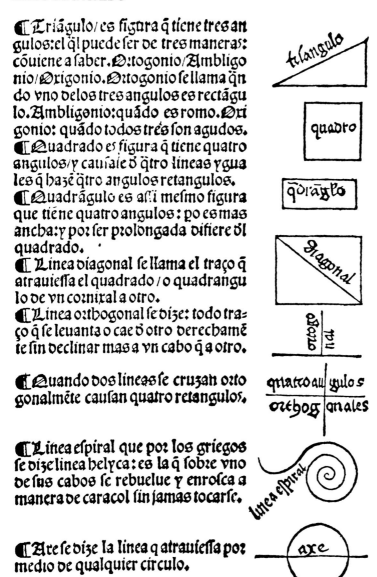

❡ Triágulo/ es figura q̃ tiene tres an
gulos:el q̃l puede fer de tres maneras:
cõuiene a faber. Ø:togonio/Ambligo
nio/Ørigonio. Ø:togonio fe llama q̃n
do vno delos tres angulos es rectágu
lo. Ambligonio:quãdo es romo. Ø:ri
gonio: quãdo todos trés fon agudos.
❡ Quadrado es figura q̃ tiene quatro
angulos/y cauíafe õ q̃tro lineas ygua
les q̃ bazẽ q̃tro angulos retangulos.
❡ Quadrágulo es afíi mefmo figura
que tiéne quatro angulos: po es mas
ancha:y po: fer p:olõgada difiere õl
quadrado.   ·
❡ Linea diagonal fe llama el traço q̃
atrauieffa el quadrado / o quadrangu
lo de vn co:ni:al a otro.
❡ Linea o:tbogonal fe dize: todo tra=
ço q̃ fe leuanta o cae õ otro derecbamẽ
te fin declinar mas a vn cabo q̃ a otro.

❡ Quando dos lineas fe cruzan o:to
gonalmẽte caufan quatro retangulos.

❡ Linea efpiral que po: los griegos
fe dizelinea belyca: es la q̃ fob:e vno
de fus cabos fe rebuelue y enrofca a
manera de caracol fin jamas tocarfe.

❡ Are fe dize la linea q atrauieffa po:
medio de qualquier circulo.

1   A sequence of geometrical forms, from Sagredo, *Medidas del Romano* (Toledo, 1526), sig. A.viii*v*.

cleric called 'Tampeso', who sets out to answer his pupil's questions.
Although the dialogue is often stilted, especially when Picardo assumes
a kind of characteristic naiveté in order to set up a lengthy response
from his more knowledgeable master, the device itself does succeed in
personalising the treatise. The fact that the main protagonist is a cleric,

together with the word-play implicit in the very name 'Tampeso' (Sagredo) suggests that the modern reader should be listening out for Sagredo's own voice; his is a text directed at an educated readership and the coincidence of intellectual and architectural theorist in the character of Tampeso confirms the sense that for Sagredo architecture was a polite activity requiring more than manual facility.

The moral aspect of what is essentially a social agenda is hinted at in the opening chapter of the *Medidas* when Tampeso outlines at some length, and in a rehearsal of the European humanist discourse on 'magnificence', his refutation of what he regards as a false censure – namely, that ambitious and costly architecture is nothing but an immoral display of opulent vanity (Onians 1988, 122–6; Thomson 1993). Clearly, Sagredo is protecting the interests of great building patrons such as the Fonseca by means of his morally apologetic argument that splendid church building simply glorifies God and splendid secular architecture glorifies the city. Perhaps mindful of political sensitivities, Sagredo remains silent on the theme of magnificence in relation to Spain's Islamic inheritance (for the Islamic interest in an art of broken surfaces and small glittering elements, an art symbolising the transience of mundane things, was directed at a topic central to the discourse on magnificence).

After a further important discussion about the status of the architect (a liberal artist, one whose mind and intellect controls the work of the builders as might the mind of an artist control his hands in the act of creativity), Sagredo embarks on the core subject of the treatise, his account of the parts of architecture, starting with an explanation of the cornice. We should not underestimate the significance of this starting point; clearly these forms and Sagredo's choice have to be read symbolically. The mind is located in the head and it controls the architect's deployment of forms; in turn, the head is represented anthropomorphically by the cornice (Llewellyn 1977, 292–3). The very ordering of Sagredo's account of architecture is thus a realisation of the idea that building should be modelled on the perfect forms of God and humankind. For Sagredo described the forms of Classical architecture as originating in geometry, thus giving a rational basis for the correct principles of design, and he takes an explanation of the cornice's moulded form as his starting point. He goes on to discuss column bases, pedestals, capitals and the elements of the architrave (sigs. c.iiir ff., c.vi*v* c.vii*r* and D.v*r*).

The Orders of columns, which Sagredo calls *generos* (from the Latin *genus*, 'family') are then treated in order of degree: Doric, Ionic, Tuscan, Corinthian and Attic. Once this basic canon is established, Sagredo sets out rules for embellishment, by means of entasis or the tapering of the shaft and by the disposition of fluting, and then in a

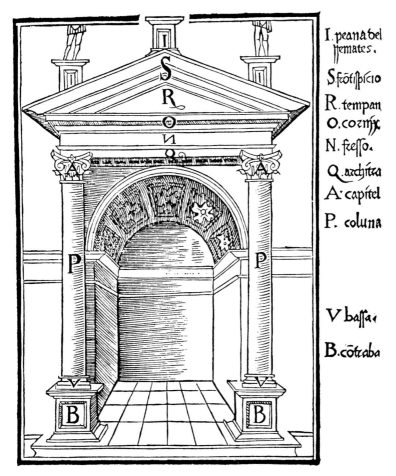

I. peana bel ffematcs.

S fcotifpício

R. tempan

O. cozníjc

N. fçeffo.

Q. azchítea

A: capítel

P. coluna

V baffa‹

B. côteaba

2   The identification of parts of the Classical portal, from Sagredo, *Medidas* (Toledo, 1526), sig. A.iiir.

long *excursus* he describes what he regards as the most interesting of all column types, the baluster. Balusters were already popular motifs in Spanish architecture and Sagredo's celebration of them carries with it the implication that they are decorative and structural forms with a particular Spanish suitability and even origin (Llewellyn 1977, 294–300). The treatise continues with an explanation of the rules of vertical diminution which must be followed if columns set high on the façade of a building are to appear correctly proportioned from below, and the book closes with brief entries on foundations, materials, and the terms and conditions of an architect's employment.

Throughout the *Medidas* there is a strong didactic tone; Sagredo uses as simple a terminology and language as he can and explains specialist architectural terminology as he goes. He also makes as full a use as is possible of illustrations and diagrams to clarify his verbal discourse (plate 2). In fact, the *Medidas* is the first original printed architectural treatise to rely so heavily on illustrated material and it is clear that Sagredo was influenced in this respect by the recently published editions of Vitruvius by Cesariano and Fra Giocondo.

PUBLISHING HISTORY

There were many editions of the *Medidas del Romano* and the text has a place in the history of architectural theory in France as well as in Spain. The first edition having appeared in Toledo in 1526, a French translation was published in about 1537 in Paris in a version reprinted on five further occasions before 1608. These French versions are all translations of what is in effect a second edition, for they all contain an extra, late, inserted chapter about intercolumniation, that is, the ratio of column to space in horizontal series, together with some new pedestal designs and an alternative sequence of column proportions. The author of the addition remains a mystery but was almost certainly not Sagredo and was probably French. A third set of editions is in Castilian and again includes the extra material. These books were published in Lisbon in 1541 and 1542 and in Toledo in 1549 and 1564 (Sagredo 1541; 1549). Ironically, given the proselytising intentions of the first edition, the French version of the *Medidas* remained in print rather longer than did the Castilian version; however, for the purposes of this chapter it is the first Toledo edition of 1526 that is of the greatest interest.

SAGREDO'S USE OF SOURCES

Sagredo paid homage to '*el famoso Marco vitruvio*' on the opening page of the *Medidas*, just as any Renaissance author writing on philosophy or astrology might cite Aristotle or Ptolemy, and he makes direct refer-ence to the *De Architectura* throughout the book. Vitruvius is Sagredo's authority for his account of the proportions of the human body (sig. A.v*r*), the training of the architect (sig. A.vii*v*), the dimensions of the architrave (sig. D.v*r*) and of intercolumniation (sig. D.vi*v*). There are other more oblique references to the ancient text and it is understand-able that the *Medidas* has so often been catalogued as an abstract of Vitruvius (Sagredo 1541; 1549). Although Alberti is only credited once by name (with reference to a uniquely shaped Ionic base (sig. c.vi*v*)), the *De re aedificatoria* is Sagredo's main modern source and of this two

Latin editions were available (those of Rome *c*.1486 and Paris 1512). Indeed, evidence abounds throughout the *Medidas* that Alberti's book was a powerful influence not only over opinion and matters of fact but over Sagredo's very approach. For Alberti's authority is often set synthetically alongside references to Vitruvius.

A good example of Sagredo's exploitation and adaptation of source material – and one worth analysing in some detail – is his treatment of the complex rules for fluting and shaping columns (entasis). The arithmetical procedure which Sagredo sets out as the basis for fluting forms part of the decorative vocabulary available to those architects who wish to change the appearance of columns (sigs. B.viir–viiir):

> TAMPESO: the ancients took the view that where there were two columns, equal in height and width, and were one to be fluted and the other not, the fluted column would look the thicker because the eye would be deceived by the air trapped in the flutes or grooves . . .
> PICARDO: Now I understand what you said before, namely that a good architect had to be a natural philosopher as well as an artist.

The rules on fluting that are then set out accord closely with Alberti, who in turn follows Vitruvius (see Vitr.III.v.14, IV.iii.9 and IV.iv.2 on Ionic, Doric and Corinthian temples). Whereas the ancient source thus deals with fluting in the course of a commentary on each Order of temple, Alberti treats the whole topic together as an aspect of columnar ornamentation (Alberti 1966, Book IX ch. 7). Sagredo's expanded treatment is characteristic for its interest in geometrical authority as the basis for design. He includes an illustration of a set-square as a measure of the flute (sig. B.viiir; plate 3),[6] and even quotes the standard Euclidean axiom on the right-angle contained within the semi-circle (Euclid, III. Prop.31; Sagredo 1526, sig. B.viiv).[7] In countless small incidents such as this Sagredo emphasises his key argument that architecture is a matter for the educated reader since its rules are based on geometry, one of the liberal arts (sig. A.viir).

Sagredo employs similar strategies in his treatment of the distorting device (called entasis) whereby architects taper columns to correct the tendency of the eye to read parallel lines as the parameters of a concave form. There are, he writes, two species of entasis: a swelling out of the column in its middle reaches with tapering at both top and bottom; and a regular diminution of the form from bottom to top. Vitruvius's account of these procedures is, needless to say, incomplete and scattered, but the *De Architectura* does set out one important principle to

---

[6]   This is very close to that in Cesariano's *Vitruvius* 1521, sigs. H.ivr–L.iiir.

[7]   For general discussion of the true relations between geometric objects based on the axioms described in Euclid's *Elements of Geometry*, see Pedoe 1976, ch. 6.

which all Renaissance commentators appear to adhere: 'Calculations must make good where the eye fails' (Vitr.III.iii.11).[8] Vitruvius's formula for simple tapering had been repeated *verbatim* by Alberti; however, Sagredo extends the rules to cover even longer columns (up to sixty feet tall) and includes a convenient table giving the relevant numbers (sig. B.vi*v*).

Vitruvius's rules on correct entasis are lost and Alberti's elaborate account is, he claims, derived from his close study of antique buildings rather than from the writings of the ancients (Alberti 1966, Book VI ch. 13).[9] Again in emulation of Alberti, Sagredo not only establishes rules but the very principles of natural law which underlie them. Columns are like trees: the ancients, interested in nature's works, 'imitated . . . the example of the trees and plants, such as the cypress, the elm, the pine, the beech, with their thick trunks, which, as they grow upwards, naturally become thinner and narrower' (sig. B.v*v*).[10] Sagredo's adaptation of a Vitruvian principle is interesting because, in fact, the expression of the analogy with nature comes at a point in the ancient source where the Roman author is addressing the rules necessary for the disposition of rows of columns set one on top of the other, ruling that those at the top should be a quarter smaller than those below. Sagredo takes up the point and adapts it for use on a related aspect of theory. He was clearly aware of the fact that the available versions of Vitruvius lacked any thorough or useful discussion of true entasis and was clearly aware too of Alberti's complex solutions, yet his own account avoids the complications of either. In his short handbook, Sagredo has to establish a fine balance between a necessary display of competence and an excessive display of technicality. He recognises only two ways of making columns that are more slender at the top than the bottom. Some columns, 'taper equally from the middle to the top and from the middle to the bottom and these are the most ancient and most natural'[11] (sig. B.vi*v*) − and of these columns enough said since they require no advanced calculation. The second category holds diminution to be a function of column-shaft length and here the deployment of a numerical table illustrates Sagredo's principle that the forms of ancient architecture could be reduced to *medidas* (measurements) (sig. B.vi*r*). However, we should not be misled into thinking that Sagredo's architectural theory relies solely on simple arithmetic; more complex calculations are necessary to remedy the especially

[8]   'Ergo quod oculus fallit, ratiocinatione est exequendum.'
[9]   For Cesariano's alternative rules, see *Vitruvius* 1521, sigs. G.viiir–H.ivr.
[10]   'Tomavan examplo enlos arboles y plantas, como son el Cipresso, Olmo, pino, haya los quales son gruessos enel tronco y como van creciendo se van naturalmente estrechando y adelgazando.'
[11]   'Comiencan a retraerse de medio arriba y de medio abaxo son yguales, y estas son las mas antiguas y mas naturales.'

Los q̃les allẽde d̃ ſer puecboſos pa
a cõſeruar y defender las eſquinas
ariſtas d̃las eſtrias como partes q̃
nas ſe tratan:adozñã y acrecientan
ñucbo enla elegãcia delas coluñas
omo poz la pſente figura ſe mueſtra
⸿En mucbos edificios de grecia y
e ytalia ſe ballã grãdes coluñas de
iedra dura:aſſentadas ſobze baſas
e metal y con capiteles de metal:q̃=
ᵉs parecẽ en roma en ſcã maria la
edõda:pueſtas poz ⸿Darco agripa
õſul romão. Ño menos ſe balla mu
bas coluñas y muy grãdes de me=
ıl:cõ tãta diligẽcia acabadas que to
os los q̃ las veẽ ſuzgã ſer labzadas
ı tozno:y no es de marauillar: pues
ᵉ lee d̃ dos maeſtros q̃ bauiã nõbze/
Colo/y Tbeodolo q̃ teniã artificio
a toznear las coluñas:aſſi de piedra
omo de metal poz grãdes q̃ fueſſen:
q̃ vn ſolo mocbacho era ſuficiente
ara las rodear y mouer. (⸿Dicar.)
Deſſeo tẽgo de ver algũa coluna la=
zada cõ tãta diligẽcia y cuydado co
ño bas dicho:no creo q̃ los oficiales
e agoza ſe põgã a formarlas guar=
ando enellas las cõdicioẽs y leyes
requierẽ.(Tãp.)Los buenos ofi=
ales y los q̃ d̃ſſean q̃ ſus obzas tẽgan autozidad y carezcã
e repbẽſiõ:pcuran d̃ regirſe poz las medidas antiguas co
ño baze tu vezino Criſtoual de andino:poz dõde ſus obzas
ñ mas venuſtas y elegãtes q̃ ningũas otras q̃ baſta agoza
ᵒ aya viſto:ſino veelo poz eſſa reta que labza pa tu ſeñoz el

The set-square engaged with the angle of the flute, from Sagredo, *Medidas* (Toledo, 1526), sig.
iir.

complex problems that arise when columns are set out in interior spaces and so tend to appear more stout than columns of the same size disposed in the open air. By elaborating an idea he found in Vitruvius (III.iii.11), Sagredo explains that this optical distortion is caused by a greater density of air in an interior space.

Sagredo's exploitation of both Vitruvius and Alberti is mostly a matter of judicious selection and careful adaptation; his use of other source-material is more straightforward, with respect both to other architectural books and to humanist literature in general. This latter body of material is cited to impress upon the reader the argument that architecture should rightly take its place in the world of scholarship and be distanced from the prejudice associated with manual activities. Most of these general sources are ancient and almost all are cited by Tampeso in his role as didactic interlocutor. In addition, nearly all these citations are made in the opening sections of the *Medidas*, when Sagredo is concentrating on theory rather than on practice.

The opening topic in the dialogue gives us the flavour of this rhetoric, for we find Picardo bemoaning the fact that architecture is so hard to understand it reduces him to a melancholic state, a view with which, he claims, the elder Cato would concur (sig. A.iir). Immediately, Tampeso counters with a sentence from Pythagoras and then proceeds comprehensively to crush Picardo by piling on authority after authority: 'the poet' Euripides, Menander, Virgil, Xenophon, St Jerome, King David the Psalmist, Socrates and an obscure near-contemporary author, Raphael Maffei de Volterrano (sigs. A.iir, A.iiv and A.iiiv). Subsequently, Sagredo uses the same tactic when he argues that geometry is a prerequisite for an understanding of architecture, citing the support of Plato, Plutarch, Euclid and in a marginal reference even the medical texts of Galen. Such listings are not a feature of the later chapters of the book.

However, two other authors are cited who had significance for architectural theory, the Roman encyclopedist Pliny the Elder and an Italian – and near-contemporary – Pomponius Gauricus. Typifying the enormous influence of the *Historia Naturalis* on Renaissance authors, Pliny is cited three times by Sagredo, on two occasions in relation to the Temple of Diana at Ephesus; this temple exemplified the use of the ancient and original form of the Ionic column, and offers an example in Sagredo's discussion of the visual effects of densely packed columns in interior spaces (sigs. B.iiiv–vir and B.viir). However, Sagredo does not always publicise his use of Pliny, for example in his adaptation of the Roman text on the fifth or Attic species of column (sig. B.ivv).[12]

---

[12] Adapting Pliny, *Hist. Nat.* XXXVI.56. In his final chapter, and following Pliny, Sagredo mentions the ancient architect 'Tesiphon' (that is, Chersiphron from Knossus) (Sagredo 1526, sig. D.viir, and Pliny, *Hist. Nat.* VII.125).

Perhaps Sagredo's most interesting cited source is Gauricus's treatise *De Sculptura sive Statuaria* (Florence, 1504) which probably acted as a general model for the *Medidas* as much for its style as for its level of ambition. For example, both treatises set theoretical questions above practical or technical matters and, like Sagredo, Gauricus was an enthusiastic amateur rather than a practising artisan or professional. The two books also share a slightly fanciful literary style, perhaps the joint result of an exposure to Filarete's *Libro architettonico* and the *Hypnerotomachia Poliphili*. Finally, both authors create an atmosphere of individuality and personality in their discussions of what by most standards was pretty dry material. Nevertheless, Sagredo only directly cites *De Sculptura* at one point in the text, where he sets out his views on the canons of perfect human proportion (sig. A.vr).

In summary, Sagredo quotes or cites only a limited number of architectural authorities, although he is clearly knowledgeable of, if not always actually widely read in, recent architectural theory. In addition, he refers to non-specialist authors as part of his campaign to elevate the intellectual status of his subject.

THREE CHARACTERISTIC TOPICS

Three of the issues treated by Sagredo epitomise his general theory of Classical architecture, the *Medidas* revealing in these a particular compliance with both ancient and Italian literary precedents and the need for an original adaptation to Spanish circumstances: Sagredo has strong views on the character and training of the architect, on anthropomorphism and human proportion, and on the qualities of the architectural Orders.

As presented in the *Medidas*, the architect possesses an individual intellect capable of understanding the theoretical principles necessary for the application of practice. Sagredo's interest in the character of the architect was widely shared in the Renaissance, for example by Cesariano, who prioritised the topic and contributed a lengthy commentary on the relevant books in Vitruvius (Vitruvius 1521, fol. IIvff).[13] In addition, the architect's status underwent a considerable change during the period and it is quite clear that many Renaissance theorists, a large number of whom also practised as architects, were active in boosting the standing of their own professional activity. Sagredo defines the architect in his opening chapter on Euclidean geometry, a

[13]   Vitruvius defines the architect in I.i.

science which he holds in the highest regard, and he cautiously follows
the Vitruvian line on the nature of the architect's education. Geometry
will enable the architect to control events in the natural world and,
together with arithmetic, is a science containing many secrets and
subtleties (sig. A.vii*r*).[14] In antiquity, great artists (including architects)
were classed not with the artisans but with the intellectuals, for they
supplemented the work of the 'mechanicals', who worked with 'intelligence and their hands', by a contribution based 'only on the intellect
and intelligence' (sig. A.vii*v*).[15] The essential distinction here is between
the talent (*ingenio*) of the mechanical artist and the intellect (*espiritu*),
the higher faculty, of his liberal counterpart. The artist's capacity to
combine learning (*saber*) with the intellect and talent allowed painters
to present moral exemplars from history. Sagredo clearly intended both
to impress the patron class with the social and intellectual quality of the
architects he hoped they would employ and to boost the confidence of
any specialist artisans amongst his readers. The particular fascination
with number as the structural and symbolic basis for architectural
planning not only ties Sagredo's book into contemporary Italian theory
but also characterises an important tradition in the architectural history
of his own country. For example, the complex esoteric plottings of
Juan de Herrera, the architect of the Escorial, perhaps owe their origins
to Sagredo's relatively modest attempts to raise the status of his subject
by presenting a particular and relatively enlightened view of the architect's education (Wilkinson Zerner 1993).

The second theme, and a central element in Sagredo's theory of
architecture, is the anthropomorphic analogy drawn in the *Medidas*
between the form of buildings and the form of the human body.
Again, the sources of the argument lie in Vitruvius and his fifteenth-
century Italian followers. Man, created in emulation of God, is the
most complex and perfect of all mundane forms. Searching for a
rationale for architectural design, early builders looked to their own
bodies as reflections of God's original perfect design. Well-organised
buildings should therefore be arranged in ways that are comparable to
a well-built and proportionate man, whose bodily parts act both as
template and proportionate model. Typically, Sagredo argues for a
specifically Spanish variant of the Italian and ancient canons of proportion, setting his ratio for the head to the body at $1:9\frac{1}{3}$ in emulation of
Felipe de Borgona, a sculptor long resident in Burgos but a native of

---

[14] 'Es la geometria instrumento q[ue] mucho ayudô a c[om]prehe[n]der todos los saberes
del mundo . . . En estas dos scie[n]cias se contienen muchos secretos y grandes sotilezas.'
[15] 'Ingenio y co[n] las manas' and 'solamente conel espiritu y conel ingenio.'

vn tercio : eſte tercio es
o que ſube mas la cabe
ça q̃ la frẽte: el pecho cõ=
iene otro roſtro : el eſto=
nago haſta el ombligo
otro : del ombligo haſta
el miẽbro genital ay o=
ro : en cada vno delos
muſlos ſe miden dos : y
en cada vna delas eſpi=
rillas otros dos. Delos
ouillos alas plantas vn
ercio: enlas chuecas de
as rodillas otro: enel pe
cueço otro tercio. de ma
nera que ſe mõta por to=
do los dichos nueue ro
tros y vn tercio ſegũ q̃
por la preſente figura ſe
nueſtra. ¶ De muchas
naneras ſe puede medir
os miẽbros y eſtatura ðl
hõbre alléde ðla q̃ haue
nos dicho. Ay enel alto
ðl hõbre ſeys pies ðlos
ſuyos. Ay quatro codos
Ay del punto dela coro
illa de la cabeça haſta

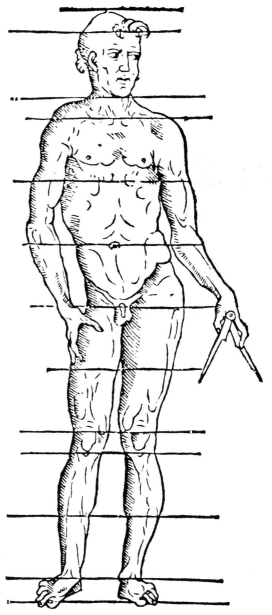

o mas baxo dela barua la octaua parte de ſu eſtatura: deſta
coronilla haſta el nacimiento dela gargãta vna quarta par
: deſte meſmo lugar haſta lo mas alto dela frente vna ſexta
arte. ¶ Contiene otroſi el ancho del hombre/ de coſtado a
oſtado/ la ſexta parte del alto: y del ombligo a los riñones
vnouena parte: y nota que eſtas medidas no tienẽ verdad

The proportionate divisions of the human male form, from Sagredo, *Medidas* (Toledo, 1526), sig.
v.

Flanders (sig. A.v*r*)[16] (plate 4). The greatest problem in tracing Renaissance arguments about proportion lies in the equation of theory with practice and in establishing consistencies of definition and terminology. When column proportion is the subject, the difference between the ratio of capital height to column shaft and the ratio of width and height of column shaft might well be critical. When the human form is the subject, the difference between the ratio of face to total height and the ratio of head to total height might well give grounds for confusion. Sagredo attempts to clarify the often contradictory evidence of ancient rules in Vitruvius by stressing the primacy of the head (sig. A.v*r*),[17] illustrating how this organ can be disposed in profile within a square, the sides of which can be divided into thirds to create a grid of nine units. These three sections correspond to the contours of the face and are given symbolic values, thus: the forehead/wisdom (*sabidura*); the nose/beauty (*hermosura*); and the mouth and chin/virtue (*bondad*). For Sagredo, architecture is a higher art, establishing as it does forms thus based on both mathematical and moral principles.

The third topic which exemplifies Sagredo's approach is his presentation of the Orders, a rational account of which came increasingly to be seen as prerequisite for any complete sixteenth-century architectural theory (Onians 1988; Guillaume 1988). Limits on space in the *Medidas* required the author to restrict himself to just one of the three main Vitruvian sub-divisions of architecture, that is *dispositio* or arrangement, and within that to what the ancient source called *orthographia* in reference to a building's elevation rather than its planilinear or perspectival qualities (on these definitions see Vitr.I.ii.2). The key element in the elevation of the Classical building is the column, which Sagredo lists in five variants, Doric, Ionic, Tuscan, Corinthian and Attic, a sequence of names to which in fact he does not always adhere. His thoughts on Attic columns can be swiftly summarised: they are square piers without strictly determined measurement, often fluted and exemplified by the pilasters which Sagredo has seen in the interior angles of the Florence Baptistery (sig. B.iv*r*; Llewellyn 1988). The other Orders are treated in a complex discussion, sometimes contradictory, which is partly an attempt to resolve conflicts in earlier theory about proportions and partly an attempt to present a particularly Spanish point of view. The set of values that Sagredo finally proposes for the canon of the Orders places the *Medidas* in a debate focused – in the pan-European sense – on Serlio's codification (Llewellyn 1988). Sagredo's discussion of the proportions of the Orders shifts from a set of values based broadly on Alberti to a final series which is uniquely his own:

[16] Vitruvius (III.i.2) and Gauricus 1969, 93, both offer a ratio of 1:10.
[17] 'La cabeça ser mas excele[u]te.'

Doric	with a ratio of 1 : 6
Tuscan	with a ratio of 1 : 7
Ionic	with a ratio of 1 : 8
Corinthian	with a ratio of 1 : 9
	(sigs. B.iii*r*–B.v*r*).

In most other respects, Sagredo's theory of the Orders of columns accords well with his colleagues amongst the Italian Vitruvians: he attributes gendered qualities to the columns (Doric and Tuscan are 'male'), and they are to be disposed on buildings and in association with one another according to the principles of decorum and in a vertical sequence based on rational notions of proportion and precedent. The only genuine novelty comes with Sagredo's extensive and unexpected discussion of the baluster column, a specifically Spanish variant on the Italianate canon which I have discussed elsewhere (Llewellyn 1977, 294–300).

In the voice which has reached us through the pages of the *Medidas*, Sagredo speaks as a teacher. His purpose is to advance the cause of an architecture that will be both ancient and contemporary but which will abandon the corrupt practices of the recent past; he wishes building to take the best from several European cultures, both Pagan and Christian. However, Sagredo's theory is unambiguously directed at the priorities of a Spanish readership; 'Roman measurements' will produce buildings that are at once morally improving and progressively rational.

Chapter Seven

ON SEBASTIANO SERLIO: DECORUM AND THE ART OF ARCHITECTURAL INVENTION

Vaughan Hart and Peter Hicks

SERLIO'S TRAVELS AND THE PUBLICATION OF HIS TREATISE

SEBASTIANO SERLIO (1475–1554) is well-known for having produced one of the most easy to use, and hence widely studied, of the illustrated treatises on architecture published in vernacular languages in the sixteenth century (Dinsmoor 1942; Thoenes 1989; Carpo 1992, 1993a&b; Serlio 1996, xi–xxxv). Twenty years or so after Serlio's death, the Mantuan antiquarian and art dealer Jacopo Strada eulogised that the author had 'renewed the art of architecture and made it easy for everyone. Indeed, he did more with his books than even Vitruvius had done before him, in that Vitruvius is obscure and not easily understood by everyone' (Serlio 1575, sig. aiiiir). Serlio was one of the first architectural writers to unite text with woodcuts, a fact which greatly facilitated the accessibility of his treatise. In his early years Serlio had himself trained as a woodcutter and a painter, working first in Pesaro between 1511 and 1514 and then moving to Rome where he studied under the artist and architect Baldassare Peruzzi. In his home town of Bologna, Serlio assisted Peruzzi between July 1522 and April 1523 on the unexecuted project for the façade of the church of San Petronio. Following the sack of Rome in 1527 Serlio moved to Venice, although it is now thought likely that he was in Bologna at the time of the sack itself.

In Venice, Serlio became part of a circle centred on Pietro Aretino, which included Titian and Jacopo Sansovino. However, despite his evidently fertile imagination and despite the expansion in building projects in the Venetian Republic, Serlio failed to find any major

architectural commissions. He executed a ceiling design in the library
of the Ducal Palace in the city between 1527 and 1531 (illustrated in
the treatise at the end of Book IV, fol. LXXIV/193v). He provided
Federico Priuli with designs for his villa at Treville, and Pietro Zen
with a design for his palace in Venice. He designed the architectural
background in a fresco of the history of Trajan by Giovanni de' Busi
Cariani in the house of Andrea di Odoni some time before 1532 when
it was seen by Marcantonio Michiel. Between 1534 and 1535 Serlio
collaborated with Titian and Fortunio Spira in the revisions made by
the Neoplatonist philosopher Francesco Giorgi to the proportioning
of Jacopo Sansovino's design for the church of San Francesco della
Vigna. Some time before 14 March 1535 Serlio was commissioned to
set the level of payment for the completed wooden ceiling which he
had designed for the Scuola di San Rocco, and in 1539 he submitted
a design with Michele Sanmicheli and Giulio Romano in the famous
competition to renovate the basilica at Vicenza which was won by
Andrea Palladio.

The limited nature of Serlio's architectural works at this time may
have been due to his preoccupation with the publication of the first
instalment of his treatise, which appeared in Venice in 1537. Serlio's
aim, declared at the start of this book, was to publish seven books (or
chapters): although all seven were completed by him, only the first five
were to be published (out of sequence) in his lifetime (Serlio 1996).
Following this initial book, which was on the five Orders and appeared
as Book IV, Book III was also published in Venice, in 1540. It principally concerned ancient monuments, but included modern work by
Peruzzi, Raphael, Bramante, Giuliano da Maiano and a fantasy project
by the author himself. This book illustrated the monuments in orthographic projection, following Raphael's famous recommendations
made to Leo X around 1519 concerning the representation of Roman
ruins. Through these woodcuts the book offered models of good, and
occasionally bad Vitruvian practices, which ranged from the position-
ing of buildings to the carving of ornaments.

Whilst the first edition of Book IV had been supported by Ercole
d'Este, and the second and third editions by Alfonso d'Avalos, Charles
V's ambassador to Venice, Book III was supported by the king of
France, François I, to whom it is dedicated. Following correspondence
between the king's sister, Marguerite d'Angoulême (the queen of
Navarre) and the French ambassador to Venice, Guillaume Pellicier,
and the promise of an elusive three hundred gold crowns, Serlio
moved to France in 1541 where he was installed as 'premier peintre et
architecte' at Fontainebleau. This period in the French king's employment coincided with the majority of Serlio's actual built work. For
between 1541 and 1550 he produced a series of designs for the king or

members of the court. At the château itself Serlio is thought to have produced a design for the Grotte des Pins, although this was certainly not built following his scheme as drawn in Book VI (Serlio 'Munich' MS, fols. 31v–33r; Serlio 'Avery' MS, XXXII–XXXIII). In Fontainebleau Serlio executed a design for the residence of Ercole d'Este's brother, Ippolito. Called the Grand Ferrara and built between 1544 and 1546 (but now destroyed), it was here that Serlio was destined to spend the last few years of his life. In Burgundy from around 1541 he designed the château of Ancy-le-Franc for count Antoine de Clermont-Tonnerre (plate 1). In Lyons he prepared a design for a merchants' courtyard with shops/workshops (*botteghe*) (illustrated in Book VII and apparently unbuilt (Serlio 1575, 184–91; Rosenfeld 1978, 25)), and a design for a merchants' exchange (or loggia, illustrated in Book VII but possibly built (Serlio 1575, 192–5)). Of these designs, only Ancy-le-Franc has survived: but with its three wings enclosing an approximately square court fronted by a low wall, Serlio's Grand Ferrara helped establish a characteristic type in French domestic architecture (illustrated in Book VI, Munich MS, fol. 14v; Avery MS, XI).

The remaining books of Serlio's treatise to be published in his lifetime all appeared in France. Books I and II were on the painterly subjects of geometry and perspective, the latter concluding with the influential section on stage design; they were published together in a bilingual Italian–French edition in Paris in 1545. These books were followed in 1547 by Book V, once again published in a bilingual edition in Paris, which contained twelve church designs. Book VI, on the design of domestic architecture ranging from peasant hut to royal palace, was never published but survives in two manuscript versions and a set of trial woodcuts (Munich MS, Avery MS: Rosci and Brizio 1966; Rosenfeld 1978; Fiore 1994). Here the Grand Ferrara and Ancy-le-Franc were illustrated as examples of French domestic 'types': evidently both houses were intended to embody Serlio's faith in the feudal (and architectural) fabric of French society, with its clearly defined classes ranging from peasant to prince.

Serlio's early problems with patronage continued during his years in France. For in reference to the representation of Ancy-le-Franc as a model 'House of the illustrious Prince in the Style of a Fortress' in Book VI (plate 2), he records that,

> subsequent to my drawing this design, which in part was made according to the wishes of the patron, he decided to use columns from top to bottom for greater richness . . . The fact is the patron of the house was not lacking in any respect, that is, he had these three qualities, knowledge, will and power . . . And he, with all his knowledge, nevertheless sought my advice and practical skill. Would

(top) Château of Ancy-le-Franc, Burgundy, designed by Serlio from *c*.1541. (above) Château of
Ancy-le-Franc, view of the courtyard.

that God made all those who take up building act as he did!
(Munich MS, fol. 16v)

Indeed, in reference to a scheme illustrated in Book VII for the loggia
fronting the Salle de Bal at Fontainebleau (the early internal work for
which has been traditionally credited to Serlio, although it was begun
by Gilles Le Breton in 1541 and completed by Philibert De l'Orme in
1548), Serlio notes rather bitterly that,

> I – I who was in that place and who lived there continuously in
> receipt of a stipend from the magnanimous King François but who
> was not even asked for the smallest piece of advice – wished to form
> a loggia in the way in which I would have arranged it had I been
> commissioned for the work. (Serlio 1575, 96)

Serlio also prepared a project for the Louvre, the rebuilding of which
François I had been considering since 1527. Serlio's palace, rejected
in favour of Pierre Lescot's, not surprisingly features in Book VI as a
model 'Palace for a King' (Munich MS, fols. 66v–73r; Avery MS, LXXI;
see Dinsmoor 1942, 150–52). With the accession of Henri II in 1547
there came a wave of nationalistic feeling in France largely hostile
to Italian artists, and in April 1548 Serlio was replaced in his post by
Philibert De l'Orme.

Some time before 1550 Serlio moved to Lyons, possibly following
Ippolito d'Este who had been Archbishop of Lyons since 1540. The
town was a centre for printing, and this move may also have been for
the purpose of publishing the remaining books of the treatise. Jacopo
Strada, when visiting Lyons in 1550 and finding our author exhausted
by his labours and impoverished, purchased Serlio's manuscript and –
on a further visit in 1553 – his woodcuts for Book VII, which Serlio
was at that time carving himself (Rosenfeld 1996, 6). The book was
edited and published posthumously by Strada in an Italian–Latin edition which appeared in Frankfurt in 1575. It represents the first publication to deal with the practical problems, or 'situations' (as the title
has it), that an architect was likely to encounter, such as the design of
buildings for irregular sites and slopes, or the re-use of columns when
refacing Gothic façades. The book illustrates Serlio's own unexecuted
project to amend François D'Agoult's partially completed château at
Lourmarin in Provence, here represented as the ideal château of
'Rosmarino' (Serlio 1575, 208–17). Serlio was evidently proud of the
novelty of the subject of this projected book, noting at the end of
Book II that it was 'something which perhaps has never been seen
before' (Serlio 1545, fol. 73v). Hence, his seven-book treatise began
with the theoretical strictures of geometry and perspective, moved
through antique building types and the five Orders to a consideration

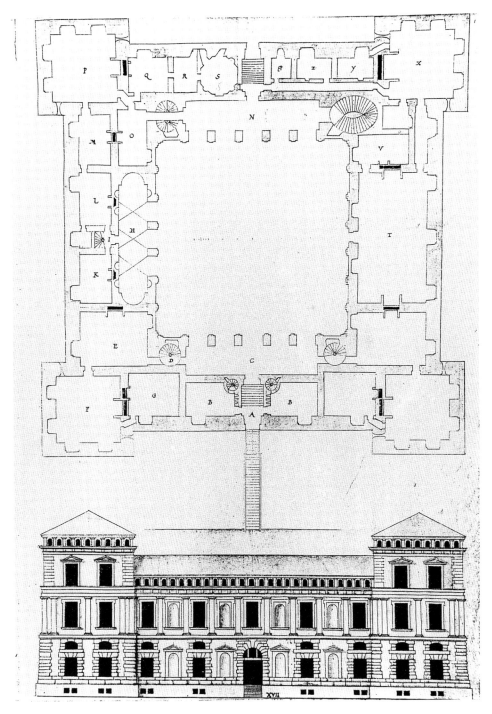

2 Château of Ancy-le-Franc, from Serlio's MS Book VI, fol. 17r. Codex Icon. 189, Munich, Bayerische Staatsbibliothek.

of a range of design models, sacred and domestic, and concluded with practical problems of planning and ornament. The structure of the treatise thus usefully followed the actual building process, from conception in drawn form to 'situations' on site.

Strada also purchased a manuscript of a book outside Serlio's original scheme as outlined in 1537, namely his treatise devoted to the Roman military camp (castrametation) as recorded by Polybius (which Strada subsequently tagged 'Book VIII') (Fiore 1994). Indeed whilst in Lyons, Serlio published a book of gate designs in 1551 (a manuscript copy of which also survives) (Carpo 1993a). This work was equally outside his seven-book scheme, a fact emphasised by its title as the *Extraordinario Libro*. The last record of Serlio's presence in Lyons was in 1552; in his introductory letter to Book VII Strada claims that Serlio's final days were spent at Fontainebleau, 'suffering from gout almost all of the time', but 'filled with joy' having seen his dream satisfied (Serlio 1575, sig. av*r*).

VITRUVIAN 'LICENCE' AND THE GENERAL RULES
OF ARCHITECTURE

Throughout his treatise, the Bolognese architect presents himself as a disciple of Vitruvius – termed 'The Great Architect' (Serlio 1540, fol. CXXXI/112*r*) – making frequent reference to the Roman's *De Architectura* by book and chapter, although remarkably enough at no point does Serlio acknowledge the writings of earlier Vitruvian commentators. This omission places in sharp relief his direct debt to Vitruvius's text as well as the fulsome acknowledgment of Peruzzi, Serlio's teacher in Vitruvian matters: at the beginning of Book IV for example Serlio notes that, 'as for all the pleasant things which you will find in this book, you should not give the credit to me but to my teacher, Baldassare Peruzzi from Siena . . . What little I know, I owe it all to his kindness and I intend to follow his example with those who do not disdain to learn from me' (Serlio 1537, fol. IIIr/126*r*). Serlio thus openly conceived his treatise as a didactic document which reflected the teachings of Peruzzi.

Serlio's reputation has however suffered from the impression given by Giorgio Vasari in his life of Peruzzi that, having inherited the great artist's drawings, our author was little more than a plagiarist. In fact Peruzzi must have sanctioned Serlio's work, since Peruzzi died in 1536 only a year before publication of Book IV, and Serlio had been preparing this work for many years. Indeed, of Peruzzi's surviving drawings, few were directly copied by Serlio. Rather, his woodcuts merely illustrate the same subject, and were in any case often of

monuments which represented the standard pilgrimage sites for Renaissance artists eager to study antiquity. Serlio's originality is perhaps
most evident in his designs of elements which had no antique precedent, such as fireplaces and house façades in the five Orders.

One of Serlio's principal purposes in publishing his treatise, and in
producing Book IV in particular, was to establish a clear set of rules
(the *regole generale* referred to in the fourth book's title) for identifying
and using the Orders. In Book IV he sought to reconcile the rules for
the Orders, as far as they were stipulated by Vitruvius, with the often
divergent appearance and arrangement of the columns on the Roman
monuments which Serlio had carefully surveyed; indeed he observes, 'I
find a great discrepancy between the buildings in Rome and other
places in Italy and the writings of Vitruvius' (Serlio 1540, fol. XIX*v*/
141*v*). Monuments such as the Colosseum and the arch of Titus in
Rome were, however, of singular importance to Serlio in establishing
the rules for the Composite column since Vitruvius was silent on this
Roman Order. As a consequence, Serlio became the first theorist
to codify rules for all five columns in a clear, consistent way, and to
describe the members of these Orders in painterly terms ranging
from 'robust' and 'solid' for the Tuscan to 'delicate' and 'ornate' for
the Corinthian and Composite (Onians 1988, 264–86; see Serlio 1575,
120–26). Indeed he is the first treatise writer to apply the now familiar
term 'Order' to the column itself (Onians 1988, 280–82; Rykwert
1996, 4).

Vitruvius had recorded rules for the carving and use of the Greek
Orders based on their imitation of certain natural models, notably those
of the human body (Vitr.III.i.3 and IV.i.6–8) and of timber construction
(Vitr.II.i.2–8 on the concept of mimesis). In attempting to codify every
architectural element from the pedestal to the entablature, Serlio
identified antique examples which departed from these models. This
form of architecture he calls 'licentious' (Jelmini 1986; Carpo
1993a&b): the appearance of bands of dentils and modillions in the
same cornice was a licentious detail, for example, since both bands
were carved representations of beam ends and in timber construction
only a single set of beams was required (see Serlio 1537, fol. XLVIII*v*/
170*r*, and Vitr.IV.ii.5–6). The Doric cornice of the Theatre of
Marcellus was used by Serlio as an example when defining architectural
'licentiousness' because,

> Even though the Doric cornice was extremely rich in members and
> highly carved, nonetheless I found it very far from Vitruvian doc-
> trine, very licentious in its members and of such a height that, in
> proportion to the architrave and frieze, two-thirds of that height
> would have been enough . . . We should uphold the doctrines of

Vitruvius as an infallible guide and rule, provided that reason does
not persuade us otherwise. (Serlio 1540, fol. XLVI/69ν)

For Serlio architectural invention should, in principle, thus respect
the (often vague) rules established by Vitruvius. In a number of cases,
however, 'reason' did indeed persuade Serlio to disagree with the
Roman author. On the height of the Corinthian capital, for example,
having taken 'account of the parallel in nature' with regard to the
capital's correspondence to the proportions of a maiden's head as
stipulated by Vitruvius (Vitr.IV.i.11), Serlio concluded that the capital
should measure one column thickness without its abacus (Serlio 1540,
fol. CXXIIII/108ν): Vitruvius had, on the other hand, included this
topmost member within the module. Hence, contrary to his normal
method, natural models and antique examples were sometimes cited
by Serlio to disprove Vitruvius and underline the importance of the
architect's own judgement.

Apparently paradoxically, however, Serlio's reputation in part rests
on the fact that he specified rules for the Composite Order, in the
absence of a description of this Roman Order by Vitruvius. Serlio
introduces the Composite in Book IV as 'almost a fifth style, a mixture
of the said "pure" ones', for it was the 'most licentious of all the
building styles' (Serlio 1537, fols. LXIν/183r and LXIIIIν/186ν). As a
mixture of elements from the Ionic and Corinthian Orders, Composite
columns possessed neither an immediate natural reference nor a
Vitruvian model. Serlio's willingness to codify beyond Vitruvian
dictates was further underlined by his 'extraordinary book' of gate
designs. Apparently completely contrary to Serlio's earlier principles,
this work illustrated fifty gates of extreme ornamentation (Carpo
1993a); this outwardly licentious character was however perfectly in
keeping with the contemporary shift from High Renaissance *all'antica*
architecture to Mannerism, whilst the text makes clear that, under-
neath the 'mask' of grotesque rustication, Vitruvian patterns prevail
(Serlio 1551, fol. 5ν).

SERLIO'S MILITARY CITY AND THE THEORY OF DECORUM

Having specified the gender of the Greek columns – ranging from
the 'masculine' Doric and 'matronly' Ionic to 'maidenly' Corinthian
(Rykwert 1996) – Vitruvius related these human types to the character,
or 'decorum', of temples dedicated to particular gods: Doric for
Minerva, Mars and Hercules; Ionic for Juno, Diana and Bacchus;
and Corinthian for Venus and Flora (Vitr.I.ii.5). Serlio developed this
principle of decorum into a 'language of use', in which particular
Orders were matched with particular modern building types according

to their dedication, function or the character and status of their patron. Hence his fourth book introduces the Tuscan as suited to fortresses and 'city gates, fortified hill towns, castles, treasuries and places where munitions and artillery are kept, prisons, sea ports and other similar things for use in war' (Serlio 1537, fol. III*v*/126*v*); the Doric as suited to buildings for 'men of arms' and 'robust characters, whether of high, middle or low rank' (fol. XVIII*r*/139*r*); Ionic to those for men of letters and 'of a quiet life' (fol. XXXVI*v*/158*v*); and Corinthian to monasteries and 'convents which cloister maidens dedicated to divine worship', as well as to houses 'for people of upright and chaste lives', so as 'to preserve decorum' (fol. XLVII*v*/169*r*). The use of the more decorative Orders was however further restricted by the Calvinist aversion to the display of luxury, a factor which restrained Serlio's own use of the Orders in his domestic designs in Book VI (Carpo 1992).

In Book VII Serlio adds that the characteristics of the Orders could be tempered by additional carving in the form of intaglios which would make the work more 'delicate' (Serlio 1575, 120–26; Onians 1988, 264–86; Carpo 1993a). Moreover, for Serlio the location of a building clearly also had an effect on the design of its ornamentation and consequent 'decorum'. For whilst ornament must always be appropriate to the rank of the patron, in the centre of towns this carving should be 'solemn and modest' whereas in more open places in the city and in the country 'a certain licence can be taken' (Serlio 1575, 232). In practice, the principle of decorum led Serlio to think in terms of 'types' (*generi*), classifying the individual examples of the ancient monuments, columns, churches, houses, gates and military buildings illustrated in his treatise principally by their show of ornament, which was seen as expressing their character (Carpo 1992). Hence a door in Book VII is described as 'of three "species"' in reference to its use of rustication, brick and reticular work (Serlio 1575, 78).

In his final book, the so-called Book VIII, Serlio again noted that an architect 'must always look to the grandeur and decorum' in design matters (Fiore 1994, fols. 21*v*–22*r*). This recommendation was given physical expression in the various buildings which make up his reconstruction of a Roman military city built by the Emperor Trajan; Serlio's friend cardinal Marco Grimani had reported that he had found the remains of this city in Dacia. Serlio made clear that the layout of this 'walled citadel', as he calls it (Fiore 1994, fol. 1*r*) (plate 3), was based on the temporary Roman camp (the *castra*) as described by Polybius and reconstructed by Serlio in a further part of the manuscript (Marconi 1969; Wischermann 1975; Rosenfeld 1978, 46–7; Johnson 1985; Thoenes 1989, 216–27; Fiore 1994). Although Serlio had provided designs of military camps in Piedmont and Flanders for François I, his city in 'Book VIII' represented an antiquarian exercise. With a perfectly square enclosure and Roman *cardo-decumanus* street layout, a

consul's palace (*praetorium*), *forum*, treasury (*quaestorium*), amphitheatre
and baths – each building decorated with the Orders – this was an ideal
city more civil than military in character: the real city with which
the architect had to work was irregular and accidental, as the various
projects of Book VII fully acknowledged. And the real, sixteenth-
century military fort was a geometric bastion which contemporary
theorists such as Girolamo Maggi considered required no ornament
(Johnson 1985). Serlio himself comments on the 'ideal' nature of his
city design in 'Book VIII' when noting that 'I did this not because I
thought that there would be anyone in this century, which is so full
to the brim with avarice, who would undertake such a project, but to
exercise the little intellect that I possess, which can find no peace unless
occupied in my beloved architecture' (Fiore 1994, fol. 1*v*). Hence,
quite unlike the content of Serlio's other books, this work was not
practical in nature and was not, therefore, principally aimed at architects. Rather, as a product of Trajan's magnificence, this imaginary
Roman city was intended by Serlio as a coherent demonstration of
what could be achieved through the generosity of patrons.

Serlio's many references to the theory of decorum make clear that
the various building types in 'Book VIII' were characterised through
the style and degree of ornament on their façades (Onians 1988, 277).
He noted on the *porta decumana* (plate 4), for example, that, 'This is
the principal gateway of the castrametation . . . and it is Corinthian
work mixed with Rustic so as to show figuratively the gentleness and
clemency of the Emperor Trajan's spirit when pardoning and his
strength and severity when punishing' (Fiore 1994, fol. 17*r*). Moreover,
on the *porta pretorea* (plate 5) Serlio applied the rule in his fourth book
that Doric was suitable for buildings 'for men of arms' and 'robust
characters', when noting,

> the praetorian gateway should be made with austere work that
> possesses a certain majesty, which befits the rank of the consul. In
> this respect Doric work is the most austere of all and truly appro-
> priate for a soldier. The entire work is therefore to be Doric but
> delicate, because of the great Emperor who was such an admirer of
> architectural beauty. (Fiore 1994, fol. 18*r*)

Indeed, on the *praetorium*, the consul's palace in the centre of the city
(marked 'A' on the plan and aligned with this gate; plate 3), Doric is,
once again, the only Order used: the upper entablature has triglyphs
whilst the pilasters on a central window and on two niches are Doric
(with ornamental pediments however to add the required 'delicacy')
(plate 6). Here, as with the praetorian gate, the use of this Order clearly
signified the consul's 'austere majesty'. The Doric 'style' is matched by
the general austerity of the façade, the walls of which are astylar. The

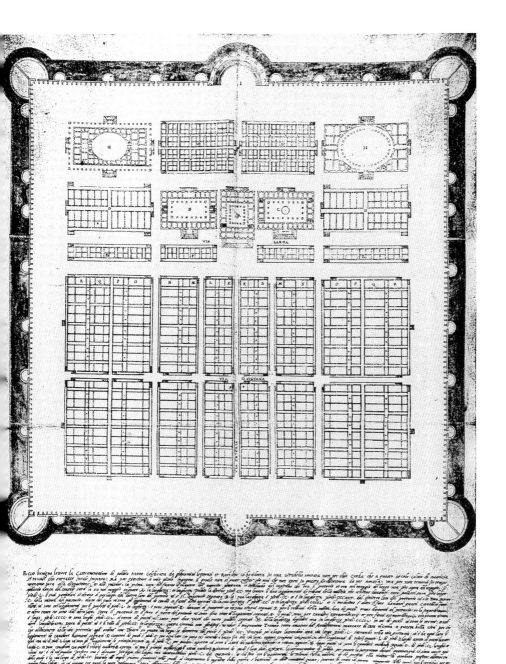

Plan of a Roman military city, after Polybius, from Serlio's MS 'Book VIII', fol. 1*v*. Codex Icon. o, Munich, Bayerische Staatsbibliothek.

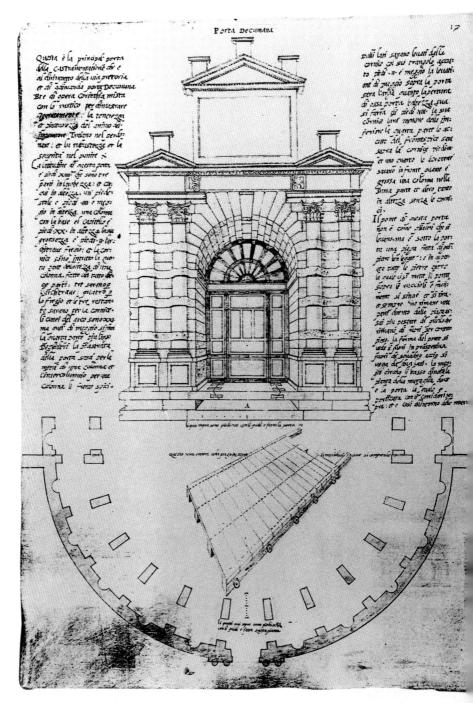

4 The *porta decumana*, from Serlio's MS 'Book VIII', fol. 17r. Codex Icon. 190, Muni
Bayerische Staatsbibliothek.

The *porta pretorea*, from Serlio's MS 'Book VIII', fol. 18r. Codex Icon. 190, Munich, Bayerische
taatsbibliothek.

6   Section parallel with the *via larga*, composite drawing reconstructed from the individual drawings in Serlio's MS 'Book VIII'. The preferred design for the *forum* is shown above.

central door and the windows are of 'mixed work' (rustic blocks and brickwork), whilst this austere character has been continued in the courtyard through the presence of a rusticated arcade befitting a military building: for elsewhere in 'Book VIII' Serlio made clear that rustication 'is very suitable' as a symbol of protection and strength (Fiore 1994, fol. 17*v*). In this way, following the theory of decorum, the most important building did not necessarily display the most ornate Order.

Indeed, the austerity of the consul's palace is in contrast to the public buildings either side of it – the *quaestorium* (treasury and quartermaster's stores, marked 'B') on the left and the *forum* (merchants' shops and temple, marked 'C') on the right (plates 3 and 6). For, whilst the courtyard of the *quaestorium* has 'strong' rusticated loggias, the front façade of this treasury building is ornamented with Doric and Ionic pilasters richly carved with intaglios – appropriately enough signifying strength but refinement. The front façade of the *forum* has Corinthian columns on its central door, tabernacled windows and a Composite cornice on the third storey. In fact, Serlio had rejected an alternative design (also illustrated in the manuscript) for this façade which was much more ornamental, with Corinthian pilasters (replaced with niches in his preferred design) and a central attic storey of Composite work (which is omitted) (plate 6). Commenting that 'after deeper reflection I felt that I wanted to change partly the arrangement of the façade' (Fiore 1994, fol. 8*v*), Serlio's revisions have the effect of simplifying and balancing the level of ornament with respect to the *quaestorium* on the other side of the consul's palace. Indeed the preferred façade is a more restrained expression of the *forum's* function and status, matching more closely the principle of decorum.

An ornamental balance is also maintained between the front façade of the baths and that of the amphitheatre (plate 6), placed further towards the wall on the left and right respectively (both marked 'H'). Whilst the baths have Doric pillars with intaglios on the first two storeys and Composite pilasters on the attic storey, the amphitheatre has Corinthian pilasters on the first two storeys and, again, Composite pilasters above. For Serlio, the use of Composite in the attic would follow the obvious precedent of the most significant Roman amphitheatre, the Colosseum, which was fully illustrated by him in Book III (Serlio 1540, fols. LXIIII/78*v*–LXIX/81*r*). Indeed, in Book IV he interpreted the Composite attic on this building as a sign of Roman military might, since its position above the Greek Ionic and Corinthian Orders indicated the fact that the Romans had 'triumphed over all those countries from which these works originated' (Serlio 1537, fol. LXI*v*/183*r*). The Roman Composite Order in an attic position would thus be particularly appropriate to the decorum of a Roman military city, matching as a sign of triumph the sculptures representing captives which Serlio tells us are displayed elsewhere in the camp.

In contrast to these public buildings, the ordinary barracks (running vertically, marked 'K'–'R') are austere, with pilasters restricted to doorways and limited to the barracks for Roman cavalrymen and the *triarii* (Fiore 1994, fol. 15*r*). The quarters for the military tribunes (the horizontal runs either side of the consul's palace, marked 'F') are the only ones to be decorated with the Orders, in the form of Doric and Ionic pilasters (Fiore 1994, fol. 11*r*). This exclusivity perfectly accords with the importance of the tribunes in the Roman army, for Serlio's principal source, Polybius, records (VI 21, 6–10) that they were magistrates responsible for the selection of troops, depending on age, to serve as the *velites*, *hastati*, *principes* and *triarii*. Indeed, as befitting the role of the military tribunes as administrators, here the severity of Doric is tempered with the more delicate Ionic – suitable, according to Serlio's fourth book, to men of letters.

Hence, each of the front façades of the public buildings are ornamented with the Orders – moving from 'military' Doric in the centre through the more 'gentle' Ionic and Corinthian either side to the Composite, the Order of Roman 'triumph', on the outermost buildings. Again as might be expected, in contrast the façades of the ordinary barracks are, with the exception of a few doorways, astylar. Moreover, true to the Vitruvian principle of decorum, the various Orders are here used selectively to express a particular building's character, status and function in the city structure. Indeed, Serlio concludes his reconstruction of Roman military building types with a design of a bridge which has a triumphal arch at either end; the arch 'which is Rustic work was on the side inhabited by the fiercest and most warlike barbarians', whilst 'the one of Corinthian work was on the side towards Italy' (Fiore 1994, fols. 19*v*–20*r*). In this way Polybius's temporary Roman camp was used by Serlio as a template for a unique exercise in *all'antica* design, turning this 'ideal city' to stone using the Vitruvian principle of decorum advanced throughout his seven-book treatise.

THE RECEPTION OF SERLIO'S TREATISE

Serlio's treatise was destined to become one of the most important architectural publications to disseminate throughout sixteenth-century Europe knowledge of Italian antique heritage and of Renaissance invention. By the early seventeenth century its various parts had been translated into seven languages and were studied by almost every European architect (Serlio 1996, 470–71). This influence was, however, largely due to the currency of what Serlio regarded as forgeries of his work. He was perturbed at reports of unauthorised translations, noting at the end of Book II that, 'I have heard rumours that in addition to the one which was reprinted in Germany, a translation is being made into French of books which I do not wish to be printed under my name. On the contrary with the authority of my Royal privilege I shall bring a prosecution' (Serlio 1545, fol. 73v). Three years after the first publication of Book IV, Serlio noted in his opening letter to the second edition that, 'some people, driven by greed for gain, have tried to re-print this book of "rules" in a smaller format, without respecting either the proportions or the measurements of my figures' (fol. IIv; Serlio 1996, 469). This was in reference to the work of the Flemish scholar Pieter Coecke van Aelst (1502–50), Serlio's main unauthorised publisher. Coecke had published a Flemish translation of Book IV just two years after Serlio's first edition, in 1539. A German-language edition of Book IV was published by him in 1542, whilst his French translation of the same work and of Book III appeared in Antwerp in 1545 and 1550 respectively.

Ironically, with his name preserved on the cover, Serlio's fame was to be assured by these free translations, although because their publication coincided with a time of financial insecurity for the author, the lack of remuneration must have especially annoyed him. The possibility of forgery had in fact been foreseen by Serlio, as his copyright applications for Book IV record in their attempt to punish any forger, at least within the Venetian domains (Howard 1973; Serlio 1996, 466–7). Coecke adapted the contents to suit various northern European practices, in the spirit of Serlio himself, and this added to the popularity of the work. A notable example of this is the addition of an alphabet at the end of Book IV to facilitate the carving of inscriptions.

Whilst the first five books were published as a set in Venice in 1551, the closest Serlio's treatise came to complete publication was in the 1584 and 1600 editions, which have no Book VI but included the 'Extraordinary Book of Doors', followed by Book VII; by the time of the 1618–19 edition, with textual alterations probably by Giovanni Domenico Scamozzi (father of the architect Vincenzo Scamozzi), the *Extraordinario Libro* had, not surprisingly, been mistaken for the (unpublished) Book VI. Giacomo Barozzi da Vignola, an erstwhile pupil of Serlio in Bologna, was to consolidate Serlio's 'invention' of the five Orders in his *Regola* of 1563 and Andrea Palladio copied the format of Serlio's treatise when he matched woodcuts with text whilst publicising his own built work in his *Quattro libri* of 1570. Serlio was thus largely responsible for establishing the format of subsequent architectural treatises.

The architectural principles outlined by Serlio were intended to be universally applicable, irrespective of local styles and building traditions. His designs for churches in Book V, and for houses in Books VI and VII, clearly demonstrate this fact by including French medieval forms and ornament. It may at first sight appear surprising that these should feature in a treatise extolling Vitruvius, but in this respect Serlio followed his fellow northern Italian theorist Cesare Cesariano who had illustrated Gothic Milan cathedral in his 1521 Italian translation of Vitruvius. This emphasis on the continuity of building practices was greatly to assist the popularity of Serlio's treatise.

In the absence of any organised architectural training, Serlio's work would establish the Renaissance treatise as a vital element of the architect's instruction in theory and practice, and assist the explanation of Vitruvian design to both the patron and the master-mason. For his was the first treatise to address the practical problems which faced the Renaissance architect in the use of the Orders, integrating contemporary construction methods and expectations of comfort with Roman concepts of utility, decorum and beauty when illustrating easy-to-use models. These designs were not to be copied slavishly, but were starting points for invention within an established architectural language: the importance of the architect's creative judgement is emphasised by Serlio's inclusion of alternative schemes for various domestic designs. In this relativity, Serlio's treatise fundamentally departed from the Albertian model whilst introducing the 'type' of the illustrated architectural manual in use today (Rosenfeld 1989).

Never overly theoretical, always practical, Serlio graphically underlined the interrelationship between theory and practice by presenting his own architectural work as models. Through these models he sought to recommend a middle path in the choice of architectural ornamentation, avoiding the temptation of licentious excess whilst fully exploiting the expressive potential of the Orders as the context demanded (Carpo 1992). For the Serlian architect should, in all matters, 'proceed very modestly and be very cautious, especially in public and solemn works, where it is praiseworthy to preserve decorum' (Serlio 1537, fol. IIIv/126v).

Chapter Eight

THE MAKING OF THE TYPOGRAPHICAL ARCHITECT

Mario Carpo

ACCORDING TO A SCHEMA that has its origins in the architectural historiography of positivism, each period in the history of architecture corresponds to a specific construction technique:[1] in the architecture of ancient Greece this is the technique of post and lintel; for Roman architecture the arch and the vault; for medieval architecture stereotomy; and so on, until we arrive at reinforced concrete and its advocates. Today this evolutionary – in a way teleological – interpretation provokes a variety of allergic reactions, understandably perhaps, but it has nevertheless been responsible for that frequently cited theory according to which the Renaissance is one of the few great eras in architectural history in which a new style emerges unrelated to any remarkable technical innovation (but see Ackerman 1991a, 3–22 [esp. 6–7]; 1991b, 361–84 [esp. 368]).

Between the beginning of the fifteenth century and the end of the sixteenth, most construction in Europe adopted a new style – without any attendant change in building methods. Admittedly, a range of medieval building techniques was indeed abandoned, but they were neither replaced nor rendered obsolete by new technical discoveries. No piece of equipment, no building material seems to be connected to the fortunes of the *all'antica* architecture of humanism and the Renaissance.

Against this standard scenario at least three arguments can be raised. First, while techniques may not have changed, the organisation and division of labour on the building site did change. The Renaissance

---

[1]   This chapter was translated by Sarah B. Benson. It anticipates several of the arguments of my forthcoming book (entitled *L'architettura dell'età della stampa. Oralità, scrittura, libro stampato e riproduzione meccanica dell'imagine nella storia delle teorie architettoniche.* Milan: Jaca Book, 1998), which will contain a more complete bibliography.

architect was no longer required to matriculate in any guild, and he was no longer an artisan but an artist. The guild system lost control of the building site and of the design process itself – whatever that process may have been in a pre-Renaissance context. Second, the techniques of representing a plan (drawings or three-dimensional models) changed because of an increasing separation and estrangement between design and building site (Carpeggiani and Patetta 1989; Frommel 1994, 113–14, 612 n. 303; Millon 1994, 19, 35). Finally, the building site is not the only locus of intersection between architecture and technology. Apart from the technical requirements of construction, and of design, architecture has always been a 'discipline' – a technical knowledge founded upon the accumulation and transmission of concepts and experiences from one generation to the next. From the alphabet to the ASCII code for electronic communication, this process of recording and transmitting has always relied upon contemporary technologies. But no means of communication is either universal or neutral. The generation of exactly repeatable architectural images, made possible by xylography and printing, necessarily transformed the architectural discipline. This chapter compares the processes of architectural composition before and after.

The organisation of medieval masons' lodges, and the secrecy that surrounded certain of their building practices, has been the subject of an endless and at times whimsically speculative body of scholarship. One thing is clear, the knowledge of medieval builders was in large part founded upon speech – on dialogue, direct observation and memory. Instruction was given *ad personam*, from master to apprentice, according to the methods of the corporate curriculum. The secret of the masons is not a romantic invention. It existed, imposed in categorical, if not always efficacious terms in the corporate statutes. Esoteric formulas were either read aloud or recited in ritual contexts, and in certain cases it was expressly forbidden to keep written documents that revealed professional techniques (Rykwert 1988; but see Freigang 1990).

In these conditions, hostile as they were to the written transmission of knowledge, some concepts were more easily passed on than others. To take a hypothetical example: a description of Strasbourg cathedral composed in verse and recited from memory, without the aid of illustrations, would not readily allow a person unfamiliar with the original to construct a mental image. Discourse records thought rather than images: verbal description can readily convey a set of abstract rules, but it cannot so easily convey a visual model. *Ekphrasis* was traditionally one of the hardest exercises of classical rhetoric.

In compensation, a geometric construct, even a complex one, can easily be verbalised. A geometric construct is a sequence; it unfolds in time like speech itself, and adapts itself easily to verbal reproduction in real time. ('Take the line segment A–B. Divide it into two equal parts with a pair of compasses. Call the middle point C. From point C . . .'.) Medieval artisans committed to memory scores of these verbal sequences. For those in the know, an elementary visual diagram could in fact be of use in jogging the memory on a difficult passage in the geometric sequence. These diagrams, incomplete and cryptic as they were, did not reveal any methods of construction to those who were not already initiated into their secrets. Consider the sketch-book (c.1225–50) of Villard de Honnecourt. It has recently been suggested that the technical designs on folios 19v–21r are examples of just this sort of encoded geometric diagram.[2]

Through a quirk of history, an illustrated book printed by Matthias Roriczer in 1486 has preserved a geometric rule for the construction of the spires of Gothic cathedrals (Roriczer 1486). These geometric rules translate themselves into schematic diagrams that determine various proportions of the building, but this method in no way determines the building's exterior appearance. By the same token, the visual aspect of the building reveals neither this set of rules nor other possible proportional schemes that its builders may have considered. The system of Roriczer would never have been known if Roriczer himself, for reasons that no one has been able to explain, had not published it in a book.

The method of oral transmission and mnemonic techniques imposed by the guilds hints at the existence of a disciplinary corpus comprising sets of rules rather than models, rules that generated plans and geometric constructions. Still, the idea of the model was not alien to medieval culture, neither was the practice of imitation. This was as true for the visual arts, including architecture, as it was for other areas. As Richard Krautheimer demonstrated in a pioneering and well-known article, many medieval structures were explicitly conceived by their builders as the imitation of a celebrated model, sometimes a Pagan building but more often a Christian one (Krautheimer 1969). From our point of view, all of these replicas have one important characteristic in common: they do not resemble each other, and they do not resemble their model. Yet medieval people, who were in principle neither better nor worse than ourselves, considered them similar.

This paradox is only an apparent one. The idea of imitation has not itself changed. An archetype and its copy are two individuals (in the epistemological sense) that have something in common. The imitator

---

[2]   Villard de Honnecourt, MS 19093, Bibliothèque Nationale, Paris, fols. 19v–21r. See the interpretation in Bechmann 1991, 150–54, 313–14, 357–60. Bechmann's thesis has recently been contested by scholars.

introduces into his or her product various elements extracted from the original matrix. Differences come in the selection of pertinent features. The elements that interested a medieval imitator are not those that would interest the imitator of today. Among other things, Krautheimer shows that in some cases the sharing of a common name (as in the case of two churches dedicated to the same saint) was enough to mark one building as the copy of another (Krautheimer 1969, 127 n. 88). In other cases, medieval imitation consisted in the approximated replication of the plan of the original (centralised, square, basilical and so on), or in sets of relationships of proportion, geometry or number (such as the number of columns or windows). Krautheimer concludes, in another important text, that medieval culture had an 'almost emphatically nonvisual' vision of antiquity (Krautheimer and Krautheimer-Hess 1956, 294; Choay 1992, 39, n. 31). Antiquity was not the only model for medieval architecture, and perhaps not even the most important. In any case the criterion was consistent: ancient or modern, the models were neither visual nor visualised.

All this changes with the culture of humanism, which brought in a metamorphosis in the figurative arts that has frequently been associated with the topos of a so-called 'new visual realism' of the first moderns. We find a complementary topos in that 'tendency toward symbolic abstraction' which many attribute, somewhat generously, to medieval art in general. Letting this traditional exegesis stand, the phenomenon of non-visual imitation in the visual arts, which we find so curious, may admit of a simpler explanation, and a more technical one. Medieval artisans, whether builders or painters, were almost always working from models that they had never seen. For they imitated models that they knew only through hearsay.

Accounts might arrive first-hand from the mouth of a witness. Sometime around 670, Bishop Arculf, on his way back to France from the Holy Land, landed instead (inexplicably) in Scotland. During his stay on the island of Iona he described the form of the buildings he had seen to Saint Adamnanus, who questioned him relentlessly on this subject. Arculf gave his account from memory; he had made neither notes nor sketches. Adamnanus took down the dictation, then made a good copy on parchment (the medieval version of publication) to which he added four diagrams including a plan of the church of the Holy Sepulchre. This juxtaposition of illustrations with handwritten text must have been extraordinary, since the author felt it necessary to comment on it – to offer instructions. He advises his readers that the drawings are not descriptions but 'descriptiunculae', 'viles figurationes' of little use (Adamnanus 1898, 230, 244, 254, 270; Delpit 1868; Krautheimer 1969, 129–30, fig. 31). Drawing did not replace verbal description. Architectural images continued to be passed on primarily by word of mouth, 'verbis solis', as Leon Battista Alberti said, many years later but in a similar context and with the same trepidation about the use of illustrations (Book III ch. 2. [Alberti 1966, 176; 1988, 62]; Choay 1997, 105).

In describing the church of Hagia Sophia in Constantinople, the Byzantine historian Procopius mentions two modes of architectural apperception, one clearly better than the other. According to Procopius, one had either to see the building at first hand or to rely upon oral or written accounts such as his own.[3] Significantly, Procopius fails to mention the possibility of reproducing appearances through visual media. Anyone who did not trust in hearsay was forced to travel to the site itself.

It is no accident that travel was to become an integral part of the education of a medieval artisan. Guild statutes required journeymen to travel from one town to another, and to work in a number of different locations. Once having seen the original, the itinerant artist had to commit it to memory. The visual memory of medieval artists must have been prodigious, since in many cases they did not make use of pictures to record or fix an image. Apparently, many considered the memory more secure or more sound than a wax tablet. Maybe they did not know how to draw; maybe they just did not want to.

An Irish chronicle of the 1180s relates the story of a miniaturist, either lazy or of mediocre talents, who was visited by an angel in a dream. The angel presented to the artist a painted image asking that he reproduce it as the frontispiece of an illuminated Bible. The artist hesitated, and in the end the angel's request was carried out thanks only to the intervention of Saint Brigid of Kildare ('angelo praesentante, Brigida orante, scriptore imitante, liber ille conscriptus est') (Giraldus Cambrensis 1955, 217; Scheller 1995, 12). The primary obstacle, so far as one can tell, was not the drawing itself. What the artist balked at was the task of memorising at night ('memoriae fideliter commendare') the image that he was asked to reproduce by day. Why did the angel not simply leave the picture on the artist's nightstand?

On the frontispiece of a Bible printed in Antwerp in 1530 the evangelists are pictured in the act of writing under divine inspiration. Traditionally the angel *dictates* to Matthew, but in this case the angel holds a book open before him from which the evangelist transcribes the Word of God.[4] This angel demonstrates a strong preference for

---

[3] 'So the church has become a spectacle of marvellous beauty, overwhelming to those who see it, but to those who know it by hearsay altogether incredible.' Procopius, *Buildings*, (*c*.560), I.i.27, English trans. H. B. Dewing (London, 1940), 13.

[4] This frontispiece was repeated in numerous editions printed in Antwerp from 1530 on by Martin Lempereur and William Vorsterman (see Gilmont 1990, 10).

written documents over speech and human memory. If the angel of Antwerp had behaved like his medieval predecessor, Matthew would have received the Word during a dream, and would then have had to remember it, verbatim, the morning after. But in 1530 printing had already started to change habits of speech, and the visual apprehension of texts had begun to replace discourse and memory.

Medieval authors, and as we have seen even medieval angels, had a thousand good reasons to be suspicious of images. Speech can be recorded thanks to the technology of writing. Furthermore, a written text can be easily reproduced. A reader dictates, twenty amanuenses take down the words, and at the end of the day there are twenty copies of the same text, which should in theory be more or less identical. An image cannot be dictated in the same way. It can always be copied, but the operation is complicated and risky, the risk being proportional to the complexity of the design. Pliny and Galen had already warned the authors of scientific texts not to use any sort of illustration (*Nat. Hist.* XXV.4; Galen 1552, vi.i, 351–3). Pliny is categorical: the destiny of an image in a manuscript is unpredictable. No one can tell how the next copyist may distort it.

The warnings of the ancients were limited, with good reason, to texts on technical and scientific subjects. Despite the risks, richly illustrated scrolls and codices, even dealing with botany and medicine, were produced and recopied again and again – and in some cases the mutation of the illustrations does not seem to have been uncontrollable. Nevertheless, the traditional mistrust of scientific and technical illustration was more than justified by an almost inevitable material condition: in the world of manuscripts, discourse can be recorded and transmitted thanks to the alphabet; images can be recorded, thanks to drawing, but drawing in general cannot be transmitted. Let the author be warned: take into account the pros and the cons – the function of the text, the intended audience, the planned distribution – and consider the consequences.

Renaissance authors, as well as more recent ones, have looked high and low for the lost illustrations of Vitruvius, inventing the most bizarre theories for their disappearance (Carpo 1993a, 128 n. 53). But the illustrations of Vitruvius never existed, with the exception of the nine to eleven elementary geometric diagrams mentioned in the text and first partially itemised by Philandrier in 1544 (I.vi, annotation 17).[5] As had so many other ancient authors, Vitruvius thought better of burdening his text with a complex iconography, knowing full well that

---

[5] Vitruvius refers to the same illustration more than once. Philandrier lists nine illustrations in his 1544 edition, and adds one to the list in his 1552 edition. His passage is translated and discussed in Lemerle 1991, 106 and notes.

such an iconography would, after the first copy, have been abandoned, manipulated or hopelessly deformed.

In the Middle Ages, as we have seen, the discipline of architecture was, for reasons both socio-cultural (the organisation of guilds) and technical (the difficulty of reproducing images), largely anti-iconic; it did not make use of images. This proscription had nothing to do with the drafting of visual project designs, a common practice especially in late-medieval architecture, and of which many examples survive. These drawings did not have any reproductive problems. Sometimes the original sufficed for the builder's purposes; if not, two or three copies could be carried out without loss of fidelity through tracing or pouncing. The risk inherent in the use of images did not affect communications between a builder and his workshop. Rather it affected the general accumulation and transmission of architectural knowledge from one architect to other architects distant in space and time.

For this sort of long-range communication images were in large measure useless, and therefore, not surprisingly, unused. The result was a theory that controlled non-visual factors and that at the same time renounced control of outward appearances. Or, as we would say today, of style. Context and technique, culture and the media of communication always interact in a complex manner: the reason for the non-existence of a technology is usually that it is of no cultural use. Reciprocally, a new technology spreads only when it is useful to someone. While it is not always easy to distinguish between cause and effect, the absence of reliable technologies for the reproduction of images must have been an essential component of the medieval architectural discipline.

However, from the beginning of the fifteenth century, especially after the invention of printing with moveable type, images became transmissible. Early modern culture adapted itself quite rapidly to a new and revolutionary phenomenon: the theoretically unlimited availability of inexpensive and, for the first time reliable images – all identical because all were obtained through the pressure on paper of the same ink-smeared wooden block. The alphabet was the first 'technologising of the word' (Ong 1995, esp. 81–3). The woodcut was the first technologising of the image. From time immemorial images could be fixed thanks to drawing, but it was only with the xylograph that images could be reproduced and transmitted. For architecture, a discipline that treats of material and visible objects, the consequences of the first technologising of the image were staggering and of long duration.

The principal consequence was a new practice and theory of imitation. The architect could now easily imitate the visible form of the model, and without embarking on any long journeys. For many

Renaissance architects, the Colosseum, before becoming a topogra-
phical site within the city of Rome, was a site within a book (Serlio's
Book III, 1540, fols. LXIIII/78v–LXIX/81r, etc.). The idea of compiling
an exhaustive graphic record of all of the eminent monuments of
antiquity, surveyed and reconstructed in plan, elevation and section,
has its origins in the second decade of the sixteenth century among
Raphael's Roman circle (Morolli 1984; Thoenes 1986). Yet it was only
in 1540, with Sebastiano Serlio's Book III, that this plan was actually
realised in the form of a printed book. Thanks to the diffusion of
printed images, antiquity ceased to be the attribute of places more or
less accessible; it was dislocated from its physical setting. Not yet
on-line, but nevertheless readily available on the printed pages of
Serlio's and other books that followed, the visual models of antiquity
were now archived in a virtual and typographic space (*bibliospace*), easy
of access, easy to use, regardless of political and geographic boundaries.

With few exceptions, it would never occur to any reasonable person
today to invent a modern architecture based on the imitation of
another pre-existing architecture that had disappeared over a millennium before. The idea of 'moving forwards looking backwards' may
seem strange, but the Renaissance version of imitation after antiquity
was in many ways innovative with respect to the medieval tradition of
which we have been speaking. The practice of imitation, which had
been of secondary importance in the general economy of medieval
architectural practice, became the keystone of Renaissance architectural
theory. Consequently, the choice of models was more pointed, and in
itself the subject of theoretical debate (what should one imitate? and
why?). Finally, Renaissance architectural imitation became a visual
process. This comes as no surprise to us, since this is the operative
notion of imitation in most fields of the figurative arts today. In
historiographic terms, however, and particularly for the history of
architecture, the passage from non-visual to visual imitation is a change
of the first importance. The mechanical reproduction of images may
not have been the only catalyst, but it is the principal one.

The technologising of images does not limit itself to transforming
architecture, or more generally the visual culture of early modern
Europe. According to some, the illustration of technical and scientific
texts lies at the origin of the scientific revolution, perhaps even of the
industrial revolution, and of still other revolutions of the modern era
(Ivins 1953; Ackerman 1991c). Before all this, the diffusion of printed
books, of images in themselves, and of printed images gave rise in the
Cinquecento to a theological debate that was to have far-reaching
consequences. From the point of view of architectural theory, the
availability of a repertoire of illustrated models of antiquity (of all of the
models of antiquity, or of carefully selected models) may have solved

one problem, but at the same time it brought about another one. The raw material of imitation, the image of the model, was now at anyone's disposal. Precisely for this reason, the theory and practice of imitation now needed to be *taught*.

It was not enough to say, look, be inspired, create. This may have sufficed for some students but not for all. There was a problem common to the discursive and the figurative arts in the Cinquecento: how to transform imitation into a rational technique, a communicable method. Some said (as many continue to do) that imitation was itself a creative act, and as such could be neither explained nor taught. Still, some persisted in looking for simple guidelines to the imitation of antiquity. Foremost among these pioneers in the field of architectural imitation was Sebastiano Serlio.

Serlio's treatise is in part the result of the author's encounter with Giulio Camillo, a Neoplatonic philosopher and linguistic theorist. Best known in his own day for his many peculiar undertakings (he was, among other things, proficient in the hypnosis of lions), Camillo is also the author of theoretical writings dedicated to a weirdly 'technological' reform of the principles of literary imitation. It seems that Camillo was convinced that composition was a kind of mechanism, and that this mechanism could be made to function in a semi-automatic fashion. Camillo also attempted to construct an actual machine for the imitation of Ciceronian style (his famous *Teatro*), an enterprise that did not improve his reputation either among his contemporaries or ours.

Serlio transposed, cautiously, Camillo's method from its application in the imitation of literary models to the imitation of architectural models (Carpo 1993b). One result is Serlio's system of the five Orders (plate 1). Serlio's Orders are meant to function as a catalogue of 'ready-made' architectural citations – decontextualised graphic micro-models, inspired by the antique, but conceived to be repeatedly recycled in modern architectural compositions. Rather than urging his readers to the creative imitation of the antique architectural models provided in his third book (1540), Serlio formalised in his fourth book (1537) a brief and easy method that allowed any architect, especially the less than brilliant ones, to construct *all'antica* without wasting any time on the study of antiquity. The system of the Orders is a short cut to imitation after the antique. Short cut and 'methodus' are in this case actually synonymous.

The third and the fourth books of Serlio are inconsistent pedagogically, even in a certain sense incompatible. The third book is for the most part an illustrated catalogue of antiquity. The reader can imitate any of these models *à la carte*, with greater or lesser degrees of creative intervention. This operation does not require any awareness, let alone use, of the Serlian Orders codified in the fourth book.

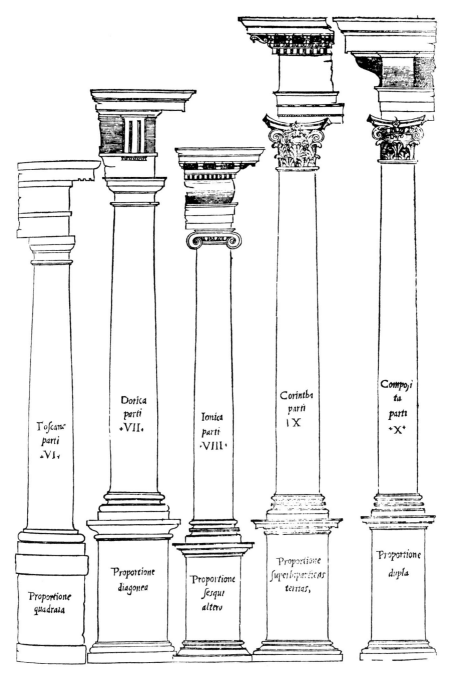

Toscana
parti
·VI·

Proportione
quadrata

Dorica
parti
·VII·

Proportione
diagonea

Ionica
parti
·VIII·

Proportione
sesqui
altera

Corintha
parti
IX

Proportione
superbipartias
tertias,

Compoji
ta
parti
·X·

Proportione
dupla

1   The five Orders according to Serlio, from Book IV (Venice, 1537), fol. IIIIr/127r. Paris,
Bibliothèque Nationale.

Similarly, the architect who adopts the system of the Orders laid out in the fourth book no longer has any need of the Classical models provided in the third book. This apparent contradiction, as I have shown elsewhere, is inherent to the method of Giulio Camillo (Carpo 1993b). From another point of view, the third and fourth books of Serlio simply represent two different stages of assimilation of the new possibilities opened up by the technologising of the image.

In a famous text of 1936, Walter Benjamin reflected on 'The Work of Art in the Age of Mechanical Reproduction' (Benjamin 1936).[6] Understandably, Benjamin was primarily concerned with the great novelties of his own day – photography and film – and the political uses of these new media. Benjamin might have observed that radio – a verbal medium – much more than film, or any other means of communication, allowed Mussolini to galvanise an illiterate public. But Benjamin was not McLuhan. Unfortunately, Benjamin made no more than a token acknowledgement of the first mechanical revolution in the history of the visual arts – the printing of images.

Benjamin distinguishes between the legitimate and illegitimate use of the new media. For example, photographing a Gothic cathedral is illegitimate because Gothic cathedrals were not conceived to be reproducible. A Gothic cathedral is a unique example that cannot be repeated. Every reproduction violates the cathedral's 'aura' and betrays its authenticity. According to Benjamin, it is only with film that 'the work of art reproduced becomes the work of art designed for reproducibility' (Benjamin 1991, 146 [1969, 224]). The film-maker knows from the outset that his or her work will be reproduced – ad libitum, identical – in different locations, and, likewise from the outset, conceives of the product according to these conditions of use.

The progressive technologising of Renaissance images can be described in the same terms. There is a primary phase in which prints reproduce pre-existing works of art – above all examples from antiquity, which were not originally designed to be reproduced. There follows a phase in which the new reproductive technology generates an 'autonomous' artistic process (Benjamin 1991, 141 [1969, 219]).[7] Precisely and knowingly formulated for distribution in a new medium, Serlio's Orders were 'destined for reproduction' right from the start. Printed ad libitum in identical copies (typographical reproduction), they were also meant to be recopied ad libitum in diverse architectural projects (architectural reproduction). Of course the Serlian Orders

---

[6]   On the history of this text (and the various titles Benjamin suggested for the first edition in French) see Benjamin 1972, 982–1020; Benjamin 1991, 117–39.

[7]   The new reproductive technology 'captures a place of its own among the artistic processes'.

standardised design, not building. The Orders are not prefabricated but predesigned. Economies of scale were alien to Cinquecento builders.

The Serlian Orders are a watershed in European architectural history, not because they come in fives or sevens or twelves, not for the forms of the capitals, the terms that describe them, or the proportions of the columns; the novelty comes in the fact that, for the first time, an architectural theory was consciously made to measure for the new and revolutionary medium of printing. Thanks to the distribution of printed books and the standardisation of the xylographic image, Serlio aspired to an 'architecture reduced to a brief and simple method' (Carpo 1993b, 83–139). The inevitable corollary to the stand taken by Serlio, a fundamentally ideological one, is his awareness of the decline in quality inherent to this programme of vulgarisation. An architecture based on the limitless repetition of identical elements is destined to a certain monotony. This is a price that Serlio was more than willing to pay. The result is an architectural programme with ideological and social implications that was received with anything but unanimity upon its publication. Condemned by some, defended by others, it has left an indelible mark.

In the brief span of the opening decades of the Cinquecento, this intersection of printing, the technologising of images, and architectural culture combined to bring about a new architecture. More generally, it created categories of modernity that remained operative until quite recently. The hypostasis of this process is probably a certain notion of visual standardisation that continues to influence – in both negative and positive ways, by being absorbed or refuted – various contemporary phenomena.

This is not an inopportune moment to begin to reflect on all that printing, and the technologising of images (up to and including the development of lithography and photography) have given to or imposed upon architecture in the course of the last five centuries. We should take stock of all that we are about to lose. That which came in with printing will probably go out with it, and we are all curious to know what will take its place. Five hundred years ago a close encounter with the Gutenberg galaxy was enough to change forever the history of architecture. There is no reason to think that the current forays into cyberspace will do any less. Time will tell.

Chapter Nine

SERLIO AND THE REPRESENTATION OF ARCHITECTURE

Vaughan Hart

SERLIO AND THE LOST ILLUSTRATIONS TO VITRUVIUS

IN PUBLISHING THE FIRST TREATISE to deal with the five Orders in a systematic way (in the form of the *Regole generali di architettura* of 1537), Sebastiano Serlio introduced the 'type' of the illustrated architectural rule-book which Hans Blum and Il Vignola (Jacopo Barrozzi) would develop (Dinsmoor 1942; Rosenfeld 1989; Serlio 1996, xi–xxxv). This chapter will discuss Serlio's adaptation of the now familiar, but in his day still relatively novel, interrelated scale projections of plan, section and elevation when illustrating Vitruvian principles. For in the clarification of good, and on occasions bad building practices, Serlio's pioneering woodcuts of architectural elements represented in these projections played a vital role. He lamented the loss of the nine to eleven illustrations to which Vitruvius refers (for example, Vitr.III.v.8), a loss which hindered the clarity of the Roman author's text. Concerning the Ionic volute for example Serlio observes that, 'the text of Vitruvius is difficult to understand, especially since that author promised that the figures of this element together with many other beautiful things would be in his last book, a book which is no longer to be found' (Serlio 1537, fol. XXXVIIv/159v). Vitruvius's enigmatic reference to figures did however provide Serlio with a perfect precedent for an illustrated treatise on the Orders.

Serlio's first known collaboration with an engraver was in 1528, when he published a series of nine plates which illustrate the base, capital and entablature of the three Orders, Doric, Ionic and Corinthian, engraved by Agostino de' Musi (called 'Veneziano') (Dinsmoor 1942, 64–5; Howard 1973; Zerner 1988). In conceiving an illustrated architectural treatise, he was fortunate that developments in the craft of printing since its introduction into Italy in 1464/5 had greatly increased the dimensional accuracy of, and detail possible with woodcut blocks. Indeed, there are very few discrepancies between the dimensions or proportions specified in Serlio's text and those represented in his woodcuts. Developments in printing had equally facilitated the full integration of figures and text, a style of layout for which Serlio's books are famed. Serlio's frequent use of the apparently tautological expression 'visible design' (*disegno visibile/disegno apparente*)[1] to describe his figures underlines the role of the text as a parallel, as it were 'invisible', expression of the design, and emphasises the novelty of his publishing enterprise in producing a fully illustrated Vitruvian treatise. His use of this phrase also points to his achievement in making the text and figures work hand in hand.

Serlio's treatise was produced by its various publishers with astonishing accuracy, as the small lists of errata in the second editions demonstrate. The complexity of production is highlighted by a number of references to the design of the figures in anticipation of the printing process, with, for example, a staircase reduced in size 'because of the narrowness of the page and the print block' (Serlio 1545, fol. 52*v*/37*r*). Serlio, himself a skilled woodcutter, used certain illustrative techniques which were unique in an architecture book: most notable are the cutaway elevational sections in Book III and Book V,[2] and, as this chapter will examine, a drawing projection called *sciografia*, which was apparently defined by Vitruvius.

SERLIO AND VITRUVIUS'S *SCAENOGRAPHIA*

Vitruvius, in the second chapter of his first book, famously specified three kinds of architectural representation (called *ideae*), in the form of icnography (*ichnographia*), orthography (*orthographia*) and scenography (*scaenographia*) (Bartoli 1978; Hui 1993). The first term is defined as the 'plan', and the second as the 'vertical image of the front', which has been interpreted variously as 'elevation' or 'section'. More puzzlingly, however, the third term (*scaenographia*) is defined by Vitruvius as, 'the sketched outline of the front and receding sides, the correspondence of all the lines to the centre of a circle' (Vitr.I.ii.2).[3] As we shall see, Serlio's interpretation of this enigmatic term was crucial in defining the

---

[1] Book IV fol. IIIr/126r; Book VI ['Munich' version, Rosci and Brizio 1966; Fiore 1994] fol. 1r; Book VII p. 1; Book 'VIII' (Fiore 1994) fols. 19v, 21v–22r; *Extraordinario libro*, sig. A2r.

[2] For example, Bramante's dome for St Peter's on fol. XL/66v. This technique was also frequently used in drawings by Giuliano da Sangallo, see Lotz 1977, 19 and fig. 23.

[3] 'Item scaenographia est frontis et laterum abscedentium adumbratio ad circinique centrum omnium linearum responsus.' Here using Harleian MS 2767, reproduced in the trans. F. Granger (1931).

types of three-dimensional projections which appear in his treatise alongside the more clearly defined two-dimensional Vitruvian projections of plan, section and elevation.

At the outset of Serlio's publishing project, in Book IV of 1537, the content of his forthcoming books is outlined. Serlio notes with reference to Vitruvius's drawing definitions that, 'in the third [book] there will be the *Icnografia* – that is, the plan – the *Ortografia* – which is the elevation – and the *Sciografia* [*sic*] – which means the receding side – of a majority of the buildings in Rome, Italy and abroad' (Serlio 1537, fol. IIIr/126r). Subsequently, in this third book, first published in 1540, Serlio repeats that, 'the first thing will be the *icnografia*, that is, the plan, the second the *ortografia*, that is, the elevation (others call it the section)[4] and the third thing will be the *sciografia*, that is, the front and the sides of whatever it is' (Serlio 1540, fol. VI/50v).

It should be noted here that rather than use the established Vitruvian term *scenografia*, Serlio on both occasions cites a variant term *sciografia* derived from the Greek word *skia* meaning 'painted shadows' (Keuls 1975). Serlio certainly did not invent this variant term, however, since it was to be found in a published version of Vitruvius's text in the enigmatic passage on architectural representation. For whilst the first two editions of Fra Giocondo's *Vitruvius* (Venice, 1511, 4–6, and Florence, 1512, 6–7) had given *scenographia* in this passage, by the third edition (Florence, 1522, fols. 10v–11r) this term had been revised to *sciographia*. Indeed, as if to emphasise the apparent interchangeability of these two terms, Serlio himself switches to using *scenographia* in his next published work, Book II (on linear perspective) of 1545. This, the more common of the two terms, is here defined with greater precision by Serlio, with direct reference to Vitruvius's famous passage, in noting, 'I would indeed say that perspective is what Vitruvius calls *scenografia*, that is the front and the sides of a building and also of any other thing, whether a plane or a body' (Serlio 1545, fol. 25r/18r).

Serlio's emphasis in this definition ('I would indeed say ...') and the revision in the later edition of Fra Giocondo's *Vitruvius* both hint at a contemporary debate concerning the interpretation and correctness of the term *scaenographia*, as opposed to *sciographia*, in Vitruvius's enigmatic and frequently corrupt text. For Ermolao Barbaro (1454–93) in his glossary to Pliny of 1492/93 had emphasised that *scaenographia*, rather than *sciographia*, was the correct term in the Vitruvian representational triad since, as he put it, 'painting is not of the plan alone, as with the ichnographia, nor of the front, as with the orthographia, but

---

[4] Cesariano had illustrated *orthographia* with a section through Milan cathedral, and is therefore one of the 'others' to which Serlio refers.

of the whole building, which the Greek custom is to call the scena, that is, small tent' (Barbaro 1492/93, glossary, sig. [fv]r).[5] And whilst Cesariano had also given *scenographia* in his Italian translation of the Roman's text (Como, 1521, fol. xiiii*v*), his commentary equated the two terms since *scaena* (or *skene*) 'for the Greeks means a small tent for making shade' and *skia* 'in Greek means to use shadow or imitation of an object illuminated'.[6]

Serlio is very scrupulous in his use of architectural terminology (Jelmini 1986) and would have been well aware of this debate. His attempt to resolve the contemporary confusion concerning the meaning of these variant Vitruvian terms by explicitly defining *scenografia* as linear perspective makes it clear that this can not be what he means by the earlier term *sciografia*, despite his apparently similar definition of this earlier term as a 'front and side view'. For although *sciografia* is occasionally translated as 'perspective' (Dinsmoor 1942, 66), it is in fact defined by Serlio not as *prospettiva* ('perspective') but somewhat enigmatically as *lo scorcio* (meaning 'the receding side' or 'the foreshortening'). Examining Serlio's woodcuts it becomes evident that *sciografia* refers to the (apparently) more sketchy type of projection, common enough in Books III and IV,[7] in which a side-face drawn to a vanishing point is combined with an *ortografia*, or 'true' elevation: on this face the details are obviously flat, as the section line shows, and as such are not distorted but can be easily measured using compasses (plate 1). Serlio thus employs two variant Vitruvian terms to make a clear distinction between this form of 'false' perspective (called *sciografia*) and that which is 'correctly' constructed and which he defines as *scenografia*.

Indeed, following the publication of Book II, with its definition of *scenografia* as 'perspective', in Book VII Serlio returns to the term *sciografia* which he uses, perfectly consistently, in reference to a figure which has no perspective in it at all (plate 2). Here for the first time Serlio helpfully defines *sciografia* with reference to a particular illustration, in noting, 'The figure above the plan represents the true view [*il vero*] of the building raised above ground . . . In this you can see . . . the *sciographia* [*sic*], that is the parts which recede and the fronts together'

---

[5] Revised in *Hermolai Barbari Patritii Veneti in C. Plinii Naturalis Historiæ Libros Castigationes* (Basle, 1534), 507. Barbaro's interpretation was to be quoted by Philandrier, Serlio's pupil, in his famous annotations to Vitruvius (Rome, 1544, 10).

[6] This interpretation was repeated in the commentary to Vitruvius by 'Durantino' (Venice, 1524).

[7] For example, Book III fols. XI/53r, XLIX/71r, LXXXI/87r, CVII/100r, Book IV fols. XLI/163r, XLIIII/164v, LI/171v.

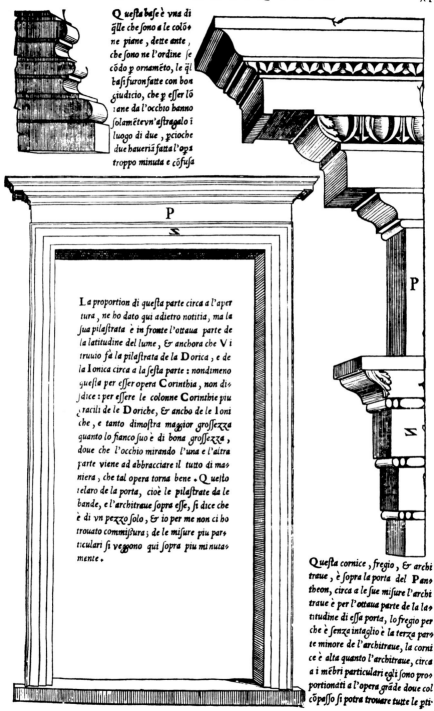

Q uesta base è vna di
q̃lle che sono a le colõ￫
ne piane, dette ante,
che sono ne l'ordine se￾
cõdo p ornamẽto, le q̃l
basi furon fatte con bon
giudicio, che p esser lõ
tane da l'occhio hanno
solamẽtevn'astragalo i
luogo di due, pcioche
due haueriã fatta l'ope
troppo minuta e cõfusa

La proportion di questa parte circa a l'aper
tura, ne ho dato qui adietro notitia, ma la
sua pilastrata è in fronte l'ottaua parte de
la latitudine del lume, & anchora che V i
truuio fà la pilastrata de la D orica, e de
la I onica circa a la sesta parte: nondimeno
questa per esser opera Corinthia, non di￾
sdice: per essere le colonne Corinthie piu
gracili de le D oriche, & ancho de le I oni
che, e tanto dimostra maggior grossezza
quanto lo fianco suo è di bona grossezza,
doue che l'occhio mirando l'una e l'altra
parte viene ad abbracciare il tutto di ma￾
niera, che tal opera torna bene ♦ Q uesto
telaro de la porta, cioè le pilastrate da le
bande, e l'architraue sopra esse, si dice che
è di vn pezzo solo, & io per me non ci ho
trouato commissura; de le misure piu par￾
ticulari si veggono qui sopra piu minuta￾
mente ♦

Questa cornice, fregio, & archi
traue, è sopra la porta del Pan￾
theon, circa a le sue misure l'archi
traue è per l'ottaua parte de la la￾
titudine di essa porta, lo fregio per
che è senza intaglio è la terza par￾
te minore de l'architraue, la corni
ce è alta quanto l'architraue, circa
a i mẽbri particulari egli sono pro￾
portionati a l'opera grãde doue col
cõpasso si potrà trouare tutte le pti·

1 *Sciografia* applied by Serlio to a detail of the Pantheon, from Book III (Venice, 1540),
fol. XI/53r. Cambridge University Library.

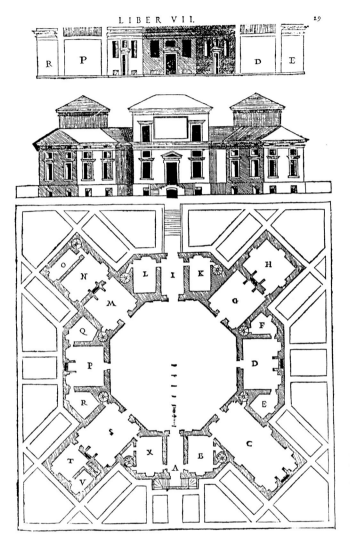

2 *Sciografia* applied by Serlio to an 'ideal' design, from Book VII (Frankfurt, 1575), p. 29. Cambridge University Library.

(Serlio 1575, 28).[8] These 'parts which recede' are obviously not shown in perspective, rather they are perpendicular or 'true', that is, drawn in elevation but concertinaed. Thus, the projection called *sciografia* is here clearly demonstrated by Serlio as being distinct from linear perspective, a fact which underlines both the status of *scenografia* as exclusively

---

[8]   The MS of Book VII (Fiore 1994) has a different text at this point, but one which helps to clarify the meaning of the expression *il vero*: 'La figura sopra la pianta dimostra tutta la massa de l'edificio, cioè quanto se ne può vedere': (The figure above the plan shows the whole mass of the building, that is, everything which can be seen).

concerned with perspective representation and Serlio's purposeful use of Vitruvian terminology.

The 'sciographic' combination of an elevation and side view is common enough in the drawings of Roman remains produced by Italian Renaissance artists and architects: the projection is, for example, frequently used by the Sangallos (Saalman 1959, 102–6; Howard 1973, 515; Lotz 1977; Frommel 1994; Evans 1995, 107–8).[9] However, the technique had rarely been used in a published architectural treatise before Serlio's books. Sagredo has a minor sketchy example (sig. Eii*r*), but none can be found in the figures of Colonna, Cesariano, Durantino, Philandrier or Lefreri.[10] Moreover, whilst Alberto Jelmini has argued (without explanation) that Serlio's variation in Vitruvian terminology reflects his particular reliance on the text in Cesariano (for the term *scenografia* or 'perspective') together with that in the revised, third edition of Fra Giocondo (for *sciografia*) (Jelmini 1986, 14), confusingly the earlier editions of Fra Giocondo had shown a front elevation with side view (of a palazzo) to illustrate not *sciographia* but *scaenographia*, whilst Cesariano famously illustrated *scaenographia* by showing Milan cathedral in what we would today describe as 'section' (Hui 1993), certainly not 'perspective'. Serlio is thus the first to exploit the established 'technical' drawing technique of *sciografia* in a printed book and, following the revised Fra Giocondo, to define this form of 'false' perspective in Vitruvian terms. Indeed Serlio's plates of 1528 illustrating the Doric and the Ionic entablature can now be identified as early experiments in the projection of *sciografia*. Just as the first printed books had imitated manuscripts (Febvre and Martin 1993, 78), so these early architectural woodcuts naturally enough imitated architectural drawings. Furthermore, Serlio is also the first treatise writer to define the Vitruvian term *scaenographia* as linear perspective. Jean Martin, who provided the parallel French translation in Serlio's book on perspective of 1545, when translating Vitruvius two years later, not surprisingly echoed Serlio by referring to *scaenographia* as 'commonly called perspective' (Vitruvius 1547, sig. [Avi]*r*).[11] And modern editors of Vitruvius have repeated this definition in their translations of the Roman's text,[12] a repetition based on a tradition which we can now see to have been either established or first recorded by Serlio, rather

---

[9]   See, for example, Sangallo drawings: Uffizi 1413*r–v* and 1716*v*.

[10]   Comprising Antonio Lefreri's *Speculum* (Rome, 1540–92) and his engravings in Antonio Labacco's *Libro* (Rome, *c.*1572).

[11]   See also Jean Goujon's 'To the Readers', where scenography is again defined as 'perspective'.

[12]   These editors include: Granger (1931); Fensterbusch (1964); Choisy (1971); and Fleury (1990).

than on any actual evidence of the knowledge of the rules of linear perspective in antiquity itself (Keuls 1975, 8; Panofsky 1927/97, 38–9).[13]

The key distinction between *sciografia* and *scenografia* as defined by Serlio clearly concerns the dimensional (and therefore proportional) accuracy of the two projections: for whilst linear perspective surrenders all claim to mensural accuracy in favour of spatial realism, *sciografia* retains orthogonal co-ordination. Alberti in *De re aedificatoria* had distinguished between the dimensionally accurate drawings necessary to the art of building and the traditional rendered perspectives of the painter: for whilst the painter,

> takes pains to emphasize the relief of objects in paintings with shading and diminishing lines and angles; the architect rejects shading, but takes his projections from the ground plan [*fundamenti descriptione*] and, without altering the lines and by maintaining the true angles, reveals the extent and shape of each elevation [*figuras frontis*] and side – he is one who desires his work to be judged not by deceptive appearances but according to certain calculated standards. (Alberti 1988, Book II ch. 1, 34; see Saalman 1959, 105)

Baldassare Castiglione and Raphael, in their famous letter of *c.*1519 to Pope Leo X, at first rejected perspective as of no use in recording the measurements of ancient monuments in Rome. However, in a revised copy of this letter, both theorists accepted the utility of perspective in representing depth, but it remained necessarily distinct from the more favoured projections of plan (cited as *la pianta*), section (*la parte di dentro*) and elevation (*la parte fuora*) (Pedretti 1962, 170–71; Bonelli 1978).

The insistence by Castiglione and Raphael on the utility and unique status of the three orthogonal projections indicates the relative infrequency of, or the lack of precision in, their combined use to the same scale in late medieval building practices. Certainly Villard de Honnecourt included plans and elevations of various cathedrals in his sketch-book (*c.*1225–50) (Bowie 1959), whilst the famous plan/section of medieval Milan cathedral dates from around 1390 (Frommel 1994, 101–3). But details were often decided on site, and then from plan and model alone (Lotz 1977, 5; Frommel 1994, 102). Saalman has even concluded that Gothic drawings and wooden models 'contain few or no precise measurements', and that plans, sections, and elevations 'began to be practically accepted only at the beginning of the sixteenth

---

[13] The rules of linear perspective were in fact rediscovered, or more likely invented, in the fifteenth century by Filippo Brunelleschi (see Kemp 1990, 9–21).

century when the old architectural system [of perspective drawings] no longer functioned effectively' (Saalman 1959, 104–5) – that is, coincident with Serlio's training by Peruzzi.

Following Cesariano's scale (or 'measured') woodcuts of Milan cathedral in plan and section (with part elevation), Serlio's pioneering scale woodcuts of buildings and fragments further reflected this emerging need for mensural accuracy in architectural representation (Frommel 1994, 114, 117). Indeed, in those instances where designs are illustrated by Serlio in plan, section and elevation, all three projections are represented to exactly the same scale (for example, in the case of the Pantheon in Book III and the churches of Book V). Since neither Alberti nor Raphael had made reference to the Vitruvian representational terms when advocating the three orthogonal projections, Serlio in so doing was amongst the first of the theorists to legitimise these renewed architectural drawing practices with direct reference to the Roman's text. Here, as elsewhere in his treatise, Serlio thus codified modern practices with reference to those of antiquity.

In his third book Serlio gives further information concerning the projections used in his woodcuts. He emphasises the need for mensural exactness when commenting on a section through the Pantheon,

> do not be at all surprised if, in these things which touch on perspective, no foreshortening, depth or plane can be seen, because I wanted to raise these things up from the plan showing only the heights in scale, so that the measurements would not be lost in the diminishing resulting from the foreshortened sides. However, later, in the book on perspective, I shall indeed show things foreshortened correctly, in different ways on surfaces and on bodies. (Serlio 1540, fol. IX/52r)

This passage makes clear that the foreshortened sides shown on the subsequent sciographic sections and elevations in Book III are not drawn 'correctly': rather, their foreshortening merely 'touches' on the art of perspective. The sketched sides serve to emphasise both depth and profile, as would shading. Indeed, the frequent representation of (impossible) shading on these (flat) elevations serves this purpose more literally, and underlines the appropriateness of the term *sciografia*, developed from the Greek original (*skia*), to define this projection. Apparently naïve, Serlio's sciographic views are in fact precise and useful projections. Moreover they are less abstract, more 'painterly', views than are the orthogonal projections of plan and section. Serlio's *sciografia* can be seen as a sister to the well-established projection which appeared to look into a bisected building, the so-called 'cavalier projection', which united the accuracy of a section with a one-point perspective visualisation of the interior (Lotz 1977, 30–32; Onians 1988, 175). This form had been popular with Peruzzi and, although less accurate than the section, is also used by Serlio (Book III, fols. XXXII–XXXIV/62v–63v). Serlio thus goes further than Raphael in his acceptance of perspective by cleverly uniting the mensurally accurate orthogonal projections as recently developed by the architect with the traditional shaded perspective as rendered by the painter (Lotz 1977, 185; Onians 1988, 175). This in effect 'corrects' the contemporary shift in architectural representation, initiated by Alberti, from three-dimensional realism towards two-dimensional abstraction (Lotz 1977; Frommel 1994, 117; Evans 1995, 107–21). *Sciografia* might also be identified as the precursor of axonometric and isonometric projections (the former of which was first used in a printed book by Antonio Rusconi), in which elements are rendered in three dimensions but to scale.

In summation, Serlio in fact uses eight types of projection in illustrating his text: namely, the plan, either of a single level or of several combined (*icnografia*), the section (*profilo*), the elevation (*ortografia*), the elevational section (elevation/section), the elevational section with depth,[14] the sectional 'perspective' ('cavalier projection'), the elevational 'perspective' (*sciografia*), and linear perspective (*scenografia*, shown in Book II only). In the case of the latter two, his terminology effectively signifies the various levels of mensural and/or perspectival accuracy in these projections. Serlio has considerable reverence for the optical power of perspective and is clearly keen that its rules be understood, a fact which might explain why he is so careful to distinguish between this precise art and the more abstract *sciografia*. For whilst *sciografia* was a practical 'tool', *scenografia* was an integral part of the scenic illusion represented in a painting or a stage scene.

Serlio's definition of the Vitruvian *scaenographia* as linear perspective has one further important consequence. For architects, scenography was specifically concerned with the design of theatrical space (the Greek word for which is *skenographia*). Hence Daniele Barbaro was to emphasise in *La pratica della perspettiva* (Venice, 1568/9) that the Vitruvian representational trio could not have included *scaenographia*; rather, Barbaro sides with those who argued that Vitruvius meant *sciografia* (but which is here interpreted as 'section'; see Bartoli 1978, 202; Pérez-Gómez 1994). Serlio's emphatic definition of *scaenographia* as 'perspective' has the effect of closely identifying this illusionistic projection with the work of the scenographer or stage designer; this work was after all commonly undertaken by architects, to whom

---

[14] For example, the Temple of Vesta, Book III fol. XXVII/60v.

Serlio's treatise was principally addressed. To a contemporary reader Serlio's terminology in Book II would have emphasised the utility of his perspective examples to the construction of theatrical scenes, a fact underlined by the presence in this book of a concluding section specifically concerned with perspective stage scenery. Indeed in describing the uses of perspective at the start, Serlio singles out the 'beautiful scenery' that Girolamo Genga painted for Francesco Maria, Duke of Urbino (Serlio 1545, fol. 25v/18v).[15] And so the use of the term *scenografia* in Book II and nowhere else in the treatise perhaps indicates that the entire book on perspective was principally intended by Serlio as a theatrical manual, and not just the book's concluding part.

SCENOGRAFIA IN PRACTICE: SERLIO'S THEATRE WOODCUTS

Book II concludes with a full realisation of the art of scenography in the form of a plan and a section of a temporary theatre, accompanied by three 'elevational perspectives' of stage scenes (plate 3).[16] Once again, these figures are all drawn to an identical scale. In these woodcuts Serlio adapted the ancient crescent-shaped theatre with its scenes for comic, tragic, and satiric drama (as described by Vitruvius, v.vi), to fit within a rectangular courtyard. Here, as elsewhere in the treatise, Serlio's woodcuts represent a theoretical 'ideal' which the architect was supposed to adapt to suit the actual conditions on site. Whilst the forward-facing stage façades were fabricated in 'true' elevation, the angled side elevations were painted and modelled in perspective drawn to a common vanishing point. This combination represented a form of three-dimensional *sciografia*, with the side elevations creating the illusion of a deep scene on a necessarily constricted stage. This illusion was further accentuated by a raked stage which was painted with a pattern of diminishing squares and drawn to the same vanishing point as the side elevations: as a result, the appearance of a horizontal base-line was given to these side faces.

In constructing this illusionary stage, Serlio establishes the vanishing point not on the rear courtyard wall, as was common practice in the Italian Renaissance, but as far behind this wall as the sloping stage extends forward of it. A physical model was first to be constructed to

---

[15] Serlio would have learnt about perspective stage design from Peruzzi: see Casotti, in Fagiolo and Madonna 1987, 339ff.

[16] Serlio built a temporary theatre at the Palazzo Porto for a production on 16 February 1539.

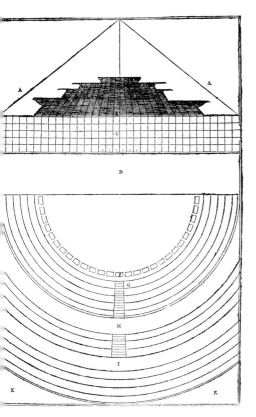

3 Serlio's theatre
section and plan, and
the comic scene,
from Book II (Paris,
1545), fols. 64r/43v,
66v/45r, and unpag./
46r. Paris,
Bibliothèque
Nationale.

Scena Comica.

4   Section through Serlio's theatre showing the actual distortion of stage buildings necessary
construct the scene. Computer model: Vaughan Hart.

enable carpenters to measure the degree of distortion necessary in the
side elements for the overall perspective scene to work. Serlio notes
that, 'since to set [the vanishing point] it would be necessary to break
down the wall – something which cannot be done – I have always
made a small, carefully measured model [*modello*] in wood and card and
easily scaled up each individual thing to a very accurate, full-size
version' (Serlio 1545, fol. 65*v*/44*v*).

   If we follow Serlio's advice and build a model of the theatre with its
comic scene, a longitudinal view down the centre-line demonstrates
the actual distortion of each element which was necessary to construct
the scenes to conform with Serlio's woodcuts (on this scale-less computer model, see Hart and Day 1995) (plate 4). Further, intentional
discrepancies between these woodcuts are highlighted by building the
model. The vanishing point of the scene woodcut is in fact much
higher than that shown on the section, for example, and represents a
raked stage floor which would have been highly impractical. The
obvious reason for this vertical adjustment of the eye level in the
perspective scenes is to make the floor squares visible for the vital
purpose of scaling-off units of height and depth when building the

scene, a method made clear by Serlio in his preceding examples of perspective (Orrell 1988; Hart and Day 1995). Certainly Serlio intended these scene woodcuts as construction diagrams, akin to his sciographic projections (in their inclusion of both receding sides and 'true' elevations), and not mere scenic 'pictures' as is often implied. It is clear, however, that these scenes should be built to the more practical vanishing point which is shown on the section and which corresponds to human proportion in matching the eye level of an actor standing on the front stage.

Serlio demarcated the seating of the theatre to correspond with the social structure of his day, as indeed he believed the Roman theatre had been arranged. Hence the most eminent nobles occupied the benches at the front, the 'noblest ladies' and lesser noblewomen were given the first tier, noblemen the second tier, lesser noblemen the back seats whilst ordinary citizens were allowed to stand at the back. A line drawn level with the vanishing point on Serlio's section shows that this optimum (undistorted) view of the stage buildings would have been enjoyed by a noblewoman sitting on the third row, although the exact position in fact coincides with a central flight of steps which is indicated on the plan alone: incidentally, the higher vanishing point of the scene woodcuts aligned with seating at the back of the theatre specified for 'lesser noblemen'.

Indeed, the model reveals the distortion of Serlio's fixed, or 'constructed', perspective scenes when viewed from seats remote from this single optimum viewing position. In other words, with this model we can for the first time test the effectiveness of the artistry of the Italian Renaissance scenographer. The model demonstrates, for example, that the scene viewed by an ordinary citizen standing in the centre at the back was in fact less distorted than were the stage buildings viewed by the noblemen seated on the outer benches (plate 5). The benches at the front give an eye level coincident with the height of the front stage – and which is indeed specified by Serlio as 'at eye level' (Serlio 1545, fol. 63r/43v) but which is obviously well below the vanishing point of the scene. This suggests that a better 'fit' between scenic coherence and status of viewer would have resulted if the seats had been organised not according to the distance from the stage but rather from the centre line, allocating the central wedge of seats opposite the vanishing point to the noblemen and those either side in decreasing order of social status. Steps could have separated the various social grades. However, these optical considerations were evidently outweighed by the precedent of the Roman theatre in which, as Vitruvius records, the senators occupied the front seats in the 'orchestra' (Vitr.v.vi.2). Indeed, the fact that the ideal viewpoint coincides with a flight of steps serves to underline the relative unimportance of this point and Serlio's faith

5   View of Serlio's stage from the back of the theatre [a] compared with that from
the front benches [b] (facing page). Computer model: Vaughan Hart.

in the entire audience's appreciation of the scenic illusion, produced by
means of the scenographic art, irrespective of any distortion. The
model mostly confirms Serlio's own observations on the comic scene
that,

> the open balconies ... are very effective on the foreshortened faces.
> Similarly, some cornices with mouldings projecting from their out-
> side corners which are cut out around and matched with other
> painted cornices are extremely effective. In the same way, houses
> that have a great projection work very well indeed – like the 'Moon
> Inn' here. (Serlio 1545, fol. 67r/46r)

Serlio's application of contemporary perspective practices to the
ancient stage was naturally legitimised by his earlier attribution to the
Romans of a full understanding of linear perspective identified as
Vitruvius's *scaenographia*. The importance of the perspective stage in
Serlio's treatise is somewhat obscured by the numerical arrangement of
the books, in which the theatre treatise is awkwardly placed before the

Roman monuments of Book III. When these books are rearranged chronologically, however, the perspective stage directly precedes the twelve sacred temples of Book V: this was published two years after Book II once again in Paris and in a bilingual edition. In Cesariano's Vitruvius the ancient theatre was itself represented as the apotheosis of the 'cosmic' building, whilst Serlio's friend Giulio Camillo conceived of the theatre as a Neoplatonic 'diagram' in which all knowledge, the entire encyclopedia, was encoded. In much the same way, the central importance to Serlio of the theatre, or rather of the art of scenography, lay in its universal application of Renaissance arts and its power to reveal the underlying order of nature. Hence he describes the construction lines in perspective drawing as *linee occulte*, whilst he remarks with evident enthusiasm that on some stages, 'the rising of the sun, its progression and then at the end of the play its setting can be seen, done with such cleverness that many of the viewers are amazed by it' (Serlio 1545, fol. 64v/44r). Scenography is Serlio's most ambitious application of the power of perspective to represent space. Moreover, his three stage perspectives are a further ingenious attempt to communicate both form *and* dimension, the essential unity between which was expressed, or so Serlio believed, in Vitruvius's concept of architectural representation.

Chapter Ten

ON GUILLAUME PHILANDRIER:
FORMS AND NORM

Frédérique Lemerle

A FRENCH HUMANIST IN ITALY

GUILLAUME PHILANDRIER PUBLISHED *In decem libros M. Vitruvii Pollionis de Architectura Annotationes* in Rome in 1544, a commentary on Vitruvius which rapidly became the fundamental reference for subsequent Vitruvian translators, commentators and publishers. That this book is also a fundamental text for the theory of the Orders in the Renaissance is however less well known. Philandrier was a renowned humanist of his day (Galle 1572, 33), a friend of François Rabelais[1] and also a scholar who had spent a long time in Italy in the service of the Bishop of Rodez and French ambassador to Venice, Georges d'Armagnac. Philandrier was initiated into architecture in Venice by Sebastiano Serlio at the same time as Serlio was engaged in publishing the *Regole generali di architettura* (Venice, 1537). Shortly after Philandrier's final return to France from Italy, he designed the Classical gable added to the Gothic west front of Rodez cathedral, a precocious realisation of the Counter-Reformation church façade of which the Gesù in Rome was a later manifestation (plate 1).

Philandrier (1505–65) was born in Châtillon-sur-Seine (France) and in 1533 became the private secretary to Georges d'Armagnac. In d'Armagnac's entourage he visited Italy three times, first in 1536 when François I appointed the bishop as ambassador to the Venetian Republic (1536–9), second when d'Armagnac was made French ambassador to Pope Paul III in Rome (1540–45), and third in 1547 when d'Armagnac, by then a cardinal resident in Rome, was called on to prepare for the election of the next Pope (1547–50). These three periods in Italy allowed Philandrier not only to associate with the

---

[1] See the 'Briefve Déclaration' (*Le Quart Livre*, Lyons, 1548).

Gable of the west front of Rodez cathedral, designed by Philandrier.

greatest artistic and literary figures of the time (Aretino, Titian, Antonio da Sangallo the Younger, Michelangelo . . .), and the most eminent members of the Roman intelligentsia such as the humanist clerics Angelo Colocci and Marcello Cervini (the future Pope Marcello II), but also to acquire direct knowledge of the most important architectural creations of the time (such as the construction of St Peter's, Palazzo Farnese, the Laurenziana library, etc.) and to combine this with detailed study of the ancient ruins in Verona, Rimini, Spoleto, Naples and, especially, Rome (Wiebenson 1988, 67–74; Lemerle 1991, vii–xv).

It was through Cervini, a keen scholar of alchemy, medicine and architecture, that Philandrier was admitted to the Accademia della Virtù (of which Cervini was a member). This Roman academy had been founded by Claudio Tolomei from Siena during the winter of 1540–41 to develop the study in, and publication of, Roman antiquities, and notably to publish an edition of Vitruvius with a commentary, destined never to see the light of day (Tolomei 1547; Pagliara 1986, 67–85). Moreover, Philandrier associated with the Sangallos: Antonio da Sangallo was interested in the theoretical problems arising from the reading of the *De Architectura*, and his brother Giovanni Battista was working on a translation of the antique treatise, annotating and illustrating a copy of the *editio princeps* (Pagliara 1988, 179–206). As a result of his dual education, humanist and architectural, Philandrier was in the perfect position to make a synthesis of Serlio's theory of the Orders and contemporary Vitruvian research.

THE *ANNOTATIONES* OF 1544 AND 1552

Philandrier published his *Annotationes* on the treatise of Vitruvius, an illustrated Latin commentary on the *De Architectura* written in note form (*annotationes*), in Rome in 1544 at the press of Andrea Dossena (Philandrier 1544). These annotations are arranged in books and chapters around short quotations of Vitruvius. In addition to the commentary, there is in Book III a 'digression' on the five architectural Orders, a text which is fundamental for the architectural theory of the Cinquecento (Lemerle 1994a, 33–41) (plate 2). As he had done for his edition of Quintilian a few years previously (Philandrier 1535), Philandrier also proposed corrections (*castigationes*) when the Vitruvian text seemed to be corrupt. The work was reprinted the year after in Paris, by the printers Jacob Kerver and Michel Fezandat (Philandrier 1545).

The *Annotationes* were published again in Lyons, in 1552, at the print shop of Jean de Tournes, in an enriched version (Philandrier 1552). In this, the text of the Roman edition was revised (and made a third longer) and has for each chapter the corresponding text from the *De Architectura*; Philandrier was not, however, responsible for the Vitruvian text. The *Annotationes* of 1552 were posthumously reprinted in 1586, in Geneva (Philandrier 1586; Lemerle 1994b, 617–29).

PHILANDRIER'S 'DIGRESSION': THE SERLIAN HERITAGE

The 'Digression', a small treatise on the Orders which Philandrier added to his commentary on Vitruvius's third book (Philandrier 1552, 96–110), is presented by its author as a synthesis derived from the *De Architectura*, contemporary treatises and observation of antique monuments. His main theoretical source was neither Alberti nor Diego de Sagredo (although he was occasionally inspired by them) but Serlio, who was the first to describe in a systematic way all five architectural Orders (Serlio 1537): that is, the three Greek Orders (Doric, Ionic, Corinthian) and the two Latin Orders (Tuscan and Composite).

The 'Digression' takes the form of an illustrated description of the five antique Orders, including the Composite (as Serlio had done in

Epiſtylio vnde pendent guttæ ſex , CAPITVLI,
Regula. Cimatium, Plinthus, Echinus, Annuli tres , Hy=
potrachelium . CO=
LVMNÆ. Aſtra=
galus , Apophygis ſupe=
rior, & Apophygis inſe=
rior. BASIS. To=
rus ſuperior , Regula ,
Scotia . Regula , Torus
inferior, Plinthus. STY
LOBAT Æ. Coro=
nicis . Regula , Cyma=
tium. Aſtragalus , Re=
gula. Quadratū diago=
nium . Baſis . Regula,
Aſtragalus, Torus, Plin
thus.

SEQVITVR ge
nus tertium. Ionicum, in
quo explicando, non licet
quod in ſuperioribus, in=
cipere à ſumma trabea=
tione, ideſt Coronice, ſed
quod ima trabs, ideſt Epi
ſtylium, eſt veluti modu=
lus quo i dimetiēdis aliis
partibus vſuri ſumus,
inde initium capere ne=
ceſſe eſt . Epiſtylii Io=
nici non eſt ſimplex ra=

2　Doric Order from Philandrier, *In decem libros M. Vitruvii Pollionis de Architectura Annotationes* (Rome, 1544), p. 79.

1537), an Order not mentioned by Vitruvius but common enough on antique architecture. Philandrier not only analyses the Orders in the same way as his master, going from the most solid to the most slender, he also follows Serlio very closely in reproducing some of the individual details. Indeed, Philandrier gives each Order the same, specific pedestal as that described by Serlio (1537) (Vitruvius never discusses pedestals); he reproduces for each Order Serlio's bases (particularly Serlio's modified Ionic base), and each Order has an identical capital to that specified by Serlio (except, that is, for the Ionic capital). The entablatures are also exactly the same as those by Serlio: the Corinthian entablature, with dentils and ovolo mouldings, matches the first Corinthian entablature illustrated in Serlio's Book IV (1537, fol. XLVIII*v*/170*r*); the Composite entablature with its characteristic modillions in the frieze also reproduces the Serlian model (plate 3). Philandrier even agrees concerning the proportions of the various mouldings rarely specified by Vitruvius, such as the astragal and necking of the Tuscan column, and the cymatium (*scima*) and band above the Ionic corona (Serlio 1537, fols. IIII*v*/127*v*, XXXIX*r*/161*r* respectively). He equally adopts the modern expression 'Composite' Order[2] (Serlio 1537, fol. LXI*v*/183*r*; Pauwels 1989, 29–46; Zampa 1993, 37–60) and the identification of the Attic base with the Doric base (Serlio 1537, fol. XVIII*r*/139*r*).

THE ORIGINALITY OF THE 'DIGRESSION'

Whilst Philandrier's debt to Serlio is obvious, this is not to say that the 'Digression' is unoriginal. The Frenchman goes into greater detail than does Serlio in discussing the members of the Orders. As for pedestals, he enumerates in detail the different elements which compose their bases and cornices, as well as their proportions, whereas Serlio merely points out the general measurements of the three parts that characterise the pedestal (i.e. base, dado, cornice), and for their respective subdivisions refers the reader to the five plates which represent each of the Orders in its entirety (Serlio 1537, fols. VI*r*/129*r*, XIX*r*/141*r*, XXXIX*v*/161*v*, XLIX*r*/170*v*, LXII*r*/183*v*). Moreover, Philandrier improves on some points. For example, his significant contribution concerning the thorny problem of how to draw the Ionic volute is an advance on both Alberti and Serlio (Günther 1988, 222–5).[3] Alberti's volute comprised only two turns (Alberti 1966, Book VII ch. 8, 577), and Serlio's, although having three turns, is rather oval in shape as a result of its

---

[2] 'Genus italicum, mixtum sive compositum.'
[3] Vitruvius only explains how to draw the first turn (III.v.5–6).

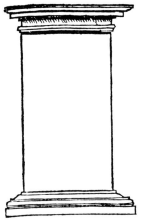

Stylobata proportionis est dupla, cui additur Vtrinque pars octaua pro Coronice, & basi, sed illa sumitur ab Ionica, aut Corinthia, hac à Corinthia.

Compositus Stylobata.

Compositi siue Italici generis partium nomina & series: Trabeationis, regula, cymatium, corona, mutili in Zophoro, fascia epistylij prima, fascia secunda, fascia tertia, Capituli, cymatium, abacus, flos in abaco scalptus, Volutæ inter abacum & echinum emergentes, echinus, caulis, folia summa, id est minima: folia media, folia ima, Columna, astragalus, apophyges cum annulis superior & inferior, Basis, torus superior, regula, scotia superior, regula, astragalus prior, astragalus posterior, regula, scotia inferior, regula, torus inferior, plinthus, Stylobatæ, Coronicis, cymatium, corona, sima, aut cymatiū, corona, Zophorus, astragalus: quadratum proportionis dupla, Basis, astragalus, sima inuersa, torulus, plinthus.

Composita integra columnatio, cum trabeatione.

Perfeci quanta potui diligentia, Vt quæ ab alijs de his quinq generibus tradita essent, ipse excolerem, aut prætermissa, ex Romanorum monimentis ruinisq adijcerem Nec tamen Velim quæ à me scripta sunt, sancta esse, Vt non liceat Vel latum Vnguem discedere. Nolim è contrario mihi obijciat quisquam, ab antiquis architectis non semper habitam esse harum omnium partium, aut dimensionis rationem. Ista à me cæterisq ita tradita sunt, Vt qui sequetur, perbelle genus à genere secernat. Eum autem Archite-

● 3   *ctum*

3   Composite Order from Philandrier, *Annotationes* (Lyons, 1552 ed.), p. 109.

construction from half-circles (Serlio 1537, fols. XXXVIII*v*–XXXVIII*r*/
159*v*–160*r*). Philandrier's volute on the other hand, taken from a spiral
by Dürer, is constructed through octants and its progressive spiral gives
it a perfectly round shape (plate 4). Furthermore, Philandrier critised
Serlio in several respects: he disapproved of the latter's Corinthian
abacus whose horns are formed outside the square used to create it
(Lemerle 1994c, 64–72). Philandrier differs from Serlio on the proportions of the columns, for although retaining for the Tuscan, Doric,
Ionic, Corinthian and Composite columns the ratios of 6, 7, 8, 9 and
10 (using the diameter as the module) recommended by Serlio, he
applies these ratios not to the entire column, that is with the base and
capital included (Serlio 1537, fols. IIII*v*/127*v*, XVIII*r*/140*r*, XXXVI*v*/158*v*,
XLVII*v*/169*r*, LXI*v*/183*r*), but to the shaft alone. The corresponding
columns are 7, 8, 8⅝, 10½, and 11½ diameters in height and are thereby
closer to antique models and contemporary practice (Frommel 1973,
124, 162). Above all, Philandrier proposes not a collection of individual
models as Serlio had done but a structured text where the forms are
described and integrated into a formalised system.

THE RULE FOR THE ORDERS: THE LINGUISTIC MODEL

The great familiarity of Philandrier with the antique monuments, his
frequent contact with the Roman Vitruvian circle, and notably his
membership of the Accademia della Virtù, opened up for him new
perspectives. There is no doubt that this influence prompted him to
revise Serlio's doctrine and to elaborate a new synthesis that took into
account new approaches. Whilst it would be simplistic to consider
Philandrier as the 'spokesperson' of the Vitruvian academy (in fact the
very multidisciplinary nature of this group, with scholars specialising in
different areas, led to its project never being realised (Pagliara 1988,
81)), nevertheless with his intellectual education Philandrier was
undoubtedly the best qualified to render explicit what Serlio had left
implicit, that is, to formulate a theory of the Orders.

As a humanist, Philandrier could not be satisfied with Serlio's
undogmatic stance. Serlio's Book IV is essentially a collection of models
intended for the practising architect who, after being initiated into the
terminology of the five Orders, may then discover fine architecture
through different examples of decorative application, such as that for
doors, windows, façades, fireplaces, and so on. The multiplicity of
theoretical, as well antique models provided by Serlio on every Order
gives the reader total freedom of choice. The rule in Serlio's Book IV
(*Regole generali*) remains 'general' and does not imply any continuity
between the elements constituting the Orders. Such flexibility in

dimittatur, spes quidem salutis superesse videri queat: id est, vt obluctetur, nec sa-
tis feliciter se hactenus circinatam iactet. Nos dum languet, periclitabimur, ecquid
possimus, vt si conficiamus, vel hinc aliquid gratia à spectatoribus expectemus : si
non succedet, hoc certè me nomine solabor : quòd fortes illi & egregij citra contro-
uersiam pugnatores, etiam re infecta, è conflictu redierunt. Et in magnis abunde est,
voluisse. Voluta itaq; rectè (nisi fallor) ad circinum inuoluetur hoc modo: Diuiso quod
restabat lineæ perpendicularis post deformatum abacum, in partes octo, in quinta,
quam magna est, describetur cyclus, qui oculus dicitur, ita vt sint supra oculum
partes quatuor, infrà verò tres. Ille ipse cyclus diuidetur in octantes, id est, partes
æquas octo, totidem ductis lineis. Describetur idem in alia charta sectus linea partium trium: ducta tertia linea à summa perpendiculari ad extremam planam, col-
locato circini pede stabili in puncto extremo planæ, ducito ad aliud ipsius punctum,
quod in centro oculi est, pedem mobilem, & circumagito dum lineam attingas, quæ
ducta est à summa perpendiculari ad extremam planam. Id circinationis diuidito
in partes sex æquas, & à puncto planæ ad perpendicularem ducito lineas rectas
per sex illas partes. Quod interuallu erit inter singulas, partieris in quatuor: ducens
item lineas à plana ad perpendicularem, vt in sex alijs feceras. Ductis his lineis,
nota puncta; vbi attigerint perpendicularem, & ijsdem distingue angustam char-
tam. Hanc vbi ad veram illam perpendicularem transtuleris, & in oculi centro
acicula affixeris, vt circumagi tamen possit, vbiuis locorum ea puncta in circum-
actione responderint ad extremum vsque, ij erunt termini volutæ, crassitudo quoq;
corrigia, seu baltheum dicere mauis, sensim in finem imminutæ quadum oportet.
Reliquum erit in octantibus cycli, id est lineis, in quas primum octo secandum oculum admonuimus, reperire vnde ductus circini mobilis pes ab octante in octan-
tem rectas circinationes efficiat: Nam locum præscribere non ita licet, cum in mul-
tis eiusdem lineæ locis plerunque id fieri possit. Hoc monere possum, initium capi
ab intrinseco octante plano, deinde sursum versus per reliquos octantes fieri circi-
nationem.

Ionicæ volutæ emendata circinatio.

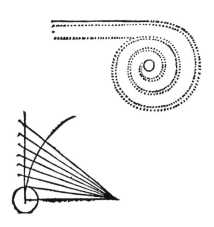

Inter pendentes vtrinq;
volutas scalpitur echinus
ouiculis vsque ad libra-
mentum summum oculi,
cum scalpto baccis, sin-
gulis intermixtis duobus
verticillis, astragalo, ali-
quando resticula, ipsius
tertia parte. Quantum
potui, rem obscuram ora-
tione ita explicare con-
tendi, vt qui legerint
me esse facilem dicend
maluisse intelligat, quàm
videri disertum. Quod
id de

Vitruvian expression may be a product of Serlio's restless mind, even
perhaps indicative of evangelical religious convictions (Tafuri 1992,
234; Carpo 1993, 85–136). Philandrier's 'Digression', on the other
hand, is a perfect example of architectural Ciceronianism where both
the structure and the content follow strict rules.

Philandrier, an expert on Quintilian, chooses the most appropriate
structure to emphasise his theories, namely the digression, a rhetorical
device of discourse interruption, used in this case to set a particular
section apart from the commentary as a whole. The 'Digression' itself
is structured like a Classical oration, with an exordium, a development
in five points (one point per Order) and a peroration. The different
parts of the Orders (entablature, column, pedestal) and their
constituent elements are described from the bottom up for the Tuscan,
following the order of construction, but from top to bottom for the
other Orders; there then follows a recapitulation. The tone is didactic,
the style concise and accurate.

Following a quasi-Platonic model, the humanist starts with the
definition of the 'idea' or 'concept' of the Order in question. The
Order (*genus*) is seen as a formal system characterised by the combination of vertical and horizontal elements (*columnatio, trabeatio*), the fundamental opposition established by Vitruvius (*De Architectura*, IV.ii.1).
Under the term *columnatio* is placed every part of the column, that is,
the pedestal, base, shaft and capital. The word *trabeatio*, with its echoes
of timber contruction, denotes the entablature composed of the architrave, the frieze and the cornice. Each Order is the representation of a
unique model defined by its specific *columnatio* and *trabeatio*. Philandrier
transcends Serlio's purely lexical presentation by integrating this presentation into a normative discourse on morphology. As with Latin
declensions, corresponding to each of the five Orders are precise forms,
in this case a succession of specific horizontal and vertical elements.
Their proportions and mouldings are definitively determined and their
application (the syntax of this architectural language) is strictly regulated. For instance the Doric column can only receive an Attic base, a
Doric capital and a frieze with triglyphs and metopes. The leaf type of
the Corinthian capital is defined: it is acanthus, with a fixed number
and disposition of leaves. The Tuscan or Ionic base cannot be used on
a column of a different Order. And even if, for the Composite, the
cornicings and base for the pedestal have to be taken from the Ionic
and/or the Corinthian, the unique proportions of the Composite
pedestal are sufficient to assure for this Order its specificity. The
proportion of the columns (as we have seen above) is also determined
by Philandrier once and for all.

According to Philandrier's theory, therefore, there can only be a
single model for each Order, that is, a single pedestal, a single column

and a single entablature. Serlio on the other hand never gives a single, definitive model for each Order. Contrary to expectations given by the inaugural plate of Book IV, reproducing as it does the models with pedestals and smooth shafts as presented in the opening of each chapter (on the sole exception see Serlio 1537, fol. XLIXr/170v), throughout the text Serlio places variants, omitting pedestals and adding fluted shafts. He also proposes several types both of Ionic entablature (a flat frieze and cornice with dentils, or a bulging frieze and a cornice with dentils and modillions), and of Corinthian entablature (a flat sculpted frieze with dentils in the cornice or an undecorated frieze and a cornice with modillions). Furthermore, when he describes and illustrates each constituent part of the Order, Serlio multiplies the forms by giving two examples of Tuscan entablature, two types of Doric capital (Vitruvian and Serlian), two Ionic bases (that described by Vitruvius and a corrected version), and two Corinthian entablatures (with either dentils or modillions). To these we might add the numerous antique examples which are appended to, and reproduced on, each Order because of their exceptional ornamental beauty, whether Vitruvian or otherwise. From amongst this diversity, Philandrier carried out a drastic selection. For the Tuscan he chose the most elaborate entablature, he followed Serlio's model for the Doric capital and base and selected an orthodox model of Corinthian entablature with dentils.

Although Philandrier provides many woodcuts, they nevertheless play a secondary role to the text. Those of 1544, which are rather poor and (because of the book's format) quite small, do not make it possible to differentiate the divers mouldings of the pedestals, bases and capitals. The woodcuts of 1552, of greater number and of higher quality, represent the text more exactly. But despite the claims of the title, the 1552 text is very similar to the first edition (Lemerle 1991, fols. LIX–LXIII), the differences being limited to some stylistic corrections, some additions essentially related to the parallels drawn between architecture in wood and stone, the mention of some antique architectural curiosities and, as a conclusion, caustic criticism of anti-Vitruvian 'heretics'. The plates are not as good as Serlio's, in which the models are reproduced so accurately that the architect can easily derive the exact proportion if necessary (for example, Serlio 1537, fol. XLIXv/171r).

By regulating the nomenclature and the relationships between elements of a particular Order, and by rejecting any admixture of elements of different origin, Philandrier writes the first grammar of the Orders, and this allows him throughout the *Annotationes* to denounce what he sees as the antique and modern 'heresies'. Every infringement of the rules, every barbarism or solecism – such as the substitution of one element for another, or the intrusion of a foreign element, whether modillions and dentils in the same cornice, an Attic base used under an Ionic or Corinthian column (Lemerle and Pauwels 1992, 7–13), or an inversion of two superimposed Orders (Corinthian under Ionic on the façade of Palazzo Farnese) (Philandrier 1552, 136, 118, 141) – is severely condemned. Such an approach is fundamentally different from that of Serlio (who trusts in the architect's good judgement to be able to adapt and combine the proposed examples), to say nothing of Serlio's mixed forms such as the antique capitals made of divers parts, whose originality could never have found favour with the French author (Philandrier 1552, 108).

PHILANDRIER AND VIGNOLA

The 'Digression', too theoretical and abstract, too humanist, was never to be as popular with practising architects as Serlio's Book IV. In the following century, a French translation of the 'Life of Vitruvius' and the 'Digression' of Book III (in its 1552 version) was included by Jean de Tournes II in a re-edition of Jean Martin's French translation of Vitruvius (*Architecture, ou Art de bien bastir de Marc Vitruve Pollion Autheur Romain Antique*), published in 1618 in Geneva and Cologne. On the other hand, the 'Digression' did influence a treatise which was to have even greater success than that of Serlio's works, the *Regola delli cinque ordini d'architettura* (1562) of Vignola. Through his desire to establish a universal rule for the Orders, Vignola made clear that he had integrated the theoretical progress made in the 'Digression'. For, henceforth, the Orders had acquired the status of the principal architectural ornament.

Vignola knew Philandrier's work and when still young had associated with him in the Accademia della Virtù; he even quoted Philandrier's method for drawing the Ionic volute. Accepting the proportions fixed by Philandrier for the Tuscan and Doric columns (7 and 8 diameters in height, respectively), Vignola more systematically (or perhaps more pragmatically) established 9 diameters for the Ionic column, and 10 for the Corinthian and Composite columns, thereby favouring the simple and more satisfactory ratios of 7, 8, 9 and 10. His suggested variants, more ornamental than structural, do not modify the fundamental nature of the Order, as with the Doric where Vignola proposes two models, one inspired by the Theatre of Marcellus, the second of his own making. Thus, whilst the use of the Orders is less fixed than that in Philandrier's 'Digression', the norm of the model remains. The success of Vignola's treatise was due to the clarity of presentation, the quality of the copperplates (Zerner 1988, 286), the use of the modular system (where the module is the half-diameter of the column), the limiting of the text to a few lines of commentary and the fact that Vignola (himself an architect) envisaged the Orders in an architectural framework (colonnade, arcade, etc.) (Thoenes 1988, 269–79).

With the rediscovery of the *Annotationes* in its own right and the recognition of its theoretical significance, we can now fully appreciate the eminent part taken by Philandrier in the elaboration of the theory of the Classical Orders through the use of the linguistic model of a strictly codified grammar – a 'rule' subsequently republished by Vignola and later established by the further theorists (notably by Palladio and Scamozzi). Regardless of the intrinsic tendency of the 'rule' to be restrictive, to limit imagination, and to condemn every infringement or transgression, it does not, paradoxically, strangle creativity. By adapting to national or vernacular practices, the 'rule' is transcended by the individual rhetoric of each great artist. Accepted or knowingly transgressed as in the work of Michelangelo and Borromini, Philandrier's 'rule' remains as a sign of culture, the yardstick against which to measure their genius.

1   Frontispiece from Vignola, *Regola delli cinque ordini d'architettura* (Rome, 1562). Florence, Biblioteca Nazionale.

Chapter Eleven

ON VIGNOLA'S *RULE OF THE FIVE ORDERS OF ARCHITECTURE*

Richard J. Tuttle

Having practised the art of architecture for many years in different countries, it has always been a pleasure for me to look at the opinion of as many writers as I could about the practice of ornament, and comparing them with each other and with ancient works still in existence, to try to extract a rule with which I could be content, and which I could be sure would completely satisfy, or at least nearly so, every scholar of this art. And this was solely to serve my own requirements, nor was there any other aim.   (Appendix 2)

WITH THESE UNASSUMING REMARKS Jacopo Barozzi da Vignola opens the one-page preface to his slender but beautifully illustrated treatise on the columnar Orders, the *Regola delli cinque ordini d'architettura*, first issued at Rome in 1562.[1] From the start Vignola makes clear his concern is practical. It is essential to study theoretical writings and the remains of ancient monuments, he maintains, in order to formulate a secure design methodology. Vignola does not attempt to justify his enterprise by lofty humanistic philosophising. He declines to rehearse the metaphysical bases or justifications for architecture, for ornament, even for the Orders in general. At a stroke, the tract is emptied of speculative discourse about the origins, historical development, social significance, expressive character and symbolism of the Orders. It is the pragmatic thrust which distinguishes the *Regola* from most other Renaissance writings about architecture.

---

[1]   The author is grateful to Vaughan Hart and Peter Hicks for invaluable assistance with the translation of the Preface to the *Regola* (Appendix 2). For the editorial history of Vignola's treatise see Thoenes 1974a, 1974b, 1983; Tuttle 1992; Vignola 1985.

The inaugural printing or *editio princeps* – which is known from only one surviving copy, in the National Library in Florence (Walcher Casotti 1976; Vignola 1985) – consists of thirty-two numbered engraved folios (Appendix 3). Its richly inventive frontispiece, without indication of date, place or publisher, presents a bust-portrait of the sober author-architect flanked by statues of Theory and Practice under the protective coat of arms and personal emblems of his wealthy and powerful patron, Cardinal Alessandro Farnese (Thoenes 1983, 360–74) (plate 1). Immediately after appears the engraved text authorising copyright privileges (in the Papal State, Tuscany, Venice, Spain and France) for ten years. There follows on plate III an obsequious but obligatory dedication to Cardinal Alessandro and, most importantly, the preface addressed to the reader (Appendix 2). Then comes the true substance of the treatise: a series of twenty-nine single-sided superbly executed analytical images of the five columnar Orders in proper order – Tuscan, Doric, Ionic, Corinthian and Composite – bearing the sparest of commentary. Vignola concludes the book with a personal invention of a palace cornice design that he claims to have 'used several times to good effect'.

The elegance, lucidity and brevity of the *Regola* helped to make it a best-seller for three centuries. Immediately accepted as the most reliable short guide to the proportions and formal vocabulary of the Orders, it became required reading in academies and schools of design throughout the world. A recent study has identified more than five hundred individual printings of the book in ten languages (Italian, Dutch, English, Flemish, French, German, Portuguese, Russian, Spanish, Swedish) between 1562 and 1974 (Vignola 1985, 539–77). Vignola's arguably ranks as the leading architectural textbook of all time. Indeed, it was only with the advent of modernism that its value was questioned. As the Classical Orders were gradually eliminated from architectural education and practice, the work lost its currency and today is nearly forgotten by architects.[2] Yet if it is no longer an indispensable professional instrument, it still retains a critical position in Renaissance architecture, one worth revisiting by way of a re-reading of the *Regola* itself.

We may begin by asking just how Vignola came to publish his work. An overview of the architect's professional itinerary – those 'many years in different countries' that constitute the pre-history of the *Regola* – discloses a career repeatedly punctuated by theoretical experiences of the first order.[3] Jacopo (or Giacomo) Barozzi was born in

[2]   The treatise is still available, albeit in inexpensive reproductions such as Ware 1977.
[3]   The primary biographical sources are Vasari's 1568 edition of his *Lives* (Vasari 1973) and (less reliably) Danti's 'Vita' in Vignola 1583; essential modern monographs are Walcher Casotti 1960, Thoenes 1974b. For a recent short biographical account in English, see Tuttle 1996.

1507 in the Modenese village of Vignola, from which he took his name, but was raised in nearby Bologna, where he was trained as a painter. Although he never gave up painting entirely, he turned to architecture at an early age, probably in the 1520s, when he is likely to have come under the spell of the painter-architects Baldassarre Peruzzi and Sebastiano Serlio, both of whom were active in Bologna. Peruzzi visited Bologna in 1522–3 to work on the unfinished civic basilica of San Petronio; his pupil Serlio, a Bolognese by birth, is documented there a little later.[4] Serlio was then laying the groundwork for a systematic presentation of the five Orders, a project that began with a series of copperplate engravings of bases, capitals and entablatures printed at Venice in 1528 (Howard 1973), and culminated nine years later with the *Regole generali di architettura sopra le cinque maniere degli edifici*, the fourth book of his architectural treatise (Serlio 1537).

Vignola undoubtedly followed Serlio's activity closely. The *Regole generali* by its subject and approach would be of capital significance for his own book. But in 1538 Vignola moved to Rome where, under the direction of Jacopo Meleghino (a former associate of both Peruzzi and Serlio as well as co-architect of St Peter's with Antonio da Sangallo the Younger), he worked as a painter and probably as a designer. The critical event of this Roman sojourn was his involvement with the Accademia della Virtù, a private association of intellectuals led by the Sienese humanist Claudio Tolomei (Pagliara 1986, 67–85). In a famous letter of 1542 Tolomei described the academy's goal as the publication of an ambitious multi-volume illustrated study of Vitruvius and ancient architecture (Tolomei 1547, 81–95; Barocchi 1971–7, 3037–46). Vignola contributed measured survey drawings. They have been lost, but the impact of this intense archeological and philological experience informs both the *Regola* and his built works. Around the time the project fell apart and the Vitruvian academy disbanded, Vignola signed on with Francesco Primaticcio to produce bronze replicas of Vatican statuary for King François I of France (Cox-Rearick 1996, 325). This enterprise took him to Fontainebleau from 1541 to 1543, where he supervised the casting of the statues, painted and perhaps practised as an architect. Though scantily documented, this episode must have been significant for Vignola's education as a theorist: for one thing it brought renewed contact with Serlio, and for another it exposed him to the practical and theoretical challenges – already met by such leading French architect-theorists as Guillaume Philandrier, Jacques Androuet du Cerceau and Philibert De l'Orme – of disseminating the Classical style in northern Europe.

---

[4] For Peruzzi in Bologna see now Tuttle 1994; Serlio's Bolognese activities are discussed in Tuttle 1989, but see now the detailed biography in Fiore 1994.

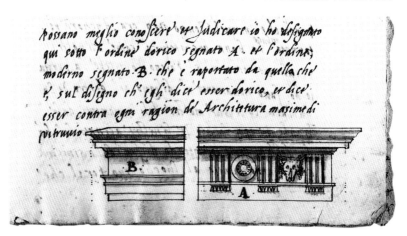

2 Vignola, Entablatures: Doric ('A') and *Moderno* ('B'). Biblioteca comunale dell'Archiginnasio, Bologna. Bibl. Gozzadini, MS 2 (Miscellanea Petroniana), fasc. 11.

Returning to Italy in 1543, Vignola became architect-in-chief of the civic basilica of San Petronio in Bologna, a prestigious post beleaguered by contentious debates about the proper style with which to complete the immense Gothic monument. Vignola's façade projects are in the Gothic style, but tempered by firm Classicist convictions. Medieval elements such as traceried gables, pinnacles, crockets and the like are fitted snugly to a system of superimposed pilasters exhibiting all of the basic canonical parts from stylobate to column to cornice (Bernheimer 1954, 278). Vignola defended his approach in a memorandum dated 1 February 1547 (Tuttle 1974, 165–9), which includes a small sketch demonstrating the differences between the true Doric entablature and the 'modern' (that is, Gothic) entabulature he deemed appropriate for San Petronio (plate 2) (Tuttle 1976, 218–20). For the correct, or Vitruvian, Doric Vignola employed a Serlian scheme (labelled 'A'), whilst for the 'modern' Doric ('B') he generated a derivative in which all of the essential Classical components (architrave, frieze and cornice) are present but profiled in non-Classical ways. Vignola's reliance upon fixed proportional schemes is thus already evident in the late 1540s. By the time he settled permanently in Rome in 1550 – at which time he re-entered the service of the Farnese family and became architect to Pope Julius III – Vignola possessed a mature grasp of architectural theory.

It is probable that the *Regola* took final form during the 1550s. These years saw the triumphant beginning of Vignola's maturity as an architect. Early in the decade he planned the famous papal Villa Giulia along with the nearby chapel of Sant'Andrea in Via Flaminia, then designed the little fortress at Norcia and the church of the Madonna

3   South-west façade of the Palazzo Farnese, Caprarola, 1558–72.

del Piano at Capranica. At the end of the decade he gained two hugely ambitious commissions from members of the Farnese family: Cardinal Alessandro's great pentagonal summer residence at Caprarola (plate 3), and the imposing (if unfinished) ducal palace of Ottavio Farnese at Piacenza. Apparently Vignola did not maintain a large workshop, which may have encouraged him to streamline and systematise design procedures for widely separated projects through a compendium of authoritative images like those brought together in the *Regola*. In any case, the book itself was not to be distributed until the early 1560s. The first known reference to it is contained in a letter Vignola sent to Giorgio Vasari in August 1561, a letter soliciting help in securing Tuscan copyright for a work done 'a long time ago . . . on the five orders of architecture taken from the antiquities of Rome' (Vasari 1981, 296–7). Now, although the first edition bears no place or date of publication, both are effectively established by another letter, this one penned by Vignola's son Giacinto Barozzi, on 12 June 1562. Addressed to Ottavio Farnese, Duke of Parma and Piacenza, it was written on behalf of the architect in Rome, who was sending a fresh copy of his book on 'these five Orders of architecture' (Vignola 1985, 501).

Let us return to the preface. After declaring the aim of finding a single rule for the Classical Orders, Vignola narrates the process by which he found it. He writes,

> To do this, leaving aside many things of the writers, where differences of no little consequence are born, and to achieve greater certainty, I decided first to study those ancient ornaments of the five Orders which appear in the antiquities of Rome. And considering all of them carefully and examining their measurements accurately, I found that those which in the general opinion are the most beautiful and appear the most graceful to our eyes also have a certain numerical agreement and proportion which is the least complex; indeed you can measure precisely the large members in all their parts with each minute member. Hence, considering further how much our senses take pleasure in this proportion, and how much the things outside it are unpleasant, as the musicians prove in their science through sensation, I undertook this task many years ago, namely to reduce the said five Orders of architecture to a concise and quick rule which was easy to use. (Appendix 2)

Vignola's quest thus begins not in the library – not with unshakable truths anchored in authoritative written texts, not even in Vitruvius – but archeologically on site, examining and searching the crumbling ancient monuments, measuring them, comparing them, judging them. This had been standard practice since the early Quattrocento, but Vignola's account is fresh in its avoidance of citing higher authorities, unless it be Rome itself. His selected models are simply the most familiar ones, those monuments which 'in the general opinion are the most beautiful and appear the most graceful to our eyes'. Unlike either Serlio or Palladio, Vignola makes no attempt to extend the archeological, historical or formal horizon beyond the *caput mundi*. However, he does follow the convention established by Serlio for the number and sequence of the Orders as Tuscan, Doric, Ionic, Corinthian and Composite. It is obvious that Vignola is uncomfortable or perhaps even incompetent when it comes to learned or academic arguments about proportion. While claiming that the most beautiful antiquities possess 'a certain numerical agreement' as well as 'proportion which is the least complex', he fails to substantiate these assertions mathematically. Simplicity, regularity and beauty simply go together 'as the musicians prove in their science through sensation'. Apparently it is the desire to compose the five Orders with simple numerical relationships, which is to say according to 'a concise and quick rule which was easy to use' that drives the argument. But the 'rule' itself is not discussed in the preface – it emerges in due course from the engraved illustrations.

Vignola then goes on to describe his approach:

> Wishing to put in this rule (by way of example) the Doric Order, I considered that of all the examples of Doric, the one in the Theatre of Marcellus was the most highly praised by everyone. This, then, I took as the basis of the rule for the said Order, that is, determining its principal parts. (Appendix 2)

The Theatre of Marcellus was greatly esteemed by Renaissance architects, both for its Doric and Ionic Orders (plate 6). Vignola takes pains to say that it is not an absolute model, but rather something like a guiding scheme. From it come the 'principal parts' of the Doric Order, which are then adjusted to accord with his system. In the sixteenth century it was generally agreed that the three main components of any architectural Order were pedestal, column and entablature. Now, although the theatre's Doric was without either pedestal or even columnar base, the appeal of its column, capital and entablature was apparently sufficient to win it acceptance as an *exemplum* for practice. In fact, Vignola refrains from claiming it or any other specific ancient work as a fixed and final formulation for any of the Orders. The rule was obtained by making fine adjustments:

> If some minor member did not entirely obey the numerical proportions (which often happens owing to the work of the stonecutters or other accidents that frequently occur with such details) I accommodated it to my rule not by altering anything of importance but by harmonising this slight licence on the authority of other examples of Doric which are also considered beautiful. From these examples I took other small parts whenever I needed to supplement the one

from the Theatre of Marcellus, not as Zeuxis did with the maidens
among the Crotons, but rather as my judgement [*giudizio*] directed.
(Appendix 2)

Like a painter, who after blocking out the overall composition
proceeds to fill in the less conspicuous details, Vignola alters and adjusts
the less critical component mouldings within the broad scheme of his
models. For this he is empowered by his personal judgement while
keeping to the authority of beautiful (and presumably well-known)
ancient examples.[5] His approach is thus quite unlike that of the Greek
painter Zeuxis, who synthesised the finest attributes of five maidens in
order to portray the ideal beauty of Helen of Troy. 'I made this choice
for all the Orders', he continues,

> extracting only from ancient works and adding nothing of my own
> save the distribution of their proportions which were based on
> simple numbers, using not the *braccia*, or feet, or palms of whatever
> locality, but an arbitrary measurement called the module, divided
> into those parts which will be seen from Order to Order in the
> appropriate place. (Appendix 2)

Practical considerations governed mensuration. To have adopted one
of the many local or national systems of measurement (in *braccia, piedi,
palmi*, etc.) available in the Renaissance would have seriously compromised the usefulness of the rule. The modular system, on the other
hand, was an efficacious means since it was universal, providing an
independent standard unit that could be translated for use in any
particular circumstance. And although the designation of the column
radius as the module – marked as '*M*' in the plates of the *Regola* –
represents a rejection of the diameter system advocated by authorities
such as Serlio, it certainly facilitated greater accuracy and ease when
calculating and projecting the smaller component mouldings. Indeed,
the salient practical feature regarding measurement was Vignola's
extension of the module to embrace not only the column, but each
and every component part of the entire Order.

The module enhanced practicality, facilitating use of the rule by
architects of modest artistic means. As Vignola puts it, 'And I have
made an otherwise difficult part of architecture so easy that every
ordinary talent, provided he has some enthusiasm for this art, can at a
glance and without much bothersome reading, understand the whole
and make use of it at opportune moments'. This passage lays bare
Vignola's openly anti-intellectual bias, or at least his unqualified reli-

---

[5]   For an introduction to the 'topos' of *giudizio* in Cinquecento artistic theory see Klein
1979.

ance upon the visual language of the engraved plates. In fact, the graphic design of the *Regola* is central to Vignola's thinking and vital to the book's success as a didactic instrument. The generous folio format – measuring about 27 by 41 cm in the early editions – while investing the work with a kind of grandeur, probably encouraged its use at the construction site, much in the traditional manner of large-scale working drawings or *modelli*. But the *Regola* ought not to be confused with pattern-books. It is, rather, to be associated with works like Labacco's book of engraved reconstructions of Roman buildings published in 1552; both works, however, are notably unlike the illustrated volumes of Serlio. Serlio's publications had set a high and influential standard for illustrated architectural treatises by establishing a fine equilibrium between image and text and by exploiting the entire range of available graphic conventions – diagrams and plans, orthographic and perspectival projections, details with or without shading, details presented as naturalistic fragments, and so on. The congenial effect of variety was further augmented by changes in the scale of images and by the inherent warmth of the woodcut medium. Yet none of these qualities appears to have interested Vignola, who rejected almost all of them for the *Regola*. He pledged himself to an exclusively visual rather than a written argument or demonstration, employed the medium of copperplate engraving over woodcut, and restricted his graphic projection to the planimetric and orthographic. If there is an extravagance it lies in the artful texturing of surfaces and in the rich nuancing of shadows. Captions, commentary, numerical relationships and nomenclature were all folded into the graphic image. The plates, single sided with blank versos, were incised with an identical border, a single framing line deftly proportioned as a $\sqrt{3}$ rectangle.[6] In scale, uniformity and elegance the *Regola* had no equal at the time it first appeared.

The exquisite engravings set forth an extraordinarily lucid and systematic organization of material, beginning with the Tuscan. The columnar Order is presented in five basic plates: colonnade, arcade, arcade with pedestals, pedestal and base alone, and capital and entablature alone. After the Tuscan, the sequence is repeated in the four remaining Orders – Doric, Ionic, Corinthian and Composite – supplemented where additional plates are required or (in the case of Composite) cutting back where fewer are needed (see Appendix 3). As might be expected, the essentials of the rule are highlighted in the opening illustrations and their captions. In plate IV, showing the Tuscan colonnade, Vignola points out that in this case the columnar

---

[6] The $\sqrt{3}$ rectangle may be generated in one of two ways: either by bisecting an equilateral triangle and then combining both halves to form the rectangle, or by enlarging a $\sqrt{2}$ rectangle (i.e. 'Golden Section') by replacing its long side with its diagonal.

proportions are based on Vitruvius (a shaft of seven diameters equals fourteen modules), and then states his own requirement that the entablature equal a quarter the height of the column in all of the Orders; in plate v, depicting the Tuscan arcade, he says that the proportions of each Order will be derived by dividing the total height by certain fixed numbers corresponding to the module; and in plate vi, illustrating the Tuscan arcade with pedestals, we read that the pedestal must be one-third the height of the column. In the Renaissance the pedestal was generally considered to be an essential component of the columnar system, undoubtedly because it was useful in situations where Orders were to be superimposed one upon another. In the present case it may or may not be used. Vignola's 'rule' – which is cited in the singular, not the plural – is finally stated fully and emphatically in the caption in plate vii: 'as a general rule in all five of the Orders I have observed that the pedestals with their ornaments should be one third of the column including base and capital, just as the whole of the upper ornament, that is the architrave, frieze, and cornice, should be a quarter.' The rule is not stated again in this fashion but is demonstrated visually and numerically in the subsequent plates. Exceptions will occur only in the taller pedestals, of the Corinthian and Composite Orders.

For the Doric, Vignola lengthened the column to sixteen modules and brought the Order's total height without pedestal to twenty (plate 4). This resulted in more slender over-all proportions than those generated according to the schemes of Vitruvius and Serlio. In plate xii a certain characteristic elongation is evident in the pedestal, with its double plinth and tall dado, but perhaps the most singular feature is the Doric base (plate 5). Lacking an authoritative ancient or modern precedent, the base is comprised of two toruses without an intervening scotia (Tuttle 1976, 212–13). The closest model would seem to be a base designed by Antonio da Sangallo the Younger for an arcade at the now-ruined city of Castro (Geiss 1981, 109–11). As we have seen, Vignola based his Doric capital and entablature on the example of the Theatre of Marcellus, a work easily identifiable by its cornice with dentils (plate 6). But in the next illustration, plate xiv, a second, alternative Doric scheme is introduced which Vignola claims is 'taken from diverse fragments of antiquities in Rome and combined in such a way that when used I found turned out very well' (plate 7). Its distinctive components, which include the flowered necking (Vignola uses Farnese lilies), abacus with egg-and-dart, the frieze with single fascia, and the powerful mutules in the cornice – all come from the ancient Basilica Aemilia in the Roman Forum. The presence of two separate and distinct Doric entablatures testifies to the flexibility of Vignola's approach to design; in fact, he used both types in his built work (plate 8).

4   Doric arcade, from Vignola, *Regola* (Rome, 1562), plate x. Florence, Biblioteca Nazionale.

5   Doric pedestal and base, from Vignola, *Regola* (Rome, 1562), plate XII. Florence,
Biblioteca Nazionale.

Questa parte d'ordine Dorico è cauata dal Teatro di Marcello in Roma come nel proemio per modo di essepio fu detto, et posta in disegno ritiene questa medesima proportione.

XIII

6 Doric capital and entablature (denticulate), from Vignola, *Regola* (Rome, 1562), plate XIII. Florence, Biblioteca Nazionale.

Looking back over the set of plates for the Doric Order, we may
easily collect, total and tabulate the number of modules apportioned to
each of its principal components. In the Order's most complete form
– with pedestal, column and entablature – the modular total comes to
$25\frac{1}{3}$:

PEDESTAL		COLUMN		ENTABLATURE	
Cornice	$\frac{1}{2}$	Capital	1	Cornice	$1\frac{1}{2}$
Dado	4	Shaft	14	Frieze	$1\frac{1}{2}$
Base	$\frac{5}{6}$	Base	1	Architrave	1
	$\overline{5\frac{1}{3}}$		$\overline{16}$		$\overline{4}$

For the Ionic Order Vignola recommends a column of eighteen
modules. While the first two Orders are shown in modular units
comprising twelve smaller parts, the module for the Ionic is presented
in units of eighteen parts – 'and this because being a more refined
Order than the Tuscan and the Doric it requires more minute divisions' (plate xv). In fact, the octadecimal system is then also applied to
the still more intricate Corinthian and Composite Orders. For the
Ionic Vignola neglects to cite formal sources, perhaps because the
scheme is so obviously derivative of the temple of Fortuna Virilis, one
of the most avidly studied Ionic temples and certainly the best preserved in Rome. The carved frieze, on the other hand, was inspired by
the Corinthian temple of Antoninus and Faustina. The Ionic capital
receives exhaustive visual and verbal treatment: in plate xix it appears
not only in front profile but from the side and in plan, and plate xx
is given over entirely to the construction of the volute, a challenging
design detail for Renaissance architects. Vignola's solution departs from
Serlio, and may be indebted to Philandrier (Lemerle 1994, 33–41).

The Corinthian Order, whose slender columns are given twenty
modules, was generated from 'diverse places in Rome, but principally
from the Rotonda, and from the three columns that are in the Roman
Forum' (plate xxvi). In fact, the capital and entablature are modelled
directly upon the celebrated Corinthian Order in the porch of the
Pantheon, while the base is derived from the 'three columns' of the
temple of Castor and Pollux. For this and for the Composite Order
Vignola inserted analytical plates for the construction of the capital,
graphic presentations that assuredly testify to the author's preference for
visual images over text (plates xxv and xxviii). The capitals are
rendered in plan and profile, with the plan further subdivided into four
different sectional views, and the profile, in corner projection, shows a
complete smooth-leaf view and a cut-away revealing the bell. In a brief
caption the laconic Vignola writes, 'the rest can be easily understood
with only a little attention' (plate xxv). Since the general proportions

7 Doric capital and entablature (mutulate), from Vignola, *Regola* (Rome, 1562), plate
XIIII. Florence, Biblioteca Nazionale.

of Corinthian and Composite are identical and differ only in the shapes of lesser components, it was unnecessary to illustrate the Composite Order in colonnade and arcades (see Appendix 3).

The Composite series concludes with an illustration (plate XXX) of two figured capitals that are classified as 'Composite' by virtue of their unique combination of motifs such as eagles, griffins, hounds and thunderbolts. One of them is featured in the aedicule framing the portrait of Vignola in the frontispiece (plate I). Below the capitals is depicted the common Attic base which, Vignola contends,

> In our days one is used to putting under the Corinthian, Composite, Ionic and Doric indifferently, but which is most appropriate for the Composite, and the Attic base may also be tolerated in the Ionic should the Ionic base not be used. Beneath the other Orders I would repudiate the use of the Attic base as definitely inappropriate, and I could adduce several reasons, but I do not want to put myself to talking about something already of such licence; it is enough with the Composite to show it and its divisions born from the module broken into 18 parts, like the Ionic and Corinthian.

The penultimate illustration (plate XXXI) proposes two different methods for determining entasis. The first, which is deemed appropriate for Tuscan and Doric columns, involves the gradual tapering of the shaft above its lower third. The less-noted second method, which Vignola claims as his own, is recommended for Ionic, Corinthian and Composite columns. Also included is a method for the construction of the twisted or Solomonic column, whose undulating profile is determined by a line projected outwardly from a spiral at the center of the shaft.

At no point in the *Regola* is there a comprehensive tabulation of the numerical relationships within or between the Orders. It is enough, Vignola seems to say, to commit his carefully rendered plates to memory in order to grasp the whole. However, a simplified table of 'the rule' of the five Orders takes the following form:

	TUSCAN	DORIC	IONIC	CORINTHIAN	COMPOSITE
Entablature	$3\frac{1}{2}$	4	$4\frac{1}{2}$	5	5
Column	14	16	18	20	20
Pedestal	$4\frac{2}{3}$	$5\frac{1}{3}$	6	7	7
	$22\frac{1}{6}$	$25\frac{1}{3}$	$28\frac{1}{2}$	32	32

To sum up, Vignola's rule is based on a simple method of subdivision. Any of the five Classical Orders may be proportioned quickly and easily to a given building or storey simply by dividing its height by the appropriate number of modules. Once this is done, the dimensions of

Within the image:
ALEXANDER · FARNESIVS
CAR · S · R · E · VICECANCEL·

Palmi. ii

Palmi Romani con li quali e' fatto il pres
ente disegno
1 2 3 4 5 6 7 8 9 10

Porta della fabrica dell'Ill.mo et R.mo Car.le Farnese a Caprarola

8 Main portal of the Palazzo Farnese at Caprarola, from Vignola, *Regola*, unnumbered addition to later editions. Biblioteca dell'Academia di Scienze, Lettere ed Arti, Modena.

the pedestals, columns and entablatures are obtained and then, with the help of the engraved plates, the shape and scale of all of the minor parts may be securely determined.

The preface concludes defensively and with an allusion to further publications,

> I would only add that should someone judge this a vain effort by saying that one cannot lay down a fixed rule, since, according to the opinion of all and especially of Vitruvius, it is often necessary to enlarge or to diminish the proportions of ornamental members in order to remedy with art where our vision has been deceived by some occurrence, to him I reply that concerning this matter it is necessary to know how much should appear to the eye – this should always be the firm rule which others have proposed to observe – and then proceed in this by certain good rules of perspective, whose practice is fundamental both here and in painting, such that I am sure you will be pleased, [and] I also hope to present that to you soon. (Appendix 2)

This last remark refers to Vignola's theoretical tract on perspective. Apparently already well advanced, it would be published posthumously as *Le due regole della prospettiva prattica* (The Two Rules of Practical Perspective) by the Dominican mathematician Ignazio Danti (Vignola 1583). It is tempting to believe that Vignola may have been pursuing a broader theoretical programme, and elsewhere in the preface he teases the reader by saying he may bring out 'other, greater things on this subject, if you accept this part in the spirit in which I believe you will' (Appendix 2). But the perspective treatise represents the natural and necessary theoretical complement to the *Regola*, insofar as it provides the means for optical refinements. Following Vitruvius, Vignola subscribes to the doctrine of the eye as the final arbiter of ornament. Even the most carefully calibrated proportions required adjustments for the sake of appearance within the final work. Vignola's precise and systematic method is not quite as absolutist as is often supposed.

As we have seen, the *Regola* was published to assist practising architects and builders as they confronted concrete design problems. In this it more closely resembles a technical manual than a theoretical tract or textbook. In fact Vignola was not seeking a particularly broad readership, as we learn from a paragraph added to subsequent editions in the margin immediately below the preface (plate III):

> As has been said, my aim was to be understood only by those who may have had some introduction to art, and for this reason I did not write the names of any of the particular members of the five Orders, believing them to be known. But after seeing by experience how

this work greatly pleases many lords moved by desire to attempt to grasp with little effort the whole of the art of these ornaments, and that the ornaments were lacking only in these particular terms, I wanted to add them here as they are commonly used in Rome and in the order that they appear. I point out only that the members which are common to several Orders, after being noted once on first appearance, will not be mentioned again in the subsequent examples. (Appendix 2)

In deference to noble patrons, then, Vignola had the original copperplates inscribed with the necessary specialised terms keyed to capital letters in the images themselves. Needless to say, this move greatly strengthened the editorial potential of the tract.

The *Regola delli cinque ordini d'architettura* documents the living linkage between research and realisation. Generated in response to practical problems rather than theoretical ones and aimed at 'those who may have had some introduction to art', it offers an archeologically informed yet efficient method of designing in the Classical style. In late Renaissance Italy there was no question that worthwhile architecture required ornament in the form of the Classical Orders. As a successful architect, Vignola was often called upon to redesign existing buildings as well as to direct construction at long distance. With speed and efficiency at a premium, the architect without a large workshop could no longer elaborate new and intricate design solutions for all of his commissions. The answer lay in making rough conceptual sketches which were then followed up by critical measured drawings. As Vignola put it regarding façade drawings at San Petronio, 'it is not the custom of architects to render a small drawing in such proportions that it may be projected in large scale by virtue of small measurements; rather one is used to making such drawings only to demonstrate the invention' (Tuttle 1993, 76). The plates of the *Regola* offered a shortcut in so far as they stood in for detailed working drawings of the Classical Orders. An era of efficient standardisation was under way. At the same time there was a growing appetite for new ideas, for models. Vignola had left open the door to supplementary illustrations with his final image, the design for a palace cornice (plate XXXII). Within a year or two of publication he was apparently preparing other such additions to enhance the book's attractiveness. At least five engravings were made after his designs for Farnese commissions in Rome and Caprarola (see Appendix 3). The first presents the reader with the principal portal to the Palazzo Farnese in Caprarola, the architect's most famous and important palace (plate 8). The portal is much more than a simple model. In it the Order is assembled or composed on the basis of Vignola's Doric arcade (plate 4), but in a manner found nowhere else in the book – as a rusticated pilaster system. The entablature follows the mutulate type (plate 7) and is embellished heraldically with Farnese fleurs-de-lis in the metopes. The Caprarola portal is thus a clear demonstration of how to work creatively according to Vignola's rule.

By the time of Vignola's death in July 1573 the *Regola* was well on its way to becoming the 'bible' of the Orders – and its author the 'law-giver' of Classical architecture. With the beauty of the plates matching the clarity and utility of the rule, the book itself did not really require changes or additions to remain alive. However later editors might choose to modify the basic scheme devised by Vignola – by altering the size or format, for example, or by multiplying the number of illustrations – demand for the *Regola* was sustained, as its author had intended, by practice.

Chapter Twelve

ON PHILIBERT DE L'ORME:
A TREATISE TRANSCENDING
THE RULES

❧

Jean Guillaume

D URING THE 1540S A NEW STYLE of architecture emerged in France. The château of St Maur and that of Anet, built by Philibert De l'Orme, and the royal château of the Louvre by Pierre Lescot, demonstrate a use of the antique Orders that was perfectly mastered and yet quite unlike that applied in Italy (Guillaume 1992; Zerner 1996) (plates 1 and 7b). It was this artistic flowering, also visible in literature with the first works by Du Bellay and Ronsard, which led to the publication of translations of Vitruvius (1547), Alberti (1553) and Serlio (1545–51), and created a demand for new architectural treatises written in the national language. These began to appear soon afterwards, with *Nouvelles inventions pour bien bastir et à petits fraiz* (1561) by Philibert De l'Orme, the *Reigle générale d'architecture des cinq manières de colonnes* (1564) by Jean Bullant, and above all De l'Orme's *Le premier tome de l'Architecture* (1567). This trend spread throughout northern Europe during this period. However, the treatises being published were for the most part limited to a presentation of the system of the Orders, much inspired by Book IV of Serlio (Blum 1550, Shute 1563, De Vries 1565) (Bury 1988). Philibert De l'Orme, on the other hand, set out to rival both Alberti and Serlio, an undertaking in which he was successful (Blunt 1958, ch. 8).

Such an ambition could be fulfilled only in France, an intellectual environment greatly influenced by Italian culture but one which was, at the same time, determined to affirm its independence, not to say its superiority. The creation of an architectural style in keeping with the teaching of the ancients, independent (or so it was believed) of Italian models and tailored to suit the expectations and tastes of the French (Guillaume 1987; Morresi 1997), called for a comprehensive treatise which provided the rules for the art of building in the French manner. It was this context and the author's own genius that explains why the *Premier tome de l'Architecture* differs so much from other treatises.

Divided into nine books, the *Premier tome* was to have been followed by a second volume. The project was, however, never finished. It had been preceded by *Nouvelles inventions* (1561), a purely practical treatise in two books devoted to a new type of roofing. These two books were incorporated into the *Premier tome* in 1626, becoming Books x and xi. But it was not until the appearance of the superb facsimile edition by Jean-Marie Pérouse de Montclos in 1988 that these two works were once again to be published separately. It is this edition (complete with a commentary, glossary and index) which must now be used as the authority.

The *Premier tome* is a remarkable work, not least because of its style. De l'Orme uses the first person throughout, as does Alberti, but in a much more spontaneous manner. In fact, De l'Orme writes as if he were speaking directly to an interlocutor (indicated by his continual use of *vous*). He is not addressing some imaginary audience but rather the French patrons and master builders who are ignorant of 'the manner of building well'.[1] De l'Orme also goes to great lengths to write 'as simply and as intelligibly as he knows how, almost in a popular way'[2] (fol. 260r), in order to be understood by every 'work-man'. The passion with which he communicates his knowledge 'for the heartfelt desire which I have to benefit the public good, and above all my country'[3] (fol. 7v), gives his writing extraordinary freshness, and a conversational tone unique in artistic literature.

The treatise, in some aspects autobiographical, is founded above all on De l'Orme's personal experience and on his direct knowledge of the art of antiquity, which he acquired in Rome from 1533 to 1536. In particular, he recalls the circumstances of his encounter with the future Pope Marcello II in the Forum (fol. 131r) (Pérouse de Montclos 1987). While Serlio, Vignola and Palladio display a knowledge which seems to predate their work, thereby acquiring a kind of objectivity, De l'Orme relates what he has seen and learned – his experiences, his *essais* ('studies') as Montaigne puts it – and explains to the French how best to adapt the models of antiquity (here he pretends to ignore contemporary Italian architecture) to 'the common practice and methods of our own architecture'[4] (fol. 62r). This is why De l'Orme in his

---

[1] 'La façon de bien bâtir.'

[2] 'Le plus facilement qu'il se peut faire, et plus intelligiblement ou si vous voulez, populairement.'

[3] 'Pour le grand désir que j'ai de faire profit au bien public et signamment à ma Patrie.'

[4] 'L'usage et pratique de notre architecture.'

Entrance pavilion, Château of Anet, c.1552.

text uses the first person, as if he is trying to create a new style of French architecture from scratch, and why as a conclusion he paints an extraordinary self-portrait, identifying himself as a wise man who reveals the true nature of things to youth (fol. 283r).

The most strikingly original aspect of De l'Orme's writings is that half of the work is devoted to technical matters (six books out of a total of eleven). Although this preoccupation brings De l'Orme's approach close to that of Vitruvius and Alberti, it nonetheless distinguishes him from all the theoreticians of the sixteenth century. Occasional remarks by Serlio and concise but short chapters by Palladio (dealing in particular with techniques from antiquity), are as little compared with De l'Orme's long sections on foundations (Book II), vaults (Books III and IV), chimneys and fireplaces (Book IX), and roofs (*Nouvelles inventions*). What is more, he does not limit himself to explaining or perfecting the methods of his time. Rather, Books III and IV and the *Nouvelles inventions* are technical treatises establishing a new science governing the construction of vaults and roofs (Potié 1996, chs. 4–9).

First published in 1561, the *Nouvelles inventions* (the 'treatise on roofs') describes ingenious techniques which replace the use of large rectilinear pieces of square section with small, flat and curved elements assembled like keystones (plate 2). This 'new invention' appears to comply with a rational approach in industrial terms, in that it keeps costs down, standardises construction and means that a relatively unqualified workforce can be employed. These innovative ideas, which were too revolutionary to achieve much success despite the persuasive force of the author, were not put into practice properly until after 1750, the date when the modern science of building properly emerged (Pérouse de Montclos 1991).

The 'treatise on vaults' (Books III and IV of the *Premier tome*) is of a different nature. Although De l'Orme did not invent a new way of constructing keystone vaults (French and Spanish master-masons having been experts in *l'art du trait* or stereotomy since the twelfth century (Pérouse de Montclos 1982, 85–95)), he was nonetheless the first to divulge the masons' 'secrets of architecture' (fol. 57*v*) and to describe these in a methodical scientific way using 'the most subtle, ingenious and inventive of all sciences',[5] namely geometry (fol. 86*v*). In fact, the chapters follow in succession like the theorems of a mathematical manual, dealing with ever more difficult examples, such as how to draw a semi-circular arch, either straight or skewed in plan, set in a rectilinear or curved plane or at an angle, on a vertical or inclined surface and so on. De l'Orme delights in combining every possible difficulty, and gives the solution 'for a door at an obtuse angle, rounded on one side and concave inside, the other half on an oblique line, skewed on both sides',[6] the same even being possible 'on a gradient' (fols. 80*v*, 81*r*) (plate 3). However, he does not demonstrate this skill for its own sake. The author knows that a French master mason might well have occasion to build such a door in a structure similar to the old, irregular one given in his example on folio 67r. De l'Orme also triumphs in the construction of rampant pendentives (*trompes*), and spiral and inclined vaults to be used in staircases (fols. 120–28). The general science of vaults which he established in Lyons in 1536 'by the means and aid of geometry and great mental travail'[7] (fol. 91*r*), when he built the two 'skewed and rampant' pendentives at the Hôtel Bullioud (plate 4), enables De l'Orme to solve every conceivable problem.

With a mind as rational and daring as De l'Orme's, capable of establishing a 'science' of building in the modern sense of the word, his approach to the subject of the Orders was bound to be an original one. In fact, the explanations of the five Orders in Books V, VI and VII

---

[5] 'La plus subtile, plus ingénieuse et plus inventive de toutes les disciplines.'

[6] 'D'une porte sur un angle obtus, ronde d'un côté et creuse en dedans, l'autre moitié sur la ligne oblique et biaise des deux côtés'.

[7] 'Par le moyen et aide de la géométrie et grand travail d'esprit.'

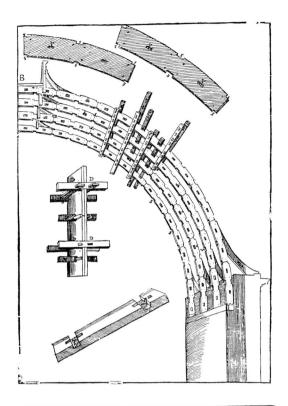

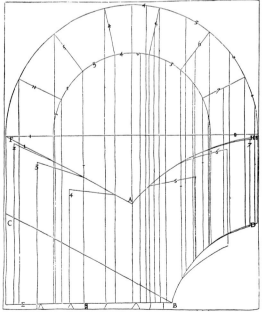

2   (above) The roof of the
Château de la Muette, from De
l'Orme, *Nouvelles inventions pour
bien bastir et à petits fraiz* (Paris,
1561), fol. 20*v*.

3   (left) Setting out of a door at
an angle. Above: setting out of
an arch. Below: a plan of the
wall from which the door opens,
from De l'Orme, *Le premier tome
de l'Architecture* (Paris, 1567),
fol. 81*v*.

4 The left pendentive,
Hôtel Bullioud, Lyons.

(Tuscan, Doric and Ionic being covered in Book v) differ considerably
from the treatment they received in contemporary treatises.

The theory of the Orders, elaborated on during the sixteenth century, came up against one essential and almost insurmountable difficulty: the examples from antiquity deemed worthy of merit differed
too much from one another – and from the instructions given by
Vitruvius (themselves not very clear) – to enable the creation of a
'system' that complied with the intellectual requirements of the new
age. Masked at first by the general imprecision associated with measurements and designs, the problem was made worse as observations
became more exact and the illustrations used in the treatises more
reliable. Theorists made efforts to get around this contradiction. Serlio
put forward Vitruvian models, or at least ones which he represents
as such, only to present immediately a number of variants. Palladio
would draft a Vitruvian text and illustrate on the opposite page a
model which differed slightly from the instructions, without commenting on the difference and without ever referring to the possibility of
variants which in fact only appear in his *Libro Quarto*. Vignola, on the
other hand, had avoided the difficulty of conflicting models by denying
their very existence, working out an abstract system which needed
no historical justification since it was justified by its own cohesive
structure.

The position adopted by De l'Orme is quite different. Like Serlio, he presents theoretical models which vary considerably from the actual examples. However, he pays particular attention to those examples which he had himself collected in Rome – and which he had also in part invented. For the first time, direct experience of the art of antiquity, in all its richness, appears to be of greater importance than a preoccupation with a particular architectural standard.

De l'Orme focuses much less on the theoretical study of the Doric Order (fols. 142–6) than on a treatment of individual examples (fols. 146–54*v*): eight pages as opposed to seventeen, one full-page illustration as opposed to five. Serlio, on the other hand, devotes five pages to theory and only two to actual examples (shown as small figures), giving neither measurements nor accompanying commentary. It is also significant to note which examples the writers choose. De l'Orme obviously includes the standard models (the inevitable Theatre of Marcellus), but he also takes great delight in very unusual examples 'in order to stimulate the minds of honest people and assist them with the most beautiful inventions'[8] (fol. 152*v*): a strange pedestal (in fact an altar) decorated with a Doric frieze comprising triglyphs with only three guttae (Pauwels 1991), capitals with 'strange ornaments' (fol. 151*v*), a cornice with a double corona found near the Palazzo Venezia (fol. 153*r*), and a remarkable architraved cornice 'taken from a marble of great antiquity' composed of 'parts which are of divers and unusual types, the sort rarely seen, and yet as beautiful and admirable as it is possible to conceive of'[9] and which bears a striking resemblance to the cornice over the courtyard of the Farnese Palace (Guillaume 1987) (plate 5).

The section on theory which comes before these pages is more mundane, and contrary to what might be expected there are no plates representing an Order in its entirety (something even De l'Orme notes 'other authors have done' in a possible reference to Vignola). The reason given by De l'Orme for their non-appearance is the poor quality of engraving, although he adds immediately afterwards that a presentation 'in parts' is better, since a single model 'would never be sufficient for use on all occasions' and could mislead the workmen. It was important for them to understand above all else 'the different ways in which the dimensions and ornaments should be rendered'[10] (fol. 141*r*).

The same method is applied to all the Orders. De l'Orme sets out three types of Ionic capital and six Corinthian entablatures, even

---

[8] 'Pour mieux réveiller les gentils esprits et les aider de toutes belles inventions.'

[9] 'Parties qui sont fort diverses et d'autres façons que l'on n'a encore accoutumé de voir, mais autant belle et admirable qu'il est possible de penser.'

[10] 'Les différences qu'on doit donner aux mesures et ornements.'

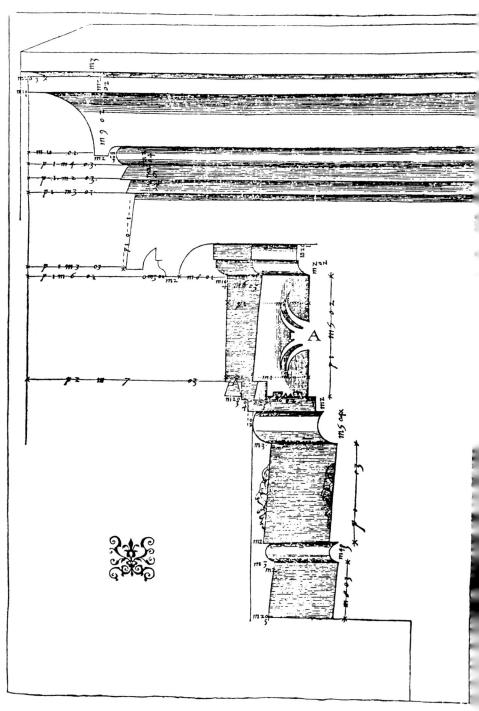

5 Antique cornice, 'unlike those which it is usual to see', from De l'Orme, *Premier tome* (Paris, 1567), fol. 154r.

6 The 'French column', from De l'Orme, *Premier tome* (Paris, 1567), fol. 219*v*.

7 (a) Entrance pavilion, Château of Anet: a chimney in the form of a sarcophagus. The body has cross-shaped plan (invented by De l'Orme), whilst the supports were inspired by the ancient sarcophagus then situated in front of the Pantheon in Rome, and the cover takes its inspiration from the Medici tombs by Michelangelo.

refusing in this latter case to give a theoretical model, since 'the difference between the cornices [is] so great that I declare I have never been able to find any two of the same proportions and measurements'[11] (fol. 197r). This passion for diversity explains the degree of interest shown in the Composite Order, alone occupying two thirds of Book VII. Under the 'Composite' are assembled, alongside the Composite Order as described by Serlio, capitals and cornices which 'belong to two or three Orders' (fol. 201v), a column in the form of a tree trunk, and lastly the 'French column', invented by the author himself (plate 6) (Pauwels 1996). Claiming his innovative right, for 'who would prevent us French from inventing a few of our own?', De l'Orme puts forward four examples of columns to serve as 'a stimulus for clever people, and to lead them to invent other sorts of columns'[12] (fols. 218v and 219r). Under De l'Orme's pen, the form of treatise devoted to the Orders consequently becomes a lesson in architectural creation, in which

[11] 'La différence des corniches [est] si diverse que je proteste n'en avoir jamais pu trouver une de même proportion et mesure.'
[12] 'D'aiguillon pour éveiller les bons esprits et les induire à inventer d'autres sortes de colonnes.'

7 (b) (left and below) Chapel, Anet: the large corner pilaster. Ionic base, and shaft with corner beading inspired by the Corinthian columns of the Pantheon: capital invented by De l'Orme.

8   Palais des Tuileries, Paris: window over the courtyard (removed to the Château La Punta). Abstra
forms are arranged around the sill, on either side of the tablet below the sill (where consoles would ha
been expected) and on the lowermost parts of the window surround. Either side is the 'French' Ion
pilaster – on these pilasters, the sculpted bands on the illustrated columns (see plate 6) have been replace
by the inset tablets of marble.

the generic 'types' are designed to stimulate the imagination and the
creation of such extraordinary inventions as the columns, doors,
dormer windows and fireplaces which are given as examples in Books
VII, VIII and IX. The whole of his architectural output testifies furthermore to the same sovereign freedom, from the chimney-sarcophaguses
and the Orders at Anet (plates 7a&b) to the window surrounds at the
Tuileries (plate 8).

However, it is important that this 'creative' teaching should not be
interpreted in too modern a sense. Everything is possible 'provided
that the measurements required by the work and the site are carefully
respected'[13] (fol. 222r). Correct proportions have an objective, ideal
reality. A man of experience, trained through studying the architecture
of antiquity – not to be confused with the 'scholar' who knows
nothing but theory (fol. 195v) – gives to the Orders their just measure,

---

[13]   'Pourvu que les mesures soient diligemment gardées ainsi que l'oeuvre et le lieu le
requerront.'

bearing in mind the conditions of use and the effect which is sought. In an apparent contradiction, De l'Orme claims both the absence of any norm *and* the existence of true proportions which the 'expert' will discover for every situation. Indeed, these can be reduced to a small number of basic proportions contained in the Bible. These 'proportions drawn from Holy Scripture', to which the author intended to devote the *Deuxième tome* of his treatise (fol. 168r), are less at odds with the freedom of creation emphasised throughout the work than might be thought. For it was no doubt De l'Orme's intention to demonstrate that the same fundamental numerical relationships could be found in all works of good quality, no matter how varied they might be. Such a discovery would have enabled him to establish a universal system of measurement, different from the fixed canon of proportions, and as objective as the science of vaults and roofs.

The quest to discover 'divine proportions' was De l'Orme's ultimate aim, although he was never to achieve it. However, this aim does at least give an indication of the scale of his ambition and of his intellectual daring, characteristics which enabled him to establish in the *Premier tome* a science of construction and a non-standard theory of the Orders, two 'inventions' which ensure him a unique place amongst the treatise authors of the Renaissance. For a work of this type to appear, cultural barriers had to be broken down, a master of stereotomy had to journey to Rome to measure the monuments there, and an architect from northern Europe with imagination and free of 'Classical' prejudices had thus to be confronted with Italian architectural thought. The originality of Philibert De l'Orme stems not only from his genius but also from his position at the convergence of two cultures.

REGINA VIRTVS

I QVATTRO LIBRI
DELL'ARCHITETTVRA
Di Andrea Palladio.

Ne' quali, dopo un breue trattato de' cinque
ordini, & di quelli auertimenti, che fono
piu neceffarij nel fabricare;
SI TRATTA DELLE CASE PRIVATE,
delle Vie, de i Ponti, delle Piazze, de i Xifti, et de' Tempij.
CON PRIVILEGI.

IN VENETIA,
Appreffo Dominico de'
Francefchi.
1570.

1   Frontispiece of Book 1 from Palladio, *Quattro libri* (Venice, 1570).

Chapter Thirteen

PALLADIO'S 'CORPUS': *I QUATTRO LIBRI DELL'ARCHITETTURA*

༺ঌঌৼৢৼ৽༻

Robert Tavernor

SINCE IT WAS FIRST PUBLISHED in Venice in 1570, *I quattro libri dell'architettura di Andrea Palladio* has appealed to connoisseurs of ancient Roman and Italian Renaissance architecture as well as to would-be practitioners of architecture *all'antica*. So successful has it been that over forty editions have been based (more or less closely) on its balanced combination of text and woodcuts; it has been translated into the main European languages, as well as Russian, Czech and Swedish. Indeed, such was its international appeal that the *Quattro libri* was the principal source-book for the architectural movement called Palladianism which, through its promotion in the eighteenth century by the English landed classes, had an impact world-wide: the architect and future American president Thomas Jefferson referred to the *Quattro libri* as 'the Bible' when designing buildings (Kimball 1968, VII; Tavernor 1991, 198). A major contribution to the popular success of the *Quattro libri* is that it appeals visually as well as intellectually. Palladio's balanced use of carefully composed woodcuts, accompanied by a direct, succinct and lucid text, has proved to be a winning combination. The quality and clarity of the images is such that lengthy and tedious descriptions are avoided, and the reader is literally drawn into the text through the compelling beauty of the woodcuts.[1]

Palladio, by appealing to the eye as well as the mind, conveyed his message clearly and memorably. He reasoned that through careful

---

[1] Over the last thirty years Palladio has probably been the most studied of all Renaissance architects. For a survey in English of Palladio's architecture with references to much of the relevant previous literature see Boucher 1994. For an Italian catalogue of Palladio's buildings see Puppi 1986/89. Recent surveys of the Palladio literature include Howard 1980 and Puppi 1990, 103–7. For a complete list of the editions of Palladio, see Palladio 1997, xix–xxii.

study and application the greatness of the architecture of antiquity can be understood and reinterpreted convincingly for the benefit and furtherance of society. He believed that an essential contribution to the 'greatness' of antique architecture was the concept of Virtue – in Latin *virtus*, and rendered in Italian at that time as *virtù* – which meant individual excellence (Tavernor 1991, 20; Palladio 1997, 347 n. 7). Alberti had considered it essential that architects should be complete individuals, and therefore virtuous, if they were to be worthy of their calling (Alberti 1988, Prologue, 3; Book IX ch. 10, 315). Virtue was acquired through disciplined study leading to a thorough knowledge of the arts and sciences. But more than academic rigour, virtue derived from individual good actions directed for the benefit and enhancement of civic life (Barbaro 1987, 2–5). Palladio highlighted this vision of the well-rounded architect in pursuit of excellence in the *Quattro libri* by depicting on the frontispiece to each of his four books *Regina Virtus* – the Queen of Virtue – as mother of the arts, presiding over his architectural deliberations within (plate 1).

The counterpart of a virtuous architect was a barbarian. This was a term of abuse which Palladio used in the *Quattro libri*, and which he equated with the perpetrators of Gothic architecture. His mentor Gian Giorgio Trissino (1478–1550) may have encouraged this unequivocal standpoint. He had written an epic poem entitled *L'Italia liberata dai Gotthi* (Italy freed from the Goths), in which an archangel called Palladio, who was an expert on architecture, was instrumental in expelling the Goths from Italy (Morsolin 1878). Trissino published the poem in 1547, though it is known he started writing it before his 'adoption' of Andrea ten years earlier (Lewis 1981). As Andrea acquired the name Palladio some time after coming into contact with Trissino, it is usually inferred, quite reasonably, that he was determined, like his fictional namesake, to revive the spirit and deeds of Roman antiquity and to overcome the 'barbarous' building practices of his contemporaries.

As part of his education, Palladio made five visits to Rome. Here he came into contact with prominent practising architects, surveyed the major ancient ruins himself and acquired, borrowed and redrew surveys of the antiquities already in circulation. He undertook this time-consuming task because he was greatly moved by the 'stupendous ruins' of antiquity, and wished to reveal to all the 'clear and powerful proof of the *virtù* and greatness of the Romans', which was still evident in their dilapidated remains, even though often partially buried under centuries of debris (Palladio 1997, 3). He made some spectacular drawings of pagan temples and shrines, basilicas and the vast Roman baths and arenas, reconstructing the ruins as entire buildings, as he imagined they had been designed. The drawings were turned into woodcuts for publication in the *Quattro libri* and presented the ancient monuments, not as damaged or imperfect relics of the past, but as potent symbols of civilised *virtù*, perfect and complete.

Palladio's mastery of the Classical language of Roman architecture and his accounts of the materials, building processes, forms and details which characterise and define its appearance, undoubtedly provided his own architectural designs, which are included in the *Quattro libri*, with great authority. He was sixty-two when the *Quattro libri* was published, and the range and sheer quantity, variety and quality of the designs he made during his lifetime provided his readers with confirmation of the flexibility and universal applicability of his approach to the Classical language of architecture. They include built and projected designs for houses and farm estates (*ville*) in the countryside of the Veneto of northern Italy; for small, medium and large town houses (palazzi) in Vicenza; and in Venice designs for a monastery (or *convento*), and (without being explicit in the text) for a bridge across the Grand Canal accommodating shops and lined with colonnades for the comfort of those it conveyed.

Book I of the *Quattro libri* outlines the preparations necessary before building can commence and which relate to foundations and materials; Palladio then proceeds to a description of the Orders of architecture. Like Serlio before him and subsequent architectural writers, he describes five column types which increase in quality from Tuscan and Doric through to Ionic, Corinthian and Composite. Their proportions are related simply, and he deliberately avoids unfamiliar Greek jargon, referring to the bulging middle of the column shaft as 'swellings', rather than by the term entasis used by Vitruvius. He concludes this book with an account of different room types and the main parts of a building. Book II characterises complete dwellings, starting with the Greek and Roman private house, and Palladio moves on to illustrate how his own designs for palazzi and villas have been adapted from these precedents for his patrons. Book III is concerned with public works – public spaces, roads, bridges and basilicas – and is again a balance of ancient example and his own project work. Book IV is given over to ancient Roman temples. However, it includes a description of Bramante's early sixteenth-century Tempietto at Montorio, Rome, which was hailed (notably by Serlio before Palladio) as an example of the best of modern sacred architecture.

For the format of the architectural treatise Palladio was undoubtedly indebted to Vitruvius, Alberti and Serlio, and he is ready to acknowledge their guidance and influence. As the principal witness of antique architecture, Vitruvius was a point of departure for anyone contemplating writing on architecture. But his *De Architectura* had some daunting shortcomings: surviving manuscripts were not illustrated; at least not in a way that could elucidate the Latin text and obscure terminology he used. In bringing Vitruvius up to date, Alberti had made more of his contemporaries aware of the value and role of an architect to society. However, the very considerable erudition embodied in his *De re aedificatoria* was aimed at the educated elite of Italian humanist society – those who could direct architects, but who were less likely to be concerned with practical issues themselves – and its unillustrated Latin text proved impenetrable and largely inaccessible to would-be architects. The translation of Alberti's scholarly Latin text into the Italian dialects of Venetian (by Pietro Lauro in 1546) and Florentine (by Cosimo Bartoli in 1550), and the inclusion of illustrations (Bartoli 1565) undoubtedly widened the treatise's appeal. But by the mid-sixteenth century it was also possible to read and understand Vitruvius more directly, through critical and well-illustrated versions of *De Architectura*. The most influential edition of Vitruvius for Palladio was published in 1556 by his patron and mentor Daniele Barbaro (1514–70). Daniele and his younger brother Marc'Antonio Barbaro had been patrons of Palladio since the late 1540s, when the architect undertook the transformation of their existing castle at Maser, turning it into the refined and exquisitely decorated Villa Barbaro (plate 2). With this work in progress Palladio and Daniele made a trip to Rome together in 1554.

The focus of each trip Palladio made to Rome (his earliest had been thirteen years before) appears to have been the objective study and representation of its ancient buildings. He wished not only to make the ruins whole again, but to relay facts about their history. He was therefore different from most other visitors to Rome, who were pilgrims concerned with the churches and the sacred relics of Christianity they contained and presumably took little more than a passing interest in architectural history. Their imaginations were stimulated by guidebook fantasies, such as those found in the medieval *Mirabilia Urbis Romae*, which perpetuated some delightful myths about the city's 'marvels'. Palladio chose to be more objective, singling out the monuments described in texts by the ancient writers such as Livy, Pliny and Plutarch, as well as more recent writers such as Biondo and Fulvio. His conclusions were published in two guidebooks to the key monuments of Rome printed during his visit there with Daniele Barbaro in 1554. One of these, published in Rome and Venice, *Le antichità di Roma di M. Andrea Palladio: Raccolta brevemente da gli auttori antichi, & moderni, nuovamente posta in luce*, is a pocket-sized book which contains descriptions of the appearance and history of the Classical ruins, organised into brief, readable sections. Similarly arranged, the *Descritione de le Chiese, Stationi, Indulgenze & Reliquie de Corpi Sancti, che sonno in la Citta de Roma* was written to provide pilgrims with a religious itinerary

LA SOTTOPOSTA fabrica è à Mafera Villa vicina ad Afolo Caftello del Triuigiano, di
Monfignor Reuerendifsimo Eletto di Aquileia, e del Magnifico Signor Marc'Antonio fratelli de'
Barbari. Quella parte della fabrica, che efce alquanto in fuori; ha due ordini di ftanze, il piano di
quelle di fopra è à pari del piano del cortile di dietro, oue è tagliata nel monte rincontro alla cafa vna
fontana con infiniti ornamenti di ftucco, e di pittura. Fa quefta fonte vn laghetto, che ferue per pe-
chiera : da quefto luogo partitafi l'acqua fcorre nella cucina, & dapoi irrigati i giardini, che fono dalla deftra, e finiftra parte della ftrada, la quale pian piano afcendendo conduce alla fabrica ; fa due pe-
chiere co i loro beueratori fopra la ftrada commune : d'onde partitafi ; adacqua il Bruolo, ilquale è
grandifsimo, e pieno di frutti eccellentifsimi, e di diuerfe feluaticine. La facciata della cafa del pa-
rone hà quattro colonne di ordine Ionico : il capitello di quelle de gli angoli fa fronte da due parti:
quai capitelli come fi facciano ; porrò nel libro de i Tempij. Dall'vna, e l'altra parte ui fono loggie,
e quali nell'eftremità hanno due colombare, e fotto quelle ui fono luoghi da fare i uini, e le ftalle, e
li altri luoghi per l'vfo di Villa.

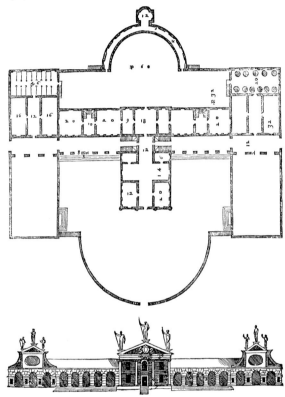

2(a) (above) The Villa
Barbaro, Maser, c. 1549–
58, from Palladio,
Quattro libri (Venice,
1570), Book II, p. 51.
(b) (left) The Villa
today.

complimented by Palladio's own appreciation of the relative artistic value of the works being visited (Palladio 1988). Both became respected and popular guidebooks to Rome, and *L'antichità di Roma* (as it is better known) was eventually to replace the *Mirabilia* as a widely read guidebook, running to more than thirty editions: in the early eighteenth century it was published with the *Quattro libri*, as the 'fifth' book (Leoni 1742).

The success of his first publishing venture can only have encouraged Palladio to proceed with the *Quattro libri*. He must also have been gratified that his ability to write succinctly and clearly – without the aid of illustrations – was well received by his readers, and he would surely have appreciated that an extensively illustrated treatise on architecture had considerable potential. For such an undertaking he needed images which would compliment his writing style, and the Barbaro *Vitruvius* (1556, and republished with expanded commentary in 1567) provided Palladio with an approach he was later to adopt for the *Quattro libri*. It contains a commentary by Daniele Barbaro illustrated by detailed figures which are remarkable for their precise reconstructions of Greek as well as Roman buildings. These are presented as woodcuts paired to the minimum of information, and are used by Daniele to elucidate rather than embellish the text. Some of the reconstructions were designed by Palladio, and Barbaro acknowledges his involvement, and specifically refers to his reconstruction of the ancient Roman theatre (plate 3).

Sebastiano Serlio (1475–1554) had provided Palladio with his most obvious model with the illustrated treatise these days known as *L'architettura*, Books I–V of which were published before the *Quattro libri*. The significance of Serlio's *L'architettura* is that it freed the architectural treatise from the model supplied by Vitruvius (from which Alberti's is derived) or critical editions of it (by Barbaro and others), and provided instead an illustrated account of ancient and modern architecture, accompanied by Serlio's own architectural inventions. The treatises by Serlio and Palladio differ in their preferred modes of presenting buildings, though this may reflect their different backgrounds. Serlio came to architecture through painting, and he represents buildings and fragments of them in a painterly way, in perspective, to give an effect of mass and depth. Also, his illustrations have a scenographic quality about them: he sometimes presents buildings in their urban setting, or details as if they were fragments of stone strewn across the ground, as he might have come across them in a field. His writing is almost equally as theatrical in effect, with long descriptive passages which, while allowing the reader to engage with his way of thinking, are less necessary in the context of such elaborate images.

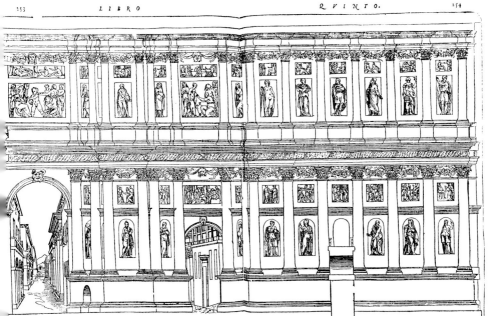

Scaenae frons of the ancient Roman theatre, from the Barbaro *Vitruvius* (Venice, 1567 ed.), pp. 53–4.

There were other contemporary influences on Palladio too. For example, the treatise by the architect Giacomo Barozzi da Vignola (1507–73), published as the *Regola delli cinque ordini d'architettura* (Rome, 1562), was composed with a short preface followed by thirty-two engravings, each with only a brief explanatory caption: later editions of Vignola's treatise also included some building designs of his own (Vignola 1985). Another useful model for Palladio, as its title suggests, was *I quattro primi libri di architettura* by the Sienese architect Pietro Cataneo (?1510–?1574), published in Venice in 1554, which considers military and civil architecture together. In 1567 he published *L'architettura di Pietro Cataneo Senese* which added four new books to those already in circulation – on ornament, water resources, geometry and perspective (Vignola 1985). Palladio knew him personally, and even claims that Cataneo appropriated his rule-of-thumb method for proportioning column shafts (Palladio 1997, 18). Such practicality and directness in matters architectural shaped Palladio's *Quattro libri*. Consequently, his treatise is simply laid out and devoid of academic and artistic pretension.

Palladio's approach may also reflect his early practical training as an apprentice stonemason. Then he would have been concerned to receive direct information about what was required, as stone was worked using precise measurements and two-dimensional templates in order to realise three-dimensional forms. Similarly, the woodcuts in his treatise are universally represented to scale, and indicate the main external elevations of buildings as vertical, orthogonal planes. Instead of perspective he used shading to indicate recessed and projecting surfaces, and sectional elevations cut through the buildings as if they were physical models. Furthermore, these woodcuts record key dimensions, and demonstrate the positions and relative sizes of columns; capitals, cornices and other details are drawn to a scale larger than the main body of the building, are often presented on separate sheets, and always carefully arranged. In this way Palladio demonstrated the beauty and ornament of the ancient buildings, as he understood or imagined them to have been, so as to be both appealing and informative.

Alberti had been the first to make clear how an architect should present the image of a building. He stated that architects' models of buildings, for instance, should not be 'accurately finished, refined, and highly decorated, but plain and simple, so that they demonstrate the ingenuity of him who conceived the idea, and not the skill of the one who fabricated the model' (Alberti 1988, Book II ch. 1, 34). We must assume, therefore, that he would have approved of Palladio's drawings. The treatment of a building as if it were a rational body which could be subjected to analysis in order to determine facts and quantities, as well as qualities, had its contemporary parallel in an increasingly scientific appraisal of the human body through anatomical studies. Correspondingly, Palladio presents sections through the body of a building with a precision, clarity and detachment that resembles the extraordinary anatomical drawings designed by artists of the school of Titian for Andreas Vesalius (1514–64) in the *De humani corporis fabrica*. Vesalius's *Fabrica* was published in Basle in 1543, though he demonstrated his anatomical skill at Padua University, in Palladio's home town. In the preface of the *Fabrica* he emphasises 'the rehabilitation of anatomy as a practical discipline and the introduction of visual material as a necessary instrument in its teaching' (Carlino 1988, 39). The twin concerns of practicality and clear drawings are echoed in Palladio's architectural treatise.

Of course, Palladio's skills were not as an anatomist of the human body. Nor was he adept at representing the human form in drawings and, like Vesalius, he possibly used artists to draw the statues represented in his treatise (Puppi 1990, 23). Nevertheless, there is a striking parallel between the representation of bodies in the *Fabrica* and of buildings in Palladio's *Quattro libri*. Palladio appears to dissect buildings as if they were equivalent to living organisms, such that he reveals the composition of walls and structure, and the inner organisation of the house (as villa or palazzo) or temple, directly relating interior spaces to

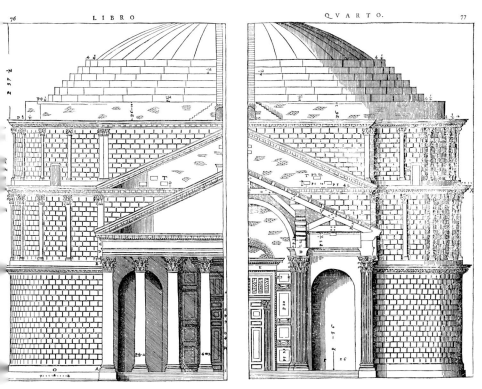

The Pantheon in part elevation, part section, from Palladio, *Quattro libri* (Venice, 1570), Book IV, pp. ⁷–77.

exterior form; in the *Fabrica* cadavers are portrayed as living, and exposing their inner workings and primary organs to the viewer (plates 4 and 5). The parallel is entirely pertinent, as Palladio, like Alberti before him, often refers to a building as if it were a body (see Alberti 1988, 421), and both architects had learnt about the qualities and characteristics of ancient buildings by effectively dissecting their remains, and identifying the activities and uses that had once invigorated them.

In the *Quattro libri* Palladio's most thorough presentation of a building commences with a plan (which is comparable to a view of the interior of the body lying prostrate on a slab), followed by a view of its principal façade in two halves – that on the left being half of the exterior elevation, and on the right a section through that half of the building. The following sheets may illustrate a side elevation and section, and ornamental details at a larger scale. His presentation of the Pantheon in Rome is a particularly stunning example of the process by which a building is revealed (Palladio 1997, 287–96) (plates 4 and 6).

VIGESIMA QVINTI LIBRI FIGVRA·

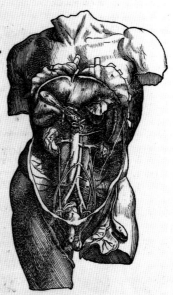

VIGESIMAE FIGVRAE EIVSDEM'QVE CHA-
racterum Index.

P R Æ S E N S *figura sectionis serie duodecimæ succedit. ab hac enim omnia intestina*
execuimus , relicta duntaxat uentriculi portione superioris orisicij uentriculi sedem common-
strante.atq; ita hæc figura pleraq; indicat,quæ nunc opportunius cum characterum indicibus se-
riatim insinuabuntur.

A,A *Septi transuersi portio peritonæo succincta, atq; una cum costis aliquot sursum reflexa.*
B,B *Caua iecoris sedes.*
C   *Iecoris ligamentum,quo ipsius sinistra pars septo alligatur.*
D   *V enæ per umbilicum iecori exporrectæ portio,ubi & sinus ille indicatur primum hanc admit-*
     tens uenam, quæ per priuatum ipsi in iecore humano incisum foramen ad iecoris usque sedem per-
     reptat,ubi hic G non procul à K adhibitum conspicis,ubiq; uena hæc in iecoris substantiam pri-
     mùm uerè digeritur.
E   *Hac sede iecur sinum obtinet,quo cedit stomacho per septum transuersum ad elatius uentriculi*
     orisicium contendenti.
F   *Superius uentriculi orisicium, uentriculiq; portio.*
G,G *Lineæ impressiones siue tuberaq; in iecoris cauo ubi partem uenam promit conspicua.*
H   *Bilis uesicula.*

I *Portæ*

5   Dissection drawings from Vesalius, *De humani corporis fabrica* (Basle, 1543), pp.
370, 605.

ANDREAE VESALII

BRVXELLENSIS, DE HVMANI CORPO-
RIS FABRICA LIBER SEPTIMVS, CEREBRO ANL
malis facultatis sedi & sensuum organis dedicatus, & mox in initio omnes
propemodum ipsius figuras, uti & duo proximè praeceden
tes libri, commonstrans.

PRIMA SEPTIMI LIBRI FIGVRA.

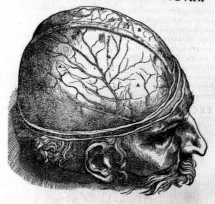

PRIMAE FIGVRAE, EIVSDEMQVE CHARACTERVM
INDEX.

PRIMA septimi libri figura humanū caput ita adaptatū exprimit, quemadmodum id
cerebro ostendēdo opportunè à collo & inferiori maxilla dissecātibus liberatur. Praeterea tan
tam caluariae partē orbiculatim serra abstulimus, quanta quoq; omniū quae in caluaria cōtinen
tur amplitudine uidendorū gratia, auferri solet. quanta uerò illa sit, liquidò dijudicabis si septi
mam figurā sexti capitis libri primi examinaueris, quae hinc ablatā caluariae partem interna su
perficie exprimit. Quēadmodū itaq; praesens figura sectionis serie caeteras omnes inuicē ordine
succedentes praecedit, ita quoq; illa septimi libri figurarū primā non inopportune inscribimus,
quae durā cerebri cōmonstrat membranam adhuc illaesam, neq; aliqua ex parte pertusam, uulne
ratam ue. quamuis interim ipsius membranae uincula diuulsimus, quae per capitis suturas ad mem
branam efformandā porriguntur. quae quod caluariā succingit, περικράνιον nuncupabitur. atque
cum his fibris pariter uascula sunt effracta, quae per caluariae foraminula & suturas deducta,
ipsi durae membranae, ac illi qua caluaria succingitur, communes censentur. Caeterum ex duobus
qui figurā ambire conspiciuntur orbibus, humiliorē, cutis & membranae ipsi subditae cōstituunt,
elatior autem ipsa est caluaria. Vniuersum uerò hoc orbe complexū, durā cerebri membranam
refert, omnibus charactèribus in figura cōspicuis uniuersim semelq; indicatam. at singuli chara
cteres in hunc modum priuatim habent.

A,A Dextrū durae cerebri membranae latus, seu eius mēbranae pars dextrā cerebri regionē ambiēs.
B,B Sinistrum durae cerebri membranae latus.
C,C C Tertius durae membranae sinus secundū capitis longitudinem exporrectus, & hic nulla ex

Ee 3   parte

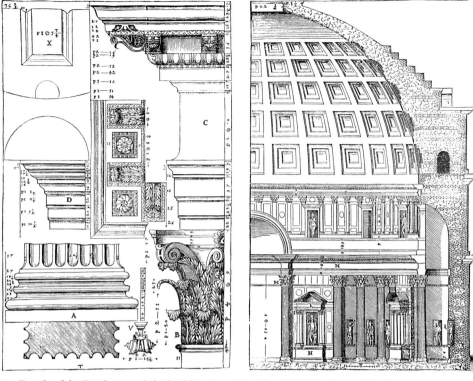

6   Details of the Pantheon and the building in section, from Palladio, *Quattro libri* (Venice, 1570), Bc
IV, pp. 80–81.

The bodily symmetry of a building *all'antica* obviates the need to
draw both halves of an elevation or section, the missing half usually
being the mirror reflection of that which is illustrated. Indeed, one may
assume that a mirror was used to reveal a façade or interior in its
entirety by placing one of the mirror's edges on the axis of symmetry
at right-angles to the page. Ultimately, the viewer 'reads' the building
as each page is turned, and the eye moves from left to right and builds
up a mental image of a complete building – its overall morphology and
the details of its parts. As in the human body, everything has its proper
place, and those skilled in dissection, as in architecture, can identify a
diseased or inappropriate member as well as healthy or appropriate
ones.

It is known that Palladio had started work on three of the books
which were to be developed into the *Quattro libri* by the mid-1550s
(Palladio 1988, 71ff.); Daniele Barbaro mentions in his *Vitruvius* a book

by Palladio on private houses (Barbaro 1556, 179; 1567, 303), and Vasari saw a version of it in 1566. Yet, for reasons unknown, Palladio was under pressure to complete these books for publication in 1570: when describing his design for the Palazzo Montano Barbarano in Vicenza he mentions that the published version was of an earlier scheme, and that he had 'not included the design of the plan which has just been completed and according to which the foundations have now been laid because I was not able to make the woodcut in time for it to be printed' (Palladio 1997, 98). Nor was the enterprise entirely complete in 1570. While the title of his treatise refers unequivocally to just four books (in fact, three different versions of it were published in 1570 – *I due libri*, *I due primi libri*, as well as *I quattro libri*), related books were to have followed: he refers specifically to one on antiquities in the *Quattro libri* (Puppi 1990, 13; Palladio 1997, 14, 56). Thus, Palladio probably intended to extend his method to describe every ancient building type. Only death, according to his seventeenth-century biographer Paolo Gualdo, Canon of Padua cathedral, prevented Palladio from publishing drawings he had already prepared of 'Ancient Temples, Arches, Tombs, Baths, Bridges, Towers, and other public buildings of Roman antiquity' (Zorzi 1958–9; Lewis 1981, 3). In 1581, a year after his death, Palladio's sons were preparing an expanded edition of the *Quattro libri* to include a fifth book he had finished, but which was left unpublished. This has tempted the suggestion that Palladio's completed treatise was intended to be longer still, and comprise ten illustrated books on architecture – which would have outdone even Vitruvius and Alberti – and that the additional six would have covered theatres, amphitheatres, triumphal arches, baths, tombs and bridges in some detail (Lewis 1981, 10 n. 16).

Palladio had certainly made provision for related books, since a large quantity of good quality measured drawings by him of various ancient building types are to be found in the Drawings Collection of the Royal Institute of British Architects (RIBA), London. As the *Quattro libri* combines his own building designs with those of ancient origin, it is equally likely he would have wished to have published his church designs for Venice in a subsequent book. Unlike Cataneo, it is unlikely Palladio would have included a book on military architecture in his treatise, for he published a commentary on the campaigns of the Roman emperor Julius Caesar quite separately, in *I Commentari di C. Giulio Cesare* (Venice, 1574–5). Palladio's fascination for military strategy had been kindled in him by his mentor Trissino, as his preface to the commentary acknowledges with gratitude (Palladio 1988, 189).

Curiously, considering Palladio deliberately wrote the *Quattro libri* in an accessible language, the first edition outside Italy was in Latin. This was published in Bordeaux in 1580, though only Book 1 was so rendered. Translations into the major European languages followed during the seventeenth century, and a common pattern was to publish only part of the four books: for example, a translation of Book I only was made into Spanish in 1625, and French in 1645; Books I and II became available in German in 1698. It was not until the French translation by Roland Fréart de Chambray was published in Paris in 1650 that all four books by Palladio became accessible to non-Italians. English-only readers had to wait until 1663 for sight of the first book of Palladio. This was published by Godfrey Richards and was translated from the Italian but relied on a version of Palladio's woodcuts taken from a 1645 French edition of Book I by Le Muet. Despite its limited scope it proved hugely successful, and was last reprinted in 1733. By then, however, complete editions of the 'Four Books' were available in English, translated by James Leoni (1715–20) and Isaac Ware (1738).

Ware's edition was the most faithful to the original, textually and visually, but Leoni's was best known in England and abroad. It provided the intellectual and visual basis for Palladian and Georgian architecture in Britain, and was used by the architects of great landowners in town and country – the British Vitruvians described by Colen Campbell (1676–1729) in his first volume of *Vitruvius Britannicus* (1715) – as an emblem of a natural hierarchy and order (Tavernor 1991, 152–6). It later took on an international and quite different dimension in Britain's American colonies. Towards the end of the eighteenth century, Thomas Jefferson (1743–1826) was instrumental in breaking these colonial ties and the notion that aristocracy should be based on the advantages of birthright alone. Moreover, he personally pursued the ancient republican belief in *virtù*, and embraced Palladio's 'Four Books' as a useful and practical means by which to give form and authority to his vision for a new society (Tavernor 1991, 188–209). Thus, the Classical language of architecture was filtered through Palladio and Jefferson into the governmental architecture of the New World. Consequently, this architecture has come to be seen by many as a potent symbol of modern democracy and individual freedom. Such has been the influence of *I quattro libri dell'architettura di Andrea Palladio*.

Chapter Fourteen

THE MIRROR THEATRE OF VINCENZO SCAMOZZI

Marco Frascari

T HE VICENTINE ARCHITECT VINCENZO SCAMOZZI (1548–1616)[1] is primarily known for having completed several of the works left unfinished by that most famous of Veneto architects, Andrea Palladio. Scamozzi is, however, largely unknown for his architectural thinking. His theory and aims have never been fully understood, and his contributions to the architectural theory of his age are still not recognised for their originality. An extraordinary architectural theoretician in his own right, Scamozzi has suffered the fate of being overshadowed by Palladio. Indeed, Scamozzi's contribution to architectural thinking is remarkably significant as regards the present unruly condition of the architectural discipline. Scamozzi emphasises the universality of tectonic propositions through the example of a specific regional architecture (with illustrations of examples of his villas in the Veneto and elsewhere in northern Italy). But Scamozzi also proposes a renewed awareness of the power of the imagination, based on a new definition of the role and responsibility of a professional architect fully engaged as an intellectual in the design process.

A particular demonstration of the lack of recognition that this remarkable architect and theorist has received can be easily made through considering the many survey texts of architectural history. These books, usually, show a central view of the stage of the Teatro Olimpico in Vicenza (1580–85), which typically includes a large part of the built perspective beyond the *scaenae frons* (plate 1). In the caption the only citation is to Palladio, although in the selected view the dominant presence is that of Scamozzi's design. For besides designing the perspectival urban structure taking up most of the stage, Scamozzi

---

[1] Scamozzi's year of birth is traditionally cited as 1552; however, it is recorded as 1548 in his will.

1   The stage of the Teatro Olimpico in Vicenza, 1580–85.

also drastically modified the *scaenae frons* itself, as completed by
Palladio, to ameliorate the view of the perspective (Tavernor 1991,
104; Magagnato 1992). The fact that Scamozzi thus finished several of
Palladio's works after the latter's death led to the false perception of
Scamozzi as a 'pupil' completing in a reasonably faithful manner the
works of his 'master'. Furthermore, an understanding of Scamozzi as a
'bad' pupil of Palladio has arisen due to the negative interpretation of
Scamozzi's establishment, through his legacy, of a fund to assist intellectually gifted students of architecture. Whilst this fund helped
Ottavio Bertotti Scamozzi (1719–90) to accomplish his wonderful
measured drawings of Palladio's buildings, published in the eighteenth
century, the legacy and this example of its subsequent influence has
strengthened the conception of Scamozzi's work as within a Palladian
heritage. The fund was construed as the project of a mischievous pupil
who had become rich by finishing the incomplete buildings of his
master and had left the funds for the study of Palladio's architecture to
alleviate his 'bad conscience'.

    In the English-speaking world, the unfortunate interpretation of
Scamozzi's Palladianism was initiated by his contemporaries. Although
Inigo Jones, for example, looked at Scamozzi's works as a source of
inspiration for several designs – and had met the aged Vicentine

architect on his travels in 1614 – the great English Palladian had a very low opinion of him: Jones famously noted in his copy of Palladio that 'this secrat[ive] Scamozio being purblind understoode nott' (I.xviii, p. 50 (Worcester College, Oxford)). Of a similarly disapproving tone is a pronouncement by an Italian contemporary critic, Giovanni Battista Agosti. In commenting on a design by Scamozzi for the façade of the Palazzo Nuovo in Bergamo, Agosti emphasised the duality of tradition and invention reflected in Scamozzi's practice of architecture, noting 'Scamozzi possessed very well the elements of the art, but he has thoughts far too peculiar and he likes novelties' (Learco 1927). In this remark Agosti does however note Scamozzi's originality of purpose, since the architect would appear to have fully articulated the work's concept even if this had appeared overtly 'novel'. Indeed, in his architectural treatise he would attempt to describe the Neoplatonic *Idea* (Panofsky 1968) or absolute conceptual basis of a universal architecture (embracing cities down to the design of the Orders) which, however, could be easily translated by an architect in particular conditions of site and construction.

SCAMOZZI'S *IDEA* OF UNIVERSAL ARCHITECTURE

Scamozzi's treatise on architecture, entitled *L'Idea della architettura universale . . . divisa in X libri* (The *Idea* of Universal Architecture), was published at the author's expense at the press of Giorgio Valentino in 1615, a year before the author-architect's death (plate 2). The treatise is a large folio volume of around eight hundred pages in length. It was written during the last twenty-five years of his life, as he informs us in the introduction (Scamozzi 1615, Proemio, vol. 1. 4). The treatise reflects Scamozzi's study of a wide range of modern architectural theorists (Scamozzi 1615, vol. 1, Book 1, 18) and Classical authors – including Plato and Aristotle but most importantly Vitruvius – and of architecture north and south of the Alps; Scamozzi's experiences of various building traditions, including particularly French Gothic, during several lengthy journeys, were recorded in his travel books (Scamozzi 1959). Indeed, the treatise's frontispiece makes explicit these two sources in the inscription which reads, 'Honest reader, consider this work [*opus*]. It is, believe me, full of labour, sweat, and grime, the result of long journeys, the inspecting of sites, and the constant turning of the pages of books. Be seated and learn, if you will. Farewell'.[2]

---

[2] 'Lector candide, viden' hoc opus? Plenum est, mihi crede, laboris, sudori, pulveris ex longa peregrinatione, locorum inspectione, librorum evolutione, suscepti. Tu sedens, si lubet, fruere. Vale.'

Divided into two parts, this ponderous treatise was conceived in ten books – emulating Vitruvius and Alberti – but is incomplete due to the author's untimely death. Scamozzi must have sensed the imminence of this event, leading him to pay for the publication of the incompleted work himself, a fact recorded in the frontispiece (*expensis auctoris*). In the closing remarks of the introduction of the first part (Scamozzi 1615, vol. 1. 4) Scamozzi outlines the intended contents of the treatise. The first book is to be devoted to a discussion of the origin, characteristics, qualities and topics which concern the discipline of architecture (defined, as in chapter 16, as *fabrica* and *edificio*): it will include a discussion of architecture's rank as a science, of the education of the architect, his moral and intellectual qualities and his supervisory role over masons and craftsmen. The second book is to deal with site analysis and the planning of cities, and of fortifications (*architettura militare*): Scamozzi here echoes Pietro Cataneo in including the art of fortification with chapters on civil architecture. The third book is assigned to a discussion of commodious private buildings (*edifici di comodo privati*), illustrated by his own designs and a reconstruction of the 'Greek' house, whereas in the fourth and fifth books Scamozzi is to consider the monumentality of, respectively, public and sacred buildings (*architettura civile*). The sixth book is to be concerned with the five canonic Orders and architectural ornament in general (which is linked, in true Neoplatonic fashion, to the order of the *macchina del mondo*), and the seventh is to deal with the relationship between form and materials. The eighth book is to be devoted to tectonic processes, from the digging of foundations to the erecting of roofs. In the ninth book, Scamozzi plans to discuss processes for finishes and embellishment (*finimenti*) whilst the tenth and final book is set aside for an analysis of the design procedures for the preservation and restoration of buildings.

In reality, however, only six books were to be included in the published treatise, three for each part: books one, two and three for the first part, books six, seven and eight for the second. Whilst the scope and structure of the planned treatise is unprecedented within the Vitruvian book tradition, the incompleteness of the published version adds to the difficulties of comprehending in totality Scamozzi's scheme for a universal architecture – his conceptual opus. Scamozzi took for granted that his readers would engage themselves in an active reading of the text: his text, diagrams and illustrations are not intended as explanations which are prescriptive in nature – offering a restricted set of paradigms – but rather they are conceived as springboards for the reader to reach the highest planes of architectural insight and invention.

Indeed, although Scamozzi illustrates and discusses his own work in the treatise, whereas this practice had dominated Palladio's four books

Frontispiece from Scamozzi, *L'Idea della architettura universale* (Venice, 1615).

in which the theory had emerged from practical examples, Scamozzi's treatise is much more focused on a theoretical narrative: it is certainly no mere catalogue of his built work. The range of his considerations is emphasised by the fact that the theoretical arguments are structured around, and centred on, a set of dualities: form and matter, architect and builder (craftsman), universal and particular (regional), theory and practice, ideal and corporeal. His ideas concerning these topics are principally intended to stimulate the imagination. Hence Scamozzi should not be seen as providing the standard didactic or sermon-like explanations regarding the discipline of architecture. He is not unfolding a path, following, say, the traditional steps of Vitruvian exercises in the Orders (of Philandrier for example): rather he is attempting to equip his reader with clues and starting-points, general patterns and devices (or even emblems) concerning the practice of architecture, in its fullest sense, as an intellectual activity. His aim is to configure an intellectual system that should yield a comprehension of a universal architecture – as the title suggests – by establishing the relationship between the universal natural order perceived by the mind (Platonic *Ideas*) and the qualities particular to buildings. His text and illustrations are thus intended as a catalyst for his reader to perceive the essence of architectural practice.

However, the originality of this treatise, providing as it does a theoretical expression of Scamozzi's built work, has never fully been understood by its editors, translators and by scholars of architectural history. The majority of them have felt that a firm editing or a healthy curtailing of the text was required to 'clarify' and make effective what was seen as nebulously correct and legitimate, from later points of view, in the context of the overwhelmingly taxing theoretical horizon set by the Vicentine architect. The result of this general approach was that the French, Dutch and English translators have kept primarily to Book VI – on the origin and proportion of the Orders – accompanied by a few excerpts and illustrations from the other books, and they have dismissed these other books as groundless speculations and superfluous digressions. Presumably the greatest obstacle Scamozzi's editors and translators found in understanding the value and merits of the treatise are its atypical configuration of the cardinal parts of *all'antica* architecture and its novel arrangement of the Vitruvian subjects. This renders a different priority to the educational programme which the treatise represented. Indeed, in an Italian edition of the treatise published in 1883 the editor, Giuseppe Ticozzi, resolutely changed the order of the books: he rearranged the treatise to begin with the sixth book in a misguided attempt to establish an apparently logical structure, on the arrogant assumption that the preferred configuration had been forfeited by the Vincentine author due to his idiosyncratic approach to the discipline and his liking for 'novelties'.

SCAMOZZI'S UNIVERSAL THEATRE OF THE MIND

In the introductory letter to the treatise Scamozzi states that his purpose in publishing the work was to reduce the complexity of architectural theory, with its manifold conflicts and contradictions, to an intelligible and ordered body of knowledge which can, he asserts, be presented and understood as analogous to an 'imaginal' theatre.[3] This theatre is a large structure (*un'ampio Theatro*) where anyone, when located in its centre, 'by turning their eyes around and stretching out their hand, could descry and retrieve the majority of the most beautiful definitions and most real and sublime understandings which the ancients had in this field and which for many years had been forgotten and almost lost . . .' (Scamozzi 1615, vol. 1. sig. a3r).[4] Scamozzi thus presents his treatise as a device for the rediscovery of architectural principles. Rather than being outlined directly to us, these principles are instead imagined as organised spatially within – and as comprising – a 'theatre' of architectural knowledge. Scamozzi here makes a distinct reference to a universal system of topical thinking common amongst the intellectuals of the Veneto during this period, that is, the memory theatre. Several Venetian architects and architectural scholars – including Serlio – had been influenced by the 'divino' Giulio Camillo, nicknamed Delminio (1480–1544), a great rhetorician, Neoplatonist and master of the art of memory (Yates 1966; Carpo 1993). Delminio had spent most of his life attempting to formulate a system of topical knowledge, and in Venice he constructed an actual memory theatre which consisted of a seven-stepped series of cabinets with painted images.[5] Delminio's basic aim was to establish an encyclopedia of human knowledge structured to reflect the workings of the human

---

[3] I should like to stress that Scamozzi's theatre is an 'imaginal', not an imaginary, construction. Corbin coined the term 'imaginal' to signify the realm of the cognitive imagination, a 'world of images in suspense', not to be confused with the realm of the imaginary. This 'imaginal' world is ontologically above the world of the senses, and below the pure intelligible world (Corbin 1976, 11).

[4] 'Di redurre in un corpo ben distinto, & ordinato tutti I Precetti di così celebre, e preclara facoltà dell'Architettura, iquali sin hora come spariti, e quasi persi se ne rimaneuano: intantoche postosi chiunque si voglia nel mezo, quasi d'un'ampio Theatro, ad un girar d'occhio, e porger di mano, potranno scorger, e ritrouare la maggior parte delle più belle Diffinitioni, e più reali, e sublimi intendimenti, c'havessero gli antichi in essa Facoltà, e già tante etadi decaduti, e quasi andati in oblivione.'

[5] Delminio's memory theatre is one of the most fascinating architectural experiments of the Veneto Renaissance. During this time the Classical art of memory underwent a transformation at the hands of 'occult' philosophers such as Delminio. His timber theatre represented an attempt to develop a memory system which would embody, as an edifice-machine, the entire encyclopedia of human thought, a theatre where the mnemonic power of images would activate the imagination and thus inspire the speech of the orator and any research into the production of human knowledge. It was to be a kind of corporeal 'time machine' where the past, present and future were related through a mnemonic building.

mind within the analogous edifice of a wooden theatre, a model *imago mundi* embodied in an *imago corpori*.[6]

Delminio's ideas lived on in Venetian circles after his death: he may well, for example, have influenced the design of the Teatro Olimpico in Vicenza (Yates 1966, 160–72). His *L'Idea del theatro dell'eccellen. M. Giulio Camillo* had been published in Florence and Venice in 1550, and was read to members of the Accademia Olimpica in their new theatre.[7] Although he could not have met Delminio, Scamozzi clearly draws on the image of the stepped memory theatre of universal knowledge, organised by subjects, as an essential structure for his 'construction' and communication of the *Idea* of a system of universal architecture (*Architettura Universale*). The architect is not a craftsman (Scamozzi 1615, vol. 1, Book 1, 6), but an intellectual (that is, one with an *intelletto*) who knows how to consider the workings of the imagination (Book 1, 7). Architecture, or rather a design for a future building, is conceived as a mental image which is based on a knowledge of the liberal arts stored artfully in the architect's memory. Hence 'the Architect reflects upon (*specula*) the Idea of the thing and within his mind (*intelletto*), and discerns the causes of all forms and parts of any building . . .' (Book 1, 7).[8] The architect's imagination is his instrument of vision, the *oculus imaginationis* at the core of his operations: the imagination's eye dissects the physiognomy, physiology and anatomy of the natural and tectonic environment.

Scamozzi's ideas concerning the operation of the imagination may be linked to the work on mnemonics by another Neoplatonic philosopher – but exact contemporary – Giordano Bruno (1548–1600) (Yates 1964; Frascari 1990). Bruno's *De umbris idearum* published in Paris in 1582, and his *De imaginum, signorum et idearum compositione* published in Frankfurt in 1591, both proposed occult mnemonic systems based on images. Although Scamozzi refers to the figurehead of the hermetic or occult arts, Hermes (Scamozzi 1615, vol. 1, Book 1, 38 margin), Bruno is not openly acknowledged in the treatise which was published fifteen years after the Neoplatonist was famously burned alive in the Campo dei Fiori in Rome (on 17 February 1600). However Scamozzi's geometric diagrams developed from Euclidean propositions can be readily compared with Bruno's Lullian mnemonic figures (Scamozzi 1615, vol. 1, Book 1, 32; Frascari 1990) (plate 3). Indeed Scamozzi's wheel of winds at the head of the treatise resembles certain Lullian mnemonic

[6] The human body was also considered by Delminio to be a 'theatre' of wisdom: Delmino equally called his theatre the *Teatro della Sapienza* (Theatre of Wisdom).

[7] *Atti dell'Accademia Olimpica* (Vicenza: Archivi Accademia), Acc. 10 (1555–86).

[8] 'L'Architetto specula nella sua Idea, e nel suo intelletto, e discorre le cause di tutte le forme, e parti di qualunque edificio.'

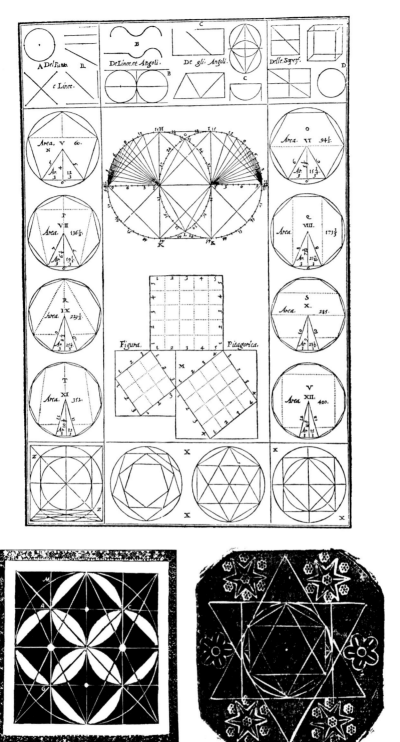

3   Scamozzi's geometric diagrams from the *Idea* (Venice, 1615), Book 1, p. 32: in comparison with Bruno's Lullian mnemonic figures.

4   Lullian graffiti in Scamozzi's Teatro Olimpico in Sabbionete, on the second row of seating step

wheels (Yates 1966, 182–3). And Lullian graffiti has been found (after recent restoration work) in Scamozzi's Teatro Olimpico in the ducal palace at Sabbionete (1590), on the second row of seating steps: it was common enough during construction for the architect to draw his 'concept' on the wall of the building for patrons and builders (plate 4). It follows that Scamozzi's villas might be conceived as 'memory buildings', passive machines in which light and shadow are harnessed to make our imagination work, just as the 'shadow of Ideas' had informed the workings of the mnemonic art (as outlined in Bruno's *De umbris idearum* (Yates 1966, 199–230; Frascari 1990, 43)). The plan and section of Scamozzi's Villa Bardellini in Monfumo near Asolo are certainly illustrated in the treatise with shadows (*skiagraphy*) expressly in mind (Scamozzi 1615, vol. 1, Book III, 279; Frascari 1990, 43–4) (plate 5).

The downfall of Giordano Bruno can be traced to the year 1591, when he moved to Venice at the invitation of Zuane Mocenigo, a wealthy Venetian collector, who wished to be instructed in the art of memory. A year later Bruno was arrested in Venice after Mocenigo had betrayed him to the Inquisition (Yates 1964, 348). It is clear from the results of this trial that Scamozzi could not openly acknowledge his debt to Bruno's work without putting himself at risk. However, during Bruno's final Venetian sojourn, both men had ample opportunity to meet. The house of Zuane Mocenigo is a possible point of contact: in

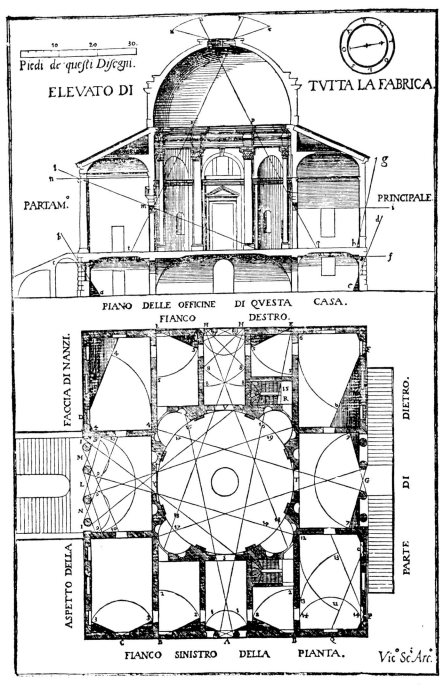

Piedi de questi Disegni.

ELEVATO DI

TVTTA LA FABRICA.

PARTAM.

PRINCIPALE.

PIANO DELLE OFFICINE   DI QVESTA   CASA.

FIANCO   DESTRO.

FACCIA DI NANZI.

DIETRO.

DI

PARTE

ASPETTO DELLA

FIANCO   SINISTRO   DELLA   PIANTA.

Vic°Sc.Arc.

5   The plan and section of Scamozzi's Villa Bardellini in Monfumo near Asolo, 1615, from the *Idea* (Venice, 1615), Book III, p. 279.

his treatise Scamozzi singles out members of the Mocenigo family during a discussion of the *galleria*, a new type of space which reflected mnemonic theory in displaying sequentially collections of artworks (Scamozzi 1615, vol. I, Book III, 305, 328–9). Equally, Scamozzi, the active bibliophile, could well have met Bruno in Giovanni Battista Ciotto's bookshop, Bruno having discussed his theory in public there (Spampanato 1933, 135; Yates 1964, 346). Alternatively, the Accademia which met in the house of Andrea Morosini may have been a point of contact, Bruno having presented his thoughts at their meetings. Scamozzi was, after all, the favourite architect of the Morosini family.

In his writings, Bruno had criticised an art of memory based solely on images, since these images rapidly become too many and were as a consequence easily forgotten. Rather, diagrams were of a higher order of efficacy as representing the underlying or 'occult' patterns of nature. The construction of such geometric diagrams, and of gridded layouts (Scamozzi 1615, vol. I, Book III, 260–61), lies at the very heart of Scamozzi's thinking (Hersey 1976).

Scamozzi divides the arts in general into two sets comprising three categories: the first set includes arts which are *dottrinali*, *liberali* and *meccaniche*: the second set embraces arts which are *imitative*, *operative* and *pratiche*. Architecture, according to Scamozzi, is neither an imitative (mimetic) nor a mechanical art, but a liberal art, since architectural forms are necessarily geometric and belong to mathematics: hence in place of the anecdotal origins of architectural order found in the hut and human body as recorded by Vitruvius, architectural forms were now seen by Scamozzi as a product of geometric/mathematical rules (Scamozzi 1615, vol. I, Book I, 41). In line with Neoplatonic philosophy, Scamozzi's emphasis on the 'universal' efficacy of regular geometric forms – the square in particular as developed in the opening chapter of the treatise's first book – is due to their status as the underlying order of nature, and hence although the 'Vitruvian man' is illustrated he is now imposed on a grid surrounded by geometric figures (Scamozzi 1615, vol. I, Book I, 40; Hersey 1976).

SCAMOZZI'S FRONTISPIECE

With its distinct full-page illustrations, Scamozzi's treatise (or 'theatre of knowledge') can be seen to comprise a number of topical and visual 'thresholds' (or 'levels' in the theatre), the most significant of which is obviously the book's frontispiece (Genette 1987). For it is through this that the reader enters Scamozzi's 'theatre'. Frontispieces were emblems which pictured the book's content and theme, and typically involved allegorical figures cast in an architectural framework befitting the virtue and grandeur of their book's subject (Barbaro's triumphal arch in his *Vitruvius*, for example, or Palladio's 'altarpiece' in his *Quattro libri*).[9] Scamozzi's frontispiece is no exception in illustrating a heroic four-sided structure of the Composite Order, which supports allegorical figures, inscriptions and a miniature of the author (plate 2). In the distance lies a landscape of *all'antica* buildings – amongst which there appears to be a church – the fruits, no doubt of the learning encapsulated in the allegorical structure pictured surrounding the great author-architect. Befitting the book's learned contents and the frontispiece's status as a 'gateway', the frieze bears the warning, 'Let no one enter here without knowledge of the liberal arts'.[10] Architecture's intellectual (that is, non-mechanical) status was thereby firmly established right from the start.

The four female figures above the pediment symbolise the virtues required in an architect, as the inscriptions make clear. The first figure on the left represents *praecognitio*, that is the knowledge of the liberal arts. This is symbolised by the open book in the hands of the statue. The second figure on the left of the arch represents the duality of *aedificatio* and *constructio*. The former term concerns the physical art of building (but can also mean enlightenment), the latter the metaphysical construction (or structure). The figure has a model or small building at her feet (perhaps symbolising *aedificatio*) and a mathematical template in one hand (perhaps symbolising *constructio*). The other hand points to the heavens: for the art of building belongs to the realm of superior forms. This second figure stares across the title block at the third, who symbolises *finitio* and *expolitio*. This figure returns the gaze of the second and might be seen to represent the aspiration towards perfection through completed works of the art of building. The fourth figure looks out on the landscape and sky, like the first, and represents *restauratio*. Her fingers are pointing upwards, indicating that the act of historic preservation (the subject of the projected tenth and last book) belongs to the realm of theory. Indeed, it enjoys equal status with the liberal arts on the pediment.

At the base of the structure we have the two figures theory (*Theoria*) and practice (*Experientia*), mirroring the frontispieces in the treatises by Vignola and Palladio and following the common Renaissance distinction between the two areas. Here Theory points to the heavens whilst Practice gestures to the ground, as befits their respective realms. Theory holds a book, and the dado of the pedestal contains an architect (perhaps Scamozzi) engaged in lofty discussion; Practice holds

---

[9] For the frontispiece of his treatise, Palladio may have employed a graphic re-elaboration of the design of one of his very early works, the family altar in Vicenza cathedral.

[10] 'Nemo huc liberalium artium expers ingrediatur.'

a measuring stick, and the dado shows the architect holding a pair of compasses and giving instruction. The source of this instruction is emphasised by the Neoplatonic inscription encircling the miniature of Scamozzi, which reads, 'Here the outward image of the author's body is revealed. Inside is shown the image of his intellect.'[11]

Scamozzi's *L'Idea della architettura universale* obviously echoed in title Delminio's *L'Idea del theatro* (1550), Lomazzo's *Idea del tempio della pittura* (1590) and Zuccaro's *L'Idea de'pittori, scultori et architetti* (1607). The 'Idea' of art was a universal truth, a concept repeated by Scamozzi in his notion of a 'universal architecture'. As the last treatise in the Vitruvian tradition of such works, Scamozzi's *L'Idea* lies at the crossroads between the old body-centred Renaissance Neoplatonism and the new age of mathematical order which would be exemplified by Perrault. In its reflection of the former it is already anachronistic, whilst in the completeness of its quest for the universal mathematical order to architecture and appeal to 'reason' (*ragione*) it is precocious. Unprecedented also is Scamozzi's conception of an architectural treatise as analogous to a mnemonic 'theatre'. The central task of the Scamozzian architect is to translate the *Idea* of his imaginary design on to paper and thence into tectonic form, a making visible that which is invisible. Scamozzi's conception of the workings of the imagination might be likened to a mirror, in which the image but not the substance of corporeal forms is visualised: indeed the first English translation of a part of Scamozzi's treatise, published in 1669 by William Fisher, was itself entitled, *The Mirror of Architecture, or, The Ground-Rules of the Art of Building*.

---

[11] 'Corporis effigies hic obvia cernitur. Intus ipsius effigies cernitur ingenii.'

Part Two

THE TREATISE IN CONTEXT

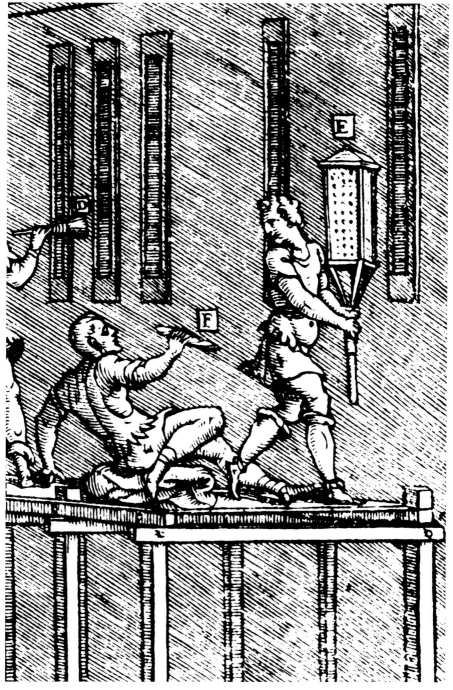

Detail of plate 4, Chapter 15.

Chapter Fifteen

TREATISES AND THE ARCHITECTURE OF VENICE IN THE FIFTEENTH AND SIXTEENTH CENTURIES

Manuela Morresi

ON 11 AUGUST, 1508, at the Venetian church of San Bartolomeo di Rialto, the mathematician and philosopher Luca Pacioli read out his introduction to Book v of Euclid's *Elementa*. More than five hundred people were present. In his text which was printed the following year, he himself lists some of his more illustrious listeners: amongst the clerics there was 'frater Iucundus Veronensis Antiquarius', and amongst the architects there was 'Petrus Lombardus' (Pacioli 1509; Nardi 1963, 116–17). During this famous lecture, Pacioli proposed mathematics as a common foundation for all the sciences and suggested that this fundamental status even extended to the truth of religious faith: in fact, the mystery of the Holy Trinity became understandable when reduced to the concept of *proportion*. This introduction to Euclid thus provided Pacioli with an opportunity to present the theoretical, philosophical and theological bases to his treatise *De divina proportione*, published in Venice in 1509 (Bruschi 1978, 25–59).

The presence of Fra Giovanni Giocondo ('Iucundus') at the lecture of August 1508 was, without doubt, motivated by his humanistic, mathematical and geometrical interests. On the other hand, the presence of Pietro Lombardo, head of Venice's main construction company in the fifteenth century and someone who was not known for his interests in theory, is less understandable (McAndrew 1980, 112–212). Nor do his architectural works reflect a particular sensitivity to proportion: taking but one example, this can be clearly seen in the

church of Santa Maria dei Miracoli (begun in 1480) whose geometric
framework comprising inlays of multi-coloured marble is contradicted
by the arbitrary widening of the central span of the façade and by the
windows, which are off-centre with respect to the front of the apse
(Lieberman 1972). It is even doubtful whether Pietro was capable of
understanding with any ease the Latin in which Pacioli gave his
lecture. We may therefore presume that the old master – nearly eighty
in 1508 – attended the lecture more because it was a particularly
important social event than for scientific reasons or because he was
looking for insights within Euclidean philosophy, as interpreted by
Pacioli, for his own professional work.

At the end of the fifteenth century and the beginning of the next,
Venetian artisans seemed in general to show little interest in theoretical
speculation, or in the very recent developments made in the field of
architectural treatises. The *De re aedificatoria* by Leon Battista Alberti
was known in the city very early on but circulated only in humanist
circles. Bernardo Bembo had a copy: in his haste to read it he ended
up personally helping with the transcription of the manuscript
(Grayson 1956, 181–8; Giambonetto 1985); the Camaldolesi monks of
San Michele in Isola, who in 1468 commissioned Mauro Codussi to
build the monastery's church, also appear to have known of Alberti's
writings. Not so the architect who realised the façade of San Michele
by imitating that of Alberti's Tempio Malatestiano in Rimini but who,
despite this, was probably incapable of reading Alberti's rhetorical Latin
nor very likely even to think such reading a necessary complement to
his skill as a stonemason. Not even the publication in Venice in 1497
of the third edition of Vitruvius's treatise – following the Roman
edition by Sulpicio da Veroli (n.d., c.1486–92) and the Florentine
edition of 1496 – seems to have had any immediate repercussions in
Venetian architectural practice. This practice remained largely faithful
to Venetian tradition and did not respond to the 'call of the antique'
with the same urgency as in Florence and Rome.

Of the counter examples, which are relatively few in number and
therefore particularly significant, those that should be mentioned are
the architectural initiatives promoted by the doge Francesco Foscari
(1423–57) for the ducal palace and the basilica of San Marco, and for
Foscari's own home (Morresi 1998), and, in the literary field,
Francesco Colonna's *Hypnerotomachia Poliphili* (Venice, 1499). In one of
the best-known woodcuts that accompany this text, concerning the
'Magna Porta', there is a representation of one of the most extraordinary pieces of *all'antica* architecture realised in Venice in the fifteenth
century, the monumental Arsenale gate of 1457 copied from the Arco
dei Sergi at Pula (Concina 1984, 51–73; Furno 1994). This is an

example of 'inverse' transmission, from a constructed piece of architecture to a theoretical text. However, neither of these exceptional works had any immediate effect in Venice itself. As a result of the *Hypnerotomachia's* courtly theme and the difficulty in understanding Colonna's 'mixed' language, the book circulated mostly amongst the nobility and was to be found more in monastic libraries than in stonemasons' workshops.

FRA GIOCONDO AND THE INFLUENCE OF HIS *VITRUVIUS*

In such a cultural context, the appearance of the *Vitruvius* published by Fra Giocondo in 1511 represents an event of quite some significance. And yet, once again it did not lead to any appreciable changes in built architecture. Giocondo the humanist, philologist and antiquarian was also an engineer, an expert in hydraulics, bridges and fortresses, and an *all'antica* architect (Fontana 1988). His knowledge of the Vitruvian treatise was so detailed that during his stay in Paris (1495–1505) he was able to give public and private lessons on the *De Architectura*, already with a commentary backed up by illustrations (Juřen 1974, 101–15). Giocondo's rich and varied knowledge enabled him to combine the two distinct avenues of Vitruvian research, namely that defined by the artistic-architectural ensemble of learning and that of the philological-humanist (Pagliara 1986, 33–4). His *Vitruvius*, emended using a sophisticated method of comparing manuscripts of different families, was thus rendered clearer than previous editions (Ciapponi 1984, 72–90), and the presence of many illustrations – for the first time in a printed edition of Vitruvius – made comprehension even easier. In fact, like Francesco di Giorgio, Giocondo attached great importance to the illustrations. So much so that their explanatory function is even stated in the title of the work: 'M. Vitruvius per Iocundum solito castigatior factus *cum figuris* et tabula ut iam legi *et intelligi* possit' (An exceptionally good text of M. Vitruvius prepared by Giocondo *with figures* and index so that it can now be read *and understood*) (my italics). The 136 woodcuts which accompany the text illustrate, for the most part, machines (for hydraulics, lifting and defence), antique buildings (with particular emphasis on houses) and architectural Orders. In these latter cases, the author shows his precise technique for orthogonal representation in plan, elevation and section – the very technique later described by Raphael in his famous letter to Leo X (Nesselrath 1986, 110–11; Camesasca 1993, 284).

In Giocondo's reconstruction of the *amplissima* (exceedingly large) Roman *domus* (fol. 64v), which was possibly influenced by Giuliano da

Sangallo's 1488 project for the palace of the King of Naples[1] (Pellecchia 1992, 405–6) or by Francesco di Giorgio's domestic reconstructions (Burns 1994, 162–3) – Giocondo had met both men in Naples – the atrium is identified as an entrance with three aisles rather than as a part of the courtyard. This particular interpretation was to be taken up and developed by the Vitruvian specialists of the 'Roman school' in the early 1500s, from Fabio Calvo to Giovanni Battista da Sangallo (Fontana and Morachiello 1975; Pagliara 1988, 179–206). The alternative design for an atrium – this time uncovered in the centre, as presented in Giocondo's reconstruction of the 'small house' (fol. 63*v*) – was much less influential since it was unsuitable for urban buildings with several floors (Pagliara 1988, 196). But even though Giocondo's 'basilica' atrium had an immediate effect on Sangallo's atrium design for the Palazzo Farnese in Rome, begun in 1514 (Frommel 1995, 7–18), no such reactions can be seen in Venetian houses until at least the second half of the 1500s. When Michele Sanmicheli planned the palace for Girolamo Grimani in 1556, his interpretation of the atrium followed the tetrastyle model preferred by Serlio, although he deformed it because of the site's irregular shape (Puppi 1986, 171–4). On the other hand, Jacopo Sansovino's unrealised plan for a palace for Vettor Grimani on the Grand Canal of 1527 proposed a structure with two courtyards (Tafuri 1987b, 41–50), thus alluding to the antique house but departing from Giocondo's and Sangallo's interpretation by including an entrance in the form of a vestibule screened by columns at the front.[2] In defining such an area as a '*porttico*', Jacopo makes an unprecedented connection between the *vestibulum* and the *portego* – the ground-floor vestibule in Venetian buildings, running through the house, connecting the canal and land entrances – thus fluently marrying antique typology with that of medieval Venetian tradition.

Despite being illustrated, Giocondo's *Vitruvius* of 1511 was only of limited use to architects, at least for the first decades of the century, due to its being written in Latin (a significant obstacle to its potential utility). This limitation was even more the case in a place such as Venice which was geographically and culturally distant from the 'centre' of Vitruvian studies. Equally, Giocondo's potential Venetian 'public' was not comprised of stonemasons, proudly based as they were on their native tradition which resisted any stimuli from Rome. The circumstances which led to Venice as the chosen place of publication for the *Vitruvius* can be explained by the fact that Giocondo was called to the city in 1506 by its highest body of magistrates, the Council of Ten (Ciapponi 1961, 152). However, the choice was most certainly

[1]   Rome, Biblioteca Apostolica Vaticana, Codex Barberinianus Latinus 4424, fol. 39*v*.
[2]   Venice, Biblioteca Civica Correr, *Disegni*, cl. II, fol. 6038*r*.

also influenced by the high quality of Venetian publishing, capable as it was of producing woodcuts to rival those of the best printing houses in Europe. In addition, in Venice Giocondo could probably find direct contacts within a small and select public: the fringe of Venetian nobility which found it hard to adapt to the law imposing equality within the city's oligarchy and which was consequently more sensitive to the stimuli of *novitas* derived from the antique. It was probably not a coincidence that the *De Architectura* of 1511 came from the press of Giovanni Tacuino, the trusted publisher of the Corner family (Ceriana 1996, 113–14); from the second half of the 1400s this patrician family had shown a keen interest in architecture and was to commission Sansovino to build a majestic palace on the Grand Canal (Howard 1987, 132–46). Indeed, the Corner family was particularly known for its promotion of the reconstruction of Udine Castle, the residence of the Venetian Lieutenant; this was proposed after the earthquake of 1511 (Tafuri 1994, 375–8; Guerra 1996, 27–37), the same year in which Fra Giocondo's *Vitruvius* was published. When Giovanni Fontana eventually constructed a residential building with *all'antica* architectural features for Lieutenant Giacomo Corner, he sent Giacomo's father, Giorgio, a letter in which he described the new building using up-to-date Vitruvian terminology – a heritage that both the author and addressee obviously had in common.[3] Echoing Alberti's *De re aedificatoria*, Giocondo's *Vitruvius* thus seemed to be addressed more to the nobility – potential patrons – than to those who would physically carry out those patrons' intentions.

It is, however, likely that Giocondo was himself a consultant for certain architectural works in Venice, such as the Fondaco dei Tedeschi and the church of San Salvador (Tafuri 1985, 53–61). The rebuilding of the Fondaco dei Tedeschi, which housed German merchants and their merchandise, commenced in the summer of 1505 after it had been destroyed by fire. Girolamo Tedesco (whose design was approved on 19 June), Giorgio Spavento and Antonio Abbondi (called 'Scarpagnino') are all mentioned in documents regarding the building, but it is very probable that Giocondo acted as 'consultant' to the administrators and supervisors of the building site. Certainly the building's formal Vitruvian composition of a square courtyard with arches on pillars (plate 1) and the general *all'antica* arrangement of the new Fondaco resemble one of the buildings illustrated in the 1511 *De Architectura* (fol. 4r) (plate 2). Indeed, powerful evidence of Giocondo's involvement is a statement to that effect, first made in 1517 – in a public oration in praise of the *capitano da terra*, Andrea Gritti, the future doge – and repeated in 1541 (Dazzi 1939–40, 873–4). Gritti had

---

[3] Udine, Archivio di Stato, *Notarile*, b. 5545, fol. 15v.

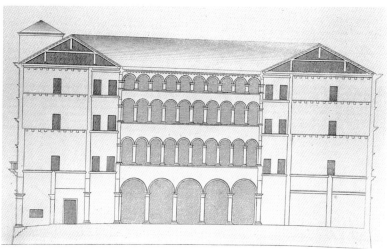

1   (a) (top) The courtyard of the Fondaco dei Tedeschi, Venice (begun in 1505).
(b) (above) Section showing the courtyard of the Fondaco (Cicognara et al., 1858,
III).

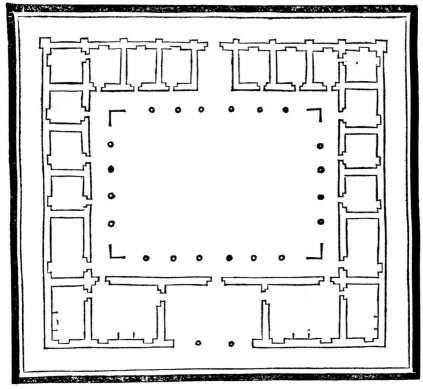

2   Fra Giocondo's plan of an ideal building illustrating the Vitruvian term *ichnographia*, from *M. Vitruvius per Iocundum solito castigatior factus* (Venice, 1511), Book I, fol. 4r. This plan is comparable with that of the Fondaco dei Tedeschi in Venice.

himself been directly involved in the reconstruction of the Fondaco in 1505 (Concina 1997, 205–6).

On realisation, the Fondaco represented an isolated *all'antica* fragment in the compact late-medieval urban fabric of Venice. But when, in 1514, a fire destroyed the Rialto market – the symbolic and functional heart of a city whose power was founded on its commerce – the project submitted by Giocondo for the market's reconstruction did not enjoy the same success. This project, known to both Marin Sanudo and Giorgio Vasari, was to have transformed the Rialto area into a Greek forum resembling that described by Vitruvius (v.i.1) – a square, with a gateway on each axis – and would have been completely surrounded by canals (Vasari 1878–85, v, 269–71). This scheme, apart from the last characteristic, is very similar to Cesariano's future reconstruction of the Greek forum (Vitruvius 1521, fol. LXXIIIv), so much so that it was probably one of Cesariano's sources (Tafuri 1978, 427).

The rigorousness of Giocondo's *all'antica* design, which would have brought a dangerous variation into the 'sanctuary' of the city,[4] led to its rejection by the Senate of the Republic. The Rialto area, which local historians held as the first region in the lagoon to be settled by Venetians (and therefore sacrosanct), was preserved in its character by the choice of the project by Scarpagnino for this site which, although not as coherent as Giocondo's, was more respectful of what had gone before (Calabi and Morachiello 1984, 291–331). Indeed, Sanudo's striking remark 'Fra Giocondo, who is not here, and who does not understand the place'[5] (Sanudo 1887, XVIII, 401) revealed the fundamental defect in the proposal rejected by the Senate. In other words, an out-of-place *all'antica* language was being superimposed upon a site regulated by age-old laws governing settlement in the lagoon. The Vitruvian approach which was accepted for a small fragment – the Fondaco dei Tedeschi – was not welcome when it was a case of intervening in, and giving form to, a part of the city itself.

'HIDDEN' TEXTS ON ARCHITECTURE

Yet, construction and urban planning in the Republic during the fifteenth and sixteenth centuries were not devoid of theoretical concerns. But the source of this theory which seemed best to express the architectural orientation of the Venetians – or rather that of some groups amongst the nobility – was a body of texts which were 'above suspicion': that is, works of a philosophic, economic and political nature which may be considered as 'hidden' treatises on architecture. Just as theories for the development of villa culture in Venetian territory can be traced in the numerous treatises on agriculture published in Venice from the end of the fifteenth century (Morresi 1988, 7–15), so too can architectural 'rules' and directions be found in these 'hidden' texts – equally unrelated, apparently, to architecture – which influenced Venetian construction and urban planning. This is certainly the case with *De oeconomia veneta* (1473) by the doctor Giovanni Caldiera, in which the description of an ideal family provides the excuse for a long digression on the characteristics which define domestic and public buildings.[6] For Caldiera, like Alberti before him, believed in the Platonic-Aristotelian analogy of the house being like a small town ('And just as every economy resembles a polity, so also the

---

[4]   Venice, Archivio di Stato, *Provveditori al Sal*, 31 May 1497, b. 6, R. 4, fol. 39*v*, cited in Calabi and Morachiello 1984, 294, n. 24.

[5]   'Fra Ziocondo, qual non é qui e locho non capisse.'

[6]   Oxford, Bodleian Library, Cod. Laud. Misc. 717, fols. 79–99*v*.

home is in the likeness of the city').[7] In other words, the family, structured on a hierarchical basis, is intrinsically assimilable to the state as a unit of public government. The private house should therefore be built skilfully and on a site worthy of it; it should have a wide entrance and a well-lit courtyard but should not be the occasion for ostentation if properly regulated by the economic criterion of *utilitas* (utility). On the other hand, *magnificentia* (magnificence) is appropriate for public buildings since they must express the virtue and wisdom of the state. The hierarchy which Caldiera establishes for the respective architectural forms of the public and private buildings is the same as that found within the family; indeed, in the family the *pater*, through his virtue, supervises the domestic rules just as the architect supervises the rules (the *principia*) of a building in the city (King 1986, 103). The distinction between public and private equally reflects the mythical law said to have been established by the founders of the settlement in the lagoon, which imposed uniformity of height for all private houses to represent 'unity and equality' (Sansovino 1581, fol. 140r) (and which therefore sets them apart from public buildings).

Such hierarchy was also accepted by the aged Procuratore of San Marco, Domenico Morosini, in his book *De bene istituta re publica*, begun in 1497, but this treatise on the state takes a critical stance towards the Republic's politics and constitution (Morosini 1969; Cozzi 1970, 405–58). Morosini did however consider the splendour of public buildings and public ceremonial a deterrent to enemies, whilst here again the *mediocritas* (standardised average) of private dwellings was seen to reflect the age-old equality which consolidated Venetian aristocracy. Morosini's urban vision projected the straightening and widening of roads, the creation of urban axes giving views of certain pivotal monuments and the institution of a civic magistrature controlling ornamentation (Morosini 1969, 80–83, 98–9, 134–5). For newly acquired territory, he projected new roads and the improvement of the site and defence systems (Morosini 1969, 172–3, 201–3, 214). That Vitruvian and Albertian themes should appear within this political programme is hardly surprising given Morosini's well-documented relationship with Venetian literary circles, in other words with those who were amongst the first to support the *De re aedificatoria* (Tafuri 1985, 157–8). But underlying the urban and territorial project contained in the treatise was Morosini's political project which opposed the Serenissima's broad system of government and was against its policy of expansion on the mainland, Morosini aiming instead at a concentration of republican power in a few 'old' hands (Morosini 1969, 423–5).

---

[7] 'Et quia omnia Iconomia Policie assimilatur, et domus etiam civitatis similitudinem gerit' (Caldiera quoted in King 1986, 105 n. 38).

URBAN RENEWAL UNDER ANDREA GRITTI

It is not, therefore, by coincidence that *De bene istituta re publica* remained unpublished until the twentieth century. Given the successive wars which occupied the Republic at the end of the fifteenth century and during the first decade of the sixteenth – culminating in the tragic defeat at Agnadello in 1509 – such an architectural programme could not hope to find a broad consensus. It was only when the title of doge fell to Andrea Gritti, in 1523, that Morosini's cultural policy was, in part, to be realised (Cozzi 1970, 441). During the fifteen years in which he was doge, Gritti promoted reforms in the areas of defence on land and at sea, in the legislative system and in scientific experimentation; furthermore, from 1536 to 1537, he encouraged a revolutionary rearrangement of the San Marco site (Tafuri 1984, 9–55). In each of these areas opposition to Gritti's policy – a policy which aimed at a conscious specialisation in the different fields of knowledge – came from factions of the nobility which preferred to remain faithful to republican traditions that were considered holy because inspired by God and as such immutable. In the field of architecture, this manifested itself in the conflict between the *proto* – a master-craftsman skilled in matters of practice, who simply executed detailed programmes which had already been specified – and the architect, who was the bearer of new theoretical and specialist knowledge. However in 1529 the new Proto of the San Marco *procuratori* was the Florentine Jacopo Sansovino, who had come from the Roman 'architectural laboratory' of the first quarter of the century. Gritti broke with tradition by appointing Sansovino, a 'very expert architect', to being responsible for the San Marco site. Moreover, by this means Gritti promoted the introduction of a well-developed *all'antica* language into the heart of a city which, until then, had been hardly touched by such *novitas*.

The gestation of the San Marco buildings, comprising the Library, the Loggetta and the Mint, coincided with the publication of the first volume of Sebastiano Serlio's treatise on architecture – *Regole generali . . . sopra le cinque maniere degli edifici* – in Venice, in 1537. As is well known, this was the fourth book of Serlio's publishing project, and it dealt (for the first time ever) with the five antique architectural Orders – Tuscan, Doric, Ionic, Corinthian and Composite – in a systematic way and with reference to their proportional relationships.

The written *all'antica* code laid down by Serlio was simultaneously being put into practice in the architecture constructed by Sansovino. On the San Marco site alone, Sansovino used rustic work (the Mint), the Doric Order (Library and Mint), the Ionic (Library and Mint) and the Composite Order (Loggetta). For the Serlian motif on the first floor of the library, he used the so-called 'Vitruvian' Ionic base, as illustrated by Serlio and described in *De Architectura* but rarely used in antique architecture (Serlio 1537, fol. xxxivv/158v; Lemerle and Pauwels 1992, 7–13). But the new San Marco architecture in no way blindly followed the Vitruvian principles and proportions described by Serlio, even though Sansovino was a close friend of the Bolognese theorist (Tafuri 1985, 90–101). This inventiveness can be seen in the tall frieze above the second – Ionic – storey of the Library, large enough to contain the windows for the mezzanine, a solution recalling the Bramantesque Palazzo Caprini in Rome of 1501 (Frommel 1973, II, 85). Sansovino clearly distances himself from Vitruvian proportions here but at the same time alludes to the *all'antica* style. In fact, the frieze's decorative motif of putti holding festoons – a motif previously used by Baldassarre Peruzzi in the second, Doric, storey of the Chigi's Palazzo Farnesina in Rome (begun in 1505) and by Jacopo himself in Palazzo Gaddi (begun in 1518) – is a copy of the decoration of a Roman sarcophagus which had come to Venice as part of an antique collection belonging to Cardinal Domenico Grimani (Zorzi 1988, 25–40).

The 'freedom from the rules' demonstrated by Sansovino on this occasion was the fruit of his ability to combine his understanding of antique teaching with the architectural experimentation in Rome of the first quarter of the sixteenth century. Serlio, on the other hand, in organising his fourth book on the *regole generali* – the general theory of the Orders – goes so far as to detach the 'rules' from the examples of antique architecture to which his third book is dedicated (published in Venice in 1540). It is only with his last books, completed not in Venice but in France and partially unpublished, that the process of applying the Orders to examples of various house types would also repeatedly force Serlio to distance himself from the Vitruvian dictates which he had used in this book on antiquities as his selection criteria for the vast and contradictory repertoire of surviving monuments (Fiore 1994, XL–XLII).

Serlio's condemnation in Book III of ancient licentiousness was made in relation to the connections he had formed in Venice with certain dilettante architects of the nobility whom he called upon to witness the superiority of the Vitruvian text compared to the 'text' constituted by the Roman ruins (Serlio 1540, fol. CLV; 1537, fol. IIIr; Pagliara 1986, 63). Yet the actual architectural knowledge of these dilettantes has probably been overrated: for example, the family palace planned by Francesco Zen, one of the noblemen praised by Serlio, reflects very little of the antique despite the supposed architectural knowledge of its author (Concina 1984, 265–90). Even the autograph fragment of the treatise on architecture written by the patrician Gian Giorgio Trissino of Vicenza, Palladio's first patron, reveals the limited capability of a nobleman who supposedly 'knows'.[8] It would appear from the single illustration which can be associated with the text that this unfinished treatise, practically contemporary with Serlio's Book IV, was to include figures. This illustration, of an ancient *domus*, seems to acknowledge the reconstructions by Fra Giocondo and the plans for houses by Francesco di Giorgio. But when Trissino puts himself to the test as 'architect' of his own house in Vicenza – represented in three further illustrations appended to the manuscript – he reveals a remarkable mediocrity in terms of planning (Morresi 1994, 116–18).

THE VITRUVIUS OF DANIELE BARBARO

Even so, the ambitions of the dilettantes testify to how the policy of urban renewal promoted by Gritti stimulated some members of the nobility to acquire the theoretical tools necessary for controlling such a process. The climax of this trend was undoubtedly reached in 1556, when Daniele Barbaro published the first edition of his translation of, and commentary on, Vitruvius. Barbaro, patriarch elect of Aquileia, educated in Padua and member of an influential Venetian family of pro-Roman political leanings, had begun working on architectural theory in 1547 (Barbaro 1556, 274). In 1554 he spent some time in Rome, together with Palladio (who helped with the illustrations in his *Vitruvius*), in order to undertake scholarly research into the correspondence (or otherwise) between the Roman's text and archaeological reality.

The date that marks the beginning of Barbaro's interest in architecture coincides with the publication in Venice of a programme of Vitruvian studies which had been formulated by the Accademia della Virtù, founded in Rome by Claudio Tolomei in 1540–41 but closed in 1545 (Tolomei 1547). It is therefore possible that the patriarch elect intended collecting Tolomei's abandoned material, thus bringing into being what for the Accademia had remained at the programmatic stage (Tafuri 1987a, XIII). But the main ambition underlying Barbaro's monumental theoretical effort can, once more, be found to be of a 'political' nature. His translation is the first to show a full understanding of the Latin text, so much so as to be held an indispensable reference until at least the end of the eighteenth century. His commentary, apart from illustrating his thorough knowledge of fifteenth- and sixteenth-century architectural treatises (from Alberti to Philandrier), reveals equal familiarity with texts on mathematics, geometry, astronomy,

[8] Milan, Biblioteca Nazionale Braidense, MS Castiglioni 8/3.

navigation and agriculture, whether antique, medieval or contemporary. The resulting *summa* of technical-scientific knowledge leads us to
presume that his work was aimed at readers who were cultured and
erudite. Thus, once again, despite the use of the vernacular and the
abundance of illustrations, the main public to whom a work on
architectural theory was destined was not one of artisans. This is true
at least for the first edition, a luxury folio volume of high price. In the
second vernacular edition, of 1567, the reduction to quarto and the
simplification of text and illustrations (D'Evelin Muther 1994, 355–66)
probably signal the start of a 'second phase' in Barbaro's project, a
phase in which he seems to address himself to readers more interested
in architectural practice. It is significant, however, that this revision
follows rather than precedes the version for Venice's nobility-rulers-
patrons.

For in 1556 Barbaro had consciously addressed the nobility of
Venice, as shown by the wide coverage of specifically Venetian 'institutional' themes in the commentary – namely, the problems of the
defence of the Serenissima's frontiers, of the Arsenale, of the silting of
the lagoon, and of the Republic's building traditions (Tafuri 1987a,
XXII–XXIV). These themes were, however, partially abridged for the
1567 Latin edition destined for a 'European' public (Morresi 1987, XLI–
LIII). Characteristically it is in the violent criticisms aimed at Venetian
tradition that the patriarch elect reveals the final aim of his project:
'And if they [the Venetian people] think that their houses, as usually
built, should be considered exemplary, they are greatly mistaken,
because in fact *this custom is exceedingly bad and faulty*'[9] (Barbaro 1556,
179 [my italics]). Barbaro's target is the type of the noble house/
fondaco which had remained unchanged for centuries, with its tripar-
tite structure revealed on the façade regardless of the stylistic 'clothing'
in which the building was dressed, whether Byzantine, Gothic or
proto-humanist. His famous reconstruction of the antique *domus* – in
which, following Alberti and Cesariano, the atrium and *cavedium* are
identified as parts of a single courtyard (plate 3) – was therefore
intended for educational purposes: namely to teach the antique style to
a hostile Republic (Tafuri 1987a, XXIV).

Extending this educational aim to the whole work, it is possible to
identify in it a far broader polemical aspect. Architecture, based on
mathematical certainties, 'can be well compared with wisdom and
prudence':[10] these are the virtues of good government, and it is these
which raise architecture to a sort of *heroica virtù* above all the other arts

---

[9]   'Et se gli pare che l'usanza delle loro fabriche gli debbia esser maestra, s'ingannano
grandemente, *perché in fatti, é troppo vitiosa e mala usanza.*'
[10]   'Può essere con la Sapienza, et con la prudenza, meritamente paragonata.'

(Barbaro 1556, 15). In this notion Barbaro echoes the Aristotelian metaphor of the politician as 'architect' previously appropriated by Giovanni Caldiera: architecture becomes an instrument of government for a Republic which is *bene instituta* (well founded). Some of the polemical themes tackled by Domenico Morosini surface in Barbaro's commentary but Barbaro varies the treatment. For Barbaro, it was by reforming a 'faulty' architectural practice that the political system, supported by a philosophy upon which was based the proud claim of Venetian supremacy and sanctity, would equally be reformed. And here Barbaro's main target is the *proti*, the men of practical knowledge who were therefore subject to programmes established by the magistrature. Against these master craftsmen, Barbaro set up the heroic figure of the architect who 'knows the theory' (Barbaro 1556, 7). Hence the revolutionary potential, in political terms, of the 1556 *Vitruvius* lay in the *all'antica* architectural system as described in Vitruvius and transmitted through translation, illustration and commentary, the very system which was introduced into Venice by Andrea Gritti in the face of marked resistance.

As regards the 'rules', Barbaro gives a code which at the same time avoids the temptation to be dogmatic. The variety of the examples of antiquity guarantees a certain interpretability of the regulations: 'You see how Vitruvius makes us free from superstition, duty and slavery without reason'.[11] This remark precedes the definition of architectural virtue as the continual use of variation, an idea which was to be re-emphasised in Palladio's *Quattro libri* of 1570 (Magagnato 1980, XXIII). Rigorous archaeological research guaranteed, on the other hand, the legitimacy of architectural practice whilst both potential 'deviations' – excessive rigour and complete liberty – were equally condemned: 'I hate superstition as much as heresy'[12] (Barbaro 1556, 82).

PALLADIO AND RUSCONI

The battle between architect and *proto*, rehearsed by Barbaro in his commentary on Vitruvius, began in reality in Venice at the end of the century during two of the largest public commissions: the completion of the San Marco site and the construction of the Rialto bridge (Tafuri 1985, 245–71; Calabi and Morachiello 1987, 234–59). In both cases, architectural 'conservatism' – which defended the practical approach of the *proto* – was upheld by the *giovani* party, the faithful custodians

---

[11] 'Vedi che Vitruvio ci leva la superstitione, l'obbligo e la servitù senza ragione.'
[12] 'Io ho in odio non meno la superstizione, che la heresia.'

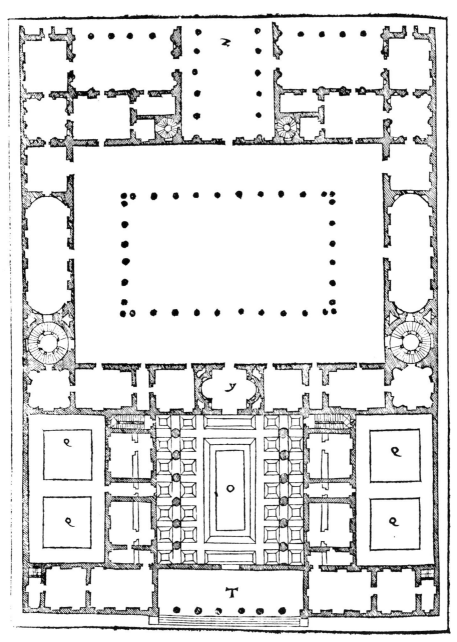

3   Daniele Barbaro's plan of the ancient house, from *I dieci libri dell'architettura di M. Vitruvio tradotti e commentati da Monsig. Daniele Barbaro* (Venice, 1567 ed.), p. 280.

of republican traditions. Radical political conflict was, therefore, expressed through opposing models of architectural practice. This was the very same conflict which in previous decades had obstructed Andrea Palladio's 'transfer' to Venice when he was rejected for the post of Proto al Sal (1554) and for the work on the Scala d'Oro of the Ducal Palace (1555). Indeed, although Palladio would eventually obtain, with the support of the pro-Roman nobility, the prestigious responsibility for the design of the façade of San Francesco della Vigna (1564–5) and for the churches of San Giorgio Maggiore (1566) and the Redentore (1575–6) in the city, nevertheless he would appear to have wished to minimise any political capital which could be had from his architectural treatise. Venice is, in fact, conspicuously absent from the *Quattro libri*. Specific references to the city are trivial, and projects which could be relevant to Venice were 'censored'. For example, there is the house 'on a triangular site' (for an irregularly shaped area very similar to a Venetian site) and there is the following project actually intended 'for a site in Venice', but here the city is only specified this once without further discussion; there is also the project for the Rialto bridge – an antique forum suspended over the water – presented by Palladio with reticence and without naming the city which had rejected him (Palladio 1570, Book II, 71, 72, Book III, 25). Such a programmatic 'absence' indicates a substantial divergence between Barbaro's commentary to Vitruvius and Palladio's *Quattro libri* – both works none the less possessing the same cultural aims (Concina 1983, 55–62) – centred around the 'absolute value' which Palladio attributes to architecture: for the lesson of antiquity, legitimised as it were by his own 'modern' interpretation, was a project *in itself* which did not allow 'other' aims (Tafuri 1985, 193–6).

The most radical of Palladio's ambitions – to define an autonomous architectural language which was indifferent to the expectations and contradictions of any particular urban reality – was to suffer in Venice a fate which its author probably did not expect. The bitter debate conducted *per architecturam* (through architecture) between rival factions of the nobility was, in fact, destined to peter out slowly as the new generation of *proti*, who straddle the turn of the century, began to assimilate and translate the antique vocabulary into 'Venetian dialect', thus freeing it from its potential to be controversial (Tafuri 1987a, XXXII). Two emblems of this process are first, concerning practice, the church of the Zitelle alla Giudecca (begun in 1581) whose designer is as yet unknown, and second, regarding the treatises, the *Vitruvius* of Giovanni Antonio Rusconi, mathematician and engineer from Bergamo and acquaintance of Palladio. The Zitelle contains certain elements, such as the centralised plan of the type that was rejected for the Redentore, the tympanum and the thermal window on the façade,

Rusconi's 'method for carefully decorating walls with painting, as is the particular custom in Venice', in *Della architettura di Gio. Antonio Rusconi* (Venice 1590), p. 111. The workmen are dressed as ʼients.

which come from the Palladian repertoire but which are used in an archaic and grammatically uncertain way (Aikema and Meijers 1989, 225–34). Rusconi's treatise, originally an illustrated translation of the *De Architectura*, was published posthumously in 1590, but without the text which was lost. The surviving illustrations were accompanied by brief notes written by the publishers (Bedon 1983, 84–90; 1996, ix–xxi). Had Rusconi's treatise been published in its entirety, it would

have coupled a translation of Vitruvius with images showing tools and
techniques found in workshops of the period and used in local construction – although paradoxically the builders are in ancient costumes
(plate 4). The treatise would have been a sort of *Vitruvius Venetus*
(Fontana 1978, 66), an ambiguous work although revelatory of the
process of assimilation of antique culture in action. But the fact that the
decision was taken to print a collection of images whose text was lost
is significant in itself: it shows a decrease in the importance of a
theoretical system and an increase in the importance of visual communication. For this last Venetian *Vitruvius* of the sixteenth century,
edited by publishers who were not experts in architecture, seems to
be an edition aimed finally at a new 'public' of artisans and their
workshops.

In a certain sense, the *Venetia città nobilissima e singolare* by Francesco
Sansovino (1581) can be thought of as consistent with this process of
assimilation occuring at the end of the century. It came out a decade
after the death of Jacopo and just a year after that of Palladio. The son
of the *proto* of San Marco illustrates, among other things, the main
public and private buildings of the city, with a correct and up-to-date
architectural vocabulary. These descriptions are so accurate as to put
this work into the category of 'hidden' treatises on architecture. However, in this erudite guide to Venice nothing appears concerning the
conflicts over the spread of the *all'antica* style in Venice which divided
the nobility at the time. The image of Venice given by Francesco
Sansovino is once again that of a 'harmonious' city, where the
fourteenth-century Ducal Palace and the sixteenth-century Libreria
Marciana co-exist peacefully, separated only by the Piazzetta di San
Marco. Both are offered to the curious traveller as 'pieces' in a
catalogue, a view anticipating the more disenchanted vision of
Canaletto and the tragic vision of Giovanni Battista Piranesi.

Chapter Sixteen

VITRUVIUS, ALBERTI AND SERLIO: ARCHITECTURAL TREATISES IN THE LOW COUNTRIES, 1530–1620

Krista De Jonge

MOST OVERVIEWS OF sixteenth-century architectural writing in the Low Countries start with Pieter Coecke van Aelst's translations of Serlio's Book IV and end with the numerous publications of Hans Vredeman de Vries. In recent studies, however, the emphasis has shifted away from the *Säulenbuch* – the 'column book' (Forssman 1956) which focuses on the Orders as the main ingredient of antique ornament – towards the 'Vitruvian tradition', characterised by a more generalised interest in all aspects of building. In a third category, the model-book illustrating antiquity, new evidence has also come to light.

Pieter Coecke van Aelst's unauthorised translations of Serlio's Book IV, published at Antwerp by Gillis Coppens van Diest, are a landmark in the history of the architectural treatise in northern Europe. Numerous editions of Serlio's Books I, II, III and V in several languages followed those of Book IV, bearing witness to Coecke's role as the chief populariser of Serlio's work north of the Alps (De la Fontaine Verwey 1975, 1976; Offerhaus 1988; Bury 1989). Robert Peake's edition – the first in English – of Books I–V (London, 1611) was based on Coecke's work, a fact which the modern user of the readily available facsimile should keep in mind.

The first, Flemish, translation of Book IV, entitled *Generale Reglen der architecturen*,[1] was published in 1539 only two years after the first Venetian edition, and does not mention Serlio on the title-page. The

---

[1]   *Generale reglen der architecturen op de vyve manieren van edificien, te weten thuscana, dorica, ionica, corinthia ende composita, met den exemplen der antiquiteiten die int meeste deel concorderen met de leeringhe van Vitruvio* (Antwerp: Pieter Coecke van Aelst, 1539), in folio.

first French translation[2] – for which Coecke had similarly not asked permission – came out in 1542 (plate 1), effectively pulling the rug from under the author's feet and causing the bitter complaint included in the Notice to Readers in Serlio's own Italian–French edition of Books I and II published in Paris (with the French translation by Jean Martin), dated 1545 (Schéle 1962, 239; Marlier 1966, 381; De la Fontaine Verwey 1976, 186–7). The first German edition by Coecke is also dated 1542:[3] the translator, a certain Jakob Rechlinger who was 'knowledgeable in architecture', can be identified as an Augsburg merchant active in Venice and Istanbul in 1533 at the time of Coecke's sojourn there. Both were involved in negotiations with Sultan Süleyman the Magnificent about a tapestry series showing Turkish scenes, the design of which would later be transformed into the woodcut series *Les Moeurs et fachon de faire des Turcz*, published posthumously by Coecke's widow at Antwerp, in 1553 (Schéle 1965, 73; Marlier 1966, 55–72; Necipoglu 1989, 419–20). According to Coecke, Jacob Seisenegger, Ferdinand I of Austria's court painter, had encouraged him to publish this version of Serlio, the first book on architecture available in High German: as Coecke himself says in the introduction, Albrecht Dürer's well-known book *Ettliche underricht, zur befestigung der Stett, Schloss und Flecken* (Nuremberg, 1527) only deals with fortification and not with architecture and antique decoration (De la Fontaine Verwey 1976, 183). How exactly Coecke gained access to Book IV so quickly is not clear, since his recorded trips to Italy predate its publication. Schéle (1962, 238) thinks in fact that Seisenegger, who travelled through Italy, Spain and the Netherlands from 1535 to 1542 and who may have had direct contact with Serlio in Venice, could have brought a copy to Coecke.

In spite of the fact that both lay-out and typography of Coecke's editions closely follow the Italian original, Coecke introduced some changes reflecting local customs: for instance the Italian coats of arms were replaced by an alphabet of Roman capitals after Dürer, Pacioli and Tory, judged to be of more practical value (Schéle 1962, 239; De la Fontaine Verwey 1976, 182–5; Rolf 1978, 38–41; Bury 1989, 95). The woodcuts are straight copies from the original illustrations and were possibly made by Cornelis Bos (Schéle 1962). For the French and German versions, Coecke used a title-page with Italianate grotesques,

[2]   *Reigles generales de l'architecture, sur les cincq manieres d'edifices, ascavoir, thuscane, doricq[ue], ionicq[ue], corinthe & co[m]posite, avec les exemples dantiquitez, selon la doctrine de Vitruve* (Antwerp: Pieter Coecke van Aelst, 1542), in folio.

[3]   *Die gemaynen reglen von der Architectur uber die funf manieren der Gebeu, zu wissen, thoscana, dorica, ionica, corinthia, und composita . . .* (Antorf [Antwerp]: P. Couck von Alst, 1542), in folio.

R eigles generales
de l'Architecture, fur
les cincq manieres d'e
difices, afcauoir, Thuf
cane, Doricq; Ionicq;
Corinthe, & Cōpo=
fite, auec les exemples
danticquitez, felon la
doctrine de Vitruue.

·ANNO·

1545

CV
MPRIVILE GII

1   Title page of the French translation by Coecke of Serlio's Book IV, 2nd edition (Antwerp, 1545). LP 2991 C, Brussels, Bibliothèque Royale Albert I.

instead of copying the original one (Schéle 1962; 1965, 42). The translator also had to invent a new terminology, since the Flemish language did not at that time have words for the elements of the Orders. In most cases Coecke preferred the Vitruvian Graeco-Latin vocabulary to more Flemish-sounding neologisms based on Serlio's vocabulary, or to technical terms from the vernacular in a new definition. It is significant that the second Flemish edition of Book IV (Antwerp, 1549) – contrary to the later editions of the French version, for instance – returns to the Gothic letter-type, whereas the use of Roman type in the 1539 edition had been a significant mark of modernism (Rolf 1978, 42–5; Offerhaus 1988, 451). At the same time the neologism *architecture* was replaced in the title-page by *metselrije* (mason's work), supposedly easier to understand; nevertheless, documents show that by the end of the century, the new term had been accepted into everyday language (Rylant and Casteels 1940; Miedema 1980; van den Heuvel 1995).

Also in 1539 Coecke published *Die Inventie der colommen*,[4] a pocket-book Vitruvius excerpt heavily dependent on, amongst others, Cesare Cesariano's 1521 Como translation of Vitruvius and especially on Diego de Sagredo's Vitruvian dialogue, *Medidas del Romano* (Toledo, 1526), a French translation of which was published in Paris around 1537 (De la Fontaine Verwey 1976, 175–6; Rolf 1978). Coecke's summary tellingly starts with the definition of 'architecture' as an intellectual activity based on scientific principles (chapters I–II) and then concentrates on the Doric, Ionic, Corinthian and Tuscan Orders (chapters III–VII). Thus, the work contains the essence of a *Säulenbuch* or book of the Orders, comparable to Serlio's Book IV. However the last chapters – on temples and proportion (VIII–X) – are uncompromisingly Vitruvian, like the terminology and the ten-part structure of the booklet, and the illustrations, drawn by Coecke himself, do not have anything to do with Serlio, but seem to have been inspired by the woodcuts in Cesariano's and Sagredo's Vitruvian treatises. Indeed, these sources are explicitly mentioned by Coecke in *Die Inventie* (Rolf 1978, 21–6). The folio format translation of Serlio's Book IV must have been relatively expensive, while *Die Inventie* was printed in large quantities, as is shown by documents relating to the bankruptcy of the distributor, Cornelis Bos, in 1545 (Schéle 1962; 1965, 14–16). Should the Vitruvius excerpt then be seen as a craftsman's manual?

Every question concerning the impact of these publications on building practice in the Low Countries has to take into account the peculiar nature of evolution in this field at that time. Sculptors and

---

[4] *Die Inventie der colommen met haren coronementen ende maten. VVt Vitruvio ende andere diversche auctoren optcortste vergadert, voer Scilders, beeltsniders, steenhouders, &c. Ende allen die ghenuechte hebben in edificien der Antiquen* (Antwerp: Pieter Coecke van Aelst, 1539), in octavo.

painters, who had not been trained in one of the traditional builders' guilds – which included those of the masons, the stonecutters and the carpenters – but who had gone to Italy, were cornering the new market in 'antique' architecture, without respecting the guilds' traditional monopoly (De Jonge 1997). Whilst traditional building techniques persisted in practice (Meischke 1952; Philipp 1989), a new type of designer gradually came into his own, in spite of many conflicts (Müller Franzo 1881; Rylant and Casteels 1940; Parmentier 1948, 13–15; Duverger et al. 1953, 68–9): this was the 'architect' as defined by Coecke following Vitruvius, in other words someone who was both a technician and a theoretician, and who knew the principles of antique architecture (Forssman 1956, 59–60; Miedema 1980, 72–4). Coecke's *Die Inventie*, destined for 'painters, sculptors, stonecutters and all who derive pleasure from antique edifices' as the title-page puts it, indeed offered a quick way to acquire the necessary antique repertory and its basic rules, without actually going to Italy. The title of Coecke's introduction to the *Generale Reglen* on the other hand – *Aenden liefhebbers der Architecturen* (To all Lovers of Architecture) – seems to indicate that this translation of Serlio's Book IV was primarily meant to educate the emerging clientele, in spite of some nods to the craftsman's specific interests (Rolf 1978; van den Heuvel 1995, 19–21): in the early 1530s the new Renaissance architecture had been exclusively a court phenomenon, which still had to gain credibility with the urban bourgeoisie. Even within court circles, the new style seems to have been the reserve of specialists. A characteristic example of this is the new staircase in front of the main wing of the Coudenberg Palace at Brussels, the emperor's most important residence in the Low Countries (1538–9). Even though the accounts prove that its execution was supervised by Lodewijk van Boghem, the style of the staircase's design seems completely foreign to this master of 'flamboyant' Gothic. It would appear therefore that the antique triumphal arch which decorates the lower landing is due to Coecke, who is mentioned as a consultant, sporting the significant title of *artiste de l'empereur* (De Jonge 1994a, 382–3; 1994b, 113–14).

Although not a treatise, the account of the *joyeuse entrée* of Philip of Spain into Antwerp in 1549, which Coecke published in 1550 in Latin,[5] Flemish[6] and French[7] at the same printer's house, Gillis

---

[5] Cornelius Scribonius. *Spectaculorum in Susceptione Philippi Hisp. Princ. Antverpiae aeditorum mirificus apparatus* (Antwerp: Pieter Coecke van Aelst, 1550), in folio.

[6] *De seer wonderlijcke schoone Triumphelijcke Incompst van den hooghmogenden Prince Philips . . . in de stadt van Antwerpen . . . Anno 1549* (Antwerp: Pieter Coecke van Aelst, 1550), in folio.

[7] Corneille Grapheus. *La très admirable . . . entrée de Prince Philippes . . . en la ville d'Anvers . . . Anno 1549* (Antwerp: Pieter Coecke van Aelst, 1550), in folio.

Coppens van Diest, deserves to be mentioned within this context because it shows the decisive influence of Serlio's Books III and IV (Roobaert 1960). The text was written by Cornelis Grapheus or Scribonius, secretary to the Antwerp city council and Coecke's friend. The illustrations have been taken only too often to be accurate versions of the real-life structures erected in the Antwerp streets in 1549, despite the many indications to the contrary in the text, and the many discrepancies which can be noted between the depicted arches and the dimensions cited by Grapheus and by other eye-witnesses of the event (Eisler 1990). Grapheus explicitly states that most of the arches were redrawn by Coecke in altered proportions to fit the format of the book (Schéle 1965, 43, 74–6), the layout of which strikingly resembles Serlio's Book IV in its systematic juxtaposition of text and woodcut on facing pages and in its manner of rendering architecture in plan and (perspective) elevation. Taken by themselves, Coecke's woodcuts – especially those depicting the decorations paid for by the town of Antwerp itself – constitute both one of the earliest manifestos of grotesque scrollwork and at the same time the first model-book of Mannerist architectural invention in the Low Countries (Schéle 1965, 54–9; Kuyper 1994, I, 7–78).

Hans Vredeman de Vries's treatise *Architectura*[8] (1577 and 1581; plate 2) is usually classified within the same category as Serlio's Book IV, that is as a 'column book' illustrated with examples which are closely linked to the most advanced architecture of its author's time, namely Antwerp Town Hall (1561–5) (Mielke 1967, 48–51). Vredeman de Vries had, in fact, competed for the design of its façade, ultimately the work of two sculptors, Cornelis Floris and Willem van den Broeck, alias Paludanus (Duverger 1941): it is here that we find the only surviving clear-cut reference in the Low Countries to Serlio in actual, three-dimensional architecture, that is, the window cornice consisting of an elongated Ionic capital (Bevers 1985, 16–30; plate 3). Vredeman de Vries undoubtedly had an impact on contemporary architecture since he was the foremost publicist of Floris's successful combination of Serlio-inspired Classicism and luxurious scrollwork decoration, as applied to traditional local building types (Forssman 1956, 87–91; Van de Winckel 1988).

The chapters on the Orders in *Architectura* closely follow the five-Order system developed by Serlio, but present in each case five heavily

---

[8]   *ARCHITECTURA Oder Bauung der Antiquen auss dem Vitruuius, woellches sein funff Collummen orden, daer auss mann alle Landts gebreuch vonn Bauuen zu accommodieren dienstlich fur alle Bawmaystren Maurer, Stainmetzlen, Schreineren Bildtschneidren, und alle Liebhabernn der Architecturen ann dag gebracht durch Johannes Vredeman Vriesae Inventor* (Getruck tzo Antorff by Geerhardt de Jode An.° 1581. Antverpiae [Antwerp]: Gerardus de Iode, 1577, 1581), in folio.

ARCHITEC TVRA

Oder

Bauung der Antiquen auss dem Vitruuius; wœlches sein funff Collumnen orden, daer auss mann alle Landts gebreuch vonn Bauuen zu accommodierē dienstlich fur alle Bawmaystren Maurer, Stainmetzlen, Schreineren Bildtshneidren, vnd alle Liebhaberinn der Architecturen ann dag gebracht durch Johannes vredeman vriesæ Inuentor

Getruck tzo Antorff by Geerhardt de Jode An.° 1581

Antwerpie Apud gerardus de Jode en platea vulgariter dicta catlyne, veste sub signo floreni aurei. 1577.

Title-page of Vredeman de Vries's *Architectura Oder Bauung der Antiquen auss dem Vitruuius* (Antwerp, 77 and 1581). VB 5321 C LP, Brussels, Bibliothèque Royale Albert I.

decorated Mannerist variations (Nuytten 1994). This part had been prepared by Vredeman de Vries in his series *Dorica Ionica* and *Corinthia Composita* (1565), but it must be stressed that these show different examples to those in the *Architectura* (Mielke 1967, 31–5, 82–4). The 1577 *Architectura* differs also in that it has a text accompanying the illustrations and in that the plates illustrating the elements of a particular Order are followed, in each case, by examples of whole buildings and not merely of relatively small-scale building components. The illustrations' titles (for example 'House for a Merchant', 'House for a Prince') even have the proper abstract, or Serlian, ring to them. It is probable that Jacques Androuet du Cerceau the Elder's model-books – the *Livre d'architecture* (Paris, 1559) with its model houses, represented in plan and elevation, and the *Second Livre d'architecture* (Paris, 1561) which shows details like chimneypieces and doors – also served as a source of inspiration as to the form of the treatise, since Vredeman de Vries mentions the author in his introduction next to Coecke, Serlio and Vitruvius (Mielke 1967, 145–9).

In the title-page, Vredeman de Vries addresses his work to building masters, masons, stonecutters, carpenters, sculptors and 'all lovers of architecture', in a manner reminiscent of Coecke's publications. In his definition of 'architecture' he also shows his dependence on Coecke's *Die Inventie der colommen* (Rolf 1978, 31). Nuytten (1994, 75–7), however, has shown that the commentary accompanying façades, bridges and fortifications is more specifically directed at the 'architect', and sometimes even the 'proprietor', than was the part on the five Orders. In the latter, construction schemes for columns and other details of the Orders have been omitted altogether, contrary to Coecke's *Die Inventie*, Serlio's Book IV or, for that matter, Hans Blum's Zurich *Säulenbuch* of 1550, which had been available in Antwerp in a Flemish edition by Hans Liefrinck since 1572 (Forssman 1956, 239). The effort Vredeman de Vries put into forging closer links with traditional, local practice should not be forgotten either, nor should the fact that most of the ground-plans illustrated are innovative adaptations and modernisations of existing typologies (Nuytten 1994; van den Heuvel 1994b, 11–14). In this he goes far beyond Coecke. In a way, the great number of his publications and especially the excessive quality of the scrollwork in his architectural perspectives, such as those in the *Variae architecturae formae* (Antwerp, 1601) (Mielke 1967, 21–5, 117–38), for instance, have obscured the real value of the *Architectura* as a treatise.

Recent analysis has revealed the existence of a final representative of the 'Serlian' model-book lineage, a book published by court architect Jacques Francart in Brussels in 1617 (plate 4). It is not unjustified to relate this work, born after the interruption caused by the Troubles and

3   'Serlian' window, Antwerp Town Hall, 1561–5. Elongated Ionic capital, after Book IV, fol. XLVIIr.

the subsequent emigration of a large part of the artistic élite to Protestant territory, to the treatises mentioned above. Francart's *Premier Livre d'architecture* shows designs for gates, portals and doors only, in elevation and plan, with a short commentary (here on the same page), much like Serlio's *Libro Extraordinario* (Lyons, 1551). The *Premier Livre* should be called late-Mannerist rather than early Baroque because of its systematic use of Michelangelo's vocabulary (De Vos 1994). It is, in fact, the only northern representative of the Michelangelo and Vignola revivals which flourished in Rome and also in France around 1600. Its links to contemporary practice still need to be explored further, but the practical nature of this book on doors seems evident: usually the only 'modern' or easily modernised element in the traditional brick-and-sandstone architecture of the cities at that time is the doorframe. The specifically 'Roman' nature of the sources of the *Premier Livre* – Michelangelo's Porta Pia, the windows in the upper floor of the courtyard of Palazzo Farnese, the windows of St Peter's – reflects Francart's years of experience in Italy. Originally educated as a painter, he only became an architect when he was called to the court of Brussels.

De la Fontaine Verwey (1976, 174) credited Coecke with being the first to introduce the Renaissance, by way of Vitruvius, into the Low Countries. Recent research has shown that this view is no longer tenable, although his *Die Inventie* (1539) remains the only work directly based on Vitruvius to be published in the Low Countries during the sixteenth century (Offerhaus 1988). In the 1530s the Vitruvian source-texts of *Die Inventie* (i.e. Cesariano and Sagredo) must have been readily available in Antwerp, the printing capital of northern Europe at that time, at least to the humanist élite. Cornelis Grapheus, who wrote the introductory poem for the Flemish translation of Serlio's Book IV, apparently was familiar with Alberti, as is shown by the introduction to his edition of Pompeus Gauricus's *De Sculptura*, published in 1528 at Antwerp (Roobaert 1960, 45). Vitruvius and Alberti are cited as authorities in a 1543 Utrecht court case for which Grapheus, as secretary to the city council, took the deposition of the Antwerp witnesses (Müller Franzo 1881; Miedema 1980; Offerhaus 1988, 443–5). From these documents it can also be inferred that the new definition of building as 'architecture', as explained by Coecke in *Die Inventie*, had become current among traditional Antwerp master-builders such as, for instance, Peter Frans, who at that time was working on the new fortifications together with Donato de'Boni Pellizuoli, a military engineer from Bergamo.

Moreover, there is important evidence that other members of the artistic avant-garde of the 1530s showed an interest in Vitruvian theory. Part of the so-called Kasseler Codex, a compilation now in the

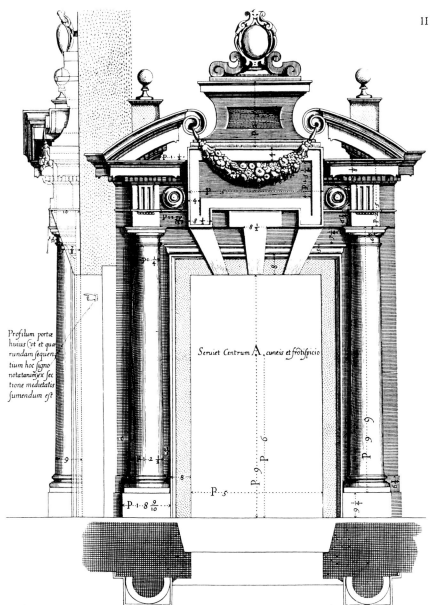

Profilum portæ
huius (vt et qua-
rundam sequen-
tium hoc signo
notatarum) ex sec-
tione medietatis
sumendum est

Seruiet Centrum A, cuneis et frotispicio

Hanc sic imitare. ùel si maiorem facies, proportionem seruabis.ùt, si latitùdo sit pedùm sex, altitudo sit. P. 10.8 ⅔ Membra cætera pariter excrescant. Cùr aùtem frontispicia diùùlsa et disrupta esse possint, et qùalis eorùndem altitùdo, libro qùarto docebo. Addam quomodo ab omni ruptura supercilium ser, uabitùr. Tabùlæ cùicùmqùe inscriptioni serùient. Præcipùa huiùs portæ membra et Notam reperies fol. VI.

4 Jacques Francart's *Premier Livre d'architecture* (Brussels, 1617), pl. II. VB 5321 C LP, Brussels, Bibliothèque Royale Albert I.

Staatlichen Kunstsammlungen at Kassel (Fol. A 45), is a copy of a Vitruvian excerpt in French dependent on the first, Spanish edition of Sagredo's *Medidas del Romano*, made by the Frisian painter Hermannus Posthumus. It is not known who wrote the original excerpt, but recently Hubertus Günther (1985; 1988a, 205, 358–9) has discovered textual links to the works of both Guillaume Philandrier and Serlio; it seems that the anonymous author also consulted the Vitruvius editions of Fra Giocondo (Venice, 1511) and Cesariano (Como, 1521). From 1535 to 1539, Posthumus's travels had brought him from Rome to Mantua (where he made the drawings of the so-called Mantuan Sketchbook now at Berlin, formerly attributed to van Heemskerck) and then (by way of Venice?) to Landshut and back to the northern Netherlands (Günther 1988b; Dacos 1989, 1995, 43–51, 75–6). During that period, he apparently had access to the most advanced material in the field.

This is not the case, however, with the only other known example of a 'Vitruvian'-type treatise in the Low Countries. In 1599 Charles De Beste, master-mason of the town of Bruges, finished his manuscript *Architectura*,[9] which he had started on (at least) three years earlier (van den Heuvel 1994a, 1995) (plate 5). This compilation combines traditional lore with excerpts from Vitruvius, Serlio and Vredeman de Vries (on the five Orders), mathematical science (as applied to surveying methods), fortification theory and instrument building (astronomical instruments, clocks, the sundial), and thus aims to cover the whole field of architecture and all related scientific issues. Amongst these should be noted the art of fortification: for De Beste, the *fortresasseur* (or military engineer) and the architect are almost synonymous. It was not usual to treat the civil and military treatise under the same heading; however, with regard to the situation in the Low Countries, such a distinction seems in some ways an artificial one, since most of the new breed of 'architects' were active in the field of fortification design (van den Heuvel 1991, 44–8, 131–3). For instance, Hans Vredeman de Vries's *Thuscana* (1578) and the chapter on the Tuscan Order in his *Architectura* (1577 and 1581), which includes designs for fortified gates, bridges and a port, are directly linked to his activities as supervisor of the Antwerp fortifications under Hans (von) Schille, 'engineer and

[9]   *Architectura. Dat is Constelicke Bouwijnghen huijt die Antijcken Ende Modernen. Waer op dat wij desen Tegenwoordghen Boeck Decideren. Ende hebben dien ghedeelt in Acht Onderscheijden Boecken Naemelicken den Eersten van Arithmetica. Den Tweeden van Geometria. Den Derden van Astronomische Instrumenten. Den Vierden van Horologien ofte Zonnenwijsers. Den vijfften van Architectura. Den sesten van perspectiva. Den sevensten van fortificatien. Den Achtsten van Artillerie. Dem welchen Beschribenn ist durch C.D. beste, Steijnmetselrnn und Mauwrrer z.w. Bruck Liebhaber der Const. 1599* (Brussels, Bibliothèque Royale Albert I, MS II 7617), in folio.

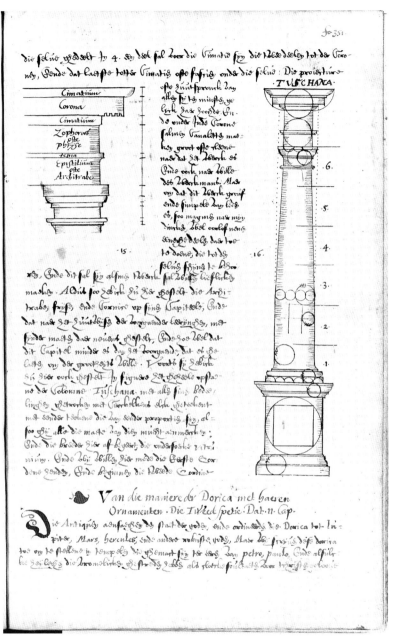

die folio gheeoelt by 4. en deel fal voor die Cimatie fyn die nederdaelen tot de Corona, ende dat leeghfte totter Cimatie, ofte faffie, onder die folio: Die proiecture · TVSCHANA ·

Cimatium
Corona
Cimatium
Zophorus ofte Phryse
tenia
Epistilium ofte Architrabe

-15-   ·16·   6. 5. 4. 3. 2. 1.

Van die maniere der Dorica met haeren
Ornamenten · Die TwEed spedie · Dat· 11· Cap·

geographer to his Majesty', in the years 1577–85 (Mielke 1967, 53–4; Nuytten 1994, 31, 51). Vredeman de Vries's application for a teaching post at Leiden University in 1604 mentions perspective, engineering and architecture in one breath (van den Heuvel 1994b, 12). At the end of the century, the title of royal engineer (*ingeniaire*), first borne in the Low Countries by Italians, represented a status coveted by many local architects, as is shown, for instance, by the careers of Jacques du Broeucq, court architect to Mary of Hungary, and Pierre Lepoivre, who worked for the Infante Isabella and Archduke Albrecht of Austria (De Jonge 1994a). The close relationship between the new architecture and the new art of fortification is also evident in the work of Simon Stevin of Bruges, the founding father of the military academy at Leiden (the *Duytsche Mathematycque*, of 1600) (Taverne 1978, 35–48; van den Heuvel 1991, 139–48). Around 1605, after some ten years' activity as a military engineer and theoretician for Maurits of Nassau, Stevin started work on an architectural treatise, *Huysbou* (On the Building of Houses), a part of which – *Vande oirdeningh der steden* (On City-Planning) – was published posthumously by his son Hendrick in his *Materiae Politicae* (Leiden, 1649) (van den Heuvel 1994b). If finished, this would have been the most original – in the sense of critical independence from Italian examples – treatise brought forth by the Low Countries. Stevin's work contains a critical reflection on Vitruvius, whom he had probably read in Daniele Barbaro's second (quarto) edition published in Venice in 1567 (Bodar 1985, 61–3). Particularly important is Stevin's rejection of the system of the Orders and its universally valid proportions as the natural basis of architecture.

In the publication of scientifically accurate studies of antique build-ings, Pieter Coecke van Aelst was again to play an important role. His translations of Serlio's Book III into Flemish (1546)[10] and into French (1550),[11] remain the only published examples of a model-book on antiquity in the Low Countries before modern times. Both were dedicated to Mary of Hungary, who is cited as being particularly interested in this type of publication (van den Boogert and Kerkhoff 1993, 248). Coecke must have known other publications of this type, like Torello Sarayna's *De origine et amplitudine civitatis Veronae* (Verona, 1540), since he used a woodcut by Giovanni Caroto from this book to illustrate the Porta dei Borsari in his translation of Serlio's Book III (Rosenfeld 1989, 103).

---

[10] *Van der antiquiteyt, dat derde boeck. Die aldervermaertste antique edificien van templen, theatren, amphiteatren* . . . (Antwerp: Pieter Coecke van Aelst, 1546), in folio.

[11] *Des antiquités, le troisièsme livre de Sebastien Serlio* . . . (Antwerp: Pieter Coecke van Aelst, 1550), in folio.

This interest was shared by Hermannus Posthumus, who carefully copied the same antique Roman examples Serlio used for Books III and IV in another part of the Kasseler Codex, the so-called Kasseler Sketchbook (Günther 1988b). However, the juxtaposition in the Kasseler Codex of the Sagredo-inspired Vitruvius excerpt mentioned above, the studies of Roman antiquity and, lastly, copies of the engraved details of the Orders which Serlio and Agostino Veneziano published in 1528, does not necessarily date back to Posthumus, but could be attributed to one of the later owners, amongst whom we find the painters Maarten van Heemskerck and Pieter Saenredam (Günther 1988a&b). It would be wrong, therefore, to interpret Posthumus's studies, which were never published in spite of circulating from workshop to workshop, as an equivalent to the popularising work of Coecke van Aelst. It is also striking that neither Vredeman de Vries's *Architectura*, nor De Beste's compilation, discuss antiquity. All the examples shown in the latter – as, for instance, the Imperial Gate at Antwerp, designed by Donato de' Boni (1545) – are contemporary. Apart from one example, the study of antiquity was thus known to the architects in the Low Countries mainly in its Serlian guise.

The one known exception represents, in fact, a major contribution to the scientific study of antique Roman buildings in the sixteenth century: the *Baths of Diocletian*, drawn by the military engineer Sebastiaan van Noyen from Utrecht for Antoine Perrenot de Granvelle and published by Hieronymus Cock at the Sign of the Four Winds in Antwerp in 1558 (Riggs 1977, 47–9, 353–4). It consists of twenty-seven engravings showing the building in plan, section (combined with perspective) and elevation, according to the principles Raphael set out in the second version of his letter on the reconstruction of ancient buildings, written for Leo X (1519–20); and thus this work differs fundamentally from the series of general views of Roman ruins which Antwerp editors like Hieronymus Cock – see for instance his *Praecipua Aliquot Romanae Antiquitatis Ruinarum Monimenta* (Antwerp, 1551) – and Philip Galle published from the middle of the century onwards (Riggs 1977; Grelle 1987).

Wenzel Coebergher, a relative of Francart and likewise engineer and architect to Albrecht of Habsburg and Isabella of Spain, had the intention to challenge the Serlian monopoly in the field of the illustration of antiquity. According to Peiresc, writing in 1606, he planned a treatise on the arts in four books, the first book of which would discuss architecture. The first part would be on ancient building techniques and the second would have measured plans to scale of antique ruins – temples, thermal complexes and mausolea at Rome, Pozzuoli and elsewhere in Italy and Europe – where he would correct all the errors found in Palladio, Serlio and others. Coebergher was going to include many of the antique buildings in Cuma, and other sites near Naples, which had never been shown before, as for instance the theatre at Capua, which he judged to be made with more 'science of architecture than everything which had been written by Vitruvius and the others' (van de Gheyn 1905). Coebergher, like Francart, had been educated as a painter and had had a career in Italy before returning to become a court artist and administrator. The plans for his treatise were unfortunately never realised, with the exception of the manuscript for the fourth book (on antique medallions).

Recent research has thus allowed us to place Coecke and Vredeman de Vries's publications on architecture in a wider context. Although no longer considered unique, their work retains a special status in the Low Countries and in northern Europe because of its popularity, as can be gauged by the high number of reprints until the mid-seventeenth century (Mielke 1967; Bury 1989). This process gradually slows to a halt with the translation of Vignola's *Regola* and Scamozzi's *Idea*, published in Amsterdam in 1619 and 1640 respectively. The advent of the new Classicism which was to dominate architecture in the northern Netherlands was heralded by Salomon de Bray in his introduction to the *Architectura Moderna ofte Bouwinge van onsen Tyt* (Amsterdam, 1631), a model-book published by Cornelis Danckerts showing mainly work of the Vredeman de Vries-inspired architect Hendrick de Keyser (Terwen and Ottenheym 1993, 216–20). In the southern Netherlands, Rubens's *Palazzi di Genova* (Antwerp, Part I 1622, Part II c.1626) takes over where Vredeman de Vries left off: the fact that, with a few exceptions, none of the residences was identified by the author, shows that this is above all a model-book. As Rubens says in his introduction, now that 'barbarous, or Gothic, architecture' is slowly giving way to architecture based on the rules of the ancient Greeks and Romans, especially in the 'famous churches of the Jesuit Order in Brussels and Antwerp', it seems useful to provide models of private houses for gentlemen, rather than princes, since they abound in the city.

Chapter Seventeen

FROM VIRGIN TO COURTESAN IN EARLY ENGLISH VITRUVIAN BOOKS

Vaughan Hart

T HE STUART AMBASSADOR Henry Wotton (1568–1639), when advocating the use of the Orders to his countrymen in 1624, noted the
'naturall imbecility of the sharpe *Angle*' and advised that any such
arches 'ought to bee exiled from judicious eyes, and left to their first
inventors, the *Gothes* or *Lumbards*, amongst other *Reliques* of that
barbarous *Age*' (Wotton 1624, 51). In the half-century prior to
Wotton's remarks, Gothic architecture (thus characterised by the
pointed arch) had been gradually replaced in England by an 'antique'
architecture built in a style ranging from Tuscan to Composite. This
change was largely stimulated by the first English architecture books,
since the *all'antica* style which they described was increasingly seen as
expressing Protestant reforms on equal terms with the continental
monuments of the Counter-Reformation (Hart 1994).

Whilst a number of early English architectural books were by native
writers, namely those by John Shute (published in 1563), John Dee (in
1570) and Henry Wotton (in 1624), English translations of continental
treatises were equally influential, namely those of Francesco Colonna
(in 1592), Giovanni Lomazzo (in 1598), Hans Blum (in 1601) and
Sebastiano Serlio (in 1611).[1] The less clearly organised, although more
fundamental, Latin treatises by Vitruvius and Alberti were not translated into English until the eighteenth century, despite their having
been rendered into other European languages and their early citation
by Dee: these authors thereby remained inaccessible to the majority of

---

[1] These translations in order are: Colonna: 'R.D.' [Roger Dallington?], *Hypnerotomachia:
The Strife of Love in a Dreame* (London, 1592). Lomazzo: Haydocke, R., *A tracte containing the
Artes of Curious Painting Carvinge & Buildinge* (Oxford, 1598). Blum: 'I.T.' [John Thorpe?],
The Booke of five collumnes of Architecture (London, 1601). Serlio: Peake, R., *The first (-fift) booke
of Architecture* (London, 1611).

artisans since only a few of their number could read a foreign language (Harris and Savage 1990, 421, 422 n. 27).

One theme in particular in these early English treatises, the characterisation of the Orders as human 'types', can be seen as central to the goal of their authors to make acceptable an essentially Italian – and therefore by implication an (at best) Pagan and (at worst) Catholic – architectural style to Protestant builders and patrons. When adopted, this new Christian architecture would, theorists hoped, renew the pristine bond of man with nature in harmony with the aspirations of the Protestant Church (Hart 1994). This chapter will illustrate how the Vitruvian body–column analogy was equated with Protestant moral truths by treatise writers in their attempt to formulate this architecture 'true' to nature.

JOHN SHUTE'S FIVE ORDERS AND HESIOD'S FIVE AGES OF THE WORLD

John Shute's *The First and Chief Groundes of Architecture used in all the auncient and famous monymentes*, published in London in 1563, was the first ever English treatise on architecture (Harris and Savage 1990, 418–22). As such, it was the earliest book to describe in English the 'five antique pillers or Columnes' (sig. Aiij*r*) as Shute's preface calls the Orders. The body–column analogy is freely adapted by Shute with reference to Vitruvius and Serlio in unprecedented illustrations of five human figures which characterise the Orders (plates 1–5). The mythological nature of these figures is emphasised by the absence of a scale which might relate them to the actual human body. The work of Hans Vredeman de Vries is frequently suggested as a source for these figures (Wittkower 1974, 100; Rykwert 1996, 32),[2] but such a licentious influence runs counter to Shute's use of the strict Vitruvian sources of Serlio and Philandrier in his text. Rykwert notes that 'the close parallel of column and figure seems Shute's own contribution . . . to an understanding of the nature of the orders in a northern land where they seemed quite alien' (Rykwert 1996, 33). What follows will show exactly how Shute overcame this native prejudice through his unique interpretation of what he calls the 'depe secretes' (Preface, sig. Aij*v*) of the Orders and their human 'types'.

Echoing Vitruvius, Shute observes that the five Orders were 'comonly named of the places and persones partely where and of

---

[2] Harris and Savage 1990, 420, suggest that the figures 'are ultimately inspired by Cesariano's 1521 illustrated edition of Vitruvius but are stylistically closer to Flemish or French mannerist sources'.

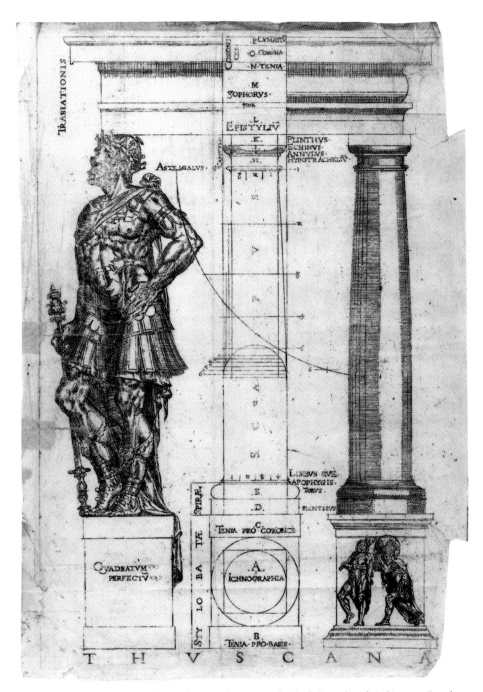

The labels within the illustration include:

TRABIATIONIS

CORONI P·CYMATI O·CORONA N·TENIA

M ZOPHORVS

L EPISTYLIV

ASTRAGALVS CAPITVLI K· PLINTHVS· ECHINVS· ANNVLVS· HYPOTRACHELIV·

LIMBVS·SIVE APOPHYGIS· TORVS·

PLINTHVS

SPIRÆ TENIA·PRO·CORONICE C

STYLOBATÆ A· ICHNOGRAPHIA

QVADRATVM·PERFECTV·

B TENIA·PRO·BASIS·

T H V S C A N A

1   Tuscan Order as Atlas, from Shute's *The First and Chief Groundes of Architecture* (London, 1563), facing fol. iiiir. Cambridge University Library.

whom they were invented, and partly of their vertues & properties of
those that they wer likned unto' (sig. Aiijr). He then emphasises that
this interpretation was dependent both on the columns' 'beautye and
comlines' and on their 'fortitude and strength' (sig. Biir). In describing
the characteristics of the three Greek Orders, that is the Doric, Ionic
and Corinthian, Shute closely follows Vitruvian precedent as codified
by Serlio. Vitruvius describes the male and female characteristics of
these Orders in the first chapter of his fourth book, having matched
their characteristics to different gods and goddesses in book one
(Vitr.i.ii.5).[3] Following Vitruvius's narrative as developed in Serlio's
fourth book (Serlio 1537, fol. IIIr/126r), Shute describes the 'manly'
Doric as signifying Hercules and Mars, and therefore appropriate for
temples dedicated to these gods, the 'matronly' Ionic as appropriate for
temples to Diana or Apollo, and the 'maidenly' Corinthian for those to
Vesta and virgins in general.

Shute's illustrations of the Orders freely interpret these Vitruvian
attributes. The Doric is shown, following the conventional emblematic
representation of the heroic Hercules, as a noble savage (plate 2). The
Ionic is represented probably not as Diana but as the Greek moon-
goddess Hera, wife of Zeus (and identified with the Roman goddess
Juno) – the peacock shown at her feet was sacred to Hera – whilst
Apollo, illustrated in the dado of the pedestal, returns Shute's Ionic
column to Vitruvian sources (plate 3). The Corinthian is shown as a
maiden, possibly the beautiful Aphrodite (Rykwert 1996, 34), again a
free interpretation of Vitruvian precedent (plate 4). All these 'types'
were named, according to Shute, in reflection 'of their vertues' and
possessed varied degrees of moral fitness and fortitude.

Shute thus follows Vitruvius when illustrating the three Greek
Orders: however, the Tuscan and Composite Orders were not Greek
but Roman inventions which, somewhat paradoxically, Vitruvius fails
to ascribe to particular gods; indeed the Roman author does not even
discuss the Composite. Serlio, Shute's other main architectural source,
is equally unspecific as regards figurative models for the Roman
Orders. Shute's unprecedented characterisation of these, the first and
last Orders, might thus be seen to say the most about his overall
adaptation of the columns to Elizabethan culture, in his position as the
first English Vitruvian writer.

Shute's Tuscan is 'likned unto Atlas, kynge of Maurytania' (sig.
Biiiiv; plate 1). Although Shute thus chooses a Greek hero (with no
Roman counterpart) for a Roman Order, at one level the attribution

---

[3]   Although there was no evidence that such a rule was applied by the Greeks and it is
most likely that it was formulated by Vitruvius chiefly in order to gratify Augustus's desire to
be associated with rigorous moral principles.

TRIGLY
PHI   G   METHO
FA.

L·GVTTA·C

D
E
B
A

ANNVLI TRES·

X
X
V
T

S

P

P

S

C

S

R

Y·PLINTHVS·
X·ECHINVS·
V·HIPOTRACHELIV·
S·ASTRAGALVS·

TORVS SVPERIOR·
TORVS INFERIOR P
PLINTHVS· N

ASTRAGLVS· I

L·
K

M
E

QVADRA TVM·
DIAGONIVM·

A

L·REGVLA
K·CYMATIV

N

ASTRAGALVS· H
TORVS· G
PLINTHVS· F

BASI

D

2   Doric Order as Hercules, from Shute's *The First and Chief Groundes of Architecture* (London, 1563), facing fol. vir. Cambridge University Library.

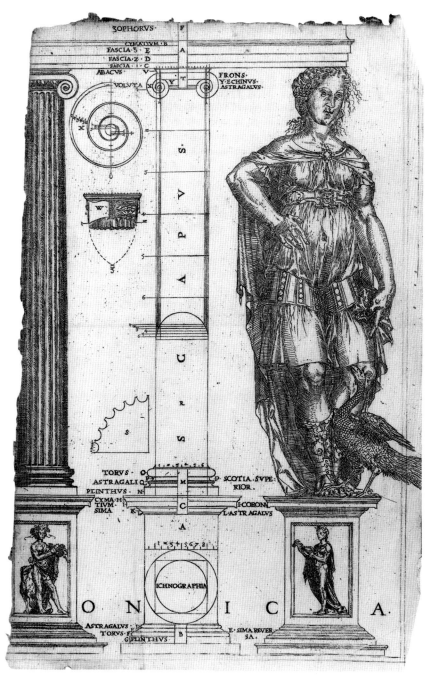

3 Ionic Order as Hera, from Shute's *The First and Chief Groundes of Architecture* (London, 1563), facing fol. viiir. Cambridge University Library.

4   Corinthian Order as Aphrodite, from Shute's *The First and Chief Groundes of Architecture* (London, 1563), facing fol. xv. Cambridge University Library.

is quite natural, since Atlas had supported the heavens according to Hesiod and the Tuscan Order was by tradition the 'strongest' of the five columns. Indeed, the plural of Atlas, 'Atlantes' (Latin *telamones*), is the term for male statues used to support an entablature. The Atlas mountains border Mauritania, where the Greek hero was supposed to have dwelt, and so Shute's identification is consistent with mythology. What is particularly noteworthy, however, is his depiction of the Tuscan figure as a king whose mace and crown would clearly signify English royalty to an Elizabethan reader. Here surely we have the Tuscan transformed into an ancient Romano-British king, complete with Roman military uniform (resembling figures by Cesariano) and English royal insignia (Hart 1993). This transformation is despite the traditional humble status of the Tuscan, the simplest in detail of the Orders described by Vitruvius (Vitr.IV.vii), and takes us some way from Serlio's treatment in marrying the Tuscan with rustic work. Shute's royal Tuscan thereby dramatically usurped the traditionally more noble Doric, rendered by Shute as a club-carrying savage cloaked in lion-skin (the standard emblematic costume of Hercules).

Shute's ennobling of the least ornate Order is in contrast to his treatment of the most decorative of the Orders, the Composite (plate 5). In the absence of a Vitruvian figurative model, Shute was again at liberty either to omit any reference to a specific deity (as Serlio had done) or to select a god which he saw as most personifying the decorum of this Order. Despite the perversity of once more assigning a Greek deity with no Roman cult to a Roman Order, he chooses as the figurative model 'Pandora, of Hesiodus' (sig. Biir). On the surface this was again an obvious choice, since Pandora's name means the 'all-endowed'. Significantly Shute is thus quite explicit that Hesiod is his source for the character of the Composite: for this reference excludes any ambiguity as to Pandora's character, given that later, Roman writers had identified her famous jar as a bringer of blessings and not, as had Hesiod, of evils.[4] Hesiod thus ranks alongside Vitruvius, Serlio and Philandrier as a source for the columns' meaning in this, the first native explanation of the Orders, and as such the Greek poet is Shute's only non-architectural source. Shute's text thereby invites his literate artisan and patrician reader to consult Hesiod for the meaning of the Composite column's character, since Shute does not develop this himself (Harris and Savage 1990, 421; Bennett 1993, 28).

Hesiod's poetry contrasted the blessings which Righteousness brings to a nation with the punishment Heaven sends down upon immorality. Hesiod's *Theogonia* is thus considered the first attempt at systematic theology. His reflections might be expected to fit easily within a

---

[4]   For example, Babrius in the *Fables*, 58.

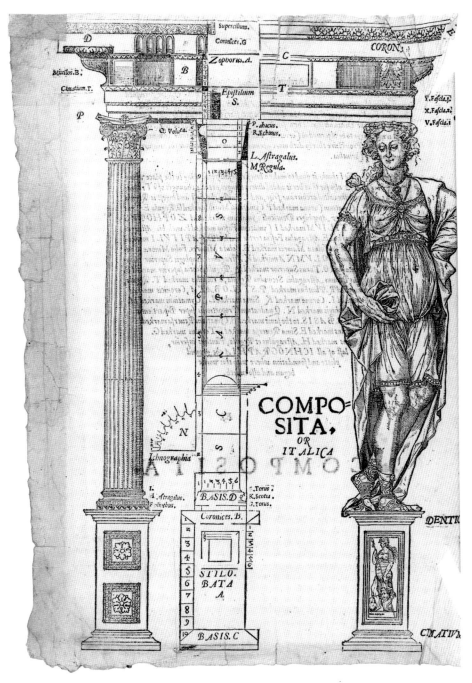

5   Composite Order as Pandora, from Shute's *The First and Chief Groundes of Architecture* (London, 1563), fol. xiii*v*. Cambridge University Library.

Christian framework in their conformity to Protestant theology and
view of human development. Shute's reader, eager to discover the
meaning of the Composite Order thus characterised as 'Pandora, of
Hesiodus', would find that according to the poet's 'Works and Days',
the first woman, called Pandora, had been created by Zeus following
the theft of fire by Prometheus and his gift of it to mortals. Zeus rages,
'I will give men as the price for fire an evil thing in which they may
all be glad of heart while they embrace their own destruction' (Hesiod
1967, ll. 54–105). Whilst Pandora appeared as 'a sweet, lovely maiden-
shape, like to the immortal goddesses in face', Aphrodite bestowed on
her 'cruel longing and cares that weary the limbs'. Hesiod continues,
'the goddess bright-eyed Athene girded and clothed [Pandora], and the
divine Graces and queenly Persuasion put necklaces of gold upon her,
and the rich-haired Hours crowned her head with spring flowers'.
Indeed these ornaments can clearly be seen in Shute's characterisation
of Composite (plate 5). Hesiod further relates that Zeus 'called this
woman Pandora, because all they who dwelt on Olympus each gave a
gift, a plague to men who eat bread'. In this way Pan-dora was indeed
'all endowed', although with vices. Hesiod continues that, before
Pandora's box was opened, 'the tribes of men lived on earth remote
and free from ills', but following the opening of the jar these vices
became scattered.

    First codified by Serlio, the Composite Order was uniquely licen-
tious among the five Orders, in that as a 'composite' it lacked a direct
prototype in nature or human types upon which the rules for its
carving could be based (one reason, perhaps, for Vitruvius's silence on
the Order). As a figure of evil in the ancient world, Pandora was an
appropriate symbol of such 'unnaturalness' and clearly stood apart from
Shute's pantheon comprising the 'noble' Atlas, 'strong' Hercules,
'matronly' Hera, and 'maidenly' Aphrodite.[5] Furthermore, since the
Composite was formed from the Corinthian and the Ionic Orders,
Shute's representation of the Corinthian as Aphrodite perfectly reflected Hesiod's story of her role as an element in Pandora's composite
character.

    Vitruvius hinted that the Orders signified the five ages of man
(Rykwert 1996, 32), although obviously the actual chronology of the
Orders' invention, as described by him (Vitr.IV.i.6–8) and repeated by
Shute, is not reflected by the columns' ornamental hierarchy, which
places Roman Tuscan before the Greek trio. Reflecting Vitruvius's
'five ages' metaphor, Shute's five Orders can be interpreted as a group
with reference to Hesiod, and the poet's description of the five ages of

---

[5] Curiously enough this distinction is emphasised in Shute's book by the fact that the
Composite is illustrated with a woodcut whilst the other four Orders are engraved.

the world which immediately follows the fable of Pandora in 'Works and Days' (Hesiod 1967, ll. 110–200). Hesiod relates that the world began with a pure, noble arcadian age of gold in which men 'lived like gods'. Shute's possible identification of the Tuscan column with this first age would explain his break with Vitruvian tradition in depicting the Tuscan in noble, indeed godly form. In any case, the rustic Tuscan would be an appropriate sign of the Golden Age since, following Serlio, Shute determines that it was 'named after the sayde countrey Tuscana' (sig. Biir), and Etruria/Tuscany was considered the cradle of the Italian race traced back to the fabled Golden Age of Troy (Hart 1994, 53). According to Hesiod, the world then went through two stages of self-indulgence and savagery (well-enough indicated by the club-carrying Hercules) to a partial renewal of a Golden Age, which can be seen as an heroic Corinthian age ruled by Vesta and her virgins. In Shute's illustration of this virginal Order, the heroic figure and floral motifs in the pedestal were standard Golden Age imagery, whilst the possible identification of the column with Aphrodite emphasised its role as the ultimate in maidenly beauty (eclipsing Composite in this regard). Hesiod relates that the world finally descended into absolute immorality in the fifth age, the age of Pandora. As we have seen, Shute clearly identifies Pandora with the fifth column, the Composite. Indeed Hesiod's myth of Pandora prefigured his historical scheme, since this myth also charted the passing of an age of naked purity into one of corruption, brought about by the opening of Pandora's box. This is to read the ornamental sequence of the five columns as characterised by Shute alongside the narrative of the world as outlined by one of his acknowledged sources, Hesiod. More exactly, Hesiod is cited by Shute to claim that one particular column bears the features of Pandora, the personification of Hesiod's historical scheme explaining the rise of evil.

At the start of his treatise Shute identifies the birth of architectural ornamentation, and therefore by implication the Orders, as bound up with the Fall of humankind. Such a view would have accorded with Elizabethan Puritan attitudes to human works and ornament (Phillips 1973). Shute makes reference to Vitruvius on the origin of building (Vitr.II.i), noting with regard to primitive man that,

> some succoured themselves under the shadowe of trees, and others taking occasion thereby, devised to set up forked stakes ... they compassed them about wyth ringes of Iron, and called them Pillers or Columnes. The forme and shape of which Pillers, they did imitate, fashioning them of stone. And then they callynge to theyr remembraunce the fludde of Noe, which had drowned all the world, devised to build the towre of Babilon. So they added in steede of the rynge above at the toppe of their pillers, those, which our author Vitruvius calleth Astragali, and Apophigis ... Then ...

they . . . buylded a great parte of the tower. In which buylding came
the devision of tounges, or languages, whereby these buylders were
parted and scattered abrode upon the face of the earth . . . And
immediately after a wittie man named Dorus . . . made the firste
piller drawen to perfection, and called it Dorica, after his owne
name (sig. Bi*r*).

The Tower of Babel thus spawned the Orders since, following its
construction, mankind divided into different nations and tongues, and
the Orders, with their various regional and dialectic origins, were an
indirect product and sign of this division. Shute adds later that the
Greeks had received their knowledge of the Orders from the Jews,
who in turn had learnt it from the Babylonians (sig. Bii*r*). He thus
accounts for the rise of the Orders with reference to biblical history,
and thereby conferred a general, albeit fallen, biblical virtue to the
otherwise Pagan columns. This architecture had, however, 'through
ignoraunce' remained 'secret and not spoken of' until Shute's own age,
when many incorrectly maintained 'this order of building to be of the
new facion' (sig. Bii*v*).

Moreover, Shute's story concerning the growing use of artifice not
surprisingly reflected the wider historical scheme cultivated by the
Elizabethan age: and in turn both accounts can be seen to be structured
around five ages. For Tudor mythology emphasised a primitive, necessarily Protestant Church and monarchy whose antiquity was established with reference to Geoffrey of Monmouth's tale of English
Trojan ancestry (and which was equated with the general Golden Age
ideal at which Hesiod's work was seen to hint) (Yates 1985, 30; Hart
1994, 32–3); a Fall and subsequent division of tongues matched by
Catholic corruption of this early Church; a Protestant Golden Age
restored by the Reformation and by Elizabeth; and an apocalyptic end
towards which all of humankind was predestined.

Shute's opening narrative simply married Vitruvian and biblical
archetypes to this Elizabethan mythology, a mythology that can be
seen to have informed his characterisation of the five Orders as symbols
of this past. Hence the huts of primitive society and its Tuscan/Trojan
British monarchy were reflected by the nobility of the first age and
architectural Order. The rise of ornament, the equivalent to the post-
Fall human need for clothing, together with the division of tongues
symbolised by the Tower of Babel, was reflected by the Doric and
subsequent Ionic Orders or the second and third age. The partially
restored antique age of gold under Elizabeth (popularly cast as the
virgin queen Astraea, herald of a new Golden Age (Yates 1985)) would
be represented by the rebirth of antique architecture urged upon the
queen by Shute, and in particular by the virginal Corinthian Order

carved in imitation of a beautiful maiden. Whilst the final apocalyptic age, that of human licentiousness, was reflected by the licentious Composite Order through its signification of Pandora.

Indeed, Shute's reference to the Corinthian as resembling 'Vesta or some lyke virgin' (sig. Biir) would surely have made the Order particularly representative to his Elizabethan readers of their own age, ruled as it was by a 'virgin queen' in the form of Shute's dedicatee, Queen Elizabeth. Certainly the dedication to Elizabeth as the 'defendor of the faith' (sig. Aijr) gives the treatise, and the Orders which it so vividly depicts, a particularly Protestant imperial introduction. Elizabeth was to be directly identified with imperial Corinthian columns by Crispin de Passe Senior in an heraldic image of 1596 (Hart 1993; 1994, 67–8). Elizabethan artists thus used the Corinthian Order in particular to represent the renaissance under their queen of a supposed Protestant English antiquity of which the first Order, the Tuscan, could be seen as the original and 'base' in signifying the much-cultivated national Trojan antiquity. Shute's depiction of the Tuscan Order as a specifically English antique king might thus reflect not just Atlas but the Trojan prince called Brute who, according to Geoffrey and Tudor mythology, founded the nation as the first king of 'Britain'. The Tuscan was indeed to be identified with this national antiquity by Inigo Jones in 1620, when discussing his Romano-British 'Tuscan' temple, Stonehenge, whose supposed dedication was moralised by Jones to conform once again to Protestant theology (Orgel 1971, 122–3; Hart 1994, 56). Subsequently, Jones was to use the Tuscan for the first Protestant Church built in Britain, St Paul's in Covent Garden.

Shute provides a clear description of the columns' parts and their modular proportions (their 'First and Chief Groundes'), and he logically organises his text to follow the ornamental hierarchy of the Orders, quite unlike Vitruvius's random textual arrangement but mirroring Serlio's fourth book. In the face of the many alternative proportions for the five Orders, Shute also replicates Serlio's clear modular progression from six to ten. In this clarity and in paralleling the five Orders with the five ages, Shute in effect 'rationalises' the columns' meaning to correspond more closely to their ornamental hierarchy. For Shute's unprecedented characterisations had the effect of emphasising the five columns' relationship as a group over their individual origins and therefore meanings, dependent as these origins were by tradition on local circumstance and indeed chance. This randomness was exacerbated by Vitruvius's exclusion of the Composite from his treatise and his isolation of the Tuscan Order in omitting any figurative model or story of origin. Shute's equality of emphasis and sequential arrangement of the five columns clearly served to reinforce their ornamental hierarchy over that implied by the legend of their invention, starting as this story did with Greek Doric. This 'rationalisation' was also perfectly compatible with Shute's identification of architecture with the high-brow mathematical sciences (Bennett 1993, 26–8). For, on Vitruvian architecture, Shute explains that 'it hath a natural societie and as it were by a sertaine kinred & affinitie is knit unto all the Mathematicalles which sciences and knowledges are frendes and a maintayner of divers rationall artes' (sig. Aij*v*). Shute therefore praises 'the prudent lady Scientia . . . wherfore naturall love hath drawne me to advaunce her reputation and honour' (sig. Aiij*r*).

Shute's five characters would have been understood by contemporaries as equivalent to moral emblems, or 'trikes and devises' (sig. Aij*r*) as he himself called the architectural drawings which he brought back from Italy. These emblem collections were frequently used by Elizabethan artists in creating frontispieces and other didactic signs capable of moral instruction, with the Orders themselves frequently appearing in such emblematic frontispieces: in the frontispiece to Walter Raleigh's *The History of the World* (London, 1614), for example, a column emblazoned with books forms a pillar of knowledge (Corbett and Lightbown 1979, 128–35). The Orders were thus to play their part in the instruction of a Gentleman, as Peacham's inclusion of architecture in *The Compleat Gentleman* (London, 1622) made clear. This link between instruction, necessarily with a moral purpose, and the column is also to be found expressed in the tomb in Merton College Chapel of Thomas Bodley (d. 1612), in which books laid flat comprise the pilasters, whilst thinner and thicker volumes are used for the capital and base (Anderson 1995, 250). Shute's main aim was to advocate the Vitruvian manner, that is the Orders, to patrons and educated builders, and in so doing, as we have seen, he gives equally detailed attention to the 'evil' Composite as he does to the other four Orders.[6] This implies that it was possible, indeed desirable, to unite all the five pillars, that is including Composite. They were first so united in England in the gate of the Old Schools in Oxford, resurfaced between 1613 and 1624, which leads to Thomas Bodley's library (plate 6); in signifying a moral range, from rustic nobility to licentiousness, the five Orders when displayed together might thus be seen to perform a didactic and mnemonic role perfectly appropriate on a gate to a University library.

In this way the largely practical nature of Shute's text can be seen to bely its underlying moral purpose. The text only hints at the Orders' 'depe secretes', which are surely signified by the five emblematic

[6] This followed the arrangement of Serlio's Book IV: later, in 1601, the English *Blum* had the same arrangement, and concluded with advice on how to build the five Orders, one on top of the other.

6(a) (left) The gate of the Old Schools in Oxford, resurfaced between 1613 and 1624, which leads to Thomas Bodley's library. (b) (below) The gate of the Old Schools in Oxford, illustrated by David Loggan in *Oxonia Illustrata* (Oxford, 1675), plate V. Cambridge University Library.

figures unique to his treatise. But even emblems were decipherable only to those well-versed in their signs. Such an allusive strategy might be understood in the context of the esoteric nature of building mythology and rules cultivated by medieval masons' guilds. To know the Orders' 'secrets', Shute's reader must consult the author's sources, and it follows that only those well-educated enough to read Hesiod's 'Works and Days' – at this time untranslated into English but widely available in Latin translation or the original Greek – could fully grasp the meaning of the Orders. Pandora would however have been familiar enough to an Elizabethan Neoplatonist as an alchemical emblem of evil. Perhaps Shute considered that a fuller description of an element of *all'antica* architecture as 'evil' would have invited censure on the whole ornamental system from the more superstitious of his Puritan readers. When displayed in sequence Shute's Orders resembled characters in a masque and were thus intended to narrate a moral fable or warning to his age, a fable of which Pandora (in her guise as Composite) served as the ultimate portent.

RICHARD HAYDOCKE'S PANDORA AND HENRY WOTTON'S PROSTITUTE

In contrast to the native treatises by Shute and Dee, the early English translations of architectural books provided less obvious scope for English interpretation of the Orders, except in their additions and omissions from the original texts. For example, Richard Haydocke's addition of illustrations to, and his textual omissions in his 1598 partial translation of, Giovanni Lomazzo's *Trattato dell'arte della pittura scultura et architettura* (Milan, 1584) are of significance in revealing contemporary prejudices towards Catholic religious iconography (Phillips 1973). Haydocke censors the more extreme manifestations of Lomazzo's Mannerist theory, imbued as this was with Counter-Reformation principles (Harris and Savage 1990, 297). A letter from Dr John Case (d. 1600), the Canon of Salisbury, which Haydocke prints after his own preface, commends Haydocke's 'corrections' for where Lomazzo 'trippeth you hold him up, and where he goeth out of the way, you better direct his foote' (sig. ★j*v*).

Haydocke's Protestantism is attested from the outset by his dedication to Thomas Bodley, in which is noted Bodley's 'vertuous desire, of increasing both the Common-wealth and Church Militant' (sig. ij*v*). The biblical quotation on Haydocke's frontispiece (plate 7) runs 'In the handes of the skilfull shall the worke be approved, Eccl. 9.19', and was specifically intended to justify the study and practice of art and architecture against Puritan iconoclasm (Corbett and Lightbown 1979, 67–78; Harris and Savage 1990, 297). However, Haydocke omitted from

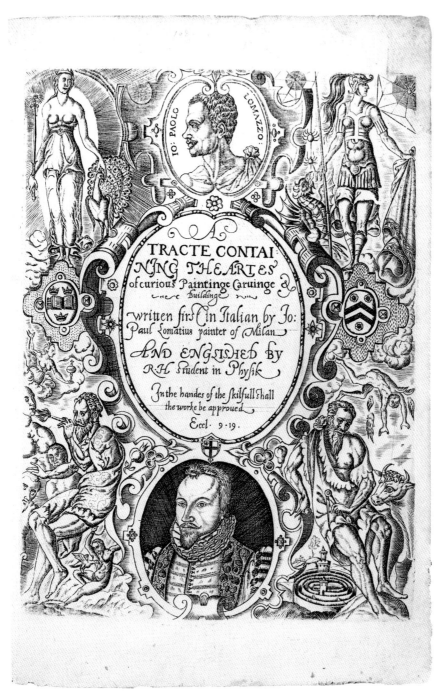

A
TRACTE CONTAI
NING THE ARTES
of curious Paintinge Caruinge &
Buildinge

written first in Italian by Jo:
Paul Lomatius painter of Milan

AND ENGLISHED BY
R:H student in Physik

In the handes of the skilfull shall
the worke be approued
Eccl. 9·19.

7   Richard Haydocke's frontispiece to Lomazzo's *Trattato*, translated as *A tracte containing the Artes of Curious Paintinge Carvinge & Buildinge* (Oxford, 1598). Cambridge University Library.

Lomazzo's preface 'a large discourse of the use of Images . . . because it
crosseth the doctrine of the reformed Churches' (Haydocke 1598, 3–4),
added to the third book 'A Briefe Censure of The Booke of Colours',
and protested in a marginal note in the fourth book against representations of God the Father (Haydocke 1598, 152). Indeed, in
Haydocke's frontispiece Pandora was again to symbolise the Puritan
principle that surface decoration was deceptive. She is pictured clasping
her box (in the middle on the left-hand side), a vessel here shaped as
a Renaissance covered cup or tazza of goldsmith's work; the evils the
box contained are thus concealed within a refined gift of tempting
aspect, of which 'deceitful' Composite work had been an earlier
example.

Lomazzo's text had urged his reader 'to represent any columne after
the similitude of mans body, which is the most perfect of all Gods
creatures' (Haydocke 1598, I, 85). His section on the Orders was not
excluded by Haydocke and they must therefore have been considered
perfectly appropriate for Protestant buildings, but Haydocke's sensitivity to the charge of idolatry has the effect of 'justifying' their use
alongside the other arts of Puritan censure which he includes but
amends. The only English treatise on the Orders to be published
during the Stuart period, Wotton's *The Elements of Architecture*
(London, 1624), avoids any open association of religion with the
Vitruvian creed until the closing section. Here Wotton would appear
to urge architects to adopt a general neutrality towards religious themes
when he notes the common suspicions surrounding the antique arts:

> I heare an *Objection* . . . that these delightfull *Craftes*, may be divers
> wayes ill applied in a *Land*. I must confesse indeede, there may bee
> a *Lascivious*, and there may be likewise a *Superstitious* use, both of
> *Picture* and of *Sculpture* . . . Nay, finally let mee aske, what ART can be
> more pernicious, then even RELIGION it selfe, if it selfe be converted
> into an Instrument of ART: Therefore, *Ab abuti ad non uti, negatur
> consequentia*[7] (Wotton 1624, 121–2).

The projected use of the Orders to express moral qualities, as
conceived by Shute, is however developed by Wotton. He observed
that in antiquity statues formed a 'continuall representation of vertuous
examples' (p. 106), and his Orders reflected this idea in expressing
degrees of virtue ranging from wholesomeness to sin. The Tuscan is
described as a 'plain, massie, rurall Pillar, resembling some sturdy well-
limmed Labourer, homely clad' (p. 33), whose 'principall Character [is]
Simplicity' (p. 35) and whose proportions in imitation of man were 'in
truth, the most naturall' (p. 33). In sharp contrast, the decorative

---

[7] This Latin expression reads 'The abuse of a thing is no argument against the use of it'.

Corinthian is described as 'laciviously decked like a Curtezane, and therein much participating (as all Inventions doe) of the place where they were first borne: *Corinthe* having been without controversie one of the wantonest Townes in the world' (p. 37). Wotton's source on the undoubted licentiousness of Corinth was probably St Paul's letters to the Corinthians (I.5,i/xii) (Hersey 1988, 66; Rykwert 1996, 320). Despite his admiration for the Roman author, Wotton thus reverses Vitruvius's 'virginal' characterisation of the Corinthian Order as introduced in the previous era by Shute, and ignores the Order's traditional heraldic association with English monarchy. Indeed, Wotton's identification of the Corinthian with the moral licentiousness of a common prostitute knows no source. As with Shute's characterisation of the Composite, however, such hostility towards the more ornamental of the Orders might easily be understood in the context of the widespread Puritan rejection of the decorative arts as idolatrous (Phillips 1973, 121–40; Hart 1995).

It is clearly the richness of Corinthian decoration which leads Wotton to identify the Order with immorality. Hence the Composite Order is next dismissed as 'nothing in effect, but a *Medlie*, or an *Amasse* of all the precedent *Ornaments*, making a new kinde, by stealth, and though the most richly tricked, yet the poorest in this, that he is a borrower of all his Beautie' (Wotton 1624, 38). Just as the relative simplicity of Wotton's Tuscan would accord with Adam's naked purity, especially since Adam was held by theorists as the origin of human proportion as applied to the Orders, so greater degrees of decoration would accord with mankind's post-Fall need for clothing. Indeed on the Composite Order Wotton observes that 'to know him will be easie by the verie mixture of his *Ornaments*, and *Cloathing*' (p. 39), and in this way his Tuscan labourer was 'homely clad'.

With the decorative 'upper' Orders thus dismissed, Wotton emphasises that despite Composite's lofty position in the hierarchy of the Orders, 'few *Palaces* Auncient or Moderne exceed the third of the Civill *Orders*' (p. 39). Wotton, like Shute before him, implies that if the Orders were arranged vertically in order then a moral architecture displaying a range of human behaviour and 'types' would result, from virtue to vice, from labourer to prostitute: his text even 'builds' such a structure, since he notes that the Ionic is 'in degree as in substantialnesse, next above the *Dorique*, sustayning the third, and adorning the second Story' (p. 36).

Wotton's moral censure of the Composite is despite, or perhaps because of, Jones's use of that Order on the upper part of the façade of the most prominent Stuart building, the Banqueting House at Whitehall palace, which had been erected just two years before the publication of Wotton's treatise. Far from agreeing, as is sometimes maintained (Wittkower 1974, 143; Harris and Savage 1990, 502), the two Stuart courtiers evidently fundamentally disagreed as to the desirability of the use, if not the meaning, of the Orders. Wotton's association of the Corinthian with immorality, and his distaste for the decorative Composite, might well have been a reaction to Jones's intentions: the Banqueting House has been seen as an emblem for an emerging Catholic court culture, and I have argued elsewhere that Jones subsequently used the full range of Orders, from a 'Puritan' Tuscan to a 'Catholic' Corinthian, on the refacing of St Paul's cathedral to express but unite religious extremes (Palme 1957; Hart 1995). As a committed Protestant, Wotton would naturally have identified any such expressions of Catholicism with immorality.

In concluding the *Elements*, Wotton promises a further treatise entitled *A Philosophicall Survey of Education* and which he described as 'a second *Building*, or repairing of Nature, and . . . a kinde of *Morall Architecture*' (Wotton 1624, 122);[8] here again he underlines the didactic, 'moral' purpose of architecture. Indeed, whilst Provost of Eton College, Wotton erected a double row of wooden columns in the Lower School, and placed on them pictures of ancient orators and poets (Smith 1907, 1, 204). This 'moralising' of Roman architecture is emphasised in the contemporary works of Ben Jonson, which equate the language of Vitruvian theory – harmony, proportion, symmetry – with terms of moral 'solidity' in the form of virtue, valour and justice (Johnson 1987, 170). And an attempt to equate the antique philosophy of ethics and morality to the Vitruvian notion of decorum in particular is evident in Jones's annotations in his Barbaro *Vitruvius*, his Xenophon, Aristotle, Piccolomini and Plutarch (Higgott 1992, 63; Hart forthcoming 1998).

Hence, although the Corinthian had been introduced into England as a virginal Order, suitable for the Protestant iconography of Elizabeth I, within the space of sixty years it became associated under the Stuarts with vice and possibly even Catholicism. Both conditions are however opposite extremes of a consistent moral order, an order which would naturally lead the two main Protestant treatise writers in the Tudor and Stuart era to condemn the impurity of Composite as 'licentious'.

TOWARDS A PROTESTANT 'TEMPERATE CLASSICISM'

This chapter has illustrated how the erstwhile Pagan and Catholic Orders were made compatible with Protestant morality in England. In

---

[8]   Wotton, H., *A Philosophical Survey of Education, or, Moral Architecture, and The Aphorisms of Education*, ed. H. S. Kermode (Liverpool, 1938). This work was unfinished when Wotton died in 1639.

this spirit, Vitruvius's treatise was presented by Dee as recording a Christian Golden Age, since Vitruvius 'did write ten bookes . . . to the Emperour *Augustus* (in whose daies our Heavenly Archemaster, was borne)' (sig. diij*r*). In introducing the 'First and Chief Groundes' of the Orders to England in 1563, John Shute reflected norms of, and indeed attempted to symbolise, the new theological order in the wake of the Reformation. Shute performs this task for the health of the Common-wealth, as his dedication to Elizabeth as the 'head' of the body-politic makes clear (sig. Aij*r*).

Architectural writers and translators were thus bound up with the wider attempts by court artists to find an appropriate expression for Protestant mythology in the context of the Counter-Reformation Mannerist architecture of Rome. The English writer-translators of treatises can be seen to have aimed to establish a 'temperate classicism', comprising neither an architecture without Order (that is, astylar) nor a licentious architecture retaining the Orders but in a mixed or abused form (Carpo 1992, 148–9). It would surely have been perfectly natural for the more Puritan-minded reformers to have identified such abuse of Vitruvian rules (that is, Mannerism) with the Catholic religion. But it has been seen that in England moral licentiousness could be ex-pressed by staying within the bounds of the five Orders, that is without recourse to the grotesque Vitruvian licentiousness of the columns created by Dietterlin or Sambin.

Whilst the universality and simplicity of the primitive hut and the human body as ornamental 'models' assisted the acceptability of Vitruvian architecture to the Protestant outlook, helping to divorce the *all'antica* style from specific Pagan and Catholic prototypes, more par-ticularly in early English treatises the Vitruvian body became clothed in national dress in the form of Shute's statues and Wotton's heraldic and lascivious columns. The ancient principle of mimesis, the truthful representation of nature, thus came to emphasise a form of 'Vitruvian morality' in the treatises of Protestant England. This equation of nature's moral truths with Vitruvian mimesis would, theorists hoped, be expressed by the (renewed) 'correct' use of the Orders in English building practice.

Sebastiano Serlio had been the strictest of Vitruvian commentators in the first five books of his treatise, laying down clear rules on how to avoid licentious (*licentioso*) designs (Serlio 1996, 458). Hence for Serlio, the Composite was the 'most licentious of all the building styles' (Serlio 1537, fol. LXIIII*v*/186*v*). Shute's dependence on Serlio and the translation into English of Serlio's first five books in 1611 perhaps reflected a general desire in European Protestant circles for a temperate classicism associated in particular with Serlio's treatise (Carpo 1992). Serlio's fifth book (on temples) had been dedicated to the pro-

Protestant Marguerite of Navarre,[9] and Robert Peake dedicated the English *Serlio* to the Protestant Prince Henry. Serlio's treatise and the Vitruvian code it described thereby became part of the cultivation of Henry's self-image as a Protestant prince. Curiously enough Henry VIII had promised three hundred *scudi* towards the publication of a second edition of Serlio's third book (on Roman antiquities), although probably not in Venice where it was destined to be published.[10] For Henry to part with money, the importance of this foreign book and its Vitruvian theory must surely have been explained to the Protestant king. Indeed a marginal reference to Serlio in James I's funeral sermon of 1625 (Williams 1625, 8 n. a) serves to illustrate just how central the Vitruvian architectural treatise had become to the image of the Protestant monarch since Shute's dedication of his 'first grounds' to Elizabeth just over sixty years earlier.

[9] Serlio's dedication of a book containing designs based on Vitruvian principles to a pro-Protestant noble is perfectly balanced according to this argument by his dedication of a subsequent book containing 'licentious' gate designs to the Catholic monarch of France, Henri II.

[10] Henry's promise is recorded in an undated letter (*c*.1538–9) from Serlio to Pietro Aretino, now in the Pierpont Morgan Library, New York (reproduced in Dinsmoor 1942, 128 n. 57). The Reformation in England cut off the book trade with European Catholic states, see Febvre and Martin 1993, 191–2.

Conclusion

BEYOND THE RENAISSANCE TREATISE

1   Frontispiece, Claude Perrault's Vitruvius translation, *Les dix livres d'architecture de Vitruve* (Paris, 1673). Collection Centre Canadien d'Architecture/Canadian Centre for Architecture, Montréal.

Chapter Eighteen

ON CLAUDE PERRAULT:
MODERNISING VITRUVIUS

Indra Kagis McEwen

IN 1673 A NEW FRENCH TRANSLATION of Vitruvius's *De Architectura* was published in Paris. It had been commissioned in 1667 by Jean-Baptiste Colbert (1619–83), Louis XIV's minister of finance and superintendant of buildings – after the king, to whom the work was dedicated and whose arms appeared on the title-page, the most powerful man in France. Its author was Claude Perrault (1613–88), doctor of medicine, founding member of the French Académie des Sciences established by Colbert in 1666, and elder brother of Charles Perrault who was Colbert's administrative assistant.[1]

The chief aim of the new translation was to provide the Académie Royale d'Architecture, which Colbert had founded in 1671 to regulate French architectural production, with the means for doing so, Jean Martin's translation of 1547 being judged too obscure for the purpose (*Procès verbaux* 1, 21). Read aloud in the Academy's sittings from June 1674 onwards (*Procès verbaux* 1, 76), Perrault's extensively annotated translation met with immediate success at home and abroad, both as an impressive work of scholarship and as a magnificent folio. Like the luxury volumes giving pictorial accounts of royal celebrations, or publications such as Perrault's own work on comparative anatomy issued by the Académie des Sciences (1671–76), the lavishly illustrated new Vitruvius was also meant to diffuse the splendour of the Sun King's reign throughout the royal courts of Europe and the emerging republic of letters. If, as it was claimed, Perrault made Vitruvius speak

[1] Many thanks for friendly assistance to the library of the Canadian Centre for Architecture and to the Blackader-Lauterman Library of Architecture and Art at McGill University. Thanks also to Vaughan Hart and Peter Hicks for helpful suggestions.
Charles Perrault was also a prominent man of letters, whose posthumous fame rests mainly on his *Contes du temps passé*, a collection of fairy tales. See especially Soriano 1972.

French, it was as much through the book's splendid illustrations as through its text. The frontispiece is an unequivocal epitome of the intention (plate 1).

On a dais at the right-hand side of the gallery in the foreground sit two allegorical figures: France and Abundance. They are instructed by Architecture, on the left, who points to Perrault's translation. Abundance gestures toward the scene beyond, where three works of architecture dominate a middle ground filled with tiny toiling figures: the triumphal arch of the Faubourg Saint-Antoine, the east façade of the Louvre and in the distance, rising like a fortress just above the geometrical centre of the composition, the Paris Observatoire. All three designs are attributed to Claude Perrault, although his authorship of the Louvre colonnade has often been contested (Picon 1988, 157–69) (plate 2), and the never-completed triumphal arch was demolished in 1716 (Picon 1988, 230).

All three, moreover, were Parisian projects, commissioned more or less concurrently with the translation, and were a vital part of Jean-Baptiste Colbert's vision of a centralised France, embodied in the person of the king.[2] 'Your majesty knows,' wrote Colbert to Louis XIV in a famous letter of 1665, 'that failing glorious deeds of war, buildings, more than anything else, are the measure of a prince's greatness and spirit' (Clément 1861–82, 5, 269). This greatness, he continued, would be far better measured by the yardstick of the Louvre than by the (in 1665) pitiable yardstick of Versailles which he considered an appalling waste of money. It was largely thanks to Charles Perrault's influence with Colbert that the great Bernini, brought from Rome in 1665 to design the Louvre's new east wing, lost the commission and was eventually replaced by Charles's brother, Claude (Charles Perrault 1909, 59–89).

'Triumphal arch for conquests of the earth. Observatoire for the heavens', noted Colbert in a memorandum of 1669 (Clément 1861–82, 7, 290). The gigantic triumphal arch of the Faubourg Saint-Antoine, just outside the eastern gate of the city, was to commemorate the king's recent military victories, while the Observatoire, standing on a hill overlooking the southern part of Paris, was meant not only for astronomical observations but also to house the new Académie des Sciences (Berger 1994, 45–52). In Colbert's opinion, 'sciences and the fine arts contribute no less to the glory of a reign than do arms and military prowess' (Clément 1861–82, 5, 515).

---

[2] Perrault received the commission for the Observatoire in 1667; he won the competition for the triumphal arch in 1669 and, according to his brother Charles, gained royal approval for his Louvre design in 1667. See Petzet 1967 and 1982; Picon 1988, 197ff; Charles Perrault 1909, 86. On Colbert: Clément 1861–82, *Colbert* 1983 and Murat 1984.

The Louvre colonnade. East front of the Louvre, Paris.

The self-contained visual logic of the frontispiece is a closed circle whose circumference, reading counterclockwise, travels through the writings of Vitruvius, the wealth and power of France, the three Parisian monuments, and back again to Vitruvius who, in this context, does indeed – inescapably – speak French. Claude Perrault and his brother Charles were convinced 'Moderns', adversaries of the 'Ancients' in the seventeenth-century controversy about the relative merits of antiquity and modernity (Charles Perrault 1688–97; Gillot 1914), and this conviction, as much as any other, was what directed the deliberate reshaping of Vitruvius's ancient Roman identity into a modern French one.

Then why bother with Vitruvius? Perrault's preface to the translation is very clear about why. Vitruvius was needed for his authority.

The precepts of this excellent author, whom critics class among the greatest minds of antiquity, were absolutely necessary to guide those who wished to become expert in this art. The great authority his writings have always had, made his precepts the ones that established the true rules of beauty and perfection in buildings, for beauty having scarcely no basis other than fancy . . . rules are needed in order to shape and to rectify it. And it is certain that . . . if nature does not supply such rules, as for example in language . . . human institutions must do so, and in order to accomplish this, agreement must be reached as to some authority which will take the place of positive reason (Perrault 1673 and 1684, Preface, unpaginated).

Perrault explains what he means by 'positive' in one of his translation notes: 'All architecture is founded on two principles. One of them is positive, the other arbitrary. The positive foundation is usage and the useful and necessary purpose for which a building is intended, such as solidity, salubrity and commodity. The foundation I call arbitrary is the beauty which depends on authority and custom' (Perrault 1673, 12, n. 3; 1684, 12, n. 13). Proportion, Perrault argues in another note, is an arbitrary beauty, and not, as most architects believe, something found in nature like the relative sizes of the stars or of the parts of the human body (1673, 100, n. 1; 1684, 105, n. 7).

This key distinction between positive and arbitrary beauty, and the classification of proportion as an arbitrary matter established by custom and underwritten by authority, form the core of Claude Perrault's architectural theory, tersely reiterated in his abridged Vitruvius published a year later (1674), and most fully elaborated in the *Ordonnance des cinq espèces de colonnes selon la méthode des anciens* of 1683. More than anything else, his is a theory about the role of architectural theory itself. His aim was to establish methodological foundations for architectural practice as certain and invariable as those developed for science by René Descartes in his *Discourse on Method* of 1637.

Although Vitruvius used many Greek words, the word *theoria* is not one of them. In the opening lines of *De Architectura*, he writes that an architect's knowledge arises from *fabrica* and *ratiocinatio* (Vitr.I.i.1). In the translation that the Académie Royale d'Architecture considered too obscure, Jean Martin rendered this as *fabrique et discours* (1547, fol. 1*v*), loosely, 'fabrication and discussion'. Perrault, however, translates *fabrica et ratiocinatio* as *pratique et théorie*, 'practice and theory' (1673 and 1684, 2).

It has been argued recently that of all the translations of this line, Jean Martin's comes closest to Vitruvius's intentions (Schrijvers 1989). This argument seems correct, but be that as it may, it is the shift from Jean Martin's *discours* to Claude Perrault's *théorie* that is of particular interest here, and what it reveals about Perrault's position at the crossroads between the Renaissance and modernity. According to Jean Martin's interpretation, what an architect knew (his *scientia*), grew out of his first-hand knowledge of the craft of building (*fabrica*) and the *ratiocinatio* or 'discussion' that reflected on it to give it meaning in a world order where all branches of learning were linked by a common *logos* or *ratio* (Vitr.I.i.12). For Perrault, over a century later, 'theory' was to direct 'practice' by supplying architects with methods and any 'discussion' not related to that end was superfluous.

Just how superfluous Perrault makes trenchantly clear by eliminating all such discussion from his abridgement of 1674 (1674, 2–5). The contrast with, for example, the earliest work on Vitruvius published in French is radical (Sagredo *c*.1537 and 1539). What this Spanish abridgement of Vitruvius, anonymously translated as *Raison d'architecture antique, extraicte de Vitruve*, considers important for an architect to know is precisely what Perrault insists must be excised. 'Thus, buildings that are well-proportioned according to the rules of the ancients, are as close to the form of man, as man himself is to the form and manner of the world, and first work of God', wrote Sagredo (1539, fols. 6r–*v*). In Renaissance theory, men were part of the natural, cosmic order,[3] and to build was to praise the Creator by imitating the proportions of that order (Sagredo 1539, fol. 51*v*). Renaissance men understood themselves as belonging to this order through the mediation of their microcosmic bodies (Vitr.III.i). Hands and upright posture gave people their human specificity within the natural order (Vitr.II.i.2).

After Descartes, man's defining essence became that of a freely rational 'thinking thing'. According to the taxonomy developed by Perrault and the Académie des Sciences, speech replaced hands as the organ of intelligence, and speech, not hands, was what made humans human (Picon 1988, 67). As a 'thinking thing' that uses language – which is without natural foundation, as Perrault claims, and, like proportion, shaped by arbitrary rules – man no longer shared in any cosmic identity. Uniquely equipped with reason, he stood above and apart from a nature made up of inert 'extended things' that, unlike him, were mechanically bound by causal laws (Toulmin 1990, 107ff). These laws, once understood, could be manipulated to his own ends so that, Descartes asserted near the end of the *Discourse on Method*, 'we might become as masters and possessors of nature' (Descartes 1953, 168). A Renaissance man who was *part* of a cosmic whole could not have aspired to becoming its 'master' or 'possessor'.

When Perrault maintains that proportions have no natural foundation his reference is to this reified Cartesian nature, not to the one in which the *discours* of humanists like Sagredo or Jean Martin was grounded. In late seventeenth-century France not everyone embraced the new Cartesian understanding of nature. Among architects most, as yet, did not and this is what made Perrault's position so revolutionary. François Blondel, director of the Académie Royale d'Architecture, and professor of the course given there, was among those who adhered firmly to the traditional view (Blondel 1675–83, 761–74). No wonder

---

[3] I use the words 'man' and 'men' deliberately: the discourse, overwhelmingly, was about men and not about women.

Perrault and Blondel could not agree about the natural foundations of architectural beauty. They were not talking about the same nature.

Although the Academy was established by Colbert to be arbiter of the French building industry, and although this charge was accepted by its director (Blondel 1675–83, Preface, unpaginated), Blondel's appreciation of traditional cosmic unity was fundamentally at odds with the Academy's own mandate. If architectural beauty is founded in a natural order bound together by a common *logos*, as Blondel and the academicians clearly believed (*Procès verbaux* 1, 321–2), then how could any human agency possibly arbitrate on it? All an architect can do is consult the authorities who seem to have penetrated the mysteries of such relationships and then make the most judicious decision possible in any given case (Blondel 1675–83, 787). However, if nature is a Cartesian collocation of manipulable 'extended things', proportions, the product of the uniquely rational human mind, cannot possibly be natural. Freed from any natural foundation, 'arbitrary' beauties do indeed become arbitratable.

Claude Perrault's theory – of whose intentions the Vitruvius frontispiece provides such a graphic elucidation – underpins the following agenda. Buildings must be built so that France will be great and wealthy. For this rules are needed. Where there is no 'positive reason' to justify these rules, some agreed-upon authority such as Vitruvius must underwrite them. The implication is that if consensus could be obtained as to the greater weight of some other authority, other rules could apply.

Jean-Baptiste Colbert aimed for increased production in all domains, not just architecture (Murat 1984, 129–70), and for this, uniform standards were required. His radical reformation of French industry involved not only supplanting local, guild control of trades with centralised, royal control, but also the passing of innumerable regulations that established strictly enforced norms for the production of all goods throughout the country.[4] As a result of the 'grand design' which Colbert proposed to Louis XIV in 1665,[5] French civil law, with its tangle of varying local codes, customs and accompanying abuses, was centralised and systematised through the *Ordonnance civile* of 1667; criminal justice, by the *Ordonnance criminelle* passed three years later.

---

[4] Cloth, for example, which did not conform to precise royal standards of length, width and thickness was to be pilloried along with a placard denouncing its producer. Repeated offences were to be punished by the pillorying of the producer himself, along with samples of the offending goods. (*Colbert* 1983, 152–3).

[5] 'Mais si Vostre Majesté s'est proposé quelque plus grand dessein, comme seroit celuy de réduire tout son royaume sous une mesme loi, mesme mesure et mesme poids, qui seroit assurément un dessein digne de la grandeur de Vostre Majesté, digne de son esprit et de son âge . . .' (Clément 1861–82, 6, 14).

Waterways and forests came under royal jurisdiction in 1669 with the *Ordonnance portant reglement sur les eaux et forêts*. In 1673, the *Ordonnance du commerce* regularised trade. Under the *ancien régime*, an *ordonnance* was royal edict, emanating from the king. An *ordonnance* was meant to establish order, and Colbert's overriding ambition was that a *maxime de l'ordre* should replace the *maxime de la confusion* he claimed had held sway when he first entered the king's service.

   Although Louis's arms do again appear on the title-page, as they did on that of the Vitruvius translation, Claude Perrault's *Ordonnance for the Five Kinds of Columns after the Method of the Ancients* (Paris, 1683) was not dedicated to the king, but to Jean-Baptiste Colbert (plate 3; Appendix 4). Now an *ordonnance* in architecture is not a royal edict, of course.[6] In architecture, the *ordonnance* is the arrangement or ordering of the parts of a building, as Perrault himself explains (1683, 1–2; 1993, 65–6). At the beginning of his *Cours*, François Blondel suggests that one might also call an *ordonnance* a *columnaison*, a coinage of his own which has specifically to do with the column because it is 'the column that gives the rule and measure to everything else' (Bondel 1675–83, 4). This common understanding of the role of columns as regulators is what made Perrault's *Ordonnance*, ostensibly a work on the Orders, exactly the right vehicle for a theory meant to justify bringing architecture into line with the systematising intentions of other absolutist reforms. And, within the context of this agenda, the regulating role of columns brings their *ordonnance* very close indeed to the royal *ordonnances* just discussed. In fact, Perrault's is the only work on the Orders in French that calls itself an *ordonnance*,[7] and the only one, moreover, that refers to the Orders as *espèces*: 'kinds' of columns to be sure, but also 'species', and subject to the same rigorous taxonomy as that being applied in Claude Perrault's biological research with the Académie des Sciences under whose auspices, significantly enough, the *Ordonnance* was prepared (the king was shown the manuscript at the Académie in 1681; Herrmann 1973, 33).

   Written, Perrault claims in the dedication, as 'a kind of supplement to what Vitruvius has dealt with in insufficient detail', the aim of the *Ordonnance* was the establishment of fixed rules for the 'proportions of those elements on whose beauty the ornament and majesty of great buildings entirely depend' (Perrault 1683, *Epistre*, unpaginated). These fixed rules, he says, are needed to achieve Colbert's goal, which is to provide lovers of architecture with the means for contributing 'to the

----

   [6]   An *ordonnance*, as in royal edict, is 'ordinance' in English. An architectural *ordonnance* is an 'ordonnance'. In French the same word, *ordonnance*, is used for both.

   [7]   Jean Bullant (1564): *Reigle générale d'architecture des cinq manières de colonnes*; Jacques Ier Androuet du Cerceau (1583): *Petit traité des cinq ordres de colonnes*; Abraham Bosse (1664): *Traité des manières de dessiner les ordres d'architecture*.

glory of our invincible monarch in everlasting monuments' (*Epistre*). It was in the provision of such rules that, despite the hopeful message of its frontispiece, the Vitruvius translation had proved deficient. But Vitruvius, as already noted, was *the* agreed-upon authority. Perrault is aware his project is 'bold and unusual'. 'Paradoxical' is a word he uses on a number of other occasions, which in the seventeenth century meant beyond the pale of consensus. On their own, his proposals were not only at odds with prevailing opinion, they had no authority to speak of.

Like the Vitruvius translation, the *Ordonnance* was written at Colbert's orders,[8] and its dedication repeatedly intimates that his is the authority which will induce acceptance of its unorthodoxy (see Appendix 4). In the initial 'M' of '*Monseigneur*', a snake, Colbert's personal emblem (*coluber* is 'snake' in Latin), rears up toward the radiance of the sun (plate 3). The legend on the banner reads, 'from him comes all my force': to Colbert from the Sun King, from Colbert to Perrault.

The *Ordonnance* has three main sections. The Preface, where Perrault gives final definition to his theory; Part I, where he establishes his method and gives general rules for such things as pedestals and entablatures; and Part II, where he lays down specific rules for each of the five Orders in turn. Part II concludes with two chapters on 'abuses' – licentious practices which architects ought to avoid, among them the practice known as optical adjustment.

After a perfunctory allusion to the human body as the source of the proportions that 'give buildings their beauty' (1683, i; 1993, 47), Perrault begins with an assessment of the confusion concerning those proportions, for proportions are completely inconsistent both among the built works of antiquity and as recommended in the treatises of modern authors such as Alberti and Philibert De l'Orme. Architectural proportions vary greatly, and yet the works where these variations are visible meet with uniform general approval.

> This shows just how ill-founded is the opinion of people who believe that the proportions supposed to be preserved in architecture are as certain and invariable as the proportions that give musical harmony its appeal, proportions that do not depend on us but that nature has established with absolutely immutable precision and that cannot be changed without immediately offending even the least sensitive ear (1683, iii; 1993, 48).

Given his intention of cutting architectural proportion loose from its traditional moorings, Perrault is quite right to begin by debunking the

---

[8] 'Ce qui m'oblige d'avantage à faire sçavoir qu'un Ouvrage qui apparamment doit estre si utile, a esté fait par vostre ordre.' (*Epistre*).

A MONSEIGNEUR
COLBERT
MARQUIS DE SEIGNELAY,
BARON DE SEAUX, &c.

MINISTRE ET SECRETAIRE D'ESTAT
& des Commandemens du Roy , Commandeur , & Grand
Threforier des Ordres de Sa Majefté , Contrôleur General
des Finances , Surintendant & Ordonnateur General des
Baftimens & Jardins de Sa Majefté , Arts & Manufactures
de France.

ONSEIGNEVR,

*Après avoir travaillé par vos Ordres à la tra-
duction & à l'explication de Vitruve, avec un fuccez*

3 Dedication to Jean-Baptiste Colbert. Claude Perrault, *Ordonnance
des cinq espèces de colonnes selon la méthode des anciens* (Paris, 1683).
Collection Centre Canadien d'Architecture/Canadian Centre for
Architecture, Montréal.

so-called musical analogy. That the proportional relationships which
establish musical harmonies, allegedly discovered by Pythagoras, are the
same as those governing architectural harmony had been virtually
axiomatic in the Renaissance. But the analogy did not end there. The
proportions rendered audible in music, whereby precise mathematical
quantities encounter the ineffability of qualitative human response,
were a key to the whole harmonious cosmic order. Architecture's

place in that order was, in a sense, guaranteed by the musical analogy above all others.[9]

Musical harmonies are positive not so much because they are 'established by nature', but because they are invariable. Positive beauties do exist in architecture, but proportions, being variable, are not among them. There are, writes Perrault, taking up the theme already broached in his Vitruvius and in the 1674 abridgement,

> two kinds of beauty in architecture . . . beauties based on convincing reasons and [those] which depend only on prejudice. I call beauties based on convincing reasons those whose presence in works is bound to please everyone. They include the richness of the materials, the size and magnificence of the building, the precision and cleanness of execution, and [bilateral] symmetry . . . Against the beauties I call positive and convincing, I set those I call arbitrary, because they are determined by our wish to give a definite proportion, shape, or form to things that might well have a different form without being misshapen and that appear agreeable not by reasons within everyone's grasp but merely by custom . . . (1683, vi–vii; 1993, 50–51).

Although he argues that proportions are among the beauties that appear agreeable 'merely by custom', Perrault is no relativist. In a project driven by the objective to attain 'something fixed, constant, and established in architecture, at least insofar as the proportions of the five Orders are concerned' (1683, xv; 1993, 55), one custom is as good as another only if taken on the basis of their equal lack (for Perrault) of intrinsic merit. One custom is *not* as good as another if taken on the basis of what Perrault understands as the positive value of consistency and systematisation. Originally, he claims, arbitrary beauties attained positive status by their association with the true positive beauties, invariably understood as such: size and magnificence, clean execution, rich materials and bilateral symmetry. Similarly, court clothes become fashionable because powerful people wear them and beliefs are adopted because respected people defend them (1683, viii; 1993, 51). But like laws and unlike fashions, proportions once established should remain unchanged.

Positive beauties are easily understood by everyone. Knowledge of arbitrary beauties, however, is the specific domain of the architect.

---

[9] Vitruvius (I.i.9) cites music as the strongest link in the chain that binds all of the branches of human knowledge into coherence. The musical analogy had recently been given a new lease of life with the publication in 1679 of René Ouvrard's *L'Architecture harmonique*. François Blondel writes appreciatively of it in his *Cours* (1675–83, 756–61), although objective grounds for cosmic harmony had already been seriously undercut by Marin Marsenne in his *Traité de l'Harmonie universelle* of 1627. See Fichet 1979, 175–6.

Like a lawyer who must know the articles of civil codes, an architect's task is, essentially, to know the rules and how to apply them, and not to bother about why: 'Just as in civil law there are rules dependent on the will of legislators and on the consent of nations that a natural understanding of fairness will never reveal' (1683, xiii; 1993, 54).

No one, Perrault laments, so far has succeeded in establishing such rules, once and for all (1683, xiv; 1993, 55). His hope is to succeed where his predecessors have failed and in the last pages of the preface, Perrault deals with what he perceives as the final obstacle to his success: excessive reverence for the ancients. 'The extent to which architects make a religion of venerating the works they call ancient is inconceivable. They admire everything about them but especially the mystery of proportions' (1683, xvii; 1993, 57), he fumes, writing as a scientist and exasperated modern. The sense of the proportions written into the built 'texts' of antiquity are as open to question as the truth of what is dealt with in the texts of, say, Aristotle who, as the pioneers of the scientific revolution were discovering, had been wrong on so many counts. In architecture, as in experimental science, 'texts' as such are owed no particular reverence. Reverence is counter-productive, and owed exclusively to the mysteries of religion.

If one understands proportion the way Vitruvius and his Renaissance interpreters did, which is to say as the *analogia*, or binding force that guaranteed the coherence of the universal harmony in which François Blondel continued to profess such unshakeable faith, it is no wonder that Perrault was determined to demystify it. Application of the scientific method depends for its success on the isolation of the phenomenon under study. Galileo's study of motion, for example, depended on the postulation of a perfect vacuum. To conduct 'controlled' experiments under laboratory conditions means cutting through the web of analogies which constitutes the very fabric of universal harmony. Allow the 'mystery' of proportion, and you disallow modern science.

'The putting together [*compositio*] of temples depends on symmetry [*symmetria*]. Architects must grasp this principle thoroughly. It arises from proportion, which is called *analogia* in Greek', wrote Vitruvius at the opening of Book III, which is more or less how Jean Martin rendered the passage in the sixteenth century.[10] Claude Perrault translates the same passage as follows: 'To regulate [*ordonner*] a building properly one must respect proportion which is something architects should, above all, observe exactly. Proportion depends on the relation

[10] 'Aedium compositio constat ex symmetria, cuius rationem diligentissime architecti tenere debent. Ea autem paritur a proportione, quae graece analogia dicitur' (Vitr. III.i.1). Jean Martin: 'La composition des Temples consiste en symmetrie, delaquelle tous Architectes doyvent diligemment entendre le secret. Ceste symmetrie est engendree de proportion, que les Grecz nomment Analogie' (1547, fol. 27v).

the Greeks call "analogy".[11] Vitruvius's 'temple' has become a 'building', whose 'putting together' is, for Perrault, its *ordonnance*. Architects no longer need to understand the principle of *symmetria*;[12] they must, above all, observe proportions exactly. The ancient text has been rewritten as a modern one.

One of the many inconsistencies inherent in Perrault's position as a modern is its seeming incompatibility with his avowed respect for Vitruvius. There is no incompatibility once one realises that this respect is for the French-speaking Vitruvius mirrored in passages such as the one just examined – which is to say that this respect is for Claude Perrault himself. The apparent anomaly of advertising the *Ordonnance* as being 'after the method of the ancients' can be accounted for on similar grounds.

Perrault classifies architecture into three categories: first, the works of the 'ancients', true originals, now missing, to which Vitruvius's rules refer; second, the built works of antiquity, faulty copies of those originals whose varying proportions are the result of careless craftsmanship; and third, architecture as prescribed by the moderns, whose proportions are also inconsistent with one another (1683, xviii–xx, 8; 1993, 57–60, 72). His claim is that his method will restore the rules of the 'ancients' (first category) to their original simplicity and unambiguous exactitude (1683, xxi; 1993, 62). His claim, in other words, is that these ancients shared his own concern for rationality; that they were modern, as he is; or, conversely and more to the point, that he himself is in fact an ancient.[13] 'After the method of the ancients', means after *his* method.

Armed with Antoine Desgodets's meticulous measured drawings of the principal Roman monuments (1682) and with Fréart de Chambray's *Parallèle de l'Architecture antique avec la moderne* (Paris, 1650) which provided a convenient compilation of the rules established by the moderns, and using a legal formula known as 'splitting the difference',

[11] 'Pour bien ordonner un Edifice il fault avoir égard à la Proportion qui est une chose que les Architectes doivent surtout observer exactement. Or la Proportion dépend du Rapport que les Grecs appellent Analogie' (Perrault 1673, 53; 1684, 56). Perrault, whose translation here as elsewhere is unabashedly tactical, takes overt issue with Martin's version in his note of the same page.

[12] Vitruvius's *symmetria*, which is how parts relate to one another in general terms, is not Perrault's bilateral symmetry. For Perrault *symmetria*, *proportio* and *eurythmia* are all reduced to 'proportion'.

[13] The argument that, because the moderns have the benefit of knowledge accrued over time, the true ancients are really the moderns was fairly common among seventeenth-century advocates of the scientific method who, like Perrault, struggled against undue reverence for antiquity (Picon 1988, 103). 'Nos premiers pères ne doivent-ils pas être regardez comme les enfans & nous comme les vieillards & les veritables Anciens du monde?' (Charles Perrault 1688–97, 1, 50).

Perrault draws up a series of comparative tables in order to establish a single consistent system of what he calls regulatory mean proportions (1683, 9; 1993, 72–3). As a further aid towards the formulation of rules that consist of whole numbers which are easy to recall, easy to calculate with and, above all, easy to apply, Perrault introduces an entirely unprecedented 'small' module of a third of a column diameter which is to replace the traditional one of either the diameter or half-diameter of the column.

The resulting system appears to be internally consistent, but erroneous calculations and falsified data are the means used to arrive at it (Herrmann 1973, 209–11). In the first plate of the *Ordonnance*, column heights increase from Order to Order by a systematic progression of two small modules each. Looking closely, however, one notices that this flawless regularity has meant making the abacus and volutes of the Corinthian capital part of the entablature and not of the column, which is a patent absurdity (plate 4). Perrault would rather alter reality than make any adjustments to his implacable order.

Of the *Ordonnance*'s two concluding chapters on abuses, chapter 7 is the crucial one, dealing as it does with the question of optical corrections: since Vitruvius, optics served as the virtually sacrosanct justification invoked for adjustments made at the decisive point where ideal proportions (the 'natural' ones that bound architecture to the cosmic order) encountered the real, complex and infinitely variable circumstances of a specific building project and where, as François Blondel taught in his course, the judgement of the architect met its ultimate challenge (1675–83, 726).

'Once . . . proportions have been established,' Perrault asserts, 'they should no longer be changed or made different in different buildings for optical reasons or because of the different aspects they may have' (1683, 96; 1993, 154). Altering proportions for reasons of 'aspect' is not only useless, it is positively vicious (1683, 106; 1993, 161). Why? Perrault says that the eye, being equipped with unerring judgement, is never really deceived, no matter what the 'aspect'. Therefore, since vision is rational and flawless (Cartesian and disembodied: see Judovitz 1993; Pérez-Gómez 1993, 26), no adjustments need to be made to compensate for its non-existant shortcomings.

The key to Perrault's hostility to optical adjustments lies in the word 'aspect'. The *aspect* of a building is at once its appearance and the angle or point of view from which it is perceived. *Aspect* covers a whole matrix of relationships: between the human subject and the built work; between the work and its specific situation. To admit that *aspect* plays a role in the architectural process would overturn the entire systematising agenda of the *Ordonnance* by admitting that unpredictable or unregulatable circumstances, and not rules, are what finally determine

4   The five Orders. Plate 1 (facing p. 34), Claude Perrault, *Ordonnance des cinq espèces de colonnes selon la méthode des anciens* (Paris, 1683). Collection Centre Canadian d'Architecture/Canadian Centre for Architecture, Montréal.

what gets built. To admit *aspect* would mean to allow that an architect, through independent judgement, plays a role beyond that of a technician who places his expert knowledge of arbitrary beauties at the service of an authority which, thus compromised, would no longer be able to stand as the guarantor of rapid and efficient production.

Nevertheless, in practice, variable criteria continued – inevitably – to take precedence over inflexible rules in Claude Perrault's built projects. In the concluding chapter of the *Ordonnance*, Perrault himself invokes 'a vast and distant aspect' (1683, 119; 1993, 171) as the reason for having used a giant Order of pilasters (normally 'abusive') on the Seine-facing side of the east wing of the Louvre. Neither the Corinthian Order of the Louvre colonnade (plate 2), nor that of the triumphal arch of the Faubourg Saint-Antoine follows the proportions Perrault gives for the Corinthian Order in the *Ordonnance* (Herrmann 1973, 115–16). The columns of the Louvre colonnade swell out slightly in the lower third of the shaft, in keeping with the practice of entasis, to which Perrault overtly objects in his writings (1673, 78; 1684, 82). The list could go on.

And yet the gap between 'theory' and 'practice' is not as wide as such inconsistencies might suggest, for maintaining the ultimately untenable fiction of absolute control was as much the overriding intention in both the Louvre colonnade and in the design for the triumphal arch as it was of Perrault's *Ordonnance*. The fiction comes closest to unassailable certainty in the Paris Observatoire, future home of the Académie des Sciences under whose auspices the *Ordonnance* was written. Its plan and south elevation illustrate the terms *ichnographia* and *orthographia* in the Perrault *Vitruvius* (plate 5).

'The construction of the Observatoire is such that the building by itself can serve as a substitute for all the principal astronomical instruments used in making observations', wrote Perrault in the margin of one of his original drawings, adding that its north–south orientation supplies a meridian line of great precision, that the faces of its two octagonal corner pavilions give the rising and setting of the sun at equinoxes and solstices, and that the opening that pierces the building from roof to foundations exactly indicates the zenith (Clément 1861– 82, 5, 516).

Situated on a hill, surrounded by a wall, stripped bare of all but positive beauties, and as rigorous in its geometry as a Vauban fort, the Observatoire's resemblance to military architecture was more immediately obvious to contemporary commentators than its incarnation of solar movement or its exactitude as an instrument of astronomical observation (Petzet 1967, 14–15; Picon 1988, 220). On the south face, reliefs flanking the central window deploy scientific and architectural instruments like battle trophies. On the other side of the building, in

5   Plan and south elevation of the Paris Observatoire. Plate 2, p. 11, Claude Perrault's
Vitruvius translation, *Les dix livres d'architecture de Vitruve* (Paris, 1673). Collection Centre
Canadian d'Architecture/Canadian Centre for Architecture, Montréal.

the pediment over the north front which overlooks the city, the arms of the Sun King herald the absolute constancy of the monarch for whose 'movements' the building is as much of an analogue as it is for those of the sun, his double (Apostolidès 1981, 155–9).

In the enchanted world where Philibert De l'Orme's good architect had operated in concert with the rhythms of pre-Cartesian nature, Vitruvius and the ancients were a wellspring of limitless invention (1567, fols. 281*v*–83*r*). Perrault's *Vitruvius* and the so-called ancients of his *Ordonnance* now arbitrate standards for increased production in a world where invention, understood as licence, has become a form of sabotage. Assuming he is there, somewhere among the toiling figures of the Vitruvius frontispiece, Perrault's architect – babbling, no doubt, and handless like Philibert's bad one (1567, fols. 280*v*–81*r*) – labours under the unerring eye of the fortress-like Observatoire.

EPILOGUE

Jean-Baptiste Colbert died in October 1683, six months after the publication of the *Ordonnance*, which the members of the Académie Royale d'Architecture only began reading five years later in December of 1688, two months after Perrault's own death from an infection he contracted while dissecting a diseased camel. The proceedings, which record the title erroneously as *Cinq espèces d'architecture selon les anciens*, convey a mixture of hostility and indifference (*Procès verbaux* 2, 170–73). The academicians gave up reading it altogether about a quarter of the way through. Had Colbert not died when he did, Perrault's 'bold and unusual' views may well have not had to wait a century before attaining currency through the mediation of less authoritative channels (Herrmann 1973, 130–89; Rykwert 1980; Pérez-Gómez 1983).

Chapter Nineteen

FROM BLONDEL TO BLONDEL: ON THE DECLINE OF THE VITRUVIAN TREATISE

✥

James McQuillan

THE EIGHTEENTH CENTURY WAS characterised by a re-evaluation of every aspect of intellectual life in the wake of new norms arising from the investigation of nature and from world navigation. By the last half of this century the Vitruvian-style treatise had all but disappeared, and it is the task of this chapter to plot the more significant reasons for this decline. This will involve the following considerations – the seventeenth-century controversy over proportion, new forms of architectural literature, the rise of historicism and 'medievalism', and in conclusion, the triumph of new theories of architecture by the mid-eighteenth century.

In dealing with the decline of the Vitruvian treatise it must be accepted that the most important change to take place was the collapse of the theory of *ordonnance*, that is the disposition of the elements of architecture and particularly the Orders. The disposition of the Orders was bound up with the theory of mimesis, the Classical theory of artistic representation through the imitation of nature as outlined by Vitruvius when advancing the human form and the construction of the primitive hut as models.[1] Whilst the principle of mimesis had been central to Renaissance treatise writers, the Baroque would be characterised by the use of forms which were only loosely related to this principle and were not treated by Vitruvius. The dome, together with such new forms as the geometry of conic sections and paired

---

[1]   The oldest authority for ordonnance was of course Vitruvius. The theory of the Orders was presented by the Roman architect as a dual argument, one based on primitive huts as a construction model which was transformed into more permanent materials, the other based on the human body as 'the positive source of the whole numerical structure of understanding, and of which the orders are one instance' (Rykwert 1972, 109).

columns, all clearly demonstrated that the scope of Vitruvius had been surpassed, and thus weakened the prestige which the Roman author had enjoyed.

Certainly after 1750 conditions were in place allowing the ascendancy of the 'first moderns', for example in the acceptance of aesthetics as a corresponding theory to the 'new philosophy' now ruling in the mathematical and material sciences (Rykwert 1980). It seems appropriate in relating the decline of the Vitruvian treatise to trace the rise of these new conditions from High Baroque to High Enlightenment, that is 'from Blondel to Blondel'. These two are François Blondel (1617–86, henceforth 'the Elder'), and his namesake Jacques-François Blondel (1705–74, henceforth 'the Younger'), once thought to be related although no connection has ever been sustained. Both were heavily engaged in academic architecture through the French Académie and both were well known because of their writings.

Blondel the Elder was amongst the first *trattatisti* to combine the legacies of Vitruvius, Vignola, Palladio and Scamozzi, so that the architect could become acquainted with the variety of measurements of the Orders and thus inform his taste and judgement (Herrmann 1982, 217). Blondel thus provided an almost encyclopedic account of Vitruvian commentators. In the first tome of his *Cours d'Architecture, enseigné dans l'Academie royale d'architecture* (Paris, 1675), Blondel began by defining architecture as 'the art of building well'. He explained that this meant that all the members must correspond and relate to the whole so that nothing was denied, and following this that the ornaments, doors and windows were applied to result in 'an agreeable proportion and appropriateness [*justesse*]' (Blondel 1675, 1). In order to discuss the elements of architecture, Blondel first demonstrated the primitive hut, for him four tree-trunks 'planted in the four corners of a square' and then enclosed. Here Blondel followed Vitruvius in celebrating the transformation of materials, from timber to stone, that attest the ancient and therefore authoritative origin and form of the Orders.

In the second tome of the *Cours*, the elder Blondel confirmed the Pythagorean doctrine of proportion and beauty as recorded by Vitruvius when he linked 'harmonious union which one calls Beauty, and which we look upon with pleasure', to the saying of Pythagoras that 'Nature is always the same in all things' (Blondel 1683, 758, 759). This discussion was even more authoritative in that Blondel called upon such important contemporaries as René Ouvrard,[2] a Master of Music of the Sainte-Chapelle, and the Abbé de Saint-Hilarion. Both theorists confirmed the role of harmony and musical proportion in

---

[2] Ouvrard published *L'art et la science des nombres en Français et Latin* (Paris, 1678); and *Lettre sur l'architecture harmonique* (Paris, 1679).

architecture, Ouvrard arguing not only from Vitruvius but from Holy
Scripture, since in the Temple of Solomon 'all the parts . . . had Harmonic numbers in proportion among themselves' (Blondel 1683, 757).
This prepared the way in Blondel's *Cours* for a critique of Claude
Perrault's re-evaluation of the Vitruvian doctrine of proportion published in his famous translation of Vitruvius of 1673, a re-evaluation
immediately denounced by Blondel as 'singular and extraordinary'
(Blondel 1683, 762). Perrault was a physician and an anatomist, an
unofficial member of the Académie Royale d'Architecture and the
designer of several important commissions for Jean-Baptiste Colbert
(chief minister to Louis XIV), as well as a member with Blondel of the
Académie des Sciences. Blondel quoted Perrault in the matter of the
transmission of proportions from one master to another – for Perrault
this was a practice of weakness giving rise to mistakes in copying, but
a notion rejected by Blondel. Blondel was therefore alert to any
possible criticism of the Vitruvian doctrine of proportion, replying in
the most assertive terms, and thus provides excellent evidence of the
reaction to Perrault's 'reform' of theory at the highest level of French
officialdom.

Perrault never retracted his doctrine as to the relativity of proportions through their transmission in the face of this criticism. His
confidence was lodged in his promotion of the 'Moderns' against the
'Ancients' and was secured by what Herrmann notes was 'justified
pride in scientific achievement and the writings of the new philosophy'
(Herrmann 1973, 51, 52). Perrault's major departure from Vitruvian
canonics as supported by Blondel was his theory of a dualistic nature of
beauty, positive and arbitrary. The first was to be found in 'richness of
material, the size and magnificence of the building, precision and
neatness of execution, and symmetry', whilst the second, arbitrary
qualities were those beauties which 'depend on one's own volition to
give things which could be different a certain proportion, form and
shape' (Perrault 1683, p. VI). The coherence of the last concept was
held together by a faculty of the mind already denoted by Descartes's
liaison des traces and Malebranche's *liaison des idées,* but Perrault is the
first to introduce the notion of 'arbitrary beauty' into art theory,
closely followed by Locke's 'association of ideas' (Herrmann 1973, 56).
Perrault's attack on the role of absolute beauty as maintained by the
Vitruvian tradition was accompanied by his recognition of the power
of custom in the affairs of men that, as Herrmann notes, 'effects the
transference of attributes with a finality that almost bars us from
recognising that proportions, originally and in themselves, have no
positive beauty at all' (Herrmann 1973, 61). The recognition of arbitrary beauty validated any range of local customs or even fashions that
now needed no link to Vitruvian principles for legitimacy.

The most dramatic of Perrault's innovations not to be found in Vitruvius, that of coupled giant Order columns (as displayed on the east front of the Louvre), fell under Blondel's censure in the *Cours*, though Perrault's name was not mentioned. In his critique, Blondel was well aware that Bramante, Michelangelo, Sangallo and later Serlio and De l'Orme, all used coupled columns in what he described as perfecting the rebirth of architecture, but he found it a remnant of Gothic practice and even ancient examples did not have enough authority to warrant the practice in his own day (Blondel 1675, 228–30). Both theorists argued over the merits of counter-perspective, that is the adjustment of proportions to take account of the foreshortening of the upper elements of a large building (Wright 1983, 146–56), which according to Perrault were the blind fumblings of the ancient architects. For Blondel, however, it was long experience and knowledge of Vitruvius that allowed an architect to make the required adjustments in proportion which conferred indispensable grace to the building, rather than, as Herrmann has noted, 'by the mechanical application of Perrault's proposed proportions, rationally arrived at by working out an average' (Herrmann 1982, 218). In the tension between the mimetic argument of the elder Blondel and the empiricism of Perrault we can see what Max Weber called 'the disenchantment of the world' (Lichtheim 1968, 266–7), or more precisely, see the rise of 'divided representation' between the symbolic and the instrumental (Vesely 1985). As we shall discover, the latter came to dominate the art of architecture by the mid-eighteenth century and dealt a decisive blow to the Vitruvian form of treatise with its Pythagorean, mimetic basis.

NEW FORMS OF ARCHITECTURAL LITERATURE

In the great expansion of the medieval European intellectual world brought about first by printing and then by global travel and conquest, it was natural that many new subjects claimed the attention of scholars and thinkers, either to conserve the *status quo* of their position or to advance fresh interpretations at the behest of new evidence (Grafton 1992). The authority of antiquity which had been bolstered by medieval scholastics was inevitably undermined by these discoveries, and as an important part of this process Vitruvian treatises were increasingly rendered irrelevant in their ignorance of new cultures and exclusive maintenance of a Roman antiquity. In the wake of this, new forms of architectural literature would emerge, including cosmologies embracing exoticism, mathematical compendia and encyclopedias more comprehensive and less Classical than any seen before.

1   Noah instructs the builders of the Ark concerning the divine proportions to be used. Fr
Athanasius Kircher's *Arca Noë* (Amsterdam, 1675), following p. 28. Cambridge Univers
Library.

In the midst of these tumultuous events, no group appeared
with greater rigour and devotion to tradition than the élite Counter-
Reformation religious orders of Rome. The Clerks Regular or
Theatines and subsequently their much more successful rivals, the
Society of Jesus, were energetic in the field of art, as well as in that of
education – the Jesuits' favoured enterprise of cultural penetration in
Europe by the end of the sixteenth century. The leading polymath
who represented the manifold intellectual force of the late Renaissance,
or rather the High Baroque, was the German Jesuit Athanasius Kircher
(1620–80). Kircher was professor of mathematics at the Collegio
Romano and also papal librarian. He expanded the work of the earlier
Jesuit exegetist Juan Bautista Villalpanda in writing *Arca Noë* (Amsterdam, 1675) and *Turris Babel* (Amsterdam, 1679). The work on Noah's
Ark was a typical rationalisation of the biblical account to which
religious controversialists of all kinds increasingly resorted at that time
(Allen 1963); on the basis of extensive calculation, Kircher was at pains
to reconstruct Noah's Ark with vivid illustrations (plate 1). Whilst this
reconstruction sought to defend traditional archetypes, his study of
Mesopotamia in *Turris Babel* (based on a wide familiarity with oriental

Ruins of 'Aiuan Kefra' or 'Arch of Soliman Pac', at Ctesiphon, based on a drawing and description
the traveller Petrus de Valla. This provides the only observed example of Mesopotamian (Sassanid)
hitecture in Kircher's otherwise invented imagery of Asian architecture. From Athanasius Kircher's
ris Babel (Amsterdam, 1679), p. 98. Cambridge University Library.

languages), provided in effect a new vision of an alternative and earlier
antiquity to the Classical as maintained by Vitruvius and his commentators (plate 2). Kircher's main activity, however, was the study of
ancient Egypt. This resulted in several works exploring the iconology
and meaning of this civilisation, which was taken to be the original
home of divine wisdom seen as the foundation of Mosaic teaching and
preparatio evangelica – 'preparation for the Gospel'. In these sumptous
works, Kircher provided all Europe with the richest library and most
extensive explanation of comparative iconology yet seen, thereby representing the first presentation of an exoticism which even embraced
contemporary China, and only omitted Islam.[3]

The fashion for Baroque compendia of the arts, typified by Kircher,
was upheld by the Savoyard Jesuit, Claude-François-Milliet de Challes

---

[3]   Kircher's co-operation with Bernini in the design of the Fountain of the Four Rivers
in the Piazza Navona, Rome, was codified in *Obeliscus Phamphilius* (Rome, 1650) (see
Rivosecchi 1982, 119–38).

(1621–78) (MacDonnell 1989). In his *Cursus, seu mundus mathematicus* (Lyons, 1674) he provided the greatest monument of mathematical learning to date, which encompassed all the subaltern arts such as pyrotechnics and of course architecture, military and civil. Although this work's impact was possibly lessened by its Latin text,[4] here we have a complete overview of architecture which was not just dependent on Vitruvian theory but on new considerations of materials and of structure. De Challes's treatment of carpentry, for example, bestowed unprecedented recognition on this branch of construction, usually ignored by treatise writers in favour of stereotomy or geometrical stone-cutting, and masonry. De Challes lived in France and, though not a Cartesian, was abreast with the latest physics, so his inclusiveness points the way to the subsequent French encyclopedic tradition. Above all, he applied to the Orders a mathematical system of definition on the Euclidean model, usually described as *more geometrico*, 'proceeding geometrically' in the style of Euclid. He defined the solid geometry of the column in a sequence moving from the base up to the shaft and then to the entablature, representing a significant step in the rationalisation of the Orders; however he then returned to the Vitruvian module based on the thirty divisions of the column's diameter, so ancient theory was maintained (De Challes 1674, I, 707–8).

The remainder of De Challes's treatise on architecture is dominated by the formal geometry of all types of vaulting, demonstrating the influence of geometry as the master-science of his time. The 'geometrisation' of the Orders is implicitly reductive, however, ignoring the mythological matrix with which Vitruvius had explained the origins of the Orders. The rationalisation of the column, reducing its 'elements' to specific mouldings, was repeated by Charles-Augustin Daviler whose popular treatise *Cours d'architecture* (Paris, 1691) was reprinted several times (the last one edited by Blondel the Younger). This mathematical rationalisation of the Orders prompted the view that architecture was an independent technical enterprise exclusively dominated by modern mathematical prodecures such as perspective, descriptive geometry and the new statics originating with Galileo.

The rise of Freemasonry as an institution in the eighteenth century, with its secret or quasi-secret appeal to the legend of architectural origins, represents perhaps the most intriguing application of building imagery which transcended Vitruvian limits, dependent as Freemasonry was on esoteric and scriptural authority at the expense of Vitruvian and strictly Classical sources. In 1717 the Grand Lodge of London was

---

[4]   This is in contrast to his *Elemens d'Euclide* (Lyons, 1672), which was demonstrated by a 'new and easy method'. This text was translated into Italian and English, editions of the latter being common until *c*.1750.

founded to bring order to the many constitutions of the various societies, a work entrusted to James Anderson who published his collation, *Constitutions*, in 1723. Here architectural theory was openly presented as an intellectual model of social development to those unfamiliar with the lore of craft-masonry (Vidler 1987, 85, 90). Hence, the rebuilding of Solomon's temple was to be seen as the first stage of the remaking of society itself. In this scenario, Anderson gave little importance to Adam, the first father. But in France, Couret de Villeneuve recognised Adam's primitive purity and noted that 'we work on Plans traced by Nature and compassed by Reason, to reconstruct a moral edifice, the model of which, executed in the first ages of the world, we have conserved by the universal idea of the [Masonic] order' (Vidler 1987, 91). In this fusion of the ethnological and the scriptural models of origins, the figure of Adam served to reinforce the identity of a natural primitive man, just as Jean-Jacques Rousseau was to describe him two years later. Masonic mythology had depended on this primitivism linked to architectural language and these notions of origin. The ground was prepared for the acceptance of the 'primitive hut' as an ulterior model for architecture as proposed by the Abbé Laugier in 1753, who if not a Freemason was considered to be a sympathiser (Vidler 1987, 92). Freemasonry thus exploited architectural imagery and language far beyond the antique proprieties of the Vitruvian treatise, and indeed would eventually contribute to a critique of the social fabric of the *ancien régime*.

The most forceful re-examination of art and its technical basis was launched by the emerging volumes of the *Encyclopédie* published by Diderot and d'Alembert, beginning in 1751. Many regard this event as the publishing milestone of the century, one of the reasons being the honour and attention given to the mechanical arts and trades as equivalent to the established sciences and the liberal arts. Architecture was now of course well to the fore, with Blondel the Younger serving as correspondent for architecture from the start. If some doubt remained as to architecture's exact place in the great scheme of knowledge proposed by these most modern encyclopedists, what was now certain was that architecture was to be no longer solely dependent on Vitruvius and his commentators.

In fact not just architecture, but the whole modern notion of art as a field of intellectual investigation was now incorporated into the new form of literature represented by the *Encyclopédie*, something no earlier book on art or architecture had achieved (Simowitz 1983, xi). The most striking aspect of this enterprise was to attach the new grouping of the fine arts, which radically departed from the scope of the Vitruvian treatise, to the general 'system' of human knowledge and reason (Simowitz 1983). This attachment was clearly proposed by

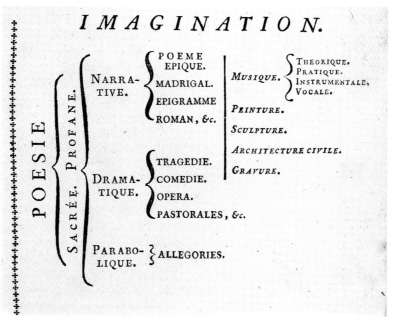

3   Detail of the 'Système figuré' from the *Encyclopédie* of 1751, vol. 1. Architecture
is now a fine art, but is related to mathematical arts in the tree of knowledge.
Cambridge University Library.

Diderot in his *Prospectus* of 1750 (reappearing a year later in the
Encyclopédie itself). Here he utilised Francis Bacon's tree of knowledge
in the now famous *Système figuré*, but revised Bacon's order of the
constituent faculties of understanding under the titles 'memory',
'reason' and 'imagination' (plate 3). Under imagination was to be
found its arts of music, painting, sculpture, civil architecture and
engraving. *Poésie* or poetry, the original fine art, embraced all the other
arts vertically on the left-hand side of the list. D'Alembert, in the
Discours préliminaire of volume 1 of the *Encyclopédie*, noted that architecture 'is confined to imitating the symmetrical arrangement that nature
observes more or less obviously in each individual thing, and that
contrasts so well with the beautiful variety of all taken together'
(Harrington 1985, 22). This meant that architecture was now to be
based on 'symmetry' understood as a visual arrangement (bilateral
symmetry), and not as in the Vitruvian concept of proportional agreement related to the human body as a microcosm.

   At the end of his article entitled 'architecture' in the *Encyclopédie*, the
younger Blondel stated that architects were now on the point of
surpassing the ancients (Harrington 1985, 32). While he emphasised a
number of common architectural qualities, those outlined by Vitruvius

– namely commodity, firmness and delight – were now omitted in Blondel's paraphrase: proportion, fitness, correctness, simplicity and beauty (Harrington 1985, 33). Most telling of all, the articles on antiquity were not written by Blondel or indeed by an architect, so that ancient monuments became in effect an autonomous feature of European history. If architecture had finally been received into the fine arts, it had lost its traditional anchor in the authority of antiquity. This loss was a fundamental blow for the validity of the Vitruvian treatise and to the continuity of architecture attached to traditional Vitruvian concerns.

After the appearance of volume VIII, the censor revoked the licence to print the *Encyclopédie* in March 1759 (Harrington 1985, 73), and so Blondel's intended article on proportion came to be written by a non-architect, the Chevalier Louis de Jaucourt.[5] Blondel's withdrawal from the *Encyclopédie* and his election to the Academy forced the editors to depend on themselves and some non-architects to supply the articles on architecture and related issues. D'Alembert wrote one on proportion and mathematics, at the end of which he reflected on the stance of Charles-Etienne Briseux that proportion in music and architecture are identical (Harrington 1985, 95); Briseux's importance lies in the fact that he was the last architectural writer to criticise the proportional system of Perrault in defence of harmonic proportion in its traditional understanding. While on the one hand d'Alembert accepted the relationship of architecture to mathematical reason, he felt that if the proportions in architecture were as simple as those in music, the observer would become very bored, and therefore architectural proportions should be more complex and difficult (Harrington 1985, 95–6). The entry on proportion by de Jaucourt aligned the subject to the laws of optics and perspective 'according to the point of view of the observer', and feigned astonishment at the division among architects on the validity of adjustments in counter-perspective (Harrington 1985, 103). Neither d'Alembert nor de Jaucourt ever sought to equate the mathematical basis of proportion with a wider view of the order of the cosmos (Harrington 1985, 104).

Jean-François Marmontel (1723–99) in the *Encyclopédie* was the first to apply the new theory of aesthetics to architecture, a theory in which art is considered as sentiment based exclusively on sensual perception. Thus he stated, 'the sense of physical beauty, whether in architecture or music, is essentially based on the relationship between these arts and our senses, and so the essential point of the critic is to determine precisely the testimony of the senses' (Harrington 1985, 106). With

---

[5]   This formed a brief note which refers to the following sources: Blondel the Elder's *Cours*, Part V, Perrault's *Vitruvius* and Daviler's *Cours*.

regard to aesthetic theory, however, Johann Georg Sulzer (1720–79) was the most important critic to contribute to the *Encyclopédie*, albeit only to the *Supplément* at first. A German and a member of the Berlin Royal Academy of Sciences, Sulzer had published his *Allgemeine Theorie der schönen Künste* (Berlin, 1771–4)[6] from which were made accurate translations for the *Supplément*. In later editions of the *Encyclopédie* such articles were combined with the original entries, such that Blondel's entry on *architecte* had Sulzer's contribution added to it (Harrington 1985, 111). Sulzer provided articles on *beaux-arts* and *architecture*, with *esthétique* as the innovatory theory of art following Alexander Gottlieb Baumgarten's establishment of modern aesthetics in his *Aesthetica* published from 1750 onwards.[7] The fundamental motive for Sulzer's position was that man may be improved through the instrumentality of the state and an enlightened ruler. This could be achieved throught the beneficial affects of the modern arts and especially mass spectacles, above all through opera as the unifier of all the arts (Harrington 1985, 122). Such attitudes were encompassed in Sulzer's question, 'since man has a natural taste for the ideas that come from the senses, how can this inclination be used to raise these feelings, and in some cases make them a means to make clear his duty?' The answer lay in the many formulations of modernity in art, with the accent on social and political reform. Such an emphasis replaced the transcendental reference of traditional art as a source of contemplation analogous to religious and philosophical reflection and dialectic; in other words the symbolic role of art was to be increasingly challenged by the instrumental in a changed cosmic order. This new order was quite foreign to the cosmology of the Vitruvian architectural treatise, and thus seriously undermined the relevance of these works.

THE RISE OF HISTORICISM AND 'MEDIEVALISM'

The triumph of humanism and the Renaissance reform of letters led to greater consideration of historical evidence and new concepts of history, beyond the apparent certainties of ancient and sacred history. However the history of art and architecture for the most part remained confined to the much-repeated recital of Renaissance glories, paraphrasing Vasari in the main, and the history of Roman magnifi-

---

[6] That is, the 'General Theory of the Fine Arts'. In 1741 Sulzer published *Moral Contemplation on the Beauties of Nature*. In 1747 he became professor of mathematics at the Berlin Royal Academy, and three years later was elected as a member; d'Alembert was also a member.

[7] Published in 2 vols. in Frankfurt-an-der-Oder, (1750–58).

cence recorded in the Vitruvian treatise tradition. The advent of exoticism and 'medievalism' in the eighteenth century saw the cultivation of new forms of architectural history and orthodoxy referred to as 'historicism', which again served to undermine this tradition (Vesely 1985, 28, 30).

Johann Bernard Fischer von Erlach, so-called father of the Austrian Baroque, is credited with the writing of the first history of world architecture, in 1721. This was facilitated by his apprenticeship in Rome, where he became familiar at first hand with Kircher and the archaeologist Jacob Spon. It is alleged that during a visit to England by Fischer, it was Sir Christopher Wren who suggested to the Austrian that he write the *Entwurff einer historischen Architectur* (Vienna, 1721) (Aurenhammer 1973, 153).[8] Fischer developed an overall account of architecture embracing the main civilisations which included the 'Arabs and the Turks', and he illustrated 'Sainte Sophia' (Hagia Sophia) whilst discussing Ottoman building. He capitalised on the latest scholarship of Alfonso Ciacconi and Raffaele Fabretti in reconstructing Roman buildings from the evidence of coins (Aurenhammer 1973, 157–8), but felt free to expand on Imperial themes, much as he was to do in his designs for his employer, the house of Habsburg, then at the height of its power in central Europe. His independence of Vitruvius in favour of rival authorities, and his debt to Kircher and to the Chinese travels of Jean Nieuhoff, presage the historicism and exoticism that would become so important by the end of the century and which thereby further aided the demise of the Vitruvian treatise. In one sentence Fischer traced the Corinthian Order back to the Solomonic temple and, apart from a brief reference to Palladio and Serlio together with the ordonnance that Fischer demonstrated in his own work in Book IV, there is no deliberate exposition of the Orders or indeed of proportion. Thus it is obvious that the novel cultural overview in the *Entwurff* has forced the usual references to the norms of the architectural treatise to almost disappear.

In the seventeenth century any recognition of the validity of the hated 'Gothick' meant a consequent loss of authority for the Classical and Vitruvian doctrine. The first significant nod to medieval architectural history was rendered by Jean-François Félibien (1658–1733), whose *Recueil historique de la vie et des ouvrages des plus célèbres architectes* (Paris, 1687) depended on his father's work on inscriptions undertaken in one of Colbert's academies. Commencing with Cain as city-builder, the *Recueil* concludes with Giotto and his contemporaries, listing many of the French Gothic masters. This historicist interest was better served

[8]   Translated into English by Thomas Lediard and entitled *A Plan of Civil and Historical Architecture* (s.n., 1730), followed by a second impression in 1737.

in Félibien's translation of Pliny's descriptions of villas, entitled *Les plans et les descriptions de deux plus belles maisons de campagne de Pline le Consul* (Paris, 1699), which was well illustrated by reconstructions in the grand manner. In the appendix to this work entitled *Une dissertation touchant l'architecture antique & l'architecture gothique*, Félibien compared Gothic and Classical architecture. He referred first to the fall of Constantinople in 1453 and to Cardinal Bessarion as the 'illustrious refugee' whose Venetian palace became a centre for all kinds of disciplines. Architecture profited in that the reading of Vitruvius became 'more familiar', leading to the revival of the architectual rules of the Roman Empire after its fall. Many experts arose to advise the better architects, to the extent that their art became 'superior to so many other arts' (Félibien 1699, 171). In the meantime, the people had become 'accustomed for many centuries' to Gothic, another way of building which was 'light, delicate, & daring work capable of giving astonishment', and still admired by the 'best architects' for good construction and 'some general proportions' (Félibien 1699, 171). Even these Gothic buildings drew qualities of 'massiveness' and 'grossness', as opposed to 'lightness', from the origin of building in nature. Félibien underlined his understanding of Gothic by describing the use of bunched shafts to support vaulting 'in the better manner of taste' (Félibien 1699, 173, 174).

Félibien's scarcely concealed admiration for Gothic prompts him to consider the 'progress of a new theory among the learned', the new 'dream of Poliphilo', which should 'open the eyes . . . of all the sensitive men of reason' (Félibien 1699, 178–84). It was not enough that 'a building should be ornamented by very exquisite works, it is necessary that ornaments be used as by necessity, & such as the character, the use and the dignity of the building seem to require' (Félibien 1699, 185). This remedy of contemporary theory was to serve as an augmentation of the 'unique' Vitruvius, and stood for the new emphasis on the related notions of *bienséance, convenance* and 'character' that had begun to animate French architectural thinking. The possibility of an alternate set of principles to the Vitruvian was underlined by Félibien when he compared the imitation of tree-trunks by Classical columns as equal to the 'flexible branches of Gothic works' (Félibien 1699, 185), suitable for garden bowers and tents, although not all that out of place in a book on the gardens of Pliny.

In Rome the antiquarian search for historical continuity between ancient and modern through the excavation of antiquity was given a major impetus by the efforts of Giovanni Ciampini, a prominent figure in the Vatican and in the intellectual circle of the exiled Queen Christina of Sweden (Middleton 1975, 141–3). His attention focused first on the ecclesiastical buildings of Constantine the Great and these comprised his *Vetera Monumenta . . . Pars Prima* (Rome, 1690), which included the Basilica of the Nativity, Bethlehem, and a plan of Hagia Sophia. A second volume dealt with early Christian architecture generally, especially Ravenna and its mosaics, and these writings and illustrations were finally brought together in his *Opera* (Rome, 1747). In a period of reassessment of medieval architecture, Ciampini's publications filled in the gap from the fall of Rome to the beginnings of northern architecture, and have been undeservedly overlooked in accounting for the rise of historicist awareness of early Christian and Byzantine architecture and iconology in the early eighteenth century. The authority of the Classical models dear to Vitruvius and his commentators (Serlio in particular) could now be compared with a diversity of architectural exemplars of unimpeachable Christian authorship, a comparison that favoured the latter in the eyes of the devout.

Guarino Guarini (1624–83), the Theatine scholar-architect of the High Baroque, demonstrated in his posthumous treatise *Architettura civile* (Turin, 1737) an appreciation of the achievement of the Gothic cathedral, noting especially the cathedral's structural daring. Having lived in Paris, Guarini's sentiment is analogous to that of the younger Félibien. An amateur commentator, Michel de Frémin took this stance further in his *Mémoires critiques d'architecture* (Paris, 1702), where for the first time the importance of the Orders was slighted in favour of Gothic architecture. For him the five Orders were the 'least part' of architecture, and he held up as premier examples two medieval Parisian buildings, Notre-Dame and the Sainte-Chapelle, because of their 'taste of simplicity' instead of the 'taste of false beauty' (Frémin 1702, 39–40).

The Abbé Jean-Louis de Cordemoy, canon of Soissons (1631–1713), confirmed this rational approach to design through emphasing the importance of site restrictions, the nature and qualities of materials, cost and the patron's needs. In comparison, the Orders and their proportions were of no importance to architecture, and Gothic buildings were preferable because of their 'lightness'. In the first edition of his *Nouveau traité de toute l'architecture* (Paris, 1706) there was no mention of proportion and Cordemoy described other treatises as 'so dubious, & in such confusion, that it is impossible for them to be able to teach anything' (Cordemoy 1706, 2). He praised Perrault's *Ordonnances* as the only treatise from which the craftsman could benefit, despite its being 'a little obscure', and he reproduced Perrault's modular system of proportion (Pérez-Gómez 1983, 51). Hence Perrault's influence was linked to 'distribution' or *bienséance* as a new articulation of architectural theory, now free of the traditional reference to proportion and its mimetic meaning, and thus setting the pattern for so many later writers. In churches Cordemoy desired a common constructional principle derived from Greek and Gothic precedent, that of an inserted gallery and a double superimposed system of Orders as used in

Boffrand's chapel for the château of Lunéville (Kalnein and Levey 1972, 208–11). Cordemoy's thinking was to be echoed by the influential functionalist theories of the Venetian friar, Carlo Lodoli (1690–1751), which were brought to public attention with the publication of Andrea Memmo's *Elementi dell'architettura Lodoliana* (Rome, 1786) (Salerno 1967, 300).

Animated by their claim to have invented stereotomy, the French considered the geometrical setting-out of stones in masonry to be a national art and a special technique and legacy from the late medieval period. Following Philibert De l'Orme, French architects had developed this procedure to include Gothic vaulting, so that it is no surprise that Blondel the Younger gave a thorough account of medieval vaulting in his *Cours d'Architecture* (Paris, 1771–7) (plate 4). Intellectual forces such as the picturesque and the cult of ruins became aspects of this general eighteenth-century French interest in medieval culture, culminating in Voltaire's recognition of this culture's importance by 1746 (Collins 1965, 36). The most serious consideration of medieval history was that by the Benedictines, whose studies included their own architectural heritage. Although not published until the following century, Dom Michel Germain (1645–94) prepared his *Le Monasticon Gallicanum* (Paris, 1870),[9] which gave aerial views of the Benedictine monasteries of France and even illustrated the sculptured portal of the great Abbey of Dijon. This represented a decisive acceptance of Gothic taste and artistic practice over that of the Vitruvian.

THE DECLINE OF VITRUVIAN MIMESIS

The reductive 'geometrisation' of architecture and the increasing understanding of statics and the strength of materials were two processes that developed from the late seventeenth century with a significant negative impact on the Vitruvian canon (Pérez-Gómez 1983). Blondel the Elder and his gifted contemporary Germain Boffrand had been perfectly capable of designing and building bridges, but the changing needs of the French state required a cadre of engineers and this resulted in the establishment of the École des Ponts et Chaussées in 1747, and with it the specialist profession of civil engineering as we now know it (Middleton and Watkin 1987, 22). Even architects became involved in these developments, as testified by Jacques-

---

[9] This followed the model of Sir William Dugdale's *Monasticon Anglicanum* (3 vols., London, 1655–73) (Watkin 1980, 22). Neither Dugdale nor Mervyn Archdall's *Monasticon Hibernicum* (Dublin and London, 1786) addressed monastic building beyond foundation dating.

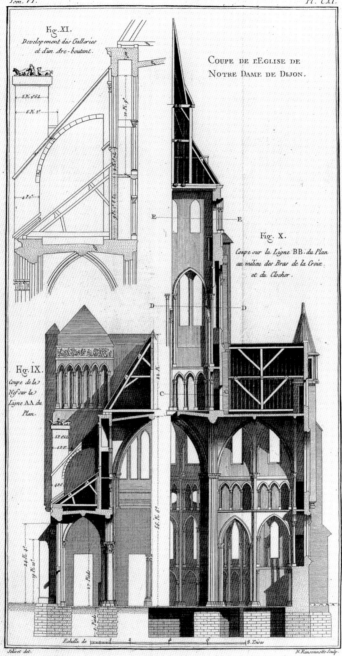

Fig. XI.
Developement des Galleries
et d'un Arc-boutant.

COUPE DE L'EGLISE DE
NOTRE DAME DE DIJON.

Fig. X.
Coupe sur la Ligne BB. du Plan
au milieu des Bras de la Croix
et du Clocher.

Fig. IX.
Coupe de la
Nef sur la
Ligne AA du
Plan.

Echelle de

Solvet del.

N. Ransonnette Sculp.

4   An accurate realisation by Blondel's assistant, Pierre Patte, of the
Gothic form of Dijon cathedral makes clear the structural implications for
vaulting and support (other plates give plans). From Jacques-François
Blondel's *Cours d'Architecture* (Paris, 1777), vol. VI of plates, Pl. CXI.
Cambridge University Library.

Germain Soufflot's setting-up of machinery for testing the strength of materials during the design of the church of Sainte-Geneviève in Paris (Middleton and Watkin 1987, 22). For these new disciplines, the Vitruvian treatise had little importance.

The general requirement for a registered architectural profession with a recognised level of competence was established in 1729 by Victor Amedeus II, the ruler of Savoy and Piedmont, when architects, surveyors and engineers could enjoy state registration only after a university examination. In contrast, the French Academy educated architects exclusively for royal employ, and Blondel the Younger's private school was designed to widen the scope of the profession, even attracting foreign students such as William Chambers. The demand for such professional institutionalised education was in itself a challenge to the exclusive reign of the Vitruvian treatise and its doctrines as the traditional source for an architect's education.

The reductive rationalism that drove these tendencies was expressed in the work of the most controversial architectural theorist of the eighteenth century, the Abbé Laugier, whose work spelled the end of the traditional architectural treatise. Marc-Antoine Laugier (1714–69) was an historian, a royal preacher and an erstwhile Jesuit who, a half-century after Cordemoy and the other early rationalists, applied his theoretical attention to the primitive hut in his famous *Essai sur l'architecture* (Paris, 1753). This return to the essentials of architecture was animated by frustration at the riot of conflicting contemporary opinion as to proportion and ornament in architecture. Blondel the Elder's description of four posts on a square plan was, in the second edition of 1755, now illustrated by Laugier as trees rooted in the ground (plate 5). The structural explicitness of the trunks and branches were understood to be the origin of the Orders or, as had been vaguely suggested by Félibien the Younger, the origin of Gothic architecture whose structural daring and 'truth' had long been vaunted. By taking the hut as a formal norm, Laugier had a model of a purified style of architecture. On this basis he argued for the primacy of the column in comparison to the wall, an argument which may be seen as a response to the glazed clerestories of the Gothic, and which he applied in turn to his own vision of a church. Such a vision was soon at hand in Soufflot's Sainte-Geneviève, whose design was begun in 1755. Laugier's *Essai* made a great impact, welcomed by the young but bitterly rejected by the older architects (Kalnein and Levey 1972, 301). Blondel the Younger recommended the book to his students and reflected its teaching in his own designs.

No longer a contributor to Diderot's *Encyclopédie*, Blondel the Younger had been giving public lectures since 1746, and had become recognised as a pre-eminent educator having taught many architects

5 The genius of Architecture points to the primitive hut as the exemplar of a rational architecture. The four-square plan of the trunks had already been prescribed by Blondel the Elder. Frontispiece from Marc-Antoine Laugier's *Essai sur l'architecture* (Paris, 1755 ed.). Department of Architecture Library, Cambridge University.

including Ledoux and Chambers. As a means of avoiding the Academy's approval, though he was by now a member, his *Cours* was described as 'notes' taken by a student (Gallet 1985, 737a). Under the aegis of 'universal utility', the work began with a sketch of architectural history, an awkward account which ignored the Italian Renaissance completely – Blondel had never crossed the Alps. The foremost token of his modernity was the choice of 'sublimity' as the first intellectual aspect of architecture, thus outbidding Boffrand with his earlier promotion of 'taste' (Boffrand 1745, 3–15).[10] Although sublimity may have had a long antecedence, it was not seen as an attribute of a work of art until Edmund Burke described it as such.[11] Blondel rendered the sublime as *terrible* and as a particular attribute of prisons, just as other buildings should have identifiable characters – the building for a tax-collector should be *aimable*, that of a country noble, *champêtre* (Gallet 1985, 737a). Unlike his elder namesake, he did not give any value to harmonic proportion, thereby endorsing Perrault's reformalisation of the Orders and his implicit status as the 'first modern'.

The demise of the Vitruvian treatise from 'Blondel to Blondel' can be further dramatised by comparing two Italian theorists who personify the past and the emerging sensibility of the nineteenth century. Bernardo Vittone (1702–70) was the last great architect of the Baroque, both in his extensive oeuvre in Piedmont and in his *Istruzioni* of civil architecture published in 1760 and 1766. His attachment to harmonics and number speculation was sustained by a full theological explanation in terms of the Church Militant.[12] In contrast, the Rome-based historian and critic Francesco Milizia (1725–98) became one of the first exponents of Neoclassicism, a movement that established its rationale by a negative assessment of the Baroque. This desk-bound historian and theorist never visited Turin yet mercilessly condemned Guarini, even for what was unexecuted,[13] as the worst exponent of the Borromini school.

Describing himself as a 'mosaicist', Milizia espoused the aesthetics of Sulzer yet insisted that architecture was still subordinate to geometry: in his *Elementi di Matematiche Pure* (Venice, 1771), Milizia described geometry as 'a science which is absolutely necessary for proceeding

---

[10] Boffrand also implied the concept of *architecture parlante*, whereby buildings should signify their purpose to the onlooker, thus anticipating modern notions on expressive function.

[11] Published in *A Philosophical Enquiry into the Origin of our Ideas of the Sublime and the Beautiful* (London, 1757).

[12] Published in *Istruzioni diverse* (Lugano, 1766), 320–24.

[13] For example, the Church of San Filippo Neri, Turin, for which Guarini prepared designs, but which was completed by others.

from theory to practice' (Milizia 1771, 248).[14] His mathematics was dominated by calculus, now deemed necessary for architectural education but divorced from the cosmological context of traditional mathematics. Milizia defined architecture as the 'bond of civilised society', and expanded Vitruvian 'distributio' within his *Principj di Architettura Civile* (Finale, 1781) to consider human progress and its critical expression in functional building types, thereby producing a model series of classifications which would become largely binding in nineteenth-century Europe (Oechslin 1982, 198a).

After nearly two millennia, the traditional European architectural treatise and its intrinsic connection to the concept of mimesis came to an end. The powerful meaning of mimesis had found its setting in a continuous cosmos, surviving until the rupture of such a world-view by the mid-eighteenth century. The last representative of the traditional Latin treatise, published as *Universae architecturae civilis elementa* (Vienna, 1756) by the Jesuit, Christian Rieger (1714–80),[15] upheld Vitruvius but also ironically approved of Perrault and Laugier as well as a small number of French Enlightenment *trattatisti* of little import. As with the decline of the importance of Euclid in mathematics, a glorious heritage of doctrine and philosophical reference collapsed from within as their respective central principles became distorted and then ignored. For Euclid, this collapse is demonstrable with respect to the ineffable point, which disappeared in mercantile mathematical treatises in the mid-seventeenth century, and eventually from many serious treatments in the eighteenth. Even the Book of Books, the Bible itself, became the territory of reductive interpretation, threatening the very integrity of the Judaeo-Christian tradition.

As to the other two books which completed the Western experience, that of nature was already subject to radical revision and subjection as we have seen, leaving the Book of the Soul as the final territory for the attention of reductive modernity in the nineteenth century. And in architecture, the authority of its textual tradition dissolved into the confusing mosaic of Milizia, while the irrelevant Latin of Rieger lay untranslated and unread.

---

[14] Milizia was citing the spherical trigonometry of Roger J. Boscovich, which was 'una scienza assolutamente necessaria per passare dalla Teoria alla Pratica'.

[15] Translated into Spanish by Michel Benavente, SJ. Rieger was a mathematician, cosmographer and teacher of architecture in Vienna, called to Madrid in 1760 as Royal Cosmographer (Sommervogel 1890–1900, vol. 6, 1841a).

Appendix I

THE DATING OF THE CODICES OF
DI GIORGIO'S *TRATTATI*

In the absence of firm evidence as to the dating of any of the codices, many differences of critical opinion have arisen. None of the main codices contains a dedication, even though it appears clear that all of them, apart from S (a codex left without illustrations, since it was a study copy), were meant to contain one. In addition, in L and M (unlike in T) blank spaces were left at the start of each chapter for the initial capitals. None of the codices is an autograph; as was customary, reproduction was entrusted to a copyist who transcribed a text prepared separately. The codex T, however, contains di Giorgio's autograph corrections, and the composite *Traduzione Vitruviana* (Translation of Vitruvius) (Fiore 1985; Scaglia 1985), bound with the codex M, was also copied in his own hand.

Furthermore, many scholars are uncertain as to whether the marginal illustrations are the work of di Giorgio himself. However, even if these illustrations were by di Giorgio they would nevertheless be copies made by the author of his own originals, and so they would not have the characteristics of original autograph designs, characteristics which appear particularly clearly elsewhere, as has been correctly noted by Maltese. Nor would it be surprising if di Giorgio had taken advantage of the help of his *bottega*, as was the custom amongst painters (Bellosi 1993). As to the quality and clarity of the illustrations, the codices L, T and M are however so much superior in these respects both to those copied by di Giorgio's *bottega* and those representing halfway stages in the development of the propositions, that these factors alone argue in favour of di Giorgio's authorship for a majority of their content. The difference between his rapid autograph sketches and his fair-copy designs can be clearly demonstrated by comparing his survey sketches of antique buildings now in the Uffizi, Florence[1] (Ericsson 1980; Burns 1993) and the designs of the antiquarian additions in codex T.

Further issues and questions have arisen with the discovery of, and work on, the codices which relate to the long preparatory work for the *Trattati*, notably the primitive version of the *Trattati* preserved in the Zichy codex (Kolb 1988); the

---

[1] Uffizi, fols. 318–37 A.

Opera di Architettura (Scaglia 1976; Betts 1977) dedicated to Alfonso di Calabria and dealing exclusively with civil architecture; the *Fogli Reggiani* (Mussini 1991), the lost folios originally part of L; the *Raccolta* (the 'collection') (Fiore 1978) bound with the codex M and exclusively containing designs for machines and fortifications; the *Fogli Chigi-Saracini* (Salmi 1947) dedicated in the same way to the illustration of war-machines; and the Accademia codex (Parronchi 1982), a sixteenth-century transcription of a preparatory copy of the *Trattati*.

It is clear that the first imperative is to establish a sequence for the different phases of work as represented by these codices and folios, and scholars (with some reservations) have produced the following reconstruction. What follows attempts to avoid the philological debate which it would be unsuitable to develop in this chapter, whilst at the same time indicating the results held to be most probable, starting from the principal elements established here. The most decisive of these elements is the level of di Giorgio's comprehension of the text of Vitruvius which he brings to the *Trattati*. From this point of view, the oldest (that is, first) version of the *Trattati* is still the Zichy codex. This is followed by codices L and T. Next come the *Traduzione Vitruviana* and the *Opera di Architectura* (dedicated to Alfonso di Calabria). Only after this intermediary phase of reworking do we come to the *Trattati* codices S and M, where the comprehension of Vitruvius is much better and where almost all the passages of direct Vitruvian translation have been removed. As for the internal chronological order within these two groups of codices, L and T together with S and M, the recent discovery of the *Fogli Reggiani* has confirmed that L preceded T; and the precedence of S with respect to M is commonly accepted. If we then consider the problem from the point of view of di Giorgio's research in the field of *machinatio*, it can be added that M predates the *Fogli Chigi-Saracini* and the *Raccolta*, both of which have a representation of a rhombic fortress with acute-angled bastions, with rectilinear flanks and with ravelins, advanced features which form a prelude to Michelangelo's fortifications for Florence.

Finally there are a few external facts: none of the different versions of the *Trattati* was present in the library in Urbino, only the *Opusculum* (Mussini 1991; Scaglia 1992) (it is probable that di Giorgio, after having written the *Codicetto* and the *Opusculum*, did not create a complete and satisfactory version of the *Trattati* in Urbino, given that if he had it would certainly have found a place in either Federico's or his son Guidubaldo's library); there is a note on the plan of the Basilica of Maxentius in T (fol. 76r) which reads 'In this place there used to be a gigantic marble statue, because its head measures six and a half feet',[2] dating the note to post-1486 when the statue was discovered and brought to the Campidoglio (Buddensieg 1962); in 1492, a copy (now lost) was made in Naples of two books by di Giorgio, described as 'both written by hand on paper, one on architecture and the other on artillery and matters concerning war',[3] neither matching M even though there is the same number of illustrations; only after Federico da Montfeltro's death in 1482 did a copy of Leon Battista Alberti's *De re aedificatoria* reach Urbino, a work which influenced di Giorgio's *Trattati* in several respects; around 1504 Leonardo copied (with certain clear errors) parts of the text of M into the Codex Madrid II (Heydenreich 1974; Reti 1974). This last fact establishes for

---

[2] 'In questo luogho sedeva hun gigante di marmo che la sua testa è piei sei et mezzo.'
[3] 'In carta di papiro scripti ado mano, uno de architectura e l'altro de artigliaria et cose appartenenti a guerre.'

certain that S and M cannot be sixteenth-century copies of the *Trattati*, or even copies of the Accademia codex as claimed by Parronchi (1982). Finally, let us consider all di Giorgio's activities after his return to Siena from Urbino in the middle of 1489, and particularly his journeys in 1490 (to Lucignano, Milan and Pavia, Bracciano and perhaps Venice, Bologna and Florence), 1491 (to Naples and Lucca), 1492, 1494 and 1495 (to Naples), 1499 (to Urbino) and 1500 (to Loreto). If a first version thus seems possible around 1490, only after 1496 would di Giorgio have had the tranquillity and time to dedicate himself to a revised, second version of the *Trattati*.

Appendix 2

PREFACE TO VIGNOLA'S *REGOLA*

Vignola's relatively short but linguistically tortuous introduction to the *Regola* was often omitted from later editions and in any case is unavailable in English. This translation was based on the transcription of the *editio princeps* edited by Walcher Casotti (Vignola 1985, 515–17) and for the 'Addition', the facsimile of the later edition published in Modena (Vignola 1974).

To the Readers

The reason why I was moved to make this little work, good readers, and then to dedicate it (such as it is) to the general service of he who delights in it, I shall briefly explain for clearer understanding.

Having practised the art of architecture for many years in different countries, it has always been a pleasure for me to look at the opinion of as many writers as I could about the practice of ornament, and comparing them with each other and with ancient works still in existence, to try to extract a rule with which I could be content, and which I could be sure would completely satisfy, or at least nearly so, every scholar of this art. And this was solely to serve my own requirements, nor was there any other aim. To do this, leaving aside many things of the writers, where differences of no little consequence are born, and to achieve greater certainty, I decided first to study those ancient ornaments of the five Orders which appear in the antiquities of Rome. And considering all of them carefully and examining their measurements accurately, I found that those which in the general opinion are the most beautiful and appear the most graceful to our eyes also have a certain numerical agreement and proportion which is the least complex; indeed you can measure precisely the large members in all their parts with each minute member. Hence, considering further how much our senses take pleasure in this proportion, and how much the things outside it are unpleasant, as the musicians prove in their science through sensation, I undertook this task many years ago, namely to reduce the said five Orders of architecture to a concise and quick rule which was easy to use, and the method I kept to was as follows. Wishing to put in this rule (by way of example) the Doric Order, I considered that of all the examples of Doric, the one in the Theatre of Marcellus was the most highly praised by everyone. This, then, I took as the basis of the rule for the said Order, that is, determining its principal parts. If some minor member did not entirely obey the numerical proportions (which often happens owing to the work of the stonecutters or other accidents that frequently occur with such details) I accommodated it to my rule not by altering anything of importance but by harmonising this slight licence on the authority of other examples of Doric which are also considered beautiful. From these examples I took other small parts whenever I needed to supplement the one from the Theatre of Marcellus, not as Zeuxis did with the maidens among the Crotons, but rather as my judgment directed. I made this choice for all the Orders, extracting only from ancient works and adding nothing of my own save the distribution of their proportions which were based on simple numbers, using not the *braccia*, or feet, or palms of whatever locality, but an arbitrary measurement called the module, divided into those parts which will be seen from Order to Order in the appropriate place. And I have made an otherwise difficult part of architecture so easy that every ordinary talent, provided he has some enthusiasm for this art, can at a glance and without much bothersome reading, understand the whole and make use of it at opportune moments. And although I was far from interested in publishing this, nevertheless it has been made possible by the entreaties of many friends desiring it, and even more by the generosity of my perpetual lord, the illustrious and most reverend Cardinal Farnese. From him not only have I received the courtesies of his honorable house which have allowed me to work diligently, but he has also given me the means to satisfy my friends and in addition to present to you shortly other, greater things on this subject, if you accept this part in the spirit in which I believe you will. And as it is neither my wish nor my intent to respond here to those objections that I know will be made by some, I leave this task to the work itself which by pleasing the more judicious will lead them to take up my defence. I would only add that should someone judge this a vain effort by saying that one cannot lay down a fixed rule, since, according to the opinion of all and especially of Vitruvius, it is often necessary to enlarge or to diminish the proportions of ornamental members in order to remedy with art where our vision has been deceived by some occurrence, to him I reply that concerning this matter it is necessary to know how much should appear to the eye – this should always be the firm rule which others have proposed to observe – and then proceed in this by certain good rules of perspective, whose practice is fundamental both here and in painting, such that I am sure you will be pleased, [and] I also hope to present that to you soon.

ADDITION IN LATER EDITIONS

As has been said, my aim was to be understood only by those who may have had some introduction to art, and for this reason I did not write the names of any of the particular members of the five Orders, believing them to be known. But after seeing by experience how this work greatly pleases many lords moved by desire to attempt to grasp with little effort the whole of the art of these ornaments, and that the ornaments were lacking only in these particular terms, I wanted to add them here as they are commonly used in Rome and in the order that they appear. I point out only that the members which are common to several Orders, after being noted once on first appearance, will not be mentioned again in the subsequent examples.

Appendix 3

The academic and popular success of the *Regola* subjected Vignola's project to significant early, and subsequently drastic and occasionally misleading, alterations. For this reason it seems useful to list the contents of the original 1562 edition, followed by the plates which were apparently added to later editions by the author himself before his death in 1573. Early posthumous editions often included a synoptic plate of all five Orders on pedestals in place of the lapsed copyright. This appears contrary to the intentions and method of the author. The only known example of the *editio princeps*, preserved in the Biblioteca Nazionale in Florence, has been published by Walcher Casotti (Vignola 1985). Its thirty-two engraved plates are as follows:

Frontispiece with portrait of Vignola (unnumbered) (plate 1)
Copyright from Pope Pius IV, ii
Dedication and preface, iii
Tuscan colonnade, iv
Tuscan arcade, v
Tuscan arcade with pedestals, vi
Tuscan pedestal and base, vii
Tuscan capital and entablature, viii
Doric colonnade, ix
Doric arcade, x (plate 4)
Doric arcade with pedestals, xi
Doric pedestal, base and impost, xii (plate 5)
Doric capital and entablature (denticulate), xiii (plate 6)
Doric capital and entablature (mutulate), xiiii (plate 7)
Ionic colonnade, xv
Ionic arcade, xvi
Ionic arcade with pedestals, xvii
Ionic pedestal, base and impost, xviii
Ionic capital and entablature, xviiii
Ionic volute, xx

Corinthian colonnade, xxi
Corinthian arcade, xxii
Corinthian arcade with pedestals, xxiii
Corinthian pedestal, base and impost, xxiiii
Corinthian capital in plan and profile, xxv
Corinthian capital and entablature, xxvi
Composite pedestal and base, xxvii
Composite capital in plan and profile, xxviii
Composite capital and entablature, xxviiii
Composite figured capitals and Attic base, xxx
Entasis and Solomonic column, xxxi
Palace cornice, xxxii

VIGNOLA'S UNNUMBERED ADDITIONS
IN LATER EDITIONS

Main portal of Palazzo Farnese, Caprarola (plate 8)
Portal project for Palazzo della Cancelleria, Rome
Portal of church of San Lorenzo in Damaso, Rome
Lower portal of Palazzo Farnese, Caprarola
Mantelpiece from Palazzo Farnese, Rome

Appendix 4

DEDICATORY EPISTLE OF PERRAULT'S *ORDONNANCE*

To My Lord Colbert
Marquis of Seignelay, Baron of Sceaux, etc., Minister of State and of the King's
Commands, Executor and High Treasurer of His Majesty's Orders, Minister of
Finance, Superindentant and General Director of His Majesty's Buildings and
Gardens, and of the Arts and Factories of France.

My Lord,
It was at your orders that I completed the translation and annotation of Vitruvius
and it is chiefly to your judgement of it that I owe its success, which I would never
have dared hope for without the confidence inspired by the extraordinary skill that
invariably brings all the projects you direct to successful completion. The advantage of your having endorsed the rather bold and unusual aims of the book I take
the liberty of presenting to you today inspires me to give it to the public with the
same confidence.

Because this book is a kind of supplement to what Vitruvius has dealt with in
insufficient detail, those drawn to the art in which that learned author has schooled
us will probably view the new ideas in the book with pleasure. Those who follow
its rules will, in all likelihood, find considerable use in how easy these rules make
the matters which they formerly found difficult. Your goal is to provide lovers of
architecture with every possible means of improving their knowledge, so that they
can contribute to the glory of our invincible monarch in everlasting monuments.
To achieve this goal, it was not enough to recover from almost impenetrable
obscurity the many marvels contained in the admirable books of Vitruvius and to
have revealed with unprecedented clarity the principles and precepts of the art of
building and the features of the ancient wonders of the world he has described. It
was also necessary to unravel the difficulties and confusion to which modern
authors have consigned most of what pertains to the five kinds of columns for
which there are no certain rules, these authors being unable to agree on the
proportions of those elements on whose beauty the ornament and majesty of great
buildings entirely depend.

I am well aware that there may be difficulty in having my methods for establishing fixed rules for those proportions accepted, that those whose views oppose my own are held in high esteem, and that works which appear to contradict my own have gained general approval. Nevertheless, My Lord, I am convinced that once it is known that you have not disapproved of this undertaking it will not seem completely foolhardy. I stress these particulars, My Lord, because it is important to me that the public be aware of them, and because my book needs the support of your authority. I need hardly elaborate on what that authority is: if some are unaware that I am favoured by its support, none ignores the weight it carries. The great brilliance of the wide-ranging genius that makes you expert in so many areas has shone long enough to make all aware that the lofty matters which usually occupy your thoughts still leave room for things of lesser importance. It has also long been obvious that, among the arts for which you have the greatest attachment, architecture, queen of the fine arts, holds one of the first places: witness the great number of splendid works so speedily completed at your orders, to the admiration of experts and the utmost satisfaction of all who hold dear the glory of the great monarch who rules us and cherish the blessed century in which we have had the good fortune to be born.

It is not only the manifest utility of this work that obliges me to make known that it was written at your command. There is something of even greater importance, and that is my hope that the public which must benefit from it will help me to acknowledge my personal obligation to you for having thought fit to entrust me with a task of such importance, there being nothing on earth I desire more ardently than to present you with tokens of that profound respect with which I am,

My Lord,
Your very humble and very obediant servant,
Perrault

Bibliography

INTRODUCTION: FROM ALBERTI TO SCAMOZZI

Ackerman, J. S. 1991. '"Ars sine scientia nihil est": Gothic Theory of Architecture at the Cathedral of Milan'. In J. S. Ackerman, *Distance Points*, Cambridge, Mass.: MIT Press, 211–68 [Originally published in *Art Bulletin*, XXXI, 1949, 84–111].

Alberti, L. B. 1988. *On the Art of Building in Ten Books*. J. Rykwert, N. Leach and R. Tavernor (trans.). Cambridge, Mass.: MIT Press.

Borsi, F. 1986 trans. ed. *Leon Battista Alberti, The Complete Works*. New York: Electa/Rizzoli.

Bowie, T. 1959 ed. *The Sketchbook of Villard de Honnecourt*. Bloomington: Indiana University Press.

Bury, J. B. 1988. 'Renaissance Architectural Treatises and Architectural Books: A Bibliography'. In J. Guillaume (ed.), op. cit. 485–503.

Choay, F. 1980/97. *La règle et le modèle. Sur la théorie de l'architecture et de l'urbanisme*. Paris: Editions du Seuil [English trans. D. Bratton. Cambridge, Mass.: MIT Press, 1997].

Colonna, F. 1592 trans. 'R. D.' [? Roger Dallington]. *Hypnerotomachia. The Strife of Love in a Dreame*. London: Simon Waterson [Facsimile: New York and London: Garland, 1976].

Dee, J. 1570. *The elements of geometrie of the most aunceint philosopher Euclide of Megara . . . with a very fruitfull præface by M. I. Dee*. London: John Daye.

Eisenstein, E. 1983. *The Printing Revolution in Early Modern Europe*. Cambridge: Cambridge University Press.

Febvre, L., and H.-J. Martin. 1993 trans. ed. *The Coming of the Book: The Impact of Printing, 1450–1800*. London: Verso.

Filarete [Averlino]. 1972. *Antonio Averlino detto il Filarete, Trattato di architettura*. A. M. Finoli, L. Grassi (eds.). 2 vols. Milan: Il Polifilo [English trans. J. R. Spencer, London and New Haven: Yale University Press, 1965].

Grafton, A. 1992. *New Worlds, Ancient Texts: The Power of Tradition and the Shock of Discovery*. Cambridge Mass.: Harvard University Press.

Guillaume, J. (ed.). 1988. *Les traités d'architecture de la Renaissance*. Paris: Picard.

Hart, V. 1994. *Art and Magic in the Court of the Stuarts*. London: Routledge.

Hart, V., and N. Thwaite. 1997. *Paper Palaces: Architectural works from the collections of Cambridge University Library*, Catalogue of an Exhibition held at the Fitzwilliam Museum. Cambridge: Cambridge University Library Press.

Haydocke, R. 1598. *A tracte containing the Artes of Curious Paintinge Carvinge & Buildinge*. Oxford: Joseph Barnes [English trans. of G. P. Lomazzo, *Trattato*, 1584].

Hersey, G. L. 1976. *Pythagorean Palaces: Magic and Architecture in the Italian Renaissance*. Ithaca, NY: Cornell University Press.

Juřen, V. 1981. 'Un traité inédit sur les ordres d'architecture, et le problème des sources du Libro IV de Serlio'. *Monuments et Mémoires publiés par L'Académie des inscriptions et belles-lettres*, LXIV, 195–239.

Krinsky, C. H. 1967. 'Seventy-eight Vitruvian Manuscripts'. *Journal of the Warburg and Courtauld Institutes*, XXX, 36–70.

Kruft, H.-W. 1994 trans. ed. *A History of Architectural Theory from Vitruvius to the Present*. New York: Princeton Architectural Press/London: Zwemmer.

Onians, J. 1988. *Bearers of Meaning: The Classical Orders in Antiquity, the Middle Ages, and the Renaissance*. Cambridge: Cambridge University Press.

Palladio, A. 1997. *Andrea Palladio: The Four Books on Architecture*. R. Tavernor and R. Schofield (trans. and eds.). Cambridge, Mass. and London: MIT Press.

Panofsky, E. 1957. *Gothic Architecture and Scholasticism*. Cleveland: World Publishing Company.

Pérez-Gómez, A. 1988. *Architecture and the Crisis of Modern Science*. Cambridge, Mass.: MIT Press.

Perrault, C. 1993. *Ordonnance for the Five Kinds of Columns after the Method of the Ancients*. I. K. McEwen (trans.). Santa Monica, Ca.: The Getty Center.

Rykwert, J. 1988. 'On the Oral Transmission of Architectural Theory'. In J. Guillaume (ed.), op. cit. 31–48.

———. 1996a. *The Dancing Column: On Order in Architecture*. Cambridge, Mass.: MIT Press.

———. 1996b. 'The Roots of Architectural Bibliophilia'. *Scroope: Cambridge Architecture Journal*, VIII, 111–17.

Serlio, S. 1537. *Regole generali di architettura: Sopra le cinque maniere degli edifici*. Venice: Francesco Marcolini.

———. 1540. *Il terzo libro di Sebastiano Serlio bolognese*. Venice: Francesco Marcolini.

———. 1996. *Sebastiano Serlio on Architecture*. vol. 1 [Books I–V of *Tutte l'opere d'architettura et prospetiva*]. V. Hart and P. Hicks (trans.). New Haven and London: Yale University Press.

———. Forthcoming 1999. *Sebastiano Serlio on Architecture*. vol. 2 [Books VI– 'VIII' and the *Extraordinario Libro* of *Tutte l'opere d'architettura et prospetiva*]. V. Hart and P. Hicks (trans.). New Haven and London: Yale University Press.

Sgarbi, C. 1993. 'A newly discovered corpus of Vitruvian images'. *Res*, XXIII, 31–51.

Simson, O. von. 1988 ed. *The Gothic Cathedral: Origins of Gothic Architecture and the Medieval Concept of Order*. New York: Bollingen Foundation/ Princeton University Press.

Tolomei, C. 1547. *De le lettere di M. Claudio Tolomei libri sette*. Venice: Gabriel Giolito de Ferrari.

Ungers, O. M. 1994. '*Ordo, fondo et mensura*: The Criteria of Architecture'. In H. A. Millon and V. Magnago Lampugnani (eds.). *The Renaissance from Brunelleschi to Michelangelo: The Representation of Architecture*, London: Thames and Hudson. 306–47.

Vitruvius. 1931. *De Architectura*. Books i–x. F. Granger (trans.). London and Cambridge, Mass.: Loeb [I. D. Rowland (trans.), New York: Cambridge University Press, forthcoming 1998].

Wiebenson, D. (ed.). 1982. *Architectural Theory and Practice from Alberti to Ledoux*. Chicago: Chicago University Press.

Wittkower, R. 1974. *Gothic versus Classic: Architectural Projects in the Seventeenth Century*. London: Thames and Hudson.

———. 1988 ed. *Architectural Principles in the Age of Humanism*. London: Academy Editions.

Wotton, H. 1624. *The Elements of Architecture . . . collected from the Best Authors and Examples*. London: John Bill.

ONE: LEON BATTISTA ALBERTI

Alberti, L. B. 1486. *Leonis Baptistae Alberti de re aedificatoria*. Florence: Niccolo di Lorenzo Alamani.

———. 1957. *Alberti and the Temple Malatestiano: An Autograph letter from L. B. Alberti to Matteo de'Pasti, November 18, 1454*. C. Grayson (ed.). New York: Pierpont Morgan Library.

———. 1960–73. *Opere volgari*. C. Grayson (ed.). 3 vols. Bari: G. Laterza & Figli Editore.

———. 1966. *L'Architettura*. G. Orlandi and P. Portoghesi (eds. and trans.). 2 vols. Milan: Il Polifilo.

———. 1969. *The Family in Renaissance Florence* [trans. of *Della famiglia*]. R. N. Watkins (trans.). Columbia, SC: South Carolina University Press.

———. 1972. *On Painting and On Sculpture: The Latin Texts of 'De pictura' and 'De statua'*. C. Grayson (ed. and trans.). London: Phaidon Press.

———. 1984. *Apologhi ed Elogi*. L. Malerba (ed.). Genoa: Costa & Nolan.

———. 1986. *Momo o del Principe*. R. Consolo (Italian trans. and ed.). Genoa: Costa & Nolan.

———. 1988a. *On the Art of Building in Ten Books*. J. Rykwert, N. Leach and R. Tavernor (trans.). Cambridge, Mass.: MIT Press.

———. 1988b. *Profugiorum ab Erumna Libri*. G. Ponte (ed.). Genoa: Tilgher.

———. 1993. *Momus ou le Prince*. C. and P. Laurens (French trans. and eds.). Paris: Société d'Edition 'Les Belles Lettres'.

Andrews Aiken, J. 1980. 'L. B. Alberti's System of Human Proportions'. *Journal of the Warburg and Courtauld Institutes*, XLIII, 68–96.

Baldi, B. 1824. *Vita e fatti di Federigo di Montefeltro, Duca di Urbino e memorie concernenti la città d'Urbino*. 3 vols. Rome: Perego Salvioni.

Baron, H. 1955. *The Crisis of the Early Italian Renaissance*. 2 vols. Princeton, NJ: Princeton University Press.

Baxandall, M. 1974. *Painting and Experience in Fifteenth-Century Italy*. Oxford: Oxford University Press.

Bialostocki, J. 1964. 'The Power of Beauty: A Utopian Idea of Leon Battista Alberti'. In W. Lotz and W. W. Möller (eds.), *Studien zur toskanischen Kunst: Festschrift Ludwig Heydenreich*. Munich: Prestel-Verlag. 13–19.

Borsi, F. 1986 trans. ed. *Leon Battista Alberti: The Complete Works*. New York: Electa/Rizzoli.

Buck, A. 1976. *Die Rezeption der Antike in den romanischen Literaturen der Renaissance*. Berlin: Erich Schmidt.

Burckhardt, J. 1985 ed. *The Architecture of the Italian Renaissance*. J. Plamer and P. Murray (trans. and eds.). London: Secker & Warburg.

Calzona, A., and L. Volpi Ghirardini. 1994. *Il San Sebastiano di Leon Battista Alberti*. Florence: L. S. Olschki.

Carpeggiani, P., and C. Tellini Perina. 1987. *Sant'Andrea in Mantova*. Mantua: Publi-Paolini.

Choay, F. 1979. 'Alberti and Vitruvius'. *Architectural Design*. XLIX 5–6, 26–35.

———. 1980/97. *La règle et le modèle: Sur la théorie de l'architecture et de l'urbanisme*. Paris: Editions du Seuil [English trans. D. Bratton, Cambridge, Mass.: MIT Press, 1997].

Dennistoun, J. 1851. *Memoirs of the Dukes of Urbino*. 3 vols. London: Longman, Brown, Green & Longmans.

Feuer-Tóth, R. 1978. 'The "Apertionum Ornamenta" of Alberti and the Architecture of Brunelleschi'. *Acta Historiae Artium*, XXIV/1–4, 148–52.

Gadol, J. 1969. *Leon Battista Alberti: Universal Man of the Early Renaissance*. Chicago: University of Chicago Press.

Garin, E. 1985 ed. *L'Umanesimo italiano: Filosofia e vita civile nel rinascimento*. Bari: G. Laterza.

Goldthwaite, R. A. 1980. *The Building of Renaissance Florence: an Economic and Social History*. Baltimore: Johns Hopkins University Press.

Gosebruch, M. 1957. '*Varietas* bei L. B. Alberti und der wissenschaftliche Renaissancebegriff'. *Zeitschrift für Kunstgeschichte*, XX/3, 229–38.

Grayson, C. 1960. 'The Composition of L. B. Alberti's *Decem libri de re aedificatoria*'. *Münchener Jahrbuch der bildenden Kunst*, 3rd ser. XI 152–61.

Hope, C. 1992. 'The Early History of the Tempio Malatestiano'. *Journal of the Warburg and Courtauld Institutes*, LV, 51–155.

Jarzombek, M. 1989. *On Leon Baptista Alberti: His Literary and Aesthetic Theories*. Cambridge, Mass.: MIT Press.

Krautheimer, R. 1969. 'Alberti's *Templum Etruscum*' and 'Alberti and Vitruvius'. In R. Krautheimer, *Studies in Early Christian, Mediaeval and Renaissance Art*, New York: New York University Press, 65–72, 323–32.

Lang, S. 1965. '*De lineamentis*: L. B. Alberti's use of a Technical Term'. *Journal of the Warburg and Courtauld Institutes*, XXXVIII, 331–5.

Lotz, W. 1977. *Studies in Italian Renaissance Architecture*. Cambridge, Mass.: MIT Press.

Lücke, H.-K. (ed.). 1975–9. *Alberti Index: Leon Battista Alberti, 'De re aedificatoria', Florence, 1485*. 4 vols. Munich: Prestel Verlag.

Mancini, G. 1882. *Vita di Leon Battista Alberti*. Florence: Sansoni.

Michel, P.-H. 1930. *Un idéal humain au XVème siècle. La pensée de L. B. Alberti (1404–1472)*. Paris: Société d'Edition 'Les Belles Lettres'.

Mühlmann, H. 1981. *Ästhetische Theorie der Renaissance: Leon Battista Alberti*. Bonn: Habelt Verlag.

Naredi-Rainer, P. von. 1984. *Architektur und Harmonie*. Cologne: Du Mont.

Onians, J. 1971. 'L. B. Alberti and ΦΙΛΑΡΕΤΗ: A Study in their Sources'. *Journal of the Warburg and Courtauld Institutes*, XXXIV, 96–114.

Papagano, G., and A. Quondam. 1982. *La corte e lo spazio: Ferrara Estense*. 3 vols. Rome: Bulzoni.

Ricci, C. 1974. *Il Tempio Malatestiano in Rimini*. Milan: Casa Editrice D'Arte Bestetti & Tumminelli.

Rykwert, J. (ed.). 1979. *Leonis Baptiste Alberti: Architectural Design*. A. D. Profile 21. XLIX 5–6.

Rykwert, J., and R. Tavernor. 21 May 1986. 'Alberti's church of Sant'Andrea in Mantua'. *Architects' Journal*, CLXXXIII⁄21, 36–57.

Rykwert, J., and A. Engel (eds.). 1994. *Leon Battista Alberti*. Catalogue of an Exhibition held at the Palazzo Tè, Mantua. Milan: Electa/Olivetti.

Santinello, G. 1962. *Leon Battista Alberti: Una visione estetica del mondo e della vita*. Florence: Sansoni.

Soggia, R. (ed.). 1991. *Storia e arte religiosa a Mantova: Basilica concattedrale di Sant'Andrea, l'atrio meridionale*. Mantua: Casa del Mantagna.

Soggia, R., and N. Zuccoli. 1994. 'Finiture di facciata nei construtti albertiani: San Sebastiano e Sant'Andrea a Mantova'. In J. Rykwert and A. Engel (eds.), op. cit. 392–401.

Tavernor, R. 1998. *On Alberti and the Art of Building*, New Haven and London: Yale University Press.

Tommaso, A. di. 1972. 'Nature and the Aesthetic Social Theory of Leon Battista Alberti'. *Mediaevalia et Humanistica*. Cleveland: Case Western Reserve University, n.s. 3, 31–49.

Vagnetti, L. 1973. '*Concinnitas*: Riflessioni sul significato di un termine Albertiano'. *Studi e documenti di architettura*, II, 139–61.

Westfall, C. W. 1969. 'Society, Beauty and the Humanist Architect in Alberti's *De re aedificatoria*'. *Studies in the Renaissance*, XVI, 61–79.

―――. 1974. *In This Most Perfect Paradise: Alberti, Nicholas V, and the Invention of Conscious Urban Planning in Rome, 1447–55*. University Park, Pa.: Pennsylvania State University Press.

Wittkower, R. 1988 ed. *Architectural Principles in the Age of Humanism*. London: Academy Editions.

TWO: FILARETE

Bruschi, A. 1992. 'L'antico e il processo di identificazione degli ordini nella seconda metà del Quattrocento'. In J. Guillaume (ed.), *L'emploi des ordres dans l'architecture de la Renaissance*, Paris: Picard, 11–57.

Filarete [Averlino]. 1965. *Filarete's Treatise on Architecture*. J. R. Spencer (trans.). 2 vols. London and New Haven: Yale University Press [cf. review, P. Tigler, *Art Bulletin*, XLIX, 1967, 352–60].

―――. 1972. *Antonio Averlino detto il Filarete: Trattato di architettura*. A. M. Finoli and L. Grassi (eds.). 2 vols. Milan: Il Polifilo.

Giordano, L. 1988. 'Il trattato del Filarete e l'architettura lombarda'. In J. Guillaume (ed.), *Les traités d'architecture de la Renaissance*, Paris: Picard, 115–28.

Hajnóczi, G. 1992. 'Bonfini Averulinus-fordításá és a budai Vitruvius-kézirat kérdése'. *Ars Hungarica*, xx/2, 29–34.

Hidaka, K. 1988. 'La Casa della Virtù e del Vizio nel trattato del Filarete'. In J. Guillaume (ed.), *Les traités d'architecture de la Renaissance*, Paris: Picard, 129–33.

Kruft, H.-W. 1989. *Städte in Utopia: Die Idealstadt von 15. bis zum 18. Jahrhundert zwischen Staatsutopie und Wirklichkeit*. Munich: C. H. Beck.

———. 1994 trans. ed. *A History of Architectural Theory from Vitruvius to the Present*. New York: Princeton Architectural Press/London: Zwemmer.

Lang, S. 1972. 'Sforzinda, Filarete and Filelfo'. *Journal of the Warburg and Courtauld Institutes*, xxxv, 391–7.

Lazzaroni, M., and A. Muñoz. 1908. *Filarete. Scultore e architetto del secolo XV*. Rome: W. Modes.

Oettingen, W. von. 1890. *Antonio Averlino Filarete's Tractat über die Baukunst, nebst seinen Büchern von der Zeichenkunst und den Bauten der Medici*. Vienna: Graeser.

Onians, J. 1971. 'L. B. Alberti and ΦΙΛΑΡΕΤΗ: A Study in their Sources'. *Journal of the Warburg and Courtauld Institutes*, xxxiv, 96–114.

———. 1973. 'Filarete and the "qualità": Architectural and social'. *Arte Lombarda*, xviii/38–9, 116–28.

———. 1988a. 'The System of the Orders in Renaissance Architectural Thought'. In J. Guillaume (ed.), *Les traités d'architecture de la Renaissance*, Paris: Picard, 169–77.

———. 1988b. *Bearers of Meaning: The Classical Orders in Antiquity, the Middle Ages, and the Renaissance*. Cambridge: Cambridge University Press, 158–70.

Saalman, H. 1959. 'Early Renaissance Architectural Theory and Practice in Antonio Filarete's *Trattato di Architettura*'. *Art Bulletin*, xli, 88–106.

Spencer, J. R. 1956. 'La datazione del trattato del Filarete desunta dal suo esame interno'. *Rivista d'arte* [annual], 93–103.

———. 1958. 'Filarete and Central-Plan Architecture'. *Journal of the Society of Architectural Historians*, xvii/3, 10–18.

———. 1959. 'The Dome of Sforzinda Cathedral'. *Art Bulletin*, xli, 328–30.

Tigler, P. 1963. *Die Architekturtheorie des Filarete*. Berlin: Walter de Gruyter.

Thoenes, C. 1980. '"Spezie" e "ordine" di colonne nell'architettura del Brunelleschi'. In *Filippo Brunelleschi: La sua opera e il suo tempo*, vol. 2, Florence: Centro Di, 459–69.

Tomasi Velli, S. 1990. 'Gli antiquari intorno al Circo Romano: riscoperta di una tipologia monumentale antica'. *Annali della Scuola Normale Superiore di Pisa. Classe di Lettere e Filosofia*, xx/1, 61–168.

Vasari, G. 1906 ed. *Le vite de' più eccellenti pittori scultori ed architettori (1568)*. G. Milanesi (ed.). [Filarete in vol. 2. 453–8] Florence: Sansoni [Repr. Florence: Sansoni, 1973].

THREE: FRANCESCO DI GIORGIO

Adams, N. 1993. 'L'architettura militare di Francesco di Giorgio'. In F. P. Fiore and M. Tafuri (eds.), op. cit., 126–62.

Bellosi, L. (ed.). 1993. *Francesco di Giorgio e il Rinascimento a Siena, 1450–1500*. Milan: Electa.

Bentivoglio, E. 1992. 'Per la conoscenza del palazzo della Cancelleria: la personalità e l'ambiente culturale del cardinale Raffaele Sansoni Riario'. *Quaderni dell'Istituto di Storia dell'Architettura*, n.s. 15–20/1, 365–74.

Betts, R. J. 1977. 'On the Chronology of Francesco di Giorgio's Treatises: New Evidence from an Unpublished Manuscript'. *Journal of the Society of Architectural Historians*, xxxvi/1, 3–14.

Buddensieg, T. 1962. 'Die Konstantinsbasilika in einer Zeichnung Francesco di Giorgios und der Marmorkolossos Konstantins des Grossen'. *Münchner Jahrbuch der bildenden Kunst*, xiii, 37–48.

Burns, H. 1974. 'Progetti di Francesco di Giorgio per i conventi di S. Bernardino e Santa Chiara di Urbino'. In *Studi bramanteschi: Atti del Congresso internazionale, Milano-Urbino-Roma 1970*, Rome: De Luca, 293–311.

———. 1993. 'I disegni di Francesco di Giorgio agli Uffizi dei Firenze'. In F. P. Fiore and M. Tafuri (eds.), op. cit., 330–57.

Christiansen, K., L. B. Kanter and C. B. Strehlke. 1988. *Painting in Renaissance Siena, 1420–1500.* Catalogue of an Exhibition held at the Metropolitan Museum of Art. New York: Metropolitan Museum of Art.

Dechert, M. S. A. 1990. 'The Military Architecture of Francesco di Giorgio in Southern Italy'. *Journal of the Society of Architectural Historians*, xlix/2, 161–80.

Ericsson, C. H. 1980. *Roman Architecture expressed in sketches by Francesco di Giorgio Martini. Studies in Imperial Roman and Early Christian Architecture.* Helsinki: Societas Scientiarum Fennica.

Fiore, F. P. 1978. *Città e macchine del '400 nei disegni di Francesco di Giorgio Martini.* Florence: L. S. Olschki.

———. 1985. 'La traduzione da Vitruvio di Francesco di Giorgio: Note ad una parziale trascrizione'. *Architettura, storia e documenti*, 1, 7–30.

———. 1987. 'Francesco di Giorgio e il rivellino "acuto" di Costacciaro'. *Quaderni dell'Istituto di Storia dell'Architettura*, n.s. 1–10, 197–208.

———. 1988. 'Francesco di Giorgio e le origini della nuova architettura militare'. In *L'Architettura militare veneta del Cinquecento*, Milan: Centro Internazionale di Studi di Architettura, 62–75.

Fiore, F. P. and M. Tafuri (eds.). 1993. *Francesco di Giorgio architetto.* Milan: Electa.

Gallavotti Cavallero, D. 1985. 'Francesco di Giorgio di Martino architetto, ingegnere, scultore, pittore, bronzista per la SS. Annunziata di Siena'. *Paragone*, cdxxvii, 45–56.

Galluzzi, P. (ed.). 1991. *Prima di Leonardo. Cultura delle macchine a Siena nel Rinascimento.* Milan: Electa.

Hale, J. R. 1965. 'The Early Development of the Bastion: An Italian Chronology, c.1450–c.1534'. In J. R. Hale, J. R. L. Highfield and B. Smalley (eds.), *Europe in the Late Middle Ages*, London: Faber and Faber, 466–94.

Heydenreich, L. H. 1974. 'The Military Architect'. In L. Reti (ed.), *The Unknown Leonardo.* New York: McGraw-Hill, 136–65.

Kolb, C. 1988. 'The Francesco di Giorgio Material in the Zichy Codex'. *Journal of the Society of Architectural Historians*, xlvii/2, 132–59.

Maltese, C. (ed.). 1967. *Francesco di Giorgio Martini: Trattati di architettura, ingegneria e arte militare.* L. Maltese Degrassi (transc.). 2 vols. Milan: Il Polifilo.

Marani, P. C. (ed.). 1979. *Il codice Ashburnham 361 della Biblioteca Mediceo-Laurenziana di Firenze: Trattato di architettura di Francesco di Giorgio Martini.* 2 vols. Florence: Giunti Barbèra.

Marani, P. C. (ed.). 1984. *L'architettura fortificata negli studi di Leonardo da Vinci. Con il catalogo completo dei disegni.* Florence: L. S. Olschki.

Michelini Tocci, L. (ed.). 1989. *Das Skizzenbuch des Francesco di Giorgio Martini: Vat. Urb. lat. 1757.* Zurich: Belser.

Morresi, M. 1989. 'Francesco di Giorgio e Bramante: osservazioni su alcuni disegni degli Uffizi e della Laurenziana'. In P. Carpeggiani and L. Patetta (eds.), *Il disegno di architettura: Atti del Convegno. Milano 15–18 febbraio 1988*, Milan: Guerini e Associati, 117–24.

Mussini, M. 1991. *Il Trattato di Francesco di Giorgio Martini e Leonardo: Il Codice Estense restituito.* Parma: University of Parma, Istituto di Storia dell'arte.

———. 1993. 'La Trattatistica di Francesco di Giorgio: Un problema critico aperto'. In F. P. Fiore and M. Tafuri (eds.), op. cit., 358–79.

Onians, J. 1988. *Bearers of Meaning: The Classical Orders in Antiquity, the Middle Ages, and the Renaissance.* Cambridge: Cambridge University Press, 182–91.

Parronchi, A. (ed.). 1982. [Baldassare Peruzzi], *Trattato di architettura militare.* Florence: Edizioni Gonnelli.

Pellecchia, L. 1992. 'Architects read Vitruvius: Renaissance Interpretations of the Atrium of the Ancient House'. *Journal of the Society of Architectural Historians*, LI, 377–416.

Pepper, S., and Q. Huges. 1978. 'Fortification in late 15th century Italy: The Treatise of Francesco di Giorgio Martini'. *British Archeological Reports, Supplementary Series*, XLI, 541–60.

Prager, F. D., and G. Scaglia. 1972. *Mariano Taccola and his book 'De Ingeneis'.* Cambridge, Mass. and London: MIT Press.

Promis, C. (ed.). 1841. *Trattato di architettura civile e militare di Francesco di Giorgio Martini architetto senese del secolo XV.* 3 vols. Turin: Chirio e Mina.

Reti, L. (ed.). 1974. *Leonardo da Vinci: The Madrid Codices.* Maidenhead: McGraw-Hill.

Salmi, M. 1947. 'Disegni di Francesco di Giorgio nella collezione Chigi Saracini'. *Quaderni dell'Accademia Chigiana*, XI, 7–45.

Scaglia, G. 1976. 'The "Opera de architectura" of Francesco di Giorgio Martini for Alfonso Duke of Calabria'. *Napoli Nobilissima*, XV/5–6, 133–61.

———. (ed.). 1985. *Il 'Vitruvio Magliabechiano' di Francesco di Giorgio Martini.* Florence: Edizioni Gonnelli.

———. 1992. *Francesco di Giorgio: Checklist and History of Manuscripts and Drawings in Autographs and Copies from c.1470 to 1687 and Renewed Copies (1764–1839).* Bethelehem, Pa.: Lehigh University Press/London: Associated University Presses.

Tafuri, M. 1993. 'Le chiese di Francesco di Giorgio Martini'. In F. P. Fiore and M. Tafuri (eds.), op. cit., 21–73.

FOUR: FRANCESCO COLONNA

Calvesi, M. 1983. *Il Sogno di Polifilo Prenestino.* Rome: Officina Edizioni.

Carson, A. 1986. *Eros the Bittersweet.* Princeton, NJ: Princeton University Press.

Casella, M. T., and G. Pozzi. 1959. *Francesco Colonna: Biografia e Opere.* Padua: Editrice Antenore.

Colonna, F. 1499. *Hypnerotomachia Poliphili*. Venice: Aldus Manutius.

———. 1971. *Le Songe de Poliphile*. Geneva: Slatkine. [reprint of the French 1883 ed.].

———. 1980. *Hypnerotomachia Poliphili*. Padua: Editrice Antenore. [2nd printing of critical edition (1968) of 1499 text, notes in Italian, G. Pozzi and L. Ciapponi (eds.)].

Fierz-David, L. 1987. *The Dream of Poliphilo*. Dallas: Spring Publications.

Gadamer, H. G. 1986. *The Relevance of the Beautiful*. Cambridge: Cambridge University Press.

Heidegger, M. 1977. 'The Origin of the Work of Art'. In D. F. Krell (ed.), *Basic Writings*, New York: Harper and Row.

Kretzulesco-Quaranta, E. 1986. *Les Jardins du Songe*, Paris: Société d'Edition 'Les Belles Lettres'.

Lefaivre, L. 1997. *Leon Battista Alberti's Hypnerotomachia Poliphili: Re-Cognizing the Architectural Body in the Early Italian Renaissance*. Cambridge, Mass.: MIT Press.

Onians, J. 1988. *Bearers of Meaning: The Classical Orders in Antiquity, the Middle Ages, and the Renaissance*. Cambridge: Cambridge University Press, 207–15.

Pérez-Gómez, A. 1983. *Architecture and the Crisis of Modern Science*. Cambridge, Mass.: MIT Press.

———. 1985. 'The Myth of Daedalus'. *AA Files: Annals of the Architecture Association School of Architecture*, no. 10, 49–52.

———. 1992. *Polyphilo, or the Dark Forest Revisited: An Erotic Epiphany of Architecture*. Cambridge, Mass.: MIT Press.

———. 1993. 'Introduction'. In Claude Perrault, *Ordonnance for the Five Kinds of Columns after the Method of the Ancients*. I. K. McEwen (trans.). Santa Monica, Ca.: The Getty Center.

———. 1994. 'Chora: The Space of Architectural Representation'. In A. Pérez-Gómez and S. Parcell (eds.), *Chora: Intervals in the Philosophy of Architecture* [Montreal: McGill-Queen's University Press], no. 1, 1–34.

Snell, B. 1960 trans. ed. *The Discovery of the Mind: The Greek origins of European thought*. New York: Harper and Row.

Vattimo, G. 1988. *The End of Modernity*. Baltimore: John Hopkins University Press.

Vernant, J. P. 1990. 'One . . . Two . . . Three: Eros'. In D. M. Halperin, J. J. Winkler and F. I. Zeitlin (eds.), *Before Sexuality: The Construction of Erotic Experience in the Ancient Greek World*, Princeton, NJ: Princeton University Press.

Zeitlin, F. I. 1990. 'The Poetics of Eros'. In Halperin et al. (eds.). *Before Sexuality*, Princeton, NJ: Princeton University Press.

FIVE: VITRUVIUS IN PRINT AND IN TRANSLATION

Bruschi, A. 1967. *Bramante Architetto*. Bari: Laterza.

Ciapponi, L. 1984. 'Fra Giocondo da Verona and his Edition of Vitruvius'. *Journal of the Warburg and Courtauld Institutes*, XLVII, 72–90.

Daly Davis, M. 1989. ' "Opus Isodomum" at the Palazzo della Cancelleria: Vitruvian Studies and Archaeological Antiquarian Interests at the Court of Raffaele Riario'. In S. D. Squarzina (ed.), *Roma, centro ideale della cultura* dell'Antico nei secoli XV e XVI: Da Martino V al Sacco di Roma, 1417–1527, Milan: Electa. 442–57.

Denker Nesselrath, C. 1990. Die Säulenordnungen bei Bramante. Worms: Wernersche Verlagsgesellschaft.

De Teodoro, F. P. 1994. Raffaello, Baldassar Castiglione e la Lettera a Leone X. Bologna: Nuova Alfa Editoriale.

Fiore, F. P. 1983. 'Cultura settentrionale e influssi albertiani nelle architetture vitruviane di Cesare Cesariano'. Arte Lombarda, n.s., LXIV, 43–52.

———. 1989. 'La traduzione vitruviana di Cesare Cesariano'. In S. D. Squarzina (ed.), Roma, centro ideale della cultura dell'Antico nei secoli XV e XVI. Da Martino V al Sacco di Roma, Milan: Electa. 458–66.

Frommel, C. L. 1988. 'Papal Policy: The Planning of Rome during the Renaissance'. In R. I. Rotberg and T. K. Rabb (eds.), Art and History: Images and their Meaning, Cambridge: Cambridge University Press, 39–66.

Gatti, S. 1971. 'L'attività milanese del Cesariano dal 1512–13 al 1519'. Arte Lombarda, XVI, 219–30.

———. 1991. 'Un contributo alla storia delle vicissitudini incontrate dal "Vitruvio" del Cesariano subito dopo la sua stampa a Como nel 1521'. Arte Lombarda, XCVI–XCVII, 132–3.

Krinsky, C. H. 1971. 'Cesariano and the Renaissance without Rome'. Arte Lombarda, XVI, 211–18.

Massa Pairault, F.-H. 1991. 'La stele di "Avile Tite" da Raffaele il Volterrano ai giorni nostri'. Mélanges de l'école française de Rome, CIII, 499–528.

Nesselrath, A. 1993. Das Fossombroner Skizzenbuch. London: Warburg Institute, 171–4 [figs. 50–51].

Pellecchia, L. 1992. 'Architects read Vitruvius: Renaissance Interpretations of the Atrium of the Ancient House'. Journal of the Society of Architectural Historians, LI, 377–416.

Raphael. c.1519–20. Prefatory letter from Raphael to Pope Leo X, intended to accompany a portfolio of drawings reconstructing Imperial Rome. Text by Raphael, Baldassare Castiglione and Angelo Colocci. Hand of Angelo Colocci. Munich, Staatsbibliothek, MS It. 37b.

Rowland, I. D. 1994. 'Raphael, Angelo Colocci and the Genesis of the Architectural Orders'. Art Bulletin, LXXVI, 81–104.

Salerno, L., L. Spezzaferro, and M. Tafuri. 1973. Via Giulia: Una utopia urbanistica del '500. Rome: Staderini.

Scaglia, G. 1985. Il 'Vitruvio Magliabechiano' di Francesco di Giorgio Martini. Documenti inediti di cultura toscana, vol. 6. Florence: Edizioni Gonnelli.

Tafuri, M. 1978. 'Cesare Cesariano e gli studi vitruviani nel Quattrocento'. In A. Bruschi, C. Maltese, M. Tafuri and R. Bonelli (eds.), Scritti Rinascimentali di Architettura, Milan: Il Polifilo, 387–458.

Thoenes, C. 1986. 'La "lettera" a Leone X'. In C. L. Frommel and M. Winner (eds.), Raffaello a Roma: Il convegno del 1983, Rome: Edizioni dell'Elefante, 373–81.

Verzone, P. 1971. 'Cesare Cesariano'. Arte Lombarda, XVI, 203–10.

Vitruvius. ?1486. L. Victruvii Pollionis De Architectura Libri Decem. Iohannes Sulpicius (ed.). Rome.

———. 1511. M. Vitruvius per Iocundum solito castigatior factus cum figuris et tabula ut *iam legi et intelligi possit.* Venice: [G]io[v]anni Tacuino de Tridino.

——. *c.*1516. *Victruvii De Architectura.* MS translation by Fabio Calvo da Ravenna, in the hand of Angelo Colocci, with annotations by Raphael. Munich, Staatsbibliothek, MS It. 37.

——. *c.*1519–20. *Victruvii De Architectura.* MS translation of Vitruvius, Books I–V (partial), in the hand of Angelo Colocci, with corrections probably by Colocci. Accompanied by drawings, some in the hand of Angelo Colocci, some by an unidentified hand. Munich, Staatsbibliothek, MS It. 37a.

——. 1521. *Di Lucio Vitruvio Pollione De Architectura Libri Dece traducti del Latino in Vulgare affigurati: Commentati: et con mirando ordine Insigniti.* Cesare Cesariano (ed.), with additional contributions by Benedetto Giovio and Bono Mauro. Como: Gottardus da Ponte [Facsimile: A. Bruschi (ed.), Milan: Il Polifilo, 1981].

——. 1996. *Cesare Cesariano. Volgarizzamento dei libri IX (capitoli 7 e 8) e X di Vitruvio, De Architectura secondo il manoscritto 9/2790 Sección de Cortes della Real Academia de Historia, Madrid. Centro di Ricerche Informatiche per i Beni Culturali, Accademia della Crusca. Strumenti e Testi, I.* B. Agosti (ed.). Pisa: Scuola Normale Superiore.

SIX: DIEGO DE SAGREDO

Alberti, L. B. 1966. *L'Architettura.* G. Orlandi and P. Portoghesi (eds. and trans.). 2 vols. Milan: Il Polifilo [English trans. J. Rykwert, N. Leach and R. Tavernor, Cambridge, Mass.: MIT Press, 1988].

Bury, J. B. 1976. 'The Stylistic Term "Plateresque"'. *Journal of the Warburg and Courtauld Institutes,* XXXIX, 199–230.

Euclid. 1516. *Geometricorum Eleme[n]torum libri XV.* D. Francisco (ed.). Paris: Henri Stephani.

Gauricus, P. 1969 ed. *De Sculptura sive Statuaria.* [Florence: P. Junta, 1504]. R. Klein and A. Chastel (eds.). Geneva: Droz.

Guillaume, J. (ed.). 1988. *Les traités d'architecture de la Renaissance.* Paris: Picard.

Kruft, H.-W. 1994 trans. ed. *A History of Architectural Theory from Vitriuvius to the Present.* New York: Princeton Architectural Press/London: Zwemmer.

Léon, T. T. 1960. 'El Obispo Don Juan Rodriguez Fonseca, diplomatico, mecenas y ministro de Indias'. *Hispania Sacra,* XIII, 251.

Llewellyn, N. 1975. 'Diego de Sagredo's Medidas del Romano and the Vitruvian Tradition'. Unpublished M.Phil. dissertation, Warburg Institute, University of London.

——. 1977. 'Two Notes on Diego de Sagredo'. *Journal of the Warburg and Courtauld Institutes,* XL, 292–300.

——. 1988. 'Diego de Sagredo and the Renaissance in Italy'. In J. Guillaume, op. cit., 295–306.

Lotz, W. 1995. *Architecture in Italy, 1500–1600.* 2nd ed. revised by D. Howard. New Haven and London: Yale University Press.

Marañon, J. R. 1947. 'Las ediciones de las "Medidas del Romano"'. In F. Z. Lucas and E. P. de Léon (eds.), *Bibliografia Española de Arquitectura, 1526–1880,* Madrid: Associación de Libreros y Amigos del Libro.

Marias, F., and A. Bustamente. 1986. 'Introduction'. In facsimile of *Medidas del Romano*, Madrid: Direccion General de Bellas Artes y Archivos.

O'Hara, J. 1917. 'Juan Rodriguez de Fonseca, first President of the Indias, 1493–1523'. *Catholic Historical Review*, III, 131.

Onians, J. 1971. 'L. B. Alberti and ΦΙΛΑΡΕΤΗ: A Study in their Sources'. *Journal of the Warburg and Courtauld Institutes*. XXXIV, 96–114.

———. 1988. *Bearers of Meaning: The Classical Orders in Antiquity, the Middle Ages, and the Renaissance*. Cambridge: Cambridge University Press.

Pedoe, D. 1976. *Geometry and the Liberal Arts*. Harmondsworth: Penguin.

Pita Andrade, J. M. 1958. 'Don Alonso de Fonseca y el Arte del Renacimiento'. *Cuadernos Est. Gallegos*, XIII, 173–93.

Rosenthal, E. 1958. 'The Image of Roman architecture in Renaissance Spain'. *Gazette des Beaux-Arts*, LII, 329–46.

Sagredo, D. de. 1526. *Medidas del Romano*. Toledo: Remon de Petras [Facsimiles: F. Z. Lucas and E. P. de Léon (eds.), Madrid: Associación de Libreros y Amigos del Libro, 1947; L. Cervera Vera (ed.), Valencia: Albatros Ediciones, 1976; F. Marias and A. Bustamente (eds.), Madrid: Direccion General de Bellas Artes y Archivos, 1986].

———. 1541. *Medidas del Romano*. Lisbon: Luis Rodriguez.

———. 1549. *Medidas del Romano o Vitruvio*. Toledo: Juan de Ayala.

Sánchez Cantón, F. J. 1923–41. *Fuentes Literarias para la Historia del Arte Español*, 5 vols. Madrid: C. Bermejo.

Sendin Calabuig, M. 1977. *El Colegio Mayor del Arzobispo Fonseca en Salamanca*. Salamanca: University of Salamanca Press.

Serlio, S. 1996. *Sebastiano Serlio on Architecture*, vol. I [Books I–V of *Tutte l'opere d'architettura et prospetiva*]. V. Hart and P. Hicks (trans.). New Haven and London: Yale University Press.

Thomson, D. 1993. *Renaissance Architecture: Critics, Patrons, Luxury*. Manchester: Manchester University Press.

Vitruvius. 1521. *Di Lucio Vitruvio Pollione De Architectura Libri Dece traducti del Latino in Vulgare affigurati: Commentati: et con mirando ordine Insigniti*. Cesare Cesariano (ed.). Como: Gottardus de Ponte.

Vives, J. V. 1969. *An economic history of Spain*. Princeton, NJ: Princeton University Press.

Wilkinson Zerner, C. 1993. *Juan de Herrera: Architect to Philip II of Spain*. New Haven and London: Yale University Press.

SEVEN: SEBASTIANO SERLIO

Carpo, M. 1992. 'The architectural principles of temperate classicism. Merchant dwellings in Sebastiano Serlio's Sixth Book'. *Res*, XXII, 135–51.

———. 1993a. *La maschera e il modello: Teoria architettonica ed evangelismo nell'Extraordinario Libro di Sebastiano Serlio (1551)*. Milan: Jaca Book.

———. 1993b. *Metodo ed ordini nella teoria architettonica dei primi moderni: Alberti, Raffaello, Serlio e Camillo. Travaux d'Humanisme et Renaissance*, vol. 271. Geneva: Librarie Droz S. A.

Dinsmoor, W. B. 1942. 'The Literary Remains of Sebastiano Serlio'. *Art Bulletin*, XXIV, 55–91 [pt. 1], 115–54 [pt. 2].

Fiore, F. P. (ed.). 1994. *Sebastiano Serlio architettura civile, libri sesto, settimo e ottavo nei manoscritti di Monaco e Vienna*, transc. and notes, F. P. Fiore, T. Carunchio. Milan: Il Polifilo, XI–LI.

Frommel, S. 1998. *Sebastiano Serlio*. Milan: Electa.

Howard, D. 1973. 'Sebastiano Serlio's Venetian Copyrights'. *Burlington Magazine*, CXV/2, 512–16.

Jelmini, A. 1986. *Sebastiano Serlio: il trattato d'architettura*. Fribourg: Tipografia Stazione Sa Locarno.

Johnson, J. G. 1985. *Sebastiano Serlio's Treatise on Military Architecture (Bayerische Staatsbibliothek, Munich, Codex Icon. 190)*. Michigan [facsimile PhD dissertation, University of California, Los Angeles, 1984].

Marconi, P. 1969. 'L'VIII libro inedito di Sebastiano Serlio: un progetto di città militare'. *Controspazio*, no. 1, 51–9: nos. 4–5, 52–9.

Onians, J. 1988. *Bearers of Meaning: The Classical Orders in Antiquity, the Middle Ages, and the Renaissance*. Cambridge: Cambridge University Press. 263–86.

Polybius. 1967–8. *The Histories*. W. R. Paton (trans.). 6 vols. London and Cambridge, Mass.: Loeb. [vol. 3].

Rosci, M., and A. M. Brizio (eds.). 1966. *Il Trattato di architettura di Sebastiano Serlio*. 2 vols. Milan: ITEC [vol. 2 facsimile of the 'Munich' MS, Book VI].

Rosenfeld, M. N. 1969. 'Sebastiano Serlio's Late Style in the Avery Library Version of the Sixth Book on Domestic Architecture'. *Journal of the Society of Architectural Historians*, XXVIII, 155–72.

———. 1978. *Sebastiano Serlio: On Domestic Architecture*. New York: Architectural History Foundation/MIT Press [facsimile of the 'Avery' MS, Book VI].

———. 1989. 'Sebastiano Serlio's Contributions to the Creation of the Modern Illustrated Architectural Manual'. In C. Thoenes (ed.), op. cit. 102–10.

———. 1996. Republication of Rosenfeld (1978) with new Intro. but without Serlio's Italian text, New York: Dover.

Rykwert, J. 1996. *The Dancing Column: On Order in Architecture*. Cambridge, Mass.: MIT Press.

Serlio, S. 1537. *Regole generali di architettura sopra le cinque maniere degli edifici*. Venice: Francesco Marcolini.

———. 1540. *Il terzo libro di Sebastiano Serlio bolognese*. Venice: Francesco Marcolini.

———. 1545. *Il primo libro [e secondo libro] d'architettura, di Sebastiano Serlio, bolognese*. Paris: Jean Barbé.

———. 1547. *Quinto Libro d'architettura di Sebastiano Serlio bolognese*. Paris: Michel de Vascosan.

———. 1551. *Extraordinario Libro di architettura*. Lyons: Jean de Tournes.

———. 1575. *Il settimo libro d'architettura*. Frankfurt: Andreas Wechel.

———. 1996. *Sebastiano Serlio on Architecture*, vol. 1 [Books I–V. V. Hart and P. Hicks (trans.)]. New Haven and London: Yale University Press.

———. Forthcoming 1999. *Sebastiano Serlio on Architecture*. vol. 2 [Books VI–'VIII' and the *Extraordinario Libro*, V. Hart and P. Hicks (trans.)]. New Haven and London: Yale University Press.

———. Avery/Munich MSS Book VI: Avery Architectural Library of Columbia University (AA.520.Se.619.F), and Staatsbibliothek, Munich (Codex Icon. 189) [facsimiles: 'Avery' MS, Rosenfeld 1978/96; 'Munich' MS, Rosci and Brizio 1966; transcription Fiore 1994].

Serlio, S. MS Book VII: Österreichische Nationalbibliothek, Vienna (Cod. ser. nov. 2649) [transcription: Fiore 1994].

———. MS 'Book VIII': Staatsbibliothek, Munich (Codex Icon. 190) [transcription: Fiore 1994].

———. MS 'Extraordinario Libro': Staats- und Stadtbibliothek, Augsburg (2° Cod. 496).

Thoenes, C. (ed.). 1989. *Sebastiano Serlio*. Milan: Electa.

Vitruvius. 1931. *De Architectura*, Books I–X. F. Granger (trans.). London and Cambridge, Mass.: Loeb.

Wischermann, H. 1975. 'Castrametatio und Städtebau im 16. Jahrhundert: Sebastiano Serlio'. *Bonner Jahrbücher des Rheinischen Landesmuseums in Bonn und des Vereins von Altertumsfreunden im Rheinland*, CLXXV, 171–86.

EIGHT: THE TYPOGRAPHICAL ARCHITECT

Ackerman, J. S. 1991a. 'Style'. In J. S. Ackerman, *Distance Points*, Cambridge, Mass.: MIT Press, 3–22 [Originally published in J. S. Ackerman and R. Carpenter (eds.), *Art and Archaeology*, Englewood Cliffs, NJ: Prentice-Hall, 1963, 164–86].

———. 1991b. 'Architectural Practice in the Italian Renaissance'. In *Distance Points*, 361–84 [Originally published in the *Journal of the Society of Architectural Historians*, XIII, 1954, 3–11].

———. 1991c. 'Early Renaissance "Naturalism" and Scientific Illustration'. In *Distance Points*, 185–210 [Originally published in *The Natural Sciences and the Arts* [Acta Universitatis Upsaliensis]: *Figura*, n.s. no. 22, Uppsala, 1985. 1–17].

Adamnanus. 1898. *Adamnani de locis sanctis libri tres*. In P. Geyer (ed.), *Itinera Hierosolimitana saeculi IIII–VIII* [Corpus Scriptorum Ecclesiasticorum Latinorum], Vienna, Prague and Leipzig: F. Tempsky, vol. 39, 221–97 [esp. 230, 244, 254, 270].

Alberti, L. B. 1966. *L'Architettura*, G. Orlandi and P. Portoghesi (eds. and trans.). 2 vols. Milan: Il Polifilo [English trans. J. Rykwert, N. Leach and R. Tavernor, Cambridge, Mass.: MIT Press, 1988].

Bechmann, R. 1991. *Villard de Honnecourt: La pensée technique au XIIIe siècle et sa communication*. Paris: Picard.

Benjamin, W. 1936/69. *L'oeuvre d'art à l'époque de sa reproduction mécanisée* [English trans. H. Zohn, in W. Benjamin, *Illuminations*, New York: Schocken Books, 1969, 217–51].

———. 1972. *Gesammelte Schriften*. Frankfurt: Suhrkamp, I, 3, 982–1020.

———. 1991. *Ecrits français*. Paris: Gallimard, 140–71.

Carpeggiani, P., and L. Patetta (eds.). 1989. *Il disegno di architettura: Atti del Convegno. Milano 15–18 febbraio 1988*. Milan: Guerini e Associati.

Carpo, M. 1993a. *La maschera e il modello: Teoria architettonica ed evangelismo nell'Extraordinario Libro di Sebastiano Serlio (1551)*. Milan: Jaca Book.

———. 1993b. *Metodo ed ordini nella teoria architettonica dei primi moderni: Alberti, Raffaello, Serlio e Camillo, Travaux d'Humanisme et Renaissance*, vol. 271. Geneva: Libraire Droz S. A.

Choay, F. 1980/97. *La règle et le modèle: Sur la théorie de l'architecture et de l'urbanisme.* Paris: Editions du Seuil [English trans. D. Bratton, Cambridge, Mass.: MIT Press, 1997].

———. 1992. *L'allégorie du patrimoine.* Paris: Editions du Seuil.

Delpit, M. 1868. 'Essai sur les pèlerinages à Jérusalem avant les Croisades'. In A. J. de Gourgues (ed.), *Le Saint Suaire*, Périgueux: J. Bounet, 259–304.

Freigang, C. 1990. 'Ausstellungen und neue Literatur zum gotischen Baubetrieb'. *Kunstchronik*, XLIII, 606–27.

Frommel, C.-L. 1994. 'Reflections on the Early Architectural Drawings'. In H. A. Millon and V. Magnago Lampugnani (eds.), *The Renaissance from Brunelleschi to Michelangelo: The Representation of Architecture*, London: Thames and Hudson, 100–21.

Galen. 1552. *De simplicium medicamentorum facultatibus libri undecim.* T. G. Gaudanus (Latin trans.). Lyons: Rovillium [Originally published in Paris: Gazellus, 1547].

Gilmont, J.-F. 1990. 'Introduction'. In J.-F. Gilmont (ed.), *La réforme et le livre*, Paris: Cerf.

Giraldus Cambrensis. 1955. In O. Lehmann-Brockhaus (ed.), *Lateinische Schriftquellen zur Kunst in England, Wales und Schottland vom Jahre 901 bis zum Jahre 1307.* Munich: Prestel Verlag, vol. 3.

Ivins, W. M. 1953. *Prints and Visual Communication.* Cambridge Mass.: MIT Press.

Krautheimer, R. 1969. 'Introduction to an "Iconography of Medieval Architecture"'. In R. Krautheimer, *Studies in Early Christian, Medieval, and Renaissance Art*, New York: New York University Press, 115–50 [Originally published in the *Journal of the Warburg and Courtauld Institutes*, v, 1942, 1–33].

Krautheimer, R., and T. Krautheimer-Hess. 1956. *Lorenzo Ghiberti.* Princeton, NJ: Princeton University Press.

Lemerle, F. 1991. 'Les Annotationes de Guillaume Philandrier'. Unpublished PhD dissertation, Centre d'Etudes Supérieures de la Renaissance de Tours.

Millon, H. A. 1994. 'Models in Renaissance Architecture'. In H. A. Millon and V. Magnago Lampugnani (eds.), *The Renaissance from Brunelleschi to Michelangelo: The Representation of Architecture*, London: Thames and Hudson, 18–73 [and bibliography].

Morolli, G. 1984. *'Le belle forme degli edifici antichi', Raffaello e il progetto del primo trattato rinascimentale sulle antichità di Roma.* Florence: Alinea.

Ong, W. 1995. *Orality and Literacy: The Technologizing of the Word*, London: Routledge.

Philandrier, G. 1544. *Gulielmi Philandri Castilionii Galli Civis Ro. in decem libros M. Vitruvii Pollionis de Architectura Annotationes.* Rome: Andrea Dossena.

Roriczer, M. [Matthias (or Matthäus)]. 1486. *Das Büchlein von der Fialen Gerechtigkeit.* Regensburg [Originally entitled *dz puechlein der fialen gerechtikeit*].

Rykwert, J. 1988. 'On the Oral Transmission of Architectural Theory'. In J. Guillaume (ed.), *Les traités d'architecture de la Renaissance*, Paris: Picard. 31–48.

Scheller, R. W. 1995 ed. *Exemplum: Model-Book Drawings and the Practice of Artistic Transmission in the Middle Ages, ca.900–ca.1470*, M. Hoyle (trans.), Amsterdam: Amsterdam University Press.

Thoenes, C. 1986. 'La "lettera" a Leone X'. In C. L. Frommel and M. Winner (eds.), *Raffaello a Roma: il convegno del 1983*, Rome: Edizioni dell'Elefante, 373–81.

NINE: SERLIO AND REPRESENTATION

Alberti, L. B. 1988. *On the Art of Building in Ten Books.* J. Rykwert, N. Leach and R. Tavernor (trans.). Cambridge, Mass.: MIT Press.

Barbaro, E. 1492–93. *Castigationes Pliniani Hermolai Barbari Aquileiensis Pontificis.* Rome: E. Silber.

Bartoli, M. T. 1978. 'Orthographia, Ichnographia, Scaenographia' [Due mila anni da Vitruvio]. *Studi e Documenti di Architettura*, VIII, Florence, 197–208.

Bonelli, R. (ed.). 1978. ['La "Lettera" a Leone X']. In A. Bruschi, L. Maltese, M. Tafuri and R. Bonelli (eds.), *Scritti Rinascimentali di Architettura*, Milan: Il Polifilo, 459–84.

Bowie, T. 1959 ed. *The Sketchbook of Villard de Honnecourt.* Bloomington: Indiana University Press.

Dinsmoor, W. B. 1942. 'The Literary Remains of Sebastiano Serlio'. *Art Bulletin*, XXIV, 55–91 (pt. 1), 115–154 (pt. 2).

Evans, R. 1995. *The Projective Cast: Architecture and its Three Geometries.* Cambridge, Mass.: MIT Press.

Fagiolo, M., and M. L. Madonna (eds.). 1987. *Baldassare Peruzzi: Pittura, scena e architettura nel Cinquecento.* Rome: Instituto della Enciclopedia italiana.

Febvre, L., and H.-J. Martin. 1993 trans. ed. *The Coming of the Book: The Impact of Printing, 1450–1800*, London: Verso.

Fiore, F. P. (ed.). 1994. *Sebastiano Serlio architettura civile, libri sesto, settimo e ottavo nei manoscritti di Monaco e Vienna*, transc. and notes F. P. Fiore and T. Carunchio. Milan: Il Polifilo, XI–LI.

Frommel, C.-L. 1994. 'Reflections on the Early Architectural Drawings'. In H. A. Millon and V. Magnago Lampugnani (eds.), *The Renaissance from Brunelleschi to Michelangelo: The Representation of Architecture*, London: Thames and Hudson, 100–21.

Hart, V., and A. Day. 1995. 'A Computer Model of the Theatre of Sebastiano Serlio, 1545'. *Computers and the History of Art*, V/1, 41–52.

Howard, D. 1973. 'Sebastiano Serlio's Venetian Copyrights'. *Burlington Magazine*, CXV/2, 512–16.

Hui, D. 1993. 'Ichnographia, Orthographia, Scaenographia: An analysis of Cesare Cesariano's illustrations of Milan Cathedral in his commentary of Vitruvius, 1521'. In J. Macarthur (ed.), *Knowledge and/or/of Experience: the Theory of Space in Art and Architecture*, Queensland: Institute of Modern Art, 77–97.

Jelmini, A. 1986. *Sebastiano Serlio, il trattato d'architettura.* Fribourg: Tipografia Stazione Sa Locarno.

Kemp, M. 1990. *The Science of Art: Optical themes in western art from Brunelleschi to Seurat*, New Haven and London: Yale University Press.

Keuls, E. 1975. 'Skiagraphia Once Again'. *American Journal of Archaeology*, LXXIX/1, 1–16.

Lotz, W. 1977. 'The Rendering of the Interior in Architectural Drawings of the Renaissance'. In W. Lotz (ed.), *Studies in Italian Renaissance Architecture*, Cambridge, Mass.: MIT Press. 1–65.

Onians, J. 1988. *Bearers of Meaning: The Classical Orders in Antiquity, the Middle Ages, and the Renaissance.* Cambridge: Cambridge University Press.

Orrell, J. 1988. *The Human Stage, English Theatre Design, 1567–1640*, Cambridge: Cambridge University Press.

Panofsky, E. 1927/97 trans. ed. *Perspective as Symbolic Form*. C. S. Wood (trans.), New York: Zone Books.

Pedretti, C. (ed.). 1962. 'A Letter to Pope Leo X on the Architecture of Ancient Rome' [trans. of letter]. In C. Pedretti, *A Chronology of Leonardo da Vinci's Architectural Studies after 1500*, Geneva: E. Droz, 162–71.

Pérez-Gómez, A. 1994. 'Chora: The Space of Architectural Representation.' In A. Pérez-Gómez and S. Parcell (eds.), *Chora: Intervals in the Philosophy of Architecture* [Montreal: McGill-Queen's University Press], no. 1, 1–34.

Philandrier, G. 1544. *Gulielmi Philandri Castilionii Galli Civis Ro. in decem libros M. Vitruvii Pollionis de Architectura Annotationes*. Rome: Andrea Dossena.

Rosci, M., and A. M. Brizio (eds.). 1966. *Il Trattato di architettura di Sebastiano Serlio*. 2 vols. Milan: ITEC [vol. 2 facsimile of the 'Munich' MS Book VI].

Rosenfeld, M. N. (ed.). 1978/96. *Sebastiano Serlio: On Domestic Architecture*. New York: Architectural History Foundation/MIT Press [facsimile of the 'Avery' MS Book VI]. Republished without Serlio's Italian text, New York: Dover, (1996).

———. 1989. 'Sebastiano Serlio's Contributions to the Creation of the Modern Illustrated Architectural Manual'. In C. Thoenes (ed.), *Sebastiano Serlio*, Milan: Electa, 102–10.

Saalman, H. 1959. 'Early Renaissance Architectural Theory and Practice in Antonio Filarete's *Trattato di Architettura*'. *Art Bulletin*, XLI, 88–106.

Serlio, S. 1537. *Regole generali di architettura sopra le cinque maniere degli edifici*. Venice: Francesco Marcolini.

———. 1540. *Il terzo libro di Sebastiano Serlio bolognese*. Venice: Francesco Marcolini.

———. 1545. *Il primo libro [e secondo libro] d'architettura, di Sebastiano Serlio, bolognese*. Paris: Jean Barbé.

———. 1575. *Il settimo libro d'architettura*, Frankfurt: Andreas Wechel.

———. 1996. *Sebastiano Serlio on Architecture*, vol. 1 [Books I–V of *Tutte l'opere d'architettura et prospetiva*], V. Hart and P. Hicks (trans.). New Haven and London: Yale University Press.

Vitruvius. 1511/22. *M. Vitruvius per Iocundum solito castigatior factus cum figuris et tabula ut iam legi et intelligi possit*. Venice: [G]io[v]anni Tacuino de Tridino [Florence: Giunta, 1522 revised ed.].

———. 1521. *Di Lucio Vitruvio Pollione De Architectura Libri Dece traducti del Latino in Vulgare affigurati: Commentati: et con mirando ordine Insigniti*. Cesare Cesariano (ed.), Como: Gottardus da Ponte [Facsimile: A. Bruschi (ed.), Milan: Il Polifilo, 1981].

———. 1547. *Architecture, ou Art de bien bastir de Marc Vitruve Pollion Autheur Romain Antique*. J. Martin (trans.). Paris: Jacques Gazeau, Jean Barbé.

———. 1931. *De Architectura*, Books I–X. F. Granger (trans.). London and Cambridge, Mass.: Loeb.

Zerner, H. 1988. 'Du mot à l'image: le rôle de la gravure sur cuivre'. In J. Guillaume (ed.), *Les traités d'architecture de la Renaissance*, Paris: Picard, 281–94.

TEN: GUILLAUME PHILANDRIER

Alberti, L. B. 1966. *L'Architettura*. G. Orlandi and P. Portoghesi (eds. and trans.). 2 vols. Milan: Il Polifilo [English trans. J. Rykwert, N. Leach and R. Tavernor, Cambridge, Mass.: MIT Press, 1988].

Carpo, M. 1993. *La maschera e il modello: Teoria architettonica ed evangelismo nell' Extraordinario Libro di Sebastiano Serlio*. Milan: Jaca Book.

Frommel, C. L. 1973. *Der römische Palastbau der Hochrenaissance*. 3 vols. Tübingen: Wasmuth.

Galle, P. 1572. *Virorum doctorum de disciplinis benemerentium effigies XLVIII*. Antwerp: François Raphelengien.

Günther, H. 1988. *Das Studium der antiken Architektur in den Zeichnungen der Hochrenaissance*. Tübingen: Wasmuth.

Lemerle, F. 1991. *Architecture et humanisme au milieu du XVIème siècle: Les Annotationes de Guillaume Philandrier. Introduction, traduction et commentaire, livres I–V*. Tours: Centre d'Etudes Supérieures de la Renaissance.

———. 1994a. 'Genèse de la théorie des ordres: Philandrier et Serlio'. *Revue de l'Art*, CIII, 33–41.

———. 1994b. 'Philandrier et le texte de Vitruve'. *Mélanges de l'Ecole française de Rome: Italie et Méditerranée*, CVI, 517–29.

———. 1994c. 'La théorie architecturale à la Renaissance: le tracé du tailloir corinthien'. *Annali di architettura del Centro Palladio di Vicenza*, VI, 64–72.

Lemerle, F., and Y. Pauwels. 1992. 'L'ionique: Un ordre en quête de base'. *Annali di architettura del Centro Palladio di Vicenza*, III, 7–13.

Pagliara, P. N. 1986. 'Vitruvio da testo a canone'. In S. Settis (ed.), *Memoria dell'antico nell'arte italiana*, III [Dalla tradizione all'archeologia]. Turin: Einaudi, 3–85.

———. 1988. 'Studi e pratica vitruviana di Antonio da Sangallo il Giovane e di suo fratello Giovanni Battista'. In J. Guillaume (ed.), *Les traités d'architecture de la Renaissance*, Paris: Picard, 179–206.

Pauwels, Y. 1989. 'Les origines de l'ordre Composite'. *Annali di architettura del Centro Palladio di Vicenza*, I, 29–46.

Philandrier, G. 1535. *Castigationes, atque Annotationes pauculae in XII libros institutionum M. Fab. Quintiliani, specimen quoddam futurorum in eosdem commentariorum*. Lyons: Sebastianus Gryphus.

———. 1544. *Gulielmi Philandri Castilionii Galli Civis Ro. in decem libros M. Vitruvii Pollionis de Architectura Annotationes*. Rome: Andrea Dossena.

———. 1545. *In decem libros M. Vitruvii Pollionis de Architectura Annotationes. Ad Franciscum Valesium Regem christianissimum. Cum Indicibus Graeco & Latino locupletissimis*. Paris: Jacob Kerver. Paris: Michel Fezandat.

———. 1552. *M. Vitruvii Pollionis de Architectura Libri decem ad Caesarem Augustum, omnibus omnium editionibus longe emendatiores, collatis veteribus exemplis. Accesserunt, Gulielmi Philandri Castilionii, civis Romani Annotationes castigatiores, & plus tertia parte*. Lyons: Jean de Tournes.

———. 1586. *M. Vitruvii Pollionis de Architectura libri decem, ad Caes. Augustum, omnibus omnium editionibus longe emendatiores, collatis veteribus exemplis. Accesserunt, Gulielmi Philandri Castilionii, civis Romani, annotationes castigatiores & plus tertia parte locupletiores*. Geneva: Jean de Tournes.

Serlio, S. 1537. [Book IV] *Regole generali di architettura sopra le cinque maniere degli edifici*. Venice: Francesco Marcolini.

Tafuri, M. 1992. *Ricerca del Rinascimento. Principi, città, architetti*. Turin: Einaudi.

Thoenes, C. 1988. 'La *Regola delli cinque ordini* del Vignola'. In J. Guillaume (ed.), *Les traités d'architecture de la Renaissance*, Paris: Picard, 269–79.

Tolomei, C. 1547. *De le lettere di M. Claudio Tolomei libri sette*. Venice: Gabriel Giolito de Ferrari.

Vignola, J. 1562. *Regola delli cinque ordini d'architettura*, Rome: Expensis auctoris [Reprint: Cassa di Risparmio].

Wiebenson, D. 1988. 'Guillaume Philander's Annotations to Vitruvius'. In J. Guillaume (ed.), *Les traités d'architecture de la Renaissance*, Paris: Picard, 67–74.

Zampa, P. 1993. 'L'ordine composito: alcune considerazioni'. *Quaderni del Dipartimento Patrimonio Architettonico e Urbanistico*, III/5–6. 37–50.

Zerner, H. 1988. 'Du mot à l'image: le rôle de la gravure sur cuivre'. In J. Guillaume (ed.), *Les traités d'architecture de la Renaissance*, Paris: Picard, 281–94.

ELEVEN: VIGNOLA

Barocchi, P. 1971–7. *Scritti d'arte del Cinquecento*. 3 vols. Milan and Naples: Riccardo Ricciardi.

Bernheimer, R. 1954. 'Gothic Survival and Revival in Bologna'. *Art Bulletin*, XXXVI, 263–84.

Cox-Rearick, J. 1996. *The Collection of Francis I: Royal Treasures*. New York: Harry N. Abrams.

Fiore, F. P. (ed.). 1994. 'Introduzione'. In *Sebastiano Serlio architettura civile, libri sesto settimo e ottavo nei manoscritti di Monaco e Vienna*, transc. and notes, F. P. Fiore and T. Carunchio, Milan: Il Polifilo, XI–LI.

Giess, H. 1981. 'Die Stadt Castro und die Pläne von Antonio da Sangallo dem Jüngeren (Teil II)'. *Römisches Jahrbuch für Kunstgeschichte*, XIX, 85–140 [esp. 109–111].

Howard, D. 1973. 'Sebastiano Serlio's Venetian Copyrights'. *Burlington Magazine*, CXV/2, 512–16.

Klein, R. 1979 trans. ed. 'Judgment and Taste in Cinquecento Art Theory'. In R. Klein, *Form and Meaning: Essays on the Renaissance and Modern Art*, New York: Viking Press, 161–9.

Labacco, A. 1552. *Libro D'Antonio Labacco appartenente a l'architettura*, Rome: 'Casa nostra' [i.e. expensis auctoris] & A. Blado.

Lemerle, F. 1994. 'Genèse de la théorie des ordres: Philandrier et Serlio'. *Revue de l'Art*, CIII, 33–41.

Pagliara, P. N. 1986. 'Vitruvio da testo a canone'. In S. Settis (ed.), *Memoria dell'antico nell'arte italiana*, III [Dalla tradizione all'archeologia]. Turin: Einaudi, 3–85.

Serlio, S. 1537. *Regole generali di architettura sopra le cinque maniere degli edifici*. Venice: Francesco Marcolini.

Thoenes, C. 1974a. 'Per la storia editoriale della *Regola delli cinque ordini*'. In C. Thoenes (ed.), *La vita e le opere di Jacopo Barozzi da Vignola, 1507–1573 nel 4° centenario della morte*, Bologna: Cassa di Risparmio di Vignola, 179–89.

Thoenes, C. 1974b. 'Nota introduttiva'. In Vignola 1974, op. cit.

———. 1983. 'Vignolas *Regola delli cinque ordini*'. *Römisches Jahrbuch für Kunstgeschichte*, xx, 345–76. [Partly republished in 1988 as 'La *Regola delli cinque ordini* del Vignola'. In J. Guillaume (ed.), *Les traités d'architecture de la Renaissance*, Paris: Picard, 269–79].

Tolomei, C. 1547. *De le lettere di M. Claudio Tolomei libri sette*. Venice: Gabriel Giolito de Ferrari.

Tuttle, R. J. 1974. 'Le lettere'. In C. Thoenes (ed.), *La vita e le opere di Jacopo Barozzi da Vignola, 1507–1573 nel 4° centenario della morte*, Bologna: Cassa di Risparmio di Vignola, 163–77.

———. 1976. 'A New Attribution to Vignola: A Doric Portal of 1547 in the Palazzo Comunale in Bologna'. *Römisches Jahrbuch für Kunstgeschichte*, xvi, 207–20.

———. 1989. 'Sebastiano Serlio bolognese'. In C. Thoenes (ed.), *Sebastiano Serlio*, Milan: Electa, 22–9.

———. 1992. 'Review of P. Cataneo and J. Vignola, *Trattati*'. *Journal of the Society of Architectural Historians*, LXI, 97–8.

———. 1993. 'Vignola's Facciata dei Banchi in Bologna'. *Journal of the Society of Architectural Historians*, LXII, 68–87.

———. 1994. 'Baldassarre Peruzzi e il suo progetto di completamento della basilica petroniana'. In M. Fanti, D. Lenzi (eds.), *Una Basilica per una Città. Sei Secoli in San Petronio* [Atti del Convegno di Studi per il Sesto Centenario di fondazione della Basilica di San Petronio 1390–1990], Bologna: Istituto per la storia della Chiesa di Bologna, 243–50.

———. 1996. 'Jacopo Vignola'. In J. Turner (ed.), *The Dictionary of Art*, London: Macmillan, vol. 32, 502–8.

Vasari, G. 1973 ed. *Le Opere di Giorgio Vasari*, G. Milanesi (ed.). 9 vols. Florence: Sansoni [reprint of 1878–85/1906 editions].

———. 1981. *Giorgio Vasari. Principi, letterati e artisti nelle carte di Giorgio Vasari*, L. Corti et al. (eds.), Catalogue of an Exhibition held at the Casa Vasari and S. Francesco in Arezzo, Florence: Edam.

Vignola, J. 1562/1974. *Regola delli cinque ordini d'architettura*, Rome: Expensis auctoris [Facsimile, C. Thoenes (ed.), (later) Modena ed., with 'Addition': Bologna: Cassa di Risparmio di Vignola, 1974].

———. 1583. *Le due regole della prospettiva prattica*, Rome: Francesco Zannetti.

———. 1985. '*Regola delli cinque ordini d'architettura*'. In M. Walcher Casotti (ed.), *Pietro Cataneo, Giacomo Barozzi da Vignola, Trattati*, Milan: Il Polifilo, 499–577.

Walcher Casotti, M. 1960. *Il Vignola*. 2 vols. Trieste: Università degli Studi.

———. 1976. 'Note vignolesche'. *Arte in Friuli: Arte a Trieste* [Udine]. III, 55–60.

Ware, W. R. 1902–6. *The American Vignola*, 2 vols. Scranton: International Textbook Company [Reprint: New York: W. W. Norton, 1977].

TWELVE: PHILIBERT DE L'ORME

Blunt, A. 1958. *Philibert De l'Orme*. London: Zwemmer.

Boudon, F. 1985. *Philibert Delorme et le château royal de Saint-Léger-en-Yvelines*. Paris: Picard.

Bury, J. 1988. 'Renaissance Architectural Treatises and Architectural Books: a Bibliography'. In J. Guillaume (ed.), *Les traités d'architecture de la Renaissance*, Paris: Picard, 485–503.

De l'Orme, P. 1561. *Nouvelles inventions pour bien bastir et à petits fraiz*. Paris: Frédéric Morel, Imprimeur du Roi [Facsimile in J.-M. Pérouse de Montclos (ed.), *Philibert De l'Orme: Traités d'architecture*, Paris: Léonce Laget, 1988].

———. 1567. *Le premier tome de l'Architecture*. Paris: Frédéric Morel, Imprimeur du Roi [Facsimile in J.-M. Pérouse de Montclos (ed.), *Philibert De l'Orme: Traités d'architecture*, Paris: Léonce Laget, 1988].

Guillaume, J. 1987. 'De l'Orme et Michel-Ange'. In *'Il se rendit en Italie': Études offertes à André Chastel*, Rome and Paris: Elefante-Flammarion, 279–88.

———. 1992. 'Les Français et les ordres, 1540–1550'. In J. Guillaume (ed.), *L'emploi des ordres dans l'architecture de la Renaissance*, Paris: Picard, 193–218.

Morresi, M. 1997. 'Philibert De l'Orme: Le patrie della lingua'. In A. Blunt [Italian edition], *Philibert De L'Orme*, Milan: Electa, 159–93.

Pauwels, Y. 1991. 'Cesariano et Philibert De l'Orme: le piédestal dorique du *Premier tome de l'Architecture*'. *Revue de l'Art*, XCI, 39–43.

———. 1996. 'Les Français et la recherche d'un langage: Les ordres hétérodoxes de Philibert De l'Orme et Pierre Lescot'. *Revue de l'Art*, CXII, 9–15.

Pérouse de Montclos, J.-M. 1982. *L'architecture à la française*. Paris: Picard.

———. 1987. 'Philibert De l'Orme en Italie'. In *'Il se rendit en Italie': Études offertes à André Chastel*, Rome and Paris: Elefante-Flammarion, 289–99.

———. 1991. 'La charpente à la Philibert De L'Orme: Réflexions sur la fortune des techniques en architecture'. In J. Guillaume (ed.), *Les Chantiers de la Renaissance*, Paris: Picard, 27–50.

Potié, P. 1996. *Philibert De l'Orme: Figures De la pensée constructive*. Marseilles: Parenthèses.

Zerner, H. 1996. 'Philibert De l'Orme, architecte-écrivain francais'. In H. Zerner, *L'art de la Renaissance en France. L'invention du classicisme*, Paris: Flammarion, 373–86.

THIRTEEN: ANDREA PALLADIO

Ackerman, J. S. 1966. *Palladio*. Harmonsworth: Penguin.

Alberti, L. B. 1988. *On the Art of Building in Ten Books*. J. Rykwert, N. Leach and R. Tavernor (trans.), Cambridge, Mass.: MIT Press.

Barbaro, D. 1556. *I dieci libri dell'architettura di M. Vitruvio tradotti e commentati da Monsig. Daniele Barbaro*. Venice: Francesco Marcolini.

———. 1567/1987. *Vitruvio: I dieci libri dell'architettura tradotti e commentati da Monsig. Daniele Barbaro*. Venice: Francesco de' Franceschi [Reprint: M. Tafuri and M. Morresi (eds.), Milan: Il Polifilo, 1987].

Bartoli, C. 1550. *L'architettura di Leon Battista Alberti tradotta in lingua fiorentina da Cosimo Bartoli . . . con l'aggiunta de disegni*. Florence: Lorenzo Torrentino.

———. 1565. *L'architettura tradotta in lingua fiorentina da Cosimo Bartoli*. Venice: Francesco de' Franceschi.

Boucher, B. 1994. *Andrea Palladio: The Architect in his Time*. New York and London: Abbeville Press.

Burns, H., B. Boucher and L. Fairburn 1975. *Andrea Palladio, 1508–1580. The Portico and the Farmyard:* Catalogue of an Exhibition held at the Hayward Gallery. London: The Arts Council of Great Britain.

Campbell, C. 1715–25. *Vitruvius Britannicus.* London: Joseph Smith.

Carlino, A. 1988. 'The book, the body, the scalpel: Six engraved title pages for anatomical treatises of the first half of the sixteenth century'. *Res*, XVI, 32–50.

Holberton, P. 1990. *Palladio's Villas: Life in the Renaissance Countryside*, London: Murray.

Howard, D. 1980. 'Four centuries of literature on Palladio'. *Journal of the Society of Architectural Historians*, XXXIX, 224–41.

Kimball, F. 1968. *Thomas Jefferson Architect.* Boston: Riverside Press [facsimile of 1916 ed., with intro. by F. D. Nichols].

Lauro, P. 1546. *I dieci libri dell'architettura di Leon Battista degli Alberti fiorentino novamente de la latina ne la volgar lingua con molta diligenza tradotti da Pietro Lauro.* Venice: Vincenzo Valgrisi.

Leoni, J. 1742. *The architecture of A. Palladio, in Four Books.* London: A. Ward, S. Birt, D. Browne, C. Davis, T. Osborne and A. Millar [Reprint of the 1721 edition of Leoni with 'Notes and remarks of Inigo Jones, and an appendix, containing the Antiquities of Rome, and a Discourse on the Fires of the Ancients'].

Lewis, D. 1981. *The Drawings of Andrea Palladio*, Catalogue of an Exhibition held at the National Gallery of Art. Washington, DC: International Exhibitions Foundation.

Morsolin, B. 1878. *Giangiorgio Trissino. Monografia di un gentiluomo letterato nel secolo XVI.* Vicenza: G. Burato.

Palladio, A. 1570. *I quattro libri dell'architettura.* Venice: Dominico de' Franceschi.

———. 1980. *Andrea Palladio: I quattro libri dell'Architettura*, L. Magagnato and P. Marini (eds.). Milan: Il Polifilo, XI–LXVI.

———. 1988. *Andrea Palladio: Scritti sull'architettura (1554–1579).* L. Puppi (ed.). Vicenza: Neri Pozza Editore.

———. 1997. *Andrea Palladio: The Four Books on Architecture.* R. Tavernor and R. Schofield (trans. and eds). Cambridge, Mass., and London: MIT Press.

Puppi, L. 1986/89. *Andrea Palladio: Opera completa.* Milan: Electa [Reprint in one volume of first edition in two volumes, 1973; English trans. P. Sanders, 2 vols., London: Electa/Faber and Faber, 1989].

———. (ed.). 1990. *Palladio Drawings.* New York: Rizzoli.

Tavernor, R. 1991. *Palladio and Palladianism.* London: Thames and Hudson.

Vignola, J. 1985. 'Regola delli cinque ordini d'architettura'. In M. Walcher Casotti (ed.), *Pietro Cataneo, Giacomo Barozzi da Vignola, Trattati*, Milan: Il Polifilo [499–577].

Vitruvius. 1521. *Di Lucio Vitruvio Pollione De Architectura Libri Dece traducti del Latino in Vulgare affigurati.* Cesare Cesariano (ed.), Como: Gottardus da Ponte [Facsimile: A. Bruschi (ed.), Milan: Il Polifilo, 1981].

Zorzi, G. G. (ed.). 1958–9. 'La Vita di Andrea Palladio'. *Saggi e Memorie di Storia dell'Arte*, II 91–104.

FOURTEEN: VINCENZO SCAMOZZI

Barbieri, F. 1952. *Vincenzo Scamozzi*. Vicenza: Cassa di Risparmio.

Camillo, G. 1550. *L'Idea del theatro dell'eccellen. M. Giulio Camillo*. Florence: L. Torrentino.

Carpo, M. 1993. *Metodo ed ordini nella teoria architettonica dei primi moderni: Alberti, Raffaello, Serlio e Camillo, Travaux d'Humanisme et Renaissance*, vol. 271, Geneva: Libraire Droz S. A.

Corbin, H. 1976. *Mundus Imaginalis, or, the Imaginary and the Imaginal*. Ipswich: Golgohooza Press.

Frascari, M. 1990. 'A Secret Semiotic Skiagraphy: The Corporal Theatre of Meanings in Vincenzo Scamozzi's *Idea* of Architecture'. *Via: Journal of the Graduate School of Fine Arts of the University of Pennsylvania*, XI, 32–51.

Genette, G. 1987. *Seuils*. Paris: Éditions du Seuil.

Hersey, G. L. 1976. *Pythagorean Palaces, Magic and Architecture in the Italian Renaissance*. Ithaca, NY: Cornell University Press.

Jannaco, C. 1961. 'Barocco e razionalismo nel trattato d'architettura di Vincenzo Scamozzi (1615)'. *Studi Secenteschi*, II, 47–60.

Learco, R. 1927. 'La facciata del Palazzo Nuovo di Bergamo in occasione della esecuzione del progetto dello Scamozzi'. *Rivista di Bergamo*, VI/1, 1 [Genoa].

Magagnato, L. 1992. *Il Teatro Olimpico*. Milan: Electa.

Panofsky, E. 1968 ed. *Idea: A Concept in Art Theory*. J. Peake (trans.). Columbia, SC: South Carolina University Press.

Puppi, L. 1967. 'Vincenzo Scamozzi trattatista nell'ambito della problematica del manierismo'. *Bollettino del Centro Internazionale di Studi d'Architettura A. Palladio*, IX, 310–29.

——. 1969. 'Sulle relazioni culturali di Vincenzo Scamozzi', *Ateneo Veneto*, n.s. VII, 49–66.

Scamozzi, V. 1581. *Discorsi sopra le Antichità di Roma*. Venice: Francesco Ziletti.

——. 1615. *L'Idea della architettura universale . . . divisa in X libri*. Venice: Expensis auctoris (per Giorgio Valentino) [Facsimile, 2 vols., Ridgewood, NJ: The Gregg Press, 1964].

——. 1959 ed. *Taccuino di viaggio da Parigi a Venezia (14 marzo-11 maggio 1600)*. F. Barbieri (ed.). Venice and Rome: Istituto per la Collaborazione Culturale.

Spampanato, V. (ed.). 1933. *Documenti della vita di Giordano Bruno*. Florence: L. S. Olschki.

Tafuri, M. 1985/89. *Venezia e il Rinascimento: Religione, scienza, architettura*. Turin: Einaudi [English trans. J. Levine, Cambridge, Mass.: MIT Press, 1989].

Tavernor, R. 1991. *Palladio and Palladianism*. London: Thames and Hudson.

Temanza, T. 1770. *Vita di V. Scamozzi*. Venice: G. B. Pasquali [Reprinted, L. Grassi (ed.), Milan: Edizioni Labor, 1966].

Yates, F. 1964. *Giordano Bruno and the Hermetic Tradition*. Chicago: University of Chicago Press.

——. 1966. *The Art of Memory*. Chicago: University of Chicago Press/London: Routledge.

Zorzi, G. 1956. 'La giovinezza di Vincenzo Scamozzi secondo nuovi documenti'. *Arte Veneta*, X, 119–32.

FIFTEEN: TREATISES AND THE ARCHITECTURE OF VENICE

Aikema, B., and D. Meijers. 1989. *Nel regno dei poveri: Arte e storia dei grandi ospedali veneziani in età moderna, 1474–1797*. Venice: Arsenale.

Barbaro, D. 1556. *I dieci libri dell'architettura di M. Vitruvio tradotti e commentati da Monsig. Daniele Barbaro*. Venice: Francesco Marcolini.

Bedon, A. 1983. 'Il "Vitruvio" di Giovan Antonio Rusconi'. *Ricerche di Storia dell'Arte*, XIX, 84–90.

————. 1996. 'Giovan Antonio Rusconi: Illustratore di Vitruvio, artista, ingegnere, architetto'. In G. A. Rusconi, *Della architettura di Gio. Antonio Rusconi, Venice (1590)* [Facsimile, Como: A. Dominioni, 1996], IX–XXI.

Bruschi, A. 1978. 'Nota introduttiva'. In A. Bruschi, C. Maltese, M. Tafuri and R. Bonelli (eds.), *Scritti Rinascimentali di Architettura*, Milan: Il Polifilo, 25–49.

Burns, H. 1994. '"Restaurator delle ruyne antiche": Tradizione e studio dell'antico nell'attività di Francesco di Giorgio'. In F. P. Fiore and M. Tafuri (eds.), *Francesco di Giorgio architetto*, Milan: Electa, 151–81.

Calabi, D., and P. Morachiello. 1984. 'Rialto, 1514–1538: Gli anni della ricostruzione'. In M. Tafuri (ed.), *Renovatio Urbis: Venezia nell'età di Andrea Gritti (1523–1538)*, Rome: Officina Edizioni, 291–331.

————. 1987. *Rialto: Le fabbriche e il ponte*. Turin: Einaudi.

Camesasca, E. 1993. *Raffaello: Gli scritti*. Milan: Rizzoli.

Ceriana, M. 1996. 'La cappella Corner nella chiesa dei Santi Apostoli a Venezia'. In M. Bulgarelli and M. Ceriana (eds.), *All'ombra delle volte: Architettura del Quattrocento a Firenze e Venezia*, Milan: Electa, 105–92.

Ciapponi, L. 1961. 'Appunti per una biografia di fra Giocondo'. *Italia Medioevale e Umanistica*, IV, 131–58.

————. 1984. 'Fra Giocondo da Verona and his edition of Vitruvius'. *Journal of the Warburg and Courtauld Institutes*, XLVII, 72–90.

Cicognara, L., A. Diedo and G. A. Selva. 1858. *Le Fabbriche e i monumenti cospicui di Venezia*, 3 vols, Venice: nello stabilmento nazionale di G. Antonelli.

Colonna, F. 1499/1980. *Hypnerotomachia Poliphili*. G. Pozzi and L. Ciapponi (eds.). Padua: Editrice Antenore.

Concina, E. 1983. *La macchina territoriale: La progettazione della difesa nel Cinquecento veneto*. Rome and Bari: Laterza.

————. 1984. 'Fra Oriente e Occidente: gli Zen, un palazzo e il mito di Trebisonda'. In M. Tafuri (ed.), *Renovatio Urbis: Venezia nell'età di Andrea Gritti (1523–1538)*, Rome: Officina Edizione, 265–90.

————. 1997. *Fondaci. Architettura, arte e mercatura tra Levante, Venezia e Alemagna*. Venice: Marsilio.

Cozzi, G. 1970. 'Domenico Morosini e il "De bene instituta re publica"'. *Studi Veneziani*, XII, 405–58.

Dazzi, M. 1939–40. 'Sull'architetto del Fondaco dei Tedeschi'. *Atti del Reale Istituto Veneto di Scienze, Lettere ed Arti*, XCIX, 873–96.

D'Eveline Muther, M. 1994. 'Word and Image in Architectural Treatises of the Italian Renaissance'. Unpublished PhD dissertation, Ann Arbor, Michigan: UMI.

Fiore, F. P. (ed.). 1994. 'Introduzione'. In *Sebastiano Serlio architettura civile, libri sesto, settimo e ottavo nei manoscritti di Monaco e Vienna*, transc. and notes, F. P. Fiore and T. Carunchio, Milan: Il Polifilo, XI–LI.

Fontana, V. 1978. '"Arte" e "Isperienza" nei trattati d'architettura veneziani del Cinquecento'. *Architectura*, VIII, 49–72.

———. 1988. *Fra Giovanni Giocondo architetto, 1433c.–1515*. Vicenza: Neri Pozza.

Fontana, V., and P. Morachiello. 1975. *Il 'De Architectura' di Vitruvio nella traduzione inedita di Fabio Calvo ravennate*. Rome: Officina Edizioni.

Frommel, C. L. 1973. *Der römische Palastbau der Hochrenaissance*. 3 vols. Tübingen: Wasmuth.

———. 1995. 'Palazzo Farnese a Roma: L'architetto e il suo committente'. *Annali di architettura del Centro Palladio di Vicenza*, VII, 7–18.

Furno, M. 1994. 'L'ortographie de la Porta Triumphante dans l'*Hypnerotomachia Poliphili* de Francesco Colonna: un manifeste d'architecture moderne?'. *Mélanges de l'Ecole Française de Rome, Italie et Mediterranée*, CVI, 473–516.

Giambonetto, N. 1985. *Bernardo Bembo umanista e politico veneziano*, Florence: Olschki.

Grayson, C. 1956. 'Un codice del *De re aedificatoria* posseduto da Bernardo Bembo'. In *Studi Letterari. Miscellanea in onore di Emilio Santini*, Palermo: U. Manfredi.

Guerra, A. 1996. '"Architectus venetus": Un'indagine su Giovanni Fontana (1470c.–1528)'. *Quaderni di Palazzo Te*, III, 27–37.

Howard, D. 1987. *Jacopo Sansovino: Architecture and Patronage in Renaissance Venice*. New Haven and London: Yale University Press.

Juřen, V. 1974. 'Fra Giovanni Giocondo et les debuts des études vitruviennes en France'. *Rinascimento*, ser. II, XIV, 101–15.

King, M. 1986. *Venetian Humanism in an Age of Patrician Dominance*. Princeton, NJ: Princeton University Press.

Lemerle, F., and Y. Pauwels. 1992. 'L'ionique: Un ordre en quête de base'. *Annali di architettura del Centro Palladio di Vicenza*, III, 7–13.

Lieberman, R. 1972. *The church of Santa Maria dei Miracoli*, Ann Arbor, Michigan: UMI.

McAndrew, J. 1980. *Venetian Architecture of the Early Renaissance*. Cambridge, Mass.: MIT Press.

Magagnato, L. 1980. 'Introduzione'. In *Andrea Palladio: I quattro libri dell'architettura*. L. Magagnato and P. Marini (eds.), Milan: Il Polifilo, XI–LXVI.

Morosini, D. 1969. *De bene istituta re publica*. C. Finzi (ed.). Milan: Guiffre.

Morresi, M. 1987. 'Le due edizioni dei commentari di Daniele Barbaro'. In M. Tafuri and M. Morresi (eds.), *Vitruvio: I dieci libri dell'architettura tradotti e commentati da Monsig. Daniele Barbaro*, Milan: Il Polifilo, XLI–LVIII.

———. 1988. *Villa Porto-Colleoni a Thiene: Architettura e committenza nel Rinascimento vicentino*. Milan: Electa.

———. 1994. 'Giangiorgio Trissino, Sebastiano Serlio e la villa di Cricoli: ipotesi per una revisione attributiva'. *Annali di architettura del Centro Palladio di Vicenza*, VI, 116–34.

———. 1998. 'Renovatio et Prudentia: Venezia e le città del Dominio'. In F. P. Fiore (ed.), *Storia dell'architettura italiana. Il Quattrocento*, Milan: Electa.

Nardi, B. 1963. 'La scuola di Rialto e l'Umanesimo Veneziano'. In V. Branca (ed.), *Umanesimo europeo e Umanesimo veneziano*, Florence: Sansoni.

Nesselrath, A. 1986. 'I libri di disegni di antichità. Tentativo di una tipologia'. In S. Settis (ed.), *Memorie dell'antico nell'arte italiana*, III [Dalla tradizione all'archeologia]. Turin: Einaudi, 87–147.

Pacioli, L. 1509. *Euclide megarensis . . . Opera.* Venice: Paganino de'Paganini.

Pagliara, P. N. 1986. 'Vitruvio da testo a canone'. In S. Settis (ed.), *Memorie dell'antico nell'arte italiana*, III [Dalla tradizione all'archeologia]. Turin: Einaudi, 3–85.

———. 1988. 'Studi e pratica vitruviana di Antonio da Sangallo il Giovane e di suo fratello Giovanni Battista'. In J. Guillaume (ed.), *Les traités d'architecture de la Renaissance*, Paris: Picard, 179–206.

Palladio, A. 1570. *I quattro libri dell'architettura.* Venice: Domenico de' Franceschi.

Pellecchia, L. 1992. 'Architects read Vitruvius: Renaissance Interpretations of the Atrium of the Ancient House'. *Journal of the Society of Architectural Historians*, LI, 377–416.

Puppi, L. 1986. *Michele Sanmicheli architetto: Opera completa.* Rome: Caliban.

Rusconi, G. A. 1590. *Della architettura di Gio. Antonio Rusconi, con Centosessanta Figure Dissegnate dal Medesimo secondo i precetti di Vitruvio*, Venice: I Gioliti [Facsimile, Como: A. Dominioni, 1996].

Sansovino, F. 1581. *Venetia città nobilissima e singolare.* Venice: Expensis auctoris.

Sanudo, M. 1887 ed. *I Diari.* Venice: Visentini [1879–1902].

Serlio, S. 1537. *Regole generali di architettura sopra le cinque maniere degli edifici.* Venice: Francesco Marcolini.

———. 1540. *Il terzo libro di Sebastiano Serlio bolognese.* Venice: Francesco Marcolini.

Tafuri, M. 1978. 'Cesare Cesariano e gli studi vitruviani nel Quattrocento'. In A. Bruschi, C. Maltese, M. Tafuri and R. Bonelli (eds.), *Scritti Rinascimentali di Architettura*, Milan: Il Polifilo, 387–458.

———. 1984. '"Renovatio urbis Venetiarum" il problema storiografico'. In M. Tafuri (ed.), *Renovatio urbis. Venezia nell'età di Andrea Gritti*, Rome: Officina Edizioni, 9–55.

———. 1985/89. *Venezia e il Rinascimento: Religione, scienza, architettura*, Turin: Einaudi [English trans. J. Levine, Cambridge, Mass.: MIT Press, 1989].

———. 1987a. 'La norma e il programma: il Vitruvio di Daniele Barbaro'. In M. Tafuri and M. Morresi (eds.), *Vitruvio: I dieci libri dell'architettura tradotti e commentati da Monsig. Daniele Barbaro*, Milan: Il Polifilo, XI–XL.

———. 1987b. 'Aggiunte al progetto sansoviniano per il palazzo di Vettor Grimani'. *Arte Veneta*, XLI, 41–50.

———. 1994. 'Il pubblico e il privato. Architettura e committenza a Venezia'. In *Storia di Venezia: Dal Rinascimento al Barocco*, vol. 6. Rome: Enciclopedia Italiana, 367–447.

Tolomei, C. 1547. *De le lettere di M. Claudio Tolomei libri sette.* Venice: Gabriel Giolito de Ferrari.

Vasari, G. 1878–85. *Le vite de' più eccellenti pittori scultori ed architettori (1568).* G. Milanesi (ed.). 9 vols. Florence: Sansoni [Reprinted, 1906, 1974].

Vitruvius. 1511. *M. Vitruvius per Iocundum solito castigatior factus cum figuris et tabula ut iam legi et intelligi possit.* Venice: [G]io[v]anni Tacuino de Tridino.

———. 1521. *Di Lucio Vitruvio Pollione De Architectura Libri Dece traducti del Latino in Vulgare affigurati.* Cesare Cesariano (ed.). Como: Gottardus da Ponte [Facsimile: A. Bruschi (ed.), Milan: Il Polifilo, 1981].

Zorzi, M. 1988. *Collezioni di antichità a Venezia nei secoli della Repubblica.* Rome: Istituto Poligrafico e Zecca dello Stato.

SIXTEEN: TREATISES IN THE LOW COUNTRIES

Bevers, H. 1985. *Das Rathaus von Antwerpen (1561–1565). Architektur und Figurenprogramm* [Studien zur Kunstgeschichte 28]. Hildesheim: Georg Olms Verlag.

Bodar, A. 1985. 'Vitruvius in de Nederlanden'. In *Stichting Leids kunsthistorisch jaarboek. Bouwen in Nederland – 25 opstellen over Nederlandse architectuur opgedragen aan Prof. Ir. J. J. Terwen*, Delft: Delftsche Uitgeverij, 55–104.

Boogert, B. C. van den, and J. Kerkhoff. 1993. *Maria van Hongarije. Koningin tussen keizers en kunstenaars. 1508–1558*. Zwolle: Waanders.

Bury, J. B. 1989. 'Serlio: Some bibliographical notes'. In C. Thoenes (ed.), *Sebastiano Serlio*, Milan: Electa, 92–101.

Dacos, N. 1989. 'L'Anonyme A de Berlin: Hermannus Posthumus'. In R. Harprath and H. Wrede (eds.), *Antikenzeichnung und Antikenstudium in Renaissance und Frühbarock. Akten des internationalen Symposions 8.–10. September 1986 in Coburg*, Mainz: Philipp von Zabern, 61–80.

————. 1995. *Roma quanta fuit. Tre pittori fiamminghi nella Domus Aurea*. Rome: Donzelli.

De Jonge, K. 1994a. 'Architekturpraxis in den Niederlanden in der frühen Neuzeit: Die Rolle des italienischen Militärarchitekten, der "status quaestionis"'. In G. Bers and C. Doose (eds.), *Der italienische Architekt Alessandro Pasqualini (1493–1559) und die Renaissance am Niederrhein. Kenntnisstand und Forschungsperspektiven*, Jülich: Fischer, 363–83.

————. 1994b, 'Le palais de Charles Quint à Bruxelles: Ses dispositions intérieures aux XVe et XVIe siècles et le cérémonial de Bourgogne'. In J. Guillaume (ed.), *Architecture et vie sociale: L'organisation intérieure des grandes demeures à la fin du Moyen Age et à la Renaissance*, Paris: Picard, 107–25.

————. 1997. '"Fiamminghi a Roma". Influences romaines sur l'architecture Renaissance des anciens Pays-Bas: l'état de la question'. *Bollettino d'Arte*, LXXIII.

De la Fontaine Verwey, H. 1975. 'Pieter Coecke van Aelst en zijn boeken over architectuur'. In H. De la Fontaine Verwey, *Uit de wereld van het boek I: Humanisten, dwepers en rebellen in de zestiende eeuw*, Amsterdam: N. Israel, 51–68.

————. 1976. 'Pieter Coecke van Aelst and the publication of Serlio's book on architecture'. *Quaerendo*, VI, 167–94.

De Vos, A. 1994. '"Premier Livre d'Architecture" (1617) van Jaques Francart: een post-Michelangelesk, maniëristisch traktaat'. *Belgisch tijdschrift voor oudheidkunde en kunstgeschiedenis*, LXIII, 73–90.

Duverger, J. 1941. 'Cornelis Floris II en het stadhuis te Antwerpen'. *Gentse bijdragen tot de kunstgeschiedenis*, VII, 37–72.

Duverger, J., M. J. Onghena and P. K. van Daalen. 1953. 'Nieuwe gegevens aangaande XVI^de eeuwse beeldhouwers in Brabant en Vlaanderen'. *Mededelingen van de Koninklijke Vlaamse Academie voor Wetenschappen, Letteren en Schone Kunsten van België. Klasse der Schone Kunsten*, XV/2, 3–95.

Eisler, W. 1990. 'Celestial Harmonies and Hapsburg Rule: Levels of Meaning in a Triumphal Arch for Philip II in Antwerp, 1549'. In B. Wisch and S. Scott Munshower (eds.), *'All the World's a Stage . . .' Art and Pageantry in the Renaissance and Baroque, I: Triumphal Celebrations and the Rituals of Statecraft* (Papers in Art History 6), University Park, Pa.: Pennsylvania State University Press, 332–56.

Forssman, E. 1956. *Säule und Ornament: Studien zum Problem des Manierismus in den nordischen Säulenbüchern und Vorlageblättern des 16. und 17. Jahrhunderts* (Acta Universitatis Stockholmiensis). Stockholm: Almquist & Wiksell.

Gheyn, J. van de. 1905. 'Peiresc et Coebergher'. *Annales de l'Académie Royale d'Archéologie de Belgique*, 5th ser., VII, 5–13.

Grelle, A. (ed.). 1987. *Vestigi delle antichità di Roma . . . et altri luochi. Momenti dell'elaborazione di un'immagine*. Rome: Quasar.

Günther, H. 1985. 'Gli ordini architettonici: rinascita o invenzione? Parte seconda'. In M. Fagiolo (ed.), *Roma e l'antico nell'arte e nella cultura del Cinquecento* (Biblioteca internazionale di cultura 17), Rome: Istituto della Enciclopedia Italiana, 272–310.

————. 1988a. *Das Studium der antiken Architektur in den Zeichnungen der Hochrenaissance* (Römische Forschungen der Bibliotheca Hertziana XXIV). Tübingen: Ernst Wasmuth.

————. 1988b. 'Herman Postma und die Antike'. *Jahrbuch des Zentralinstitutes für Kunstgeschichte*, IV, 7–17.

Heuvel, C. van den. 1991. 'Papiere Bolwercken': De introductie van de Italiaanse stede- en vestingbouw in de Nederlanden (1540–1609) en het gebruik van tekeningen*. Alphen aan den Rijn: Canaletto.

————. 1994a. '"De Architectura" (1599) van Charles De Beste. Een onbekend architectuurtractaat van een Brugs bouwmeester'. *Handelingen van het genootschap voor geschiedenis*, CXXXI, 65–93.

————. 1994b. 'Stevins "Huysbou" en het onvoltooide Nederlandse architectuurtractaat: De praktijk van het bouwen als wetenschap'. *Bulletin van de Koninklijke Nederlandse Oudheidkundige Bond*, XCIII, 1–18.

————. 1995. '"De Architectura" (1599) van Charles De Beste: Het vitruvianisme in de Nederlanden in de zestiende eeuw'. *Bulletin van de Koninklijke Nederlandse Oudheidkundige Bond*, XCIV, 11–23.

Kuyper, W. 1994. *The Triumphant Entry of Renaissance Architecture into the Netherlands: The Joyeuse Entrée of Philip of Spain into Antwerp in 1549, Renaissance and Mannerist Architecture in the Low Countries from 1530 to 1630*. Alphen aan den Rijn: Canaletto.

Marlier, G. 1966. *La Renaissance flamande: Pierre Coeck d'Alost*. Brussels: Robert Finck.

Meischke, R. 1952. 'Het architectonische ontwerp in de Nederlanden gedurende de late middeleeuwen en de zestiende eeuw'. *Bulletin van de Koninklijke Nederlandse Oudheidkundige Bond*, 6th ser., V, 161–230 [Reprinted in R. Meischke, *De gothische bouwtraditie*, Amersfoort: Bekking, 1988, 127–207].

Miedema, H. 1980. 'Over de waardering van de architekt en beeldende kunstenaar in de zestiende eeuw'. *Oud Holland*, XCIV, 71–87.

Mielke, H. 1967. *Hans Vredeman de Vries: Verzeichnis der Stichwerken und Beschreibung seines Stils sowie Beiträge zum Werk Gerard Groennings*. Berlin: Berlin University Press.

Müller Franzo, S. 1881. 'Getuigenverhoor te Antwerpen over het maken van ontwerpen van gebouwen in de 16ᵉ eeuw door schilders, goudsmeden, timmerlieden en metselaars'. In F. D. O. Obreen (ed.), *Archief voor Nederlandtsche Kunstgeschiedenis*, IV, Rotterdam: Martinus Nijhoff, 230–45.

Necipoglu, G. 1989. 'Süleyman the Magnificent and the Representation of Power in the Context of Ottoman-Habsburg-Papal Rivalry'. *Art Bulletin*, LXXI, 401–19.

Nuytten, D. 1994. 'Hans Vredeman de Vries' "Architectura Oder Bauung der Antiquen auss dem Vitruuius . . ." Analyse en evaluatie van een architecturaal voorbeeldenboek van de 16ᵉ eeuw'. Unpublished dissertation, Katholieke Universiteit, Leuven.

Offerhaus, J. 1988. 'Pieter Coecke et l'introduction des traités d'architecture aux Pays-Bas'. In J. Guillaume (ed.), *Les traités d'architecture de la Renaissance*, Paris: Picard, 443–52.

Parmentier, R. A. 1948. *Documenten betreffende Brugsche steenhouwers uit de 16ᵉ eeuw*. Bruges: Geschiedkundige Publicatiën der Stad Brugge.

Philipp, K. J. 1989. '"Ein huys in manieren van eynre kirchen": Werkmeister, Parliere, Steinlieferanten, Zimmermeister und die Bauorganisation in den Niederlanden vom 14. bis zum 16. Jahrhundert'. *Wallraf-Richartz Jahrbuch*, L, 69–113.

Riggs, T. A. 1977. *Hieronymus Cock (1510–1570): Printmaker and Publisher in Antwerp at the Sign of the Four Winds* (Garland Outstanding Dissertations in the Fine Arts). New York: Garland.

Rolf, R. 1978. *Pieter Coecke van Aelst en zijn architectuuruitgaves van 1539*. (PRAK 1). Amsterdam: PRAK.

Roobaert, E. J. 1960. 'De Seer Wonderlycke Schoone Triumphelycke Incompst van den Hooghmogenden Prince Philips . . . in de Stadt Antwerpen . . . Anno 1549'. *Bulletin van de Koninklijke Musea voor Schone Kunsten van België*, IX, 37–74.

Rosenfeld, M. N. 1989. 'Sebastiano Serlio's Contributions to the Creation of the Modern Illustrated Architectural Manual'. In C. Thoenes (ed.), *Sebastiano Serlio*, Milan: Electa, 102–10.

Rylant, J., and M. Casteels. 1940. 'De metsers van Antwerpen tegen Paludanus, Floris, de Nole's en andere beeldhouwers'. *Bijdragen tot de geschiedenis*, XXXI, 185–203.

Schéle, S. 1962. 'Pieter Coecke and Cornelis Bos'. *Oud Holland*, LXXVII, 235–40.
———. 1965. *Cornelis Bos: A Study of the Origins of the Netherland Grotesque*. Stockholm: Almqvist and Wiksell.

Taverne, E. 1978. *In 't land van belofte: in de nieue stadt. Ideaal en werkelijkheid van de stadsuitleg in de Republiek 1580–1680*. Maarssen: Gary Schwartz.

Terwen, J. J., and K. A. Ottenheym. 1993. *Pieter Post (1608–1669): Architect*. Zutphen: Walburg Pers.

Winckel, M. van de. 1988. 'Hans Vredeman de Vries'. In J. Guillaume (ed.), *Les traités d'architecture de la Renaissance*, Paris: Picard, 453–8.

SEVENTEEN: EARLY ENGLISH VITRUVIAN BOOKS

Anderson, C. 1995. 'Learning to Read Architecture in the English Renaissance'. In L. Gent (ed.), *Albion's Classicism: the Visual Arts in Britain, 1550–1660*, New Haven and London: Yale University Press, 239–86.

Bennett, J. A. 1993. 'Architecture and Mathematical Practice in England, 1550–1650'. In J. Bold and E. Chaney (eds.), *English Architecture: Public and Private: Essays for Kerry Downes*, London: Hambledon Press, 23–9.

Carpo, M. 1992. 'The architectural principles of temperate classicism: Merchant dwellings in Sebastiano Serlio's Sixth Book'. *Res*, XXII, 135–51.

Corbett, M., and R. Lightbown. 1979. *The Comely Frontispiece: the Emblematic Title-Page in England, 1550–1660*. London: Routledge.

Dee, J. 1570. *The elements of geometrie of the most auncient philosopher Euclide of Megara . . . with a very fruitfull præface by M. I. Dee*. London: John Daye.

Dinsmoor, W. B. 1942. 'The Literary Remains of Sebastiano Serlio.' *Art Bulletin*, XXIV, 55–91 (pt. 1), 115–54 (pt. 2).

Febvre, L., and H.-J. Martin. 1993. trans. ed. *The Coming of the Book: the Impact of Printing, 1450–1800*, London: Verso.

Harris, E., and N. Savage. 1990. *British architectural books and writers, 1556–1785*. Cambridge: Cambridge University Press.

Hart, V. 1993. 'Heraldry and the Architectural Orders as Joint Emblems of British Chivalry'. *Res*, XXIII, 52–66.

———. 1994. *Art and Magic in the Court of the Stuarts*. London: Routledge.

———. 1995. 'Imperial Seat or Ecumenical Temple? On Inigo Jones's use of "Decorum" at St Paul's Cathedral'. *Architectura*, XXV/2, 194–213.

———. (forthcoming 1998). '"Justice and equity . . . and proportions appertainyng": On Inigo Jones and the Stuart Legal Body'. In R. Tavernor (ed.), *Body/Building: Festschrift for Joseph Rykwert*, University Park, Pa.: Pennsylvania University Press.

Haydocke, R. 1598. *A tracte containing the Artes of Curious Paintinge Carvinge & Buildinge*, Oxford: Joseph Barnes [English trans. of Lomazzo, op. cit.].

Hersey, G. 1988. *The Lost Meaning of Classical Architecture*. Cambridge, Mass.: MIT Press.

Hesiod. 1967. 'Works and Days'. In *The Homeric Hymns and Homerica*, G. H. Evelyn-White (trans.). London and Cambridge, Mass.: Loeb, 2–65.

Higgott, G. 1992. '"Varying with reason": Inigo Jones's theory of design'. *Architectural History*, XXXV, 51–77.

Johnson, A. W. 1987. 'Angles, Squares or Roundes: Studies in Jonson's Vitruvianism'. Unpublished D.Phil. dissertation, Oxford University.

Lomazzo, G. P. 1584. *Trattato dell'arte della pittura scultura et architettura*. Milan: Paolo Gottardo Pontio [English trans., R. Haydocke, op. cit., 1598].

Orgel, S. 1971. 'Inigo Jones on Stonehenge'. *Prose*, III, 107–24.

Palme, P. 1957. *The Triumph of Peace: A Study of the Whitehall Banqueting House*. London: Thames and Hudson.

Phillips, J. 1973. *The Reformation of Images: Destruction of Art in England, 1535–1660*. Berkeley: University of California Press.

Rykwert, J. 1996. *The Dancing Column: On Order in Architecture*. Cambridge, Mass.: MIT Press.

Serlio, S. 1537. *Regole generali di architettura sopra le cinque maniere degli edifici*. Venice: Francesco Marcolini.

———. 1996. *Sebastiano Serlio on Architecture*, vol. 1 [Books I–V of *Tutte l'opere d'architettura et prospetiva*]. V. Hart and P. Hicks (trans.). New Haven and London: Yale University Press.

Shute, J. 1563. *The First and Chief Groundes of Architecture used in all the auncient and famous monymentes*. London: Thomas Marshe [Facsimile, L. Weaver (ed.), London: Country Life, 1912].

Smith, L. P. 1907. *The Life and Letters of Sir Henry Wotton*. 2 vols. Oxford: Clarendon Press.

Vitruvius. 1931. *De Architectura*, Books I–x. F. Granger (trans.). London and Cambridge, Mass.: Loeb.

Williams, J. 1625. *Great Britains SALOMON*. London: I. Bill.

Wittkower, R. 1974. 'English Literature on Architecture'. In R. Wittkower, *Palladio and English Palladianism*, London: Thames and Hudson, 95–112.

Wotton, H. 1624. *The Elements of Architecture . . . collected from the Best Authors and Examples*. London: John Bill.

Yates, F. 1985 ed. *Astraea: The Imperial Theme in the Sixteenth Century*. London: Routledge.

EIGHTEEN: CLAUDE PERRAULT

Apostolidès, J.-M. 1981. *Le Roi-machine: spectacle et politique au temps de Louis XIV*. Paris: Editions de Minuit.

Berger, R. W. 1994. *A Royal Passion: Louis XIV as Patron of Architecture*. Cambridge: Cambridge University Press.

Blondel, F. 1675–83. *Cours d'Architecture*. 3 vols. Paris: Lambert Roulland, Nicolas Langlois.

Clément, P. 1861–82. *Lettres instructions et mémoires de Colbert*. Paris: Imprimerie impériale.

Colbert 1619–83. 1983. Catalogue of an Exhibition held at the Hôtel de la monnaie, Paris, 4 October–30 November 1983 [Preface I. Murat]. Paris: Ministère de la Culture.

Desgodets, A. 1682. *Les edifices antiques de Rome*. Paris: Jean-Baptiste Coignard.

Descartes, R. 1953. *Discours de la méthode* (1637). In *Oeuvres et lettres*. A. Bridoux (ed). Paris: Gallimard.

De l'Orme, P. 1567. *Le premier tome de l'Architecture*. Paris: Frédéric Morel.

Fichet, F. 1979. *La théorie architecturale à l'âge classique*. Liège: Mardaga.

Fréart de Chambray, R. 1650. *Parallèle de l'Architecture antique avec la moderne*. Paris: Imprimerie d'Edme Martin.

Gillot, H. 1914. *La querelle des anciens et des modernes en France*. Paris: H. Champion.

Herrmann, W. 1973. *The Theory of Claude Perrault*. London: Zwemmer.

Judovitz, D. 1993. 'Vision, Representation, and Technology in Descartes'. In D. M. Levin (ed.), *Modernity and the Hegemony of Vision*, Berkeley: University of California Press, 63–87.

Martin, J. (Vitruvius). 1547. *Architecture, ou Art de bien bastir de Marc Vitruve Pollion Autheur Romain Antique*, Paris: Jacques Gazeau, Jean Barbé.

Murat, I. 1984. *Colbert*, R. F. Cook and J. van Asselt (trans.). Charlottesville: University of Virginia Press.

Pérez-Gómez, A. 1983. *Architecture and the Crisis of Modern Science*. Cambridge, Mass.: MIT Press.

———. 1993. 'Introduction'. In Claude Perrault 1993, op cit., 1–44.

Perrault, Charles. 1688–97. *Parallèles des anciens et des modernes*. Paris: Jean-Baptiste Coignard.

———. 1909. *Mémoires de ma vie* (1702). In P. Bonnefon (ed.), '*Mémoires de ma vie*' *par Charles Perrault; 'Voyage à Bordeaux' par Claude Perrault*. Paris: Librairie Renouard, 20–138 [= *Mémoires de ma vie*, Paris: Editions Macula, 1993].

Perrault, Claude. 1671–76. *Mémoires pour servir à l'histoire naturelle des animaux*. Paris: Imprimerie royale.

———— (Vitruvius). 1673/84. *Les dix livres d'architecture de Vitruve*. Paris: Jean-Baptiste Coignard [Revised and englarged 1684. 1673 edition reprinted Paris: Bibliothèque de l'image, 1995. 1684 edition reprinted Liège: Mardaga, 1988.]

———— (Vitruvius). 1674. *Abrégé des dix livres d'architecture de Vitruve*. Paris: Jean-Baptiste Coignard.

————. 1683. *Ordonnance des cinq espèces de colonnes selon la méthode des anciens*. Paris: Jean-Baptiste Coignard.

————. 1993. *Ordonnance for the Five Kinds of Columns after the Method of the Ancients*. I. K. McEwen (trans.). Santa Monica, Ca.: The Getty Center.

Petzet, M. 1967. 'Claude Perrault als Architekt des Pariser Observatoriums'. *Zeitschrift für Kunstgeschichte*, XXX/1, 1–54.

————. 1982. 'Das Triumphbogenmonument für Ludwig XIV, auf der Place du Trône'. *Zeitschrift für Kunstgeschichte*, XLV/2, 145–94.

Picon, A. 1988. *Claude Perrault, 1613–1688, ou La curiosité d'un classique*. Paris: Picard.

Procès verbaux de l'Académie Royale d'Architecture, 1671–1793. 1911–1929. H. Lemonnier (ed.). Paris: Jean Schemit.

Rykwert, J. 1980. *The First Moderns: The Architects of the Eighteenth Century*. Cambridge, Mass.: MIT Press.

Sagredo, D. de. 1539. *Raison d'architecture antique, extraicte de Vitruve* (anonymous trans.). Paris: Simon de Colines.

Schrijvers, P. H. 1989. 'Vitruve 1.1.1: explication de texte'. In H. Geertman and J. J. de Jong (eds.), *Munus Non Ingratum: Proceedings of the International Symposium on Vitruvius' De Architectura and the Hellenistic and Republican Architecture*. Leiden: Stichting Bulletin Antieke Beschaving. 49–54.

Soriano, M. 1972. *Le dossier Perrault*. Paris: Hachette.

Toulmin, S. 1990. *Cosmopolis: The Hidden Agenda of Modernity*. Chicago: University of Chicago Press.

NINETEEN: FROM BLONDEL TO BLONDEL

Allen, D. C. 1963. 'The *Arca Noë* of Athanasius Kircher'. In D. C. Allen, *The Legend of Noah, Renaissance Rationalism in Art, Science and Letters*, Illinois Studies in Language and Literature, Urbana: University of Illinois Press, 182–91.

Aurenhammer, H. 1973. *J. B. Fischer von Erlach*, London: Allen Lane.

Blondel, François-Nicolas. 1675. *Cours d'Architecture, enseigné dans l'Academie royale d'architecture*, 1st part (vol. I). Paris: Lambert Roulland.

————. 1683. *Cours d'Architecture*, 2nd–5th parts (vols. II–III). Paris: Nicolas Langlois.

Blondel, Jacques-François. 1771–7. *Cours d'Architecture*. 6 vols. of text and 6 vols. of plates [continued by Pierre Patte]. Paris: Chez Desaint.

Boffrand, G. G. 1745. *Livre d'Architecture*, Paris: Chez Guillaume Cavelier [Facsimile, Farnborough: The Gregg Press, 1969].

Ciampini, G. G. 1690. *Vetera Monumenta . . . Pars Prima*. Rome: Komarek.

————. 1693. *De sacris aedificiis a Constantino Magno constructis, Synopsis historica*. Rome: Komarek.

————. 1747. *Opera in tres tomos distributa*. Rome: Carolus Gianninus.

Collins, P. 1965. *Changing Ideals in Modern Architecture, 1750–1950*. London: Faber and Faber.

Cordemoy, J.-L. de. 1706. *Nouveau traité de toute l'architecture*. Paris: Jean-Baptiste Coignard [Facsimile of 2nd edition (1714), Farnborough: The Gregg Press, 1966].

Daviler, C. A. 1691. *Cours d'architecture*, 2 vols. Paris: Nicholas Langlois.

De Challes, C.-F.-M. 1674. *Cursus seu Mundus mathematicus*. 3 vols. Lyons: Anissoniana.

Félibien, J.-F. 1687. *Recueil historique de la vie et des ouvrages des plus célèbres architectes*. In J. F. Félibien, *Entretiens*, Trevoux: 'De l'Imprimerie de S.A.S.', 1725. vol. 5.

————. 1699. *Les plans et les descriptions de deux plus belles maisons de campagne de Pline le Consul*. Paris: Florentin and Pierre Delaulne.

Fischer von Erlach, J. B. 1721. *Entwurff einer historischen Architectur*. Vienna: Expensis auctoris.

Frémin, M. de. 1702. *Mémoires critiques d'architecture*. Paris: Saugrain [Facsimile, Farnborough: The Gregg Press, 1967].

Gallet, M. 1985. '[Jacques-François] Blondel'. In *Encyclopaedia Universalis*, Paris: Encyclopaedia Universalis France, vol. III, 735c–737b.

Germain, M. 1870. *Le Monasticon Gallicanum*. 2 vols. Paris: V. Palmé.

Grafton, A. 1992. *New Worlds, Ancient Texts*. Cambridge, Mass.: Harvard University Press.

Guarini, G. 1737. *Architettura civile*, 1 vol. of text, 1 vol. of plates. B. Vittone (ed.). Turin: Gianfrancesco Mairesse [Facsimile, London: The Gregg Press, 1964].

Harries, K. 1983. *The Bavarian Rococo Church: Between Faith and Aesthetics*. New Haven and London: Yale University Press.

Harrington, K. 1982. 'Jacques-François Blondel'. In A. K. Placzek (ed.), *Macmillan Encyclopedia of Architects*, New York: Macmillan. vol. 1, 220–24.

————. 1985. *Changing ideas on architecture in the 'Encyclopédie'*. Ann Arbor, Mi.: UMI.

Hautecoeur, L.-H. 1943–57. *Histoire de l'architecture classique en France*. 7 vols. Paris: Picard.

Herrmann, W. 1962. *Laugier and Eighteenth Century French Theory*. London: Zwemmer.

————. 1973. *The Theory of Claude Perrault*. London: Zwemmer.

————. 1982. 'François Blondel'. In A. K. Placzek (ed.), *Macmillan Encyclopedia of Architects*, New York: Macmillan. vol. 1, 216–19.

Kalnein, W. G., and M. Levey. 1972. *Art and Architecture of the Eighteenth Century in France*. The Pelican History of Art, Harmondsworth: Penguin.

Kircher, A. 1675. *Arca Noë*. Amsterdam: Joannem Janssonium à Waesberge.

————. 1679. *Turris Babel*. Amsterdam: Janssonio-Waesbergiana.

Kruft, H.-W. 1994 trans. ed. *A History of Architectural Theory from Vitruvius to the Present*. New York: Princeton Architectural Press/London: Zwemmer.

Laugier, M.-A. 1753/2nd ed. 1755. *Essai sur l'architecture*. Paris: Chez Duchesne.

Lichtheim, G. 1968. 'Alienation'. In D. L. Sills (ed.), *International Encyclopedia of the Social Sciences*, New York: Macmillan.

MacDonnell, J. 1989. *Jesuit Geometers: A Study of Fifty-Six Prominent Jesuit Geometers during the First Two Centuries of Jesuit History*. St Louis: Institute of Jesuit Sources.

Memmo, A. 1786. *Elementi dell'architettura Lodoliana o sia L'arte del fabbricare con solidità*. Rome: Stamperia Pagliarini.

Middleton, R. 1959. 'J. F. Blondel and the *Cours d'Architecture*'. *Journal of the Society of Architectural Historians*, XVIII, 140–48.

Middleton, R., and D. Watkin. 1987. *Neoclassical and Nineteenth Century Architecture*. London: Faber and Faber.

Middleton, W. E. K. 1975. 'Science in Rome, 1675–1700, and the Accademia Fisicomatematica of Giovanni Giustino Ciampini'. *British Journal for the History of Science*, VIII, 138–54.

Milizia, F. 1771. *Elementi di Matematiche Pure*. Venice: Expensis auctoris.

———. 1781. *Principj di Architettura Civile*. 3 vols. Finale: J. De Rossi.

Oechslin, W. 1982, 'Francesco Milizia'. In A. K. Placzek (ed.), *Macmillan Encyclopedia of Architects*, New York: Macmillan. vol. 3, 197–9.

Pérez-Gómez, A. 1983. *Architecture and the Crisis of Modern Science*. Cambridge, Mass.: MIT Press.

Perrault, C. 1683. *Ordonnance des cinq espèces de colonnes selon la méthode des anciens*. Paris: Jean-Baptiste Coignard [English trans. I. K. McEwen, Santa Monica, Ca.: The Getty Center, 1993].

Rieger, C. 1756. *Universae architecturae civilis elementa*. Vienna: Joannis Thomae Trattner.

Rivosecchi, V. 1982. *Esotismo in Roma barocca: studi sul padre Kircher*. Rome: Bulzoni.

Rykwert, J. 1972. *On Adam's House in Paradise: The idea of the primitive hut in architectural history*. The Museum of Modern Art Papers on Architecture. New York: MOMA.

———. 1980. *The First Moderns: The Architects of the Eighteenth Century*. Cambridge, Mass., and London: MIT Press.

Salerno, L. 1967. 'Treatises'. In *Encyclopedia of World Art*, New York, Toronto and London: McGraw-Hill, vol. 14, 293–311.

Simowitz, A. C. 1983. *Theory of Art in the 'Encyclopédie'*. Epping: Bowker.

Sommervogel, C. 1890–1900. *Bibliothèque de la Compagne de Jésus*. 9 vols. Brussels: Schepeus/Paris: Picard.

Vesely, D. 1985. 'Architecture and the Crisis of Representation', *AA Files: Annals of the Architectural Association School of Architecture*, no. 8, 21–38.

Vidler, A. 1987. *The Writing of the Walls: Architectural Theory in the Late Enlightenment*. Princeton, NJ: Princeton Architectural Press.

Watkin, D. 1980. *The Rise of Architectural History*. London: Architectural Press.

Wright, L. 1983. *Perspective in Perspective*. London: Routledge.

Index of Names and Places